Y0-CHN-710

Power and Policy in the PRC

Also of Interest

†*China Briefing, 1984,* edited by Steven M. Goldstein

†*The Making of Foreign Policy in China: Structure and Process,* A. Doak Barnett

†*China Through the Ages,* Franz Michael

China's Political/Military Evolution: The Party and the Military in the PRC, 1960–1984, Monte R. Bullard

†*China and the World: Chinese Foreign Policy in the Post-Mao Era,* edited by Samuel S. Kim

†*The Government and Politics of the PRC: A Time of Transition,* Jürgen Domes

The Chinese Mosaic: The Peoples and Provinces of China, Leo Moser

Three Visions of Chinese Socialism, edited by Dorothy J. Solinger

China: The 80s Era, edited by Norton Ginsburg and Bernard A. Lalor

The Making of a Premier: Zhao Ziyang's Provincial Career, David L. Shambaugh

†*China's Cultural Heritage: The Ch'ing Dynasty, 1644–1912,* Richard J. Smith

The Chinese Defense Establishment: Continuity and Change in the 1980s, edited by Paul H.B. Godwin

China's Financial System: The Changing Role of Banks, William Byrd

†*China's Economic Development: Growth and Structural Change,* Chu-yuan Cheng

The Limits of Reform in China, edited by Ronald A. Morse

Perspectives on Development in Mainland China, edited by King-yuh Chang

Mainland China: Politics, Economics, and Reform, edited by Yu-ming Shaw

†Available in hardcover and paperback.

Westview Special Studies on East Asia

Power and Policy in the PRC

edited by Yu-ming Shaw

Using a genuinely interdisciplinary approach, this collection of essays analyzes the full range of changes that have taken place in the People's Republic of China (PRC) since 1949. Topics covered include Mao Tse-tung's career and his influence on China's Communist movement, the PRC's foreign and military policies, the development of the government's economic and social policies, and prevailing methodologies in contemporary China studies. Based on a conference sponsored by the Asia and World Institute that brought together a distinguished group of international scholars, this book presents a comprehensive review of the theory and practice of Chinese communism.

Yu-ming Shaw is the director of the Institute of International Relations and a professor in the Graduate School of Diplomacy at National Chengchi University, Taiwan, Republic of China. He was formerly director of the Asia and World Institute in Taiwan.

Dr. Shaw's Chinese publications include *Sino-American Relations in the Twentieth Century* (1980); *From the Open Door to the Diplomatic Rupture Between the U.S. and the ROC* (1983); and *Discourses of Chinese Intellectuals on National Issues* (1983). He was the editor of *China and Christianity* (1979, in English) and is the author of many articles in English that have appeared in the *China Quarterly* and elsewhere. He served as the secretary-general for this international conference on power and policy in the PRC.

Published in cooperation with
The Asia and World Institute, Taipei, Republic of China

Power and Policy in the PRC

edited by Yu-ming Shaw

Westview Press / Boulder and London

Westview Special Studies on East Asia

Published in 1985 in the United States of America by Westview Press, Inc., 5500 Central Avenue, Boulder, Colorado 80301; Frederick A. Praeger, Publisher

Library of Congress Cataloging in Publication Data
Main entry under title:
Power and policy in the PRC.
(Westview special studies on East Asia)
Includes index.
1. China—Politics and government—1949–
2. Communism—China—History. I. Shaw, Yu-ming.
II. Series.
DS777.75.P69 1985 320.951 84-19538
ISBN 0-8133-0135-1

Printed and bound in the United States of America

10 9 8 7 6 5 4 3 2 1

Contents

PART SIX
INTELLECTUALS, DISSIDENCE, AND THE CULTURAL SCENE

PART SEVEN
METHODOLOGY

Tables and Figures

Tables

Figures

Preface

In the wake of the Gang of Four affair and the subsequent political and socioeconomic changes in China, many scholars and observers felt the time ripe for a thorough review of the theory and practice of Chinese Communism. Fully sharing such a feeling were the initial organizers of the Saarbrücken Conference on the Analysis of Power and Policy in the People's Republic of China Since 1949: Dr. Han Lih-wu, president of the Asia and World Institute, the Republic of China on Taiwan; Dr. Robert A. Scalapino, director of the Institute of East Asian Studies, University of California, Berkeley, U.S.A.; and Dr. Jürgen Domes, director of the Research Unit on Chinese and East Asian Politics, Saar University, Saarbrücken, Federal Republic of Germany. These three men first exchanged their ideas in late 1981 and by January 1982 had reached an agreement to hold such a conference. The organizers then enlisted two additional cosponsors: Dr. Dennis Duncanson, director of the Centre for South-East Asian Studies, University of Kent, Canterbury, United Kingdom; and Dr. King-yuh Chang, then director of the Institute of International Relations of National Chengchi University, now director general of the Government Information Office, Taipei, Republic of China.

All the cosponsors decided to share the financial and organizational responsibilities. Dr. Han agreed to serve as the organizer of the Asian participants; Dr. Scalapino, the American participants; and Dr. Domes, the European participants. Dr. Domes generously offered his university as the host institution. Because I had acted as an intermediary for the three main cosponsors during their initial discussions, they requested me to continue my services in the preparatory work as the conference's secretary-general.

The conference was held in Saarbrücken from 22 to 27 August 1982. At its end, the cosponsors agreed that given the nature and quality of the papers presented, they should be made available to a larger audience through publication in a single volume. They entrusted me with the responsibility for being the editor of these conference proceedings.

My duties as editor were completed with the assistance of many individuals. Most helpful were the contributors of the papers, who graciously revised their own work for publication and promptly answered all editorial queries. Some contributors used the pinyin system, others the Wade-Giles system in romanizing Chinese names; both were accepted in order to expedite the publication process. As this volume is published essentially for China specialists, who are usually familiar with both systems, there should not be undue confusion. Dr. Owen P. Lippert, managing editor of the Asia and World Institute, aided with the preliminary editorial work; Karen S. Chung of the Institute of International Relations assisted in the later stages of copy editing; and the staff of Westview Press coordinated the final editing and publication of this volume. I emphasize in conclusion that without the consistent and willing assistance of the conference cosponsors, especially Drs. Han, Scalapino, and Domes, this volume would not have been possible.

Yu-ming Shaw

Introduction

Jürgen Domes

The systematic observation and study of the People's Republic of China (PRC), which we loosely call "China watching," had its start on 25 August 1953. On that day in Hong Kong, Father D. Ladislao La Dany, S.J., began to publish his news bulletin *China News Analysis*, which until its temporary cessation at the end of 1982 stood as the most thoroughly researched and reliable source of information about political developments within the PRC.

It was to assess the methods applied and the results achieved in the three decades of "China watching" beginning with Father La Dany's first issue that forty scholars from three continents gathered at Saarbrücken, the Federal Republic of Germany, from 22 to 27 August 1982. They represented more than twenty-five universities and research institutions from the United States of America, the Republic of China on Taiwan, West Germany, Austria, France, Great Britain, Israel, Japan, South Korea, and Hong Kong. All are prestigious in their various fields—political science, sociology, economics, history, law, and philosophy.

This volume offers both scholars and the general public an opportunity to inspect the papers delivered at this unique conference. These essays fall into two categories. Some review broad political and economic developments in the PRC since its establishment in 1949. Others discuss the methodologies employed in "China watching": the successful ones as well as those that failed to uncover and interpret what we now know to be life in the PRC during the past thirty years or more.

At this juncture, rather than summarize the papers that the reader will soon examine, it would be more profitable to outline the course of the discussions and debates that developed during the five-day conference. The exchanges between the assembled scholars produced an intermediate balance sheet on the social sciences' study of post-1949 China and of her problems and developments. The debates concentrated on four questions:

1. In what ways and to what extent have "China watchers' " descriptions, analyses, and projections been accurate or inaccurate?

2. What are the reasons for inaccuracies in "China watching"?
3. Of the methods and methodologies adopted by China watchers, which have failed and which have succeeded?
4. What tasks now confront the discipline of contemporary Chinese studies and how are these tasks best approached?

These questions were examined in a spirit of mutual respect and friendship. Yet the conclusions reached among the various participants were by no means uniform. That would be an impossibility for a gathering of such distinctive men and women as those present at the conference. Moreover, honest confrontation, as witnessed at Saarbrücken, stands as the hallmark of a productive meeting.

As to the conference's first and most important question, an evaluation of the achievements and failures of "China watching," a general consensus emerged that a number of social scientists, since 1949, had inadequately analyzed events and trends in the PRC. Some of them misled the public by projecting a more favorable image of the PRC than was warranted by reality—even the incompletely known "reality" observable outside the country.

The conference members, after reviewing past forecasts about the PRC, inevitably had to broach the topic of current predictions. Here disagreement most obviously arose, and two opposing views emerged. One espoused some optimism that the PRC would enter an era in which its political system would experience normalization, stabilization, and institutionalization. The other saw more reason for pessimism, forecasting increased intra-elite conflicts that with the passing of the current aged Chinese leadership would escalate into new domestic crises.

The overall mood of the conference seemed to swing from the first view to the second, from optimism to pessimism. The metamorphosis occurred as the debates increasingly revealed and analyzed the hard economic, social, and political facts of contemporary China. It is worthwhile to note that the emphasis on the PRC political situation—with an accompanying note of pessimism—came more from U.S. and East Asian scholars rather than their European counterparts. This may be the result of U.S. scholars keeping in mind their nation's status as a world power and a Pacific power, and of East Asian scholars remaining aware of their nations' proximity to China.

In terms of the second debated question—in particular, the reasons for the presentation of misinformation and misconceptions to the public over the years—there was also partial disagreement. For my part, I would suggest three different motivations, all of which were discussed by the participants.

1. Leftist political opinions motivated some observers to create a positive image of the PRC. A limited number of pro-Maoist Western intellectuals desired to display the PRC as the model of a socialist system that works. To do so, they relied solely on Chinese government handouts

and interviews, and ignored any information that would tarnish the politically acceptable portrait of the PRC.

2. Professional self-interest propelled a larger group of writers to project a favorable picture of the PRC. From the mid-1960s until about 1980, "correct" analyses of the PRC (that is, in the PRC's own terms) could win the media's favor, particularly that of the television networks. Thus, one could gain elevation to the illustrious rank of "China expert." Scholars who wrote about the PRC's gruesome realities of life risked public negligence. The result was the creation in the public's imagination of a fairy-tale Middle Kingdom.

3. The largest group of scholars who tended to present misconceptions about the PRC, however, did so for reasons of neither leftist politics nor gaining fame; they had an honorable motive—a deep and sincere love of China. (Their affection for their subject distinguishes them from many "Sovietologists" who are often guided by a deep dislike for their subject. Scholarship gains from neither emotional extreme.) Affection led many scholars to identify the ruling elite with the Chinese people themselves. Subsequently, they found it difficult to emphasize that these political elites' attachments to Communist policies had hobbled economic and social development, thus condemning large numbers to poverty, and had moreover spawned repression of any dissent.

The reasons behind such misconceptions led into the third question involving the discipline's use of methodology. One crucial source of faulty judgment lay in the discipline's adoption of the "system-immanentist approach." This methodology was developed in Europe, and to a lesser extent in the United States and Japan, as a necessary reaction against the oversimplified anticommunism of the 1950s, which had placed the study of China into the methodological straitjacket of the study of "totalitarianism," its theory, and its practice. The "system-immanentist approach" assumed that totalistic single-party systems could only be judged according to the criteria they had established to monitor themselves. "Western standards" were deemed inapplicable. This method of analysis called for the formation of "empathic" standards through which to judge such states' growth and performance.

Despite a superficial coherence, the "system-immanentist approach" contained contradictions and liabilities that soon rendered it obsolete. The observer employing this methodology progressively tended to take at face value the official handouts of the ruling parties. For the PRC the resulting information was one-sided if not plainly wrong. Moreover, adherents to this method found themselves challenged by their own subjects. In China, the very media that they had relied upon would release facts about the harshness and savagery of life between 1958 and 1978, particularly about the Cultural Revolution. The PRC media's purpose was to allow one elite group to gain politically by criticizing another elite group as responsible for known atrocities. Thus, the Chinese themselves would condemn what many Western observers would not. Such condemnations, however, were usually propaganda rather than an indication of new, more humane, policies being adopted. The "system-immanentist approach" lapsed as a current methodological tool, but the damage it wrought still remains.

For various motives and as the result of poor methodological choices, "China watching" has often produced insufficient reports and analyses. Yet all through the decade of U.S. and European euphoria over China a slight majority of China scholars uncovered information and formulated analyses that time has proved relatively accurate. These scholars continued their work in a spirit of academic sincerity throughout the years when the public rarely listened to them and preferred instead to hear the amply provided rosier news about China. Yet the scholars who persisted were instrumental in the reorientation of Western "China watching" that has developed since 1980. Many of these scholars attended the Saarbrücken conference. One reason for these China watchers' analytical scores was their use of approaches that have proved superior—in particular, superior to the "system-immanentist" approach. There are at least three such approaches:

1. One approach is "textual criticism" (*Textkritik*) as applied to official PRC published sources. This methodology was first developed among German historians and theologians in the first half of the nineteenth century. In the context of "China watching," it means continuous observation over a long period of time of a wide array of PRC publications, press releases, and official statements. As Father La Dany pointed out, textual criticism involves "reading the small print."

2. As a complement to textual criticism, a number of scholars have developed sophisticated methods of qualitative content analysis. This tool approaches official statements as one form of esoteric communication among the elite groups. Careful attention is paid to changes in words, terminologies, and nuances as they may indicate the contours of intra-elite conflict.

3. To best use the information gleaned from content analysis, scholars have embarked as well on detailed and meticulous studies of the elite. These prosographies, or mass biographies, have in turn stimulated inquiries into the PRC's basic social conditions, such as access to education and political mobility within the Communist party.

The combination of these three approaches has produced reasonably reliable information and has led to analyses that, when challenged, have stood as essentially accurate. It is hardly necessary to recommend their future use in contemporary China studies. Of course, these analytical tools must be further refined.

A word should be added about the expanding number of sources for the study of China. The majority of Saarbrücken attendees, indeed a consensus, believed that new sources should be explored. They asserted that discretionary use of the PRC media will likely continue, but more use should be made of refugee interviews and of the information coming out of Taiwan and Hong Kong than in the past. The incorporation of these sources should allow for better verification, hence more reliable results.

Turning now to the fourth and last question of the conference, the future tasks of "China watching," the conference by no means reached a unanimous conclusion. However, the participants did agree that the discipline must continue to deal with five major topics: the state of society, the purpose and function of institutions, the major personalities involved, the content and shifts of ideology, and the workings of the political culture. To illuminate these five topics, four types of research projects were identified by the participants as being of primary importance:

1. The analysis of what Professor Martin Whyte in his paper has called the "life chances"—the basic circumstances and vistas for individuals living in the PRC.
2. The analysis of the political and social realities of life in the rural villages, where more than 80 percent of the Chinese still continue to live.
3. The analysis of the relations between the elites and the broad populace. This should include attempts to better understand the structures of the political culture and mechanisms in order to arrive at a workable theory of the interrelationship between social coalitions and elite groups.
4. Comparative studies incorporating thorough research and balanced judgments. Comparisons should be made between the PRC and four other societal entities: other socialist countries, the USSR in particular; other developing nations, especially those in Asia; other contemporary Chinese societies, most importantly that of Taiwan; and lastly, previous Chinese societies, the one with the most research value being the Second Republic under the Kuomintang leadership from 1928 until the outbreak of the Sino-Japanese War in 1937.

These suggestions for new research and study may constitute one of the Saarbrücken conference's most tangible contributions to the future of Chinese studies. As "China watchers" take up the challenge of producing new studies, it is hoped that the results will do honor to the example set by Father La Dany and hence surpass the sometimes inaccurate portraits and projections of China spawned over more than three decades. The discipline owes a better performance to the public, and it should strive for such improvements as are necessary.

Part 1

CCP History and the Role of Mao Tse-tung

1
The Position of the Chinese Communist Movement in Modern Chinese History

Gottfried-Karl Kindermann

From Study Association to a Provincial Soviet State

Examining the disruptive impact of colonial imperialism upon the already weakened structures of traditional China as represented by the late Ch'ing dynasty, Karl Marx predicted the response of endogenous revolutions that might in turn lead to repercussions against the imperialist industrial powers themselves. Successive Chinese movements competed with each other to find both the causes of China's internal backwardness and suppression by colonial powers and the concrete modes of action that could lead to China's reconstruction and liberation. Among these movements, the Communist party of China—cited hereafter as the CCP—is not only the youngest but also the one movement that has had greatest impact upon China in terms of intentional changes involving processes of destruction and restructuring.

The CCP's more than sixty-year history has been a dramatic roller-coaster ride, with steep ups and downs and sudden violent turns, now left, now right. And yet there are undeniable elements of relative continuity and stability. The intellectual leaders of that group of twelve men who formally established the Communist party of China in July 1921 perceived Bolshevik Marxism as an essentially internationalist movement offering a modern scientific doctrine linked to an action model for practicing socialism, antitraditionalism, and antiimperialism. They had just witnessed the final disintegration of China's traditional cultural system and the failure of the first brave experiments with republican forms of parliamentary democracy (1912/1913). The CCP's founders were left without any endemic system and practice with which they could identify. Having contributed significantly to the iconoclastic anti-Confucian wing of the cultural reform movement of 4 May 1919, they were strongly attracted by an ideology and movement that seemed to offer a rational and scientific explanation of history together with a Chinese role in an international partnership guided by the Communist world organization in Moscow. Within a surprisingly short time the initially very small CCP and its associated front organizations scored impressive successes in organizing labor in various city areas. But a shocking and sobering setback occurred in February 1923 when the allegedly progressive warlord Wu P'ei-fu reacted to an inconvenient railway workers' strike, led partly by Communists, with a massacre that produced the party's first real martyrs.

Another shock had been caused months before, when a representative of the Communist International had pressured the CCP's Central Committee into accepting a risky and most unflattering form of cooperation with the much larger national revolutionary Kuomintang (National People's Party), led by the most prestigious revolutionary leader and statesman of early republican China, Dr. Sun Yat-sen.[1] The latter, with a party, an ideology, and national development programs of his own, refused to accept the small CCP as an equal coalition partner. As a consequence the CCP was forced to submit to a compromise formula under which individual Communists were "admitted" to simultaneous "dual" party membership in the Kuomintang, where they were subjected to the organizational and ideological discipline of that party.[2] Sun Yat-sen had wanted arms, advisers, and money from the Soviet Union, but no import of Communist ideology. Submitting to his demands, Moscow had stated in the founding document of this first Sino-Soviet entente that communism was unsuitable for China and that the Soviet state would abandon Czarist Russia's unequal treaties with China and would refrain from "imperialistic policies" in Outer Mongolia.[3] Moscow's aid to China was thus given to Sun Yat-sen and the Kuomintang, not to the CCP.

The CCP's position within this triangular cooperation pattern was uneasy and ambivalent because of its two contradictory and frequently conflicting objectives. On the one hand, it was openly bound to support the Kuomintang in its struggle with domestic warlord and foreign imperialist adversaries. On the other hand, it had secretly decided to increase its own influence at the expense of the Kuomintang in order to replace the latter at a given moment as the leading force of the Chinese revolution.[4] Tensions between the CCP and the Kuomintang, which escalated after the death of Sun Yat-sen in 1925 and especially after the Kuomintang had conquered large parts of southern China in 1926/1927, led in April 1927 to Chiang Kai-shek's preventive assault upon the promising power structure of the Shanghai Commune. Those shots of April 1927 opened the long period of the Chinese civil war. Three months later, the CCP was expelled from a still existing coalition government between the Kuomintang left and the CCP in Wuhan. Mao's hastily organized Autumn Harvest Insurrection in his home province of Hunan in September 1927 failed, and in December the uprising of the Canton Commune with its red terror was crushed by the overpowering white terror of forces of the Kuomintang's previously cooperative left wing. Both wings of the Kuomintang refused to play the role of "useful idiot."[5] The year 1927 thus ended with one of the two most catastrophic defeats in the entire history of the CCP. Insult was added to injury when the responsible Moscow leadership forced the CCP at its Sixth Congress, convened in Moscow, to accept the entire blame for the disaster.

After the failure of Soviet-inspired attempts to capture larger cities, and with them parts of the urban proletariat, the CCP succeeded in the daring experiment of establishing a "Chinese Soviet Republic" chaired by Mao Tse-tung in Kiangsi Province. This socialist state within the state of the Republic of China created its own government and army as well as comprehensive regulations for socialist land and labor reform and the suppression of objective and subjective "class enemies." Such a dualism of coexisting, competing sociopolitical state systems as the Kuomintang and the CCP was suggestive of the later configuration of relations between Taiwan and the People's Republic after 1949 and was faintly reminiscent of Sun Yat-sen's attempts of 1917 and of the early 1920s to organize in South China a national government competing with the internationally recognized authorities in Peking.

Conditions of Victory

Chiang Kai-shek's 1934 conquest of the Kiangsi Soviet republic and the simultaneous breakup of numerous CCP underground cells in other provinces constituted the CCP's second-worst defeat. The party's membership declined by 90 percent to only 30,000 members at the time when most of these remaining members arrived in Shensi Province at the end of the agonizing Long March. The party's complete extinction was then a definite possibility—a danger accentuated by the Kuomintang's successful consolidation of power in its struggle with opposing warlords. However, the CCP was saved by a kind of "historical miracle." Japan's destructive eight-year war against China decimated the Kuomintang's frontally opposing military forces and crippled its economic system and morale to the point where the balance of forces between the CCP and the Kuomintang was decisively changed to the disadvantage of the latter. Mao Tse-tung's multidimensional and truly innovative forms of waging a highly mobile partisan war successfully pursued two objectives beyond fighting Japanese forces: to preserve and to expand the CCP's manpower and territorial control. Making only nominal concessions to the central government of the Kuomintang, Mao Tse-tung realistically retained full control of the CCP's armed forces. He skillfully used his wartime contacts with U.S. representatives in order to persuade the U.S. government to pressure Chiang Kai-shek into some kind of legitimization of the CCP.[6] The Soviet occupation of Manchuria aided the CCP's military preparations.[7] The Marshall mission's overly optimistic attempt to talk the two Chinese parties into forming a kind of democratic coalition government failed for obvious reasons. In the course of the reopened civil war, the CCP's armies won province by province from a progressively disintegrating enemy.

There were no decisive, spontaneous popular uprisings from the masses. In the hour of victory, when Mao Tse-tung proclaimed the establishment of the People's Republic of China on 1 October 1949, the CCP could look back upon no less than twenty-two years of conflict against a comparatively weak enemy before finally becoming able to seize power. The Japanese had done an eight-year job of weakening the Kuomintang, whose leaders would have much preferred to develop with Japan friendly relations on the basis of equality and mutual benefit that had been envisaged and proposed by Sun Yat-sen.

Visions and Realities in the Process of Revolutionary Restructuring

The "Heaven- and Earth-shaking" processes of China's revolutionary restructuring by the CCP started only after 1949, although the party could and did rely on a number of previous experiences and experiments. In one sense it was thus "a revolution from above." Yet, acting from Marxist-Leninist premises, the CCP simultaneously produced guided revolutionary processes "from below." In order to destroy its subjective political opponents as well as its objective class enemies not by the new ruling party alone but rather with popular participation, the CCP planned, organized, and unleashed one of the most formidable motive forces potentially existing in all human societies: social envy. In a series of furious, guided campaigns of grass-roots discontent with the privileges of wealth and power, the CCP liquidated with popular participation large parts of the socially and culturally determining strata of China's pre-1949 society.

The CCP was not composed of those urban industrial proletarians whom Karl Marx had encountered and envisaged. It consisted rather of self-appointed "proletarians" predominantly recruited from the ranks of an impoverished peasantry and from radical intellectuals and soldiers. Mao Tse-tung was factually correct when he claimed as early as 1927 that the poor peasants were the avant-garde of the social revolution in China.[8] Prior to its consolidation of central state power, the CCP sought to attract farmers with Sun Yat-sen's electrifying slogan: "The Land to the Tillers." By promising and initially practicing land distribution with a resulting greater equalization of land ownership, the CCP often tactically concealed its objective of imposing upon new and old land owners a multiphased process of collectivization. The latter process culminated in 1958 when the CCP experimented with total agrarian collectivization in the earliest phase of the agrarian communes. The results were not merely disappointing but abortive. Up to this day, thirty-three years after its victory, the CCP is still faced with the disturbing dilemma of wanting to have a socialized agrarian basis for the economy of the world's largest peasant country but of realizing painfully that private ownership remains by far the most potent incentive for the farmers' badly needed spontaneous productivity. From below, from the agrarian sector, there emerges a genuine danger and challenge to the CCP's image and reality of a socialist China.

After having successfully experimented with the adaptation of Soviet economic models to Chinese realities in the years from 1949 to 1957, the CCP subsequently sought to evolve and to practice for more than a decade Maoist self-development strategies. As argued by leading scholars in the field,[9] the motivational concepts were nationalistic and "populist" in the sense that China's poverty and overpopulation were comprehended as constituting a morally, ideologically, and organizationally advantageous starting point for new development strategies based upon self-reliance, will power, and mass mobilization. The centrally and locally planned mass mobilization of tens and hundreds of millions was intended to transform China's liability of overpopulation into the virtue of maximized labor intensity. Egalitarian enthusiasm was to substitute for lack of technical expertise. It was a heroic but futile revolution of "populist" voluntarism against the lessons of historical experience in human nature and the requirements of socioeconomic construction.

In the cultural sphere, Chinese Communism has remained essentially iconoclastic as far as the Confucian mainstream of China's great cultural heritage is concerned.[10] Thus the younger generation has been cut off from concrete knowledge about many major roots of China's former culture. A paradoxical aspect may be seen in the fact that the older generation of CCP leaders have used Confucian forms of conduct (e.g., the method of self-cultivation) in order to promote new and specifically anti-Confucian value systems. One result is that Mao Tse-tung himself has posthumously become the target of carefully dosed criticism. Without him the party would lose its only unifying Chinese symbol and ideology. But the party's healthy new realism has also led to a mood of ideological disenchantment.

In Defense of the National Interest

In the sphere of foreign policy it seems impossible to detect continuous linkages between the CCP's internal and external policies. Reminiscent of the Kuomintang's diplomatic history, the CCP allied itself with the Soviet Union after earlier efforts aimed at establishing a working relationship with the United States had failed, then subsequently switched sides by entering into a quasi-alliance with the United States. As argued elsewhere, the disruptive key issue in Kuomintang-Soviet alliance relations was the question of equal partnership.[11] That same issue also played a major role in the disintegration of the second Sino-Soviet alliance.

The CCP's foreign policy has successfully continued with those efforts of national reemancipation and reassertion that had been launched in the era of Sun Yat-sen and Chiang Kai-shek. Often the criticism of Soviet policies has been similar to that practiced by the Kuomintang since the twenties. One of the most astonishing feats consisted in the CCP's ability to wage in Korea a relatively successful containment war against the United States beginning only about one year after its victory in continental China. China also humiliated India and "punished" Vietnam. The CCP's Maoist "Three Worlds Theory" somehow resembles Sun Yat-sen's prognosis and advocacy of a world alliance of suppressed nations against the hegemony of imperialist powers.[12] There is again an element of populism in China's claim to be but the largest of the justly rebelling Third World countries.

After having severely criticized the Soviet Union in the early sixties for being too timid and too opportunistic in its dealings with "Western imperialism," the CCP developed toward the end of the sixties and during the seventies the new doctrine of "Social-Imperialism," again blaming the Soviet Union, but this time for being itself the world's greatest menace to peace. With Mao Tse-tung and the leaders of the Cultural Revolution still in full control, the CCP regime reversed its initial foreign policy position by moving toward a rapprochement with the United States, Japan, and—later on—also with the states of the Association of Southeast Asian Nations (ASEAN). The motive here has not been ideology, but rather a pragmatic policy in defense of the national interest. Any future rapprochement with the Soviet Union will have to be based upon coordination without even a shade of subordination. Related formulas and structures are hard to imagine but not impossible.

On the Taiwan question, the CCP's efforts to move ahead through the application of military force were twice repulsed in 1954/1955 and 1958. In the wake of Sino-American rapprochement and normalization, the CCP scored major international successes including its entry into the United Nations and the termination of the U.S.-Nationalist Chinese defense treaty of 1954. Even so, the Taiwan issue has retained its uncomfortable time-bomb character within the total structure of relevant PRC-U.S. relations.[13]

And the Future?

Was Mao right when he told the journalist Edgar Snow, his long-time acquaintance, in 1965 that the CCP might possibly become "revisionist" after his death and make common cause with the remnants of the Kuomintang? Or will he be right? What is to be expected? A party that up to now has wasted close to one-third of its governing era in China with fratricidal conflicts that have damaged the entire country by paralyzing badly needed development processes can hardly afford further excesses of self-disruption. The CCP's policies of "liberalization" have and will continue to have their definite limits wherever the party leadership perceives potential or real challenges to its exclusive rule based upon ideology as the source of legitimacy.

It was not the initial phase but rather the final phase of the daring but aborted Hundred Flowers Campaign that will yield the criteria for future civil liberties within China. Confucius once said men were not ruled by laws but rather by men. The era of Mao Tse-tung was an illustration. In the future there may be collective leadership bodies that rule, but there will be no rule of law. The failures of five PRC constitutions yield another illustration. In other words, the CCP, being what it was and now is, is unlikely to commit a leftist or rightist "harakiri." Systemic self-preservation is, after all, the most basic motivational force in all existing political systems. This observation is almost a law of history.

Notes

1. C. Martin Wilbur, *Sun Yat-sen: Frustrated Patriot* (New York, 1976). Harold Z. Schiffrin, *Sun Yat-sen and the Origins of the Chinese Revolution* (Berkeley, 1968). Gottfried-Karl Kindermann, ed., *Sun Yat-sen: Founder and Symbol of China's Revolutionary Nation-Building* (Munich: Olzog, 1982).

2. See Conradt Brandt, *Stalin's Failure in China 1924–1927* (Cambridge, Mass., 1958), ch. 2; Lydia Holubnychy, *Michael Borodin and the Chinese Revolution, 1923–1925* (Ann Arbor, 1979), pp. 172–173 and 207; and Ch'en Tu-hsiu, *Kao Ch'un-tang T'ung-chih Shu* [*Letter to all party comrades*] (Shanghai, 1929), p. 2.

3. The text is in *China Yearbook 1924/25,* (Tientsin: Tientsin Press, 1926), p. 863.

4. See the statement by the CCP's Comintern delegate Liu Jen-ch'ing at the Fourth Congress of the Communist International, in: *Protokoll des Vierten Kongresses der Kommunistischen Internationale* (Hamburg, 1923), p. 615.

5. One week prior to Chiang Kai-shek's decisive blow in Shanghai, Stalin had boasted that people like Chiang Kai-shek had to be squeezed out like lemons to the last drop of their utility; thereafter they would be thrown into the garbage dump of history. See Leon Trotzky, *Problems of the Chinese Revolution* (New York, 1931), p. 388.

6. See *Foreign Relations of the United States, Diplomatic Papers 1944,* vol. 6, *China* (Washington, D.C., 1967), pp. 604–614.

7. This was formerly denied by the Soviet government, but it is now openly admitted by prominent Soviet historians. For details see, for instance, O. B. Borissow and B. T. Koloskow, *Sowjetisch-Chinesische Beziehungen 1945–1970* (East Berlin, 1973), ch. 1.

8. Mao Tse-tung, "Report on an Investigation of the Peasant Movement in Hunan, February 1927," trans. C. Brandt, B. Schwartz, and J. K. Fairbank, *A Documentary History of Chinese Communism* (Cambridge, Mass., 1959), pp. 77–89. See also Mao Tse-tung, *Selected Works of Mao Tse-tung* (5 vols.), vol. 1 (Peking, 1965), pp. 23–62.

9. See, for instance, Maurice Meisner, "Leninism and Maoism: Some Populist Perspectives in Marxism-Leninism in China," in *China Quarterly* (London), January/March 1971.

10. Mao Tse-tung, "Talks at the Yenan Forum on Literature and Art," in *Selected Works of Mao Tse-tung,* vol. 3 (Peking, 1965), pp. 69–98. Mao argued here, as Ch'en Tu-hsiu had done before him, that the old cultural system had to be destroyed in its entirety before anything new could be established.

11. Gottfried-Karl Kindermann, *Der Ferne Osten in der Weltpolitik des Industriellen Zeitalters* (Munich, 1970), ch. 3.

12. See Sun Yat-sen's San min chu-i lectures of 27 January 1924 and 2 March 1924.

13. This problem is discussed in greater detail in Gottfried-Karl Kindermann, "Washington Between Beijing and Taipei: The Restructured Triangle 1978–80," in *Asian Survey* 20:5 (May 1980), pp. 457–476.

2
Mao Tse-tung, or, The Revolutionary Turned Rebel

Lucien Bianco

Early in 1982, a vigorous charge by an Indian scholar, Krishna Prakash Gupta, ridiculed the currently fashionable habit of slicing Mao Tse-tung's career into two contrasting parts (before and after the mid- or late 1950s) and of evaluating Mao's performance as being impressive before and unhappy after that turning point.[1] In a review essay dealing with eight recent books on Mao or his thought, Gupta reserved his perhaps most biting irony for Ross Terrill's "startling suggestion" that "China might have been better off if Mao had died twenty years earlier than he did."[2] Gupta considers that "to dismiss the Mao of the Great Leap Forward and thereafter is to dismiss the essence of the Maoist model"[3] and suggests that the revolutionary credentials of the pre-1956 Mao do not go beyond "the successful opportunism of a fiercely nationalistic Chinese, accidentally turned Communist hero."[4]

In spite of Gupta's trenchant revisionism (not in the sense given to that word in Peking under Mao), I think that the distinction between the pre- and post-1956 Mao still holds.[5] I found in Terrill's suggestion nothing to be startled at, but rather a trite and timid understatement of the consequences of the late chairman's role during his last two decades. I made the same point as Terrill did, in an article published in a French newspaper on the occasion of Mao's death.[6] However, whether or not one agrees with Gupta's emphasis on the essential continuity between the pre- and post-1956 Mao, one cannot but follow his sound advice to have "a second look at some of the popular myths of (Mao's) revolutionary genesis."[7] Before alluding briefly to this question in the concluding part of this paper, I will devote this discussion almost exclusively to Mao's last two decades, in which are to be found (here, I agree with Gupta) "the essence of the Maoist model."

Mao's Justified Worries

My purpose is not to attempt another definition of the Maoist model, which has been thoroughly analyzed, especially since the Cultural Revolution, but to try and understand Mao's impulse to promote the generally radical policies associated with that model. These policies have been variously held as unworkable or utopian by most knowledgeable observers of Communist China; and now, with official criticism from Peking,[8] almost no one would rise up to defend them. I would not, for I share the majority view, but one should nevertheless recognize that if it is hard to build a good case for the practicability of Maoist policies at that particular time in a still poor, underdeveloped country, most of these policies were at least intended to redress very real abuses or evils. In other words, if one leaves aside Mao's ideological preoccupations and acknowledges that it becomes difficult to justify on practical grounds policies such as Mao's attempts at revolutionizing the cultural superstructure, it remains easy to enumerate plenty of good reasons for arguing in favor of the desirability of reducing the major inequalities existing in Communist China or controlling the power bureaucracy. Using again the same nonideological, most un-Maoist approach, one could broadly define as "social" those policies of Mao aimed at reducing inequalities, and as "political" those dealing with bureaucratic attitudes and relationships between the leaders and the led. (However, the latter also contain some social implications.) With such a formulation, one can then credit Mao as having attempted to deal with basic social and political problems. Socially there is the huge gap between urban and rural revenues, with wide variations of income between poor and better-off communes or brigades, and even in the latter a whole range of revenues among city dwellers, from the apprentice or the workshop woman who is paid 20 to 30 yuan a month right up to the cadre or the university professor whose salary exceeds 100 and possibly 200 yuan a month. Politically, one recalls the deep grievances against the Communist bureaucracy that erupted in 1957 and 1966 as soon as Mao gave the Chinese people a chance to express themselves.

It is necessary at this point to pause at these two years of 1957 and 1966 in order to emphasize the link between their two otherwise dissimilar and in a way antithetical episodes. There is a striking continuity between the spontaneous criticisms made of Chinese bureaucrats and bureaucracy during the Hundred Flowers Campaign and the themes orchestrated by the Maoist media during the initial period of the Cultural Revolution—as well as the easily exploitable frustrations and anger of would-be Red Guards.[9] More importantly, it would be unfair to exclude the Hundred Flowers experiment from Mao's record during his last two decades and to begin, say, with the antirightist campaign that immediately followed.[10] Such a dichotomy has already been suggested by the above-mentioned criticism from Peking. The Resolution of the Sixth Plenum of the Eleventh Central Committee officially sanctioned the Hundred Flowers rectification campaign of the spring of 1957 but criticized the excesses of the subsequent antirightist campaign (Art. 17). Liberal Westerners also could be tempted to follow this official line, rationalizing that Mao's liberal overtures of early 1957 do not fit in well with the radical cultural policies he persistently advocated earlier in the fifties. The contrast is clearly documented by Mao's changing attitudes from 1957 to 1976, as analyzed in Merle Goldman's earlier and recent studies.[11]

Because one feels sorry for the young writer Wang Meng (or his like), whose stories in *People's Literature* in 1956 portrayed people who lived up to Communist ideals coming into conflict with bureaucrats who did not, one can easily sympathize with Mao's then-enlightened policies and deplore the opposition to them by "gray" (Liu Shao-ch'i) or "hard" (P'eng Chen) bureaucrats. It is equally easy to sympathize with Liu's, P'eng's, or Teng Hsiao-p'ing's responsible choices following the debacle of the Great Leap Forward, as opposed to Mao's irresponsible stand in economic matters. I do not imply that one should not approve of one leader in one circumstance and of his opponents in another, especially since men and issues change; however, there is consistency in the cautiousness that incited pragmatic bureaucrats to resist Mao's experiments in 1957 as well as later. More to the point, as I will try to make clear later, Mao's attraction (not adherence) to democratic ways was consistent with his values or was typically Maoist. This was exemplified in his impatience in the spring of 1957 to launch the rectification campaign, as well as in his subsequent retreat and the repression of dissenters.

Mao's Repeated Failures

Mao's repeated attempts to rectify the Communist bureaucracy, first mildly through the Hundred Flowers Campaign, then harshly through the Cultural Revolution, are of interest not only for China but for the Communist system as a whole. By coincidence, Djilas' book *The New Class* first appeared in the year that Mao launched the Hundred Flowers Campaign. Whatever the differences between Mao's attempts to reform the system from within and Djilas' more liberal conclusions, one cannot but pay tribute to Mao for addressing himself to one of the most basic "contradictions" (in his own language) affecting Communist revolutions and regimes. However, one must also recognize that his attempts did not succeed, that he destroyed much and achieved very little. As Benjamin Schwartz has observed, Mao's prescriptions to prevent or to correct the corruption of power were very traditional and deeply rooted in the Chinese past. Inculcating cadres with an "ethic of self-sacrifice," "self-abnegation," and so forth, or "sending them down" (hsia-fang) and making them participate in labor—these and other well-known Maoist methods to produce "newly born things" amounted to moralizing with the holders of power.[12] As eminently Confucian as they are, these methods recall in their limited effectiveness the superficial measures, amounting mainly to exhortations, that Lenin envisaged in order to cope with the problem of the incompetence, brutality, and corruptibility of Bolshevik leaders and commissars.[13] But Lenin did not live long enough to devise more effective methods or to revise some of his basic assumptions. He would perhaps have been unable to do either (especially the latter, a more drastic and painful move) although he was, as I will argue later, less inclined to wishful thinking than was the elderly Mao. Mao's launching of the Cultural Revolution was sanctioned by his failure to amend through gentler means the Chinese bureaucracy, which in his mind meant making it more responsive to his wishes. As is well known, the Cultural Revolution achieved close to nil, and subsequent Maoist efforts to produce "newly born things," while less disturbing, were equally fruitless.

As has been hinted above, it is not easy to separate the social from the political effects of Mao's attempts at making the bureaucracy conform to his vision. From his perspective the separation would even be artificial, since both aspects proceeded from a common ideological or ethical impulse. Some of the measures mentioned above, such as "sending down cadres" and making them participate in labor, as well as other assaults on social status (e.g., abolishing ranks in the army) were manifestations of a relentless attack on "symbolic inequalities," which, as Richard Kraus has remarked, were a more constant target of Mao's drive than material inequalities.[14] Mao seemed preoccupied more with dispensing to country people part of those services (health and education, for instance) that were available to city dwellers than in reducing the gap between peasant and urban incomes. There is a flagrant disproportion between Mao's denunciations of the "three great inequalities" and the mainly peripheral nature of the remedies he put forward in order to reduce them. I am not convinced by Kraus' suggestion that Mao's failure to redistribute a substantial part of urban revenues to the peasantry, as opposed to his more consistent efforts at reducing inequalities among the peasants themselves, was primarily due to the resistance of better-off cadres and workers and of those leaders who spoke on the latter's behalf.[15] One could even argue that more conservative-minded or more pragmatic officials like Teng Tzu-hui in the 1950s or Liu Shao-ch'i in the early 1960s accorded more consideration to the well-being of the peasantry than Mao did, in that Mao proved himself at times quite willing to pressure the peasants in order to increase the speed of economic development. The question, however, is not who should be awarded the prize for the most egalitarian leader, but which compromise would be best in order to implement the clearly desirable goal of reducing the blatant inequalities between the farming majority and the rest of the population. Mao simply had no ready solution to cope with such a problem. Anxious as he was to detect and resolve every kind of contradiction, he apparently failed to notice (or deliberately ignored) a contradiction close at hand: namely, the contradiction between the magnitude of the evils he repeatedly pointed out and his own prescriptions to combat them, which were more often than not either vague or beside the point. He seemed content to prophesy the worst and to enjoin other leaders to prevent it. In this context let us turn to the root of Mao's own "contradiction."

The Temptation of Permanent Revolution

What lies at the core of Maoism is the temptation of permanent revolution. Although I am much less appreciative of Mao Tse-tung's thought than John Bryan Starr is, I wholly agree with the latter's emphasis on Mao's "theory of continuing the revolution under the dictatorship of the proletariat."[16] My use of the word "permanent" rather than "continuing"[17] does not arise from any preference for the term "pu-tuan ko-ming" as opposed to "chi-hsü ko-ming," nor does it purport to describe Mao as a latter-day disciple of Parvus or Trotsky. Mao, of course, took pains to dissociate himself from Trotsky's views, and it is, conversely, highly improbable that Trotsky would have been ready to count Mao among his disciples. He might rather have considered Mao a faithful follower of Stalin, willing to start afresh in a second country the adventure of socialism, already foredoomed in the Soviet Union. More to the point, Trotsky saw in the permanent revolution a key to further uninterrupted progress from the bourgeois-democratic to the socialist stage of revolution, whereas for Mao it was nothing more than a way of preventing retrogression from socialism to capitalism following an already victorious revolution. In Trotsky's eyes, the objective weakness of the potential enemy (the bourgeoisie in such countries as Czarist Russia, where capitalism was not yet a major force) enabled "us" (the self-proclaimed representatives of the proletariat) to advance at once, without pause or stabilization, toward the next historical stage. In Mao's eyes, subjective weaknesses in "our" ranks (the human frailty and vulnerability of Communist party members and leaders who, whatever their revolutionary credentials, prove unable, once they achieve and exercise power, to withstand the "sugar-coated bullets" of the bourgeoisie) compelled a vigilant leadership (specifically the farsighted supreme leader) to incessantly rejuvenate a constantly threatened revolution. For Mao, it was a historical law and not just the sacred duty of the leadership to reinvigorate and restart the revolution; should this fail, the bourgeoisie would try a comeback and succeed. It is exactly what, according to Mao, had already happened in the Soviet Union. (It is well known that "On Khrushchev's Phony Communism and Its Historical Lessons for the World" was written with the Chinese revolution and the impending danger of its degeneration in mind.)

The "necessity to make revolution under conditions of the dictatorship of the proletariat"[18] was, of course, best illustrated by the Great Proletarian Cultural Revolution, launched by Mao two years after the writing of "On Khrushchev's Phony Communism. . . ." The way the Cultural Revolution ended, or more specifically, the means by which Mao put an end to it, considering the way he launched and managed it, points to Mao's temptation for permanent revolution.

Before trying to make clear the meaning of the word "temptation," let us analyze further Mao's impulse to launch a revolution within and against the revolution. A second revolution (but, as Mao made clear, others must periodically follow) should be directed against what the first has become or is in the process of becoming—e.g., institutionalized—in order to enable it to become again what it no longer is, i.e., revolutionary. This ambition of Mao was contradictory to the common assumption that a revolution can have enduring effects but does not itself endure, in the sense that it cannot maintain for long, far less perpetuate, the destabilization of the social system and other features of the crisis that by definition are ephemeral. Mao acted in his later years as if he desperately refused to accept the observation that the revolutionary crisis constitutes but one particular moment, that of the break with the past—the destruction of ancient structures and the acceleration of social change. Most of his actions implied that he denied the necessity of a restructuring that would enable social innovations to take shape and consolidate. Mao seemed to prefer sudden and violent changes over patient ones, rationalizing that the creativity of the masses, which is constrained by the straitjacket of fixed structures, flourishes in disorder—a disorder instigated and stopped by himself.

The decisive interventions of a leader who corrects "spontaneous" movement thanks to his almost divine status and prerogatives[19] make possible any kind of manipulation. Mao's manipulations, to which I will come back later, confirm that he was only attracted to or "tempted" by permanent revolution, but they illustrate the shrewd realism that went along with his utopian aspirations. To limit ourselves first, for the sake of analytical clarity, to only one side of Mao's contradictory leadership, let us further characterize his impulse to permanent revolution by contrasting it to Lenin's caution. From being the strategist, then the brilliant tactician of the conquest of power, Lenin rapidly transformed himself into the manager of an immense empire.[20] Within less than a year, the same leader imposed on his party first the April theses, then the acceptance of the Brest-Litovsk *diktat.* Mao, however, perpetually dreaming of new conquests of power that would miraculously solve the difficulties of *exercising* power, proved unable to complete his transformation. It is not surprising that the Great Teacher chose to capsulize, for the Red Guard's use, the whole of Marx's doctrine in one sentence: "To rebel is justified." The elderly Mao came to embody the classic figure of the romantic rebel, as opposed to the real revolutionary, always hard at the task of building a new world.

At least right after the assumption of power, Mao had been eager to build a new China, if not a new world. Although it is not well known, his record during the early fifties suggests that he was then more successful than later at collaborating with other CCP leaders. The successes of that earlier phase seem to have resulted from a collective undertaking by a still rather cohesive group of top leaders guiding the Chinese people along a not markedly original way. That way appeared to be the only way to follow during the first three years, until the reconstruction was completed. With the latter out of the way, most leaders, Mao included, probably saw it as safer to follow the pathway that had already been explored by their predecessors in the Soviet Union. I will not retrace here, as many students of Communist China have already done, how the Chinese leaders—and probably Mao to begin with—came to recognize that the Soviet model was not well suited to the task of developing China, and were thus compelled to look for a more appropriate strategy of development. Suffice it to contrast the cautious and not strikingly original approach followed until the mid-fifties with the more original and less secure set of policies that Mao began to evolve shortly thereafter.

Mao apparently began to doubt the validity of the Soviet model as early as 1955. A few months later, Stalin's posthumous fall from grace in Moscow incited Mao to question the political tenets of the Stalinist strategy; meanwhile, his acceleration of collectivization according to that strategy threatened China with a crisis similar to the one Eastern Europe was experiencing at the same time. Again, my purpose here is not to retrace step by step the building of the intellectual construction later to be known as Maoism or the Maoist model, but rather to clarify the mood and intent of the man who built it. By the spring of 1956, Mao's quest for an alternative model was also motivated by concern for his personal standing. Some CCP leaders resented the way Mao had imposed on his reticent colleagues the sudden acceleration of the pace of agricultural collectivization during the summer of 1955. As Noriyuki Tokuda has observed, "criticism of Stalin's personality cult would possibly turn into the criticism of Mao's behavioral pattern." A group of Politburo members chose to oppose the personality cult in order to "limit Mao's style of leadership, which transcended institutions, and to secure the . . . collective leadership of the party."[21]

Although an atmosphere of "opposing personality cults" made Mao feel uncomfortable,"[22] worries inspired by his ego do not appear to have been at the time more decisive than the responsible motivations of a leader elaborating an alternative strategy for socialist construction that could be more suited to China's needs. My hypothesis is that during the ensuing years, his personal motivations became more and more forceful, so that by the fateful summer of 1959 they finally overrode other, more abstract considerations, preventing him from adequately perceiving and responding responsibly to the sorry state of China. In the meantime (1956–1959), Mao had experienced a shocking series of setbacks and failures, coupled with indirect or not so veiled criticisms, that no doubt would have disturbed even a less proud and vainglorious leader. An incomplete list includes: the still bearable pains in 1956; like objections to, and disruptions caused by, the "First Leap" or writing off of Mao's Thought at the Eighth CCP Congress in September, in the wake of the subdued campaign against the personality cult; a major blunder in 1957, namely the experiment conducted against the will of Liu Shao-ch'i and others of the Hundred Flowers Campaign; and finally the Great Leap Forward of 1958, whose awful consequences should not cause us to overlook the added impact of less tragic miscalculations, including Mao's underestimate of U.S. and Taipei reactions during the Quemoy crisis.[23] Some of these episodes were first and last personal mortifications, hurting Mao alone, but others amounted to national crises that affected Mao all the more severely because the miscarried experiments were of his own making.[24]

Mao's declining prestige and personal discomfort explain but do not excuse his overreaction to P'eng Te-huai's criticisms in July 1959. The

Lushan crisis represented a decisive turning point not only in the political evolution of the Chinese Communist regime, but in Mao's personal evolution as well. During the Eighth Plenum of the Eighth Central Committee convened shortly after P'eng's attack, Mao emphasized for the first time with unmistakable firmness the persistence of class struggle under the dictatorship of the proletariat, a theme that was to become thereafter such a central element in his thought.[25] He also described the Lushan dispute as a struggle between two headquarters, with P'eng and his antiparty clique representing the bourgeois headquarters, in the same way as he would construe seven years later his purging of Liu Shao-ch'i as an attack on the headquarters of the capitalist restoration. Whatever new elements Mao added at the time to an intellectual construction that by then was already more than three years old were of less importance than the ugly side he revealed to his colleagues[26] as he undermined the political process by discarding some fundamental rules of the game, making difficult, if not impossible, future expressions of dissent by Politburo or Central Committee members.[27]

I think Mao's attitude at Lushan and during the early sixties, at a time when Great Leap policies had turned into absolute disaster, affected his authority more than anything that preceded this time, including the first manifestations of the failure of the Great Leap. After all, Liu Shao-ch'i had also shared responsibility in initiating the Great Leap, but his willingness to recognize the magnitude of the catastrophe and the implication of the central leadership in it,[28] as well as his determined advocacy of the only course then open to the rulers of a starving nation, won him only good will from his colleagues. To be sure, Mao reiterated in June 1961 and more obliquely in January 1962 the apologies he had offered at Lushan. But such a reluctant self-criticism, coupled with his criticisms of various associates, proved less impressive than his refusal to draw the obvious conclusions that many otherwise less perceptive CCP leaders had so easily reached. The resentment induced among Mao's colleagues by his attitude was further aggravated by his growing anxiety over vindicating himself, although the events had in fact dramatically vindicated P'eng Te-huai, whose verdict Mao had refused to "reverse."[29] In sum, Mao was preparing to fight for a model whose key elements had taken shape and repeatedly failed during the three previous years (1956–1959) by blaming the failure on his more pragmatic colleagues.

I do not intend to document here this well-known fight, from the Tenth Plenum of the Eighth Central Committee (September 1962) and the Socialist Education Campaign down to Mao's "last stand" against Teng Hsiao-p'ing in 1975–1976.[30] Rather, now that I have briefly recalled the dramatic alteration of both Mao's style of leadership and the functioning of the political process at the top of the regime over which he presided, I wish to add a few more general comments concerning some of the psychological roots of his attitudes and choices from the late fifties on—the time that witnessed the progressive transformation of the revolutionary leader into a rebel.

Mao's attacks on the bureaucracy, voicing familiar themes (Trotsky again), were no doubt well grounded for China as well as for other Communist states. They may also have been related to his fear of the institutionalization of the revolution—in other words, his worship of permanent revolution. As the main vehicle of institutionalization, bureaucracies after all represent a supreme means of dulling a leader's charisma. Mao's determination to prevent the institutionalization of the revolution became more obvious after the incipient erosion of his personal charisma, which he had helped maintain with the memory of his clearsightedness and perseverance in earlier years (the Kiangsi and Yenan years). This charisma was now threatened by his increasing recognition of his incompetence in matters of economic development and, more generally, his inability to live up to the various and complex tasks required in the undertaking of modernization. The necessary stabilization of the revolution, that is to say the time when serious and mundane tasks had come to predominate on the agenda, threatened the authority of a leader who was better suited to a time of tempests and of clear, simplistic, even heroic choices. Whatever the Promethean aspects of Mao's inspired Great Leap Forward, he thereafter attempted to rationalize the ideology behind it to the detriment of the pragmatic situation. Consciously or not, he tried to preserve and even accentuate his uniqueness in order to remain indispensable. At least *he* would embody faithfulness to the revolutionary ideals and values, which also meant sticking to a heroic past when he identified himself with the Chinese revolution. In that respect, his primarily defensive view of the permanent revolution (a permanent revolution that aimed at preventing the Chinese revolution from degenerating like the Soviet one) appears also nostalgic.

Whether Mao was right or wrong to fear that the Chinese revolution would regress from socialism to capitalism, this aging leader who looked back to Yenan precedents as recipes for developing the world's most populated country seemed to have himself experienced a kind of psychological retrogression. Dreaming of a golden age in the young, spartan days of the revolution, Mao fought a desperate rearguard action to preserve the original purity as cherished by the memory of a veteran. His relentless determination came close to giving the impression that he set this purity, the purity of a myth, above everything else, even above the perpetuation of an established revolution.

Only a Temptation

As noted, purity above all else was but an impression. In the last analysis Mao prized power more highly than purity. He was ready to take risks, not ultimate risks. He would never allow the disruption he initiated to take precedence over the perpetuation of the party rule. Whenever he felt that the threat to the established revolution posed by the challenge and struggle he had let loose had become too dangerous, he opted for continuity and therefore denial. He abruptly stopped the Hundred Flowers Campaign because of the growing threat it involved to the party's monopoly of power.[31] Some ten years later, during the Cultural Revolution, Mao began to reconstruct the party soon after it had incurred his wrath and punishment. He was not sure that so many Communist cadres who had just been attacked or purged had sincerely repented and satisfactorily amended their ways, but he needed them. Less than two years after the launching of the Cultural Revolution, the unacknowledged order of the day had become: "Long live the established revolution!"

Mao would certainly have disputed my characterization of his volte-faces as denials. He would have had good reasons to do so, because his brutal reversals were consistent with his long-standing priorities. These reversals were tactical retreats, which Mao was compelled to make once he was baffled and disappointed by the unforeseen consequences of his acts, but they did not mean that he had come to value power more than he had at the outset of each hazardous campaign. Instead, his power having become threatened, necessary steps in rescuing and maintaining it overrode every other consideration for the time being. Even before the threatening Wuhan incident and the growing turmoil during the summer of 1967, Mao had already made clear what he considered to be the absolute priority when he promptly and negatively reacted to the initiative taken by Chang Ch'un-ch'iao and Wang Hung-wen in establishing a replica of the Paris Commune in Shanghai. The reason was, of course, that such a move contradicted Mao's view of the necessity of a very centralized, authoritarian rule, a position he had constantly held. Challenging the uncontrolled power of the bureaucracy had never meant for him questioning the need of a supreme authority standing above both bureaucracy and the masses. Although his trenchant attack on the bureaucracy more than once evoked the virulence of previous denunciations by anarchists, Mao was decidedly not one of them. To be sure, he was impatient with rules, organization, and hierarchy. But the temperament of Mao the man was one thing, his beliefs and ultimate priorities quite another. Mao remained basically a Leninist, convinced of the necessity of both a vanguard leadership and an omnipotent "Centre" (Chung-yang). The same reason set him apart as well from liberal critics of the uncontrolled power of a potentially oppressive bureaucracy.[32]

Whatever the hopes some democrats might have entertained for a short time in May 1957, Mao could have objected to them in utmost sincerity: "I did not mean that." It was even hard for him to imagine how "bourgeois intellectuals" could indulge in such illusions. Although for the historian (at least for this historian) the most disconcerting illusion was that of the overconfident leader who thought that the criticisms he had solicited could remain confined to a discussion of the "style of party work," Mao was sincerely outraged by the critics who had exceeded his own directives. Ten years later, the threats represented by Cultural Revolutionary youths were even more menacing, and the wounds they inflicted heavier, as they erred no longer in words but in deeds. With the incipient polycentrism these Red Guards were bringing about, there could be no compromise, and Mao had to disavow his former allies (or tools). He not only disavowed them, but as suits a stern and righteous father, he punished and upbraided them for their failure to remain worthy of his trust (a breach of filial piety toward the revolution's father committed by the once but no longer "revolutionary successors"): "You have let me down."[33]

The Red Guards had every reason to consider that it was Mao who had let *them* down. Mao's deliberate manipulation of the frustrations and grievances[34] of a well-defined section of the urban masses had been preceded by a more classical and cautious move. Prior to embarking on his all-out assault against a well entrenched bureaucracy, Mao had assured for himself the support of the People's Liberation Army. To this end, he did not cultivate and mobilize rank-and-file troops. Nor did he incite them to constitute soviets of soldiers. He took the shorter path of making the defense minister his ally, an ally he duly repaid for his services first at the Eleventh Plenum of the Eighth Central Committee in August 1966, then at the Ninth Congress of the CCP in April 1969. Although such a move is reminiscent of the celebrated deals among warlords—all the more so if one takes into account the next episode of the tale of the two accomplices, that of the ultimate repayment in 1970–1971—there is nothing strange about it. It is even an entirely natural move in conducting a top-level struggle among power-holders, although it is less so from the point of view of a populist revolutionary hero inciting the masses to liberate themselves. Some of the latter came eventually to the sobering realization that they would never have been invited to participate in the exalted struggle if the not-so-supreme helmsman Liu Shao-ch'i and his crew had proved as compliant to the wishes and whims of the Great Helmsman as Lin Piao did.

Yet Mao considered himself the true representative of the masses: He spoke on their behalf and in their place; he stood for the interests of the have-nots as opposed to those of the privileged few. This conviction of Mao lies at the root of the contradiction pointed out by Lowell Dittmer: having "grown impatient with the rest of the leadership for impeding *his* initiatives," Mao "wanted the bureaucracy to be more responsive to *mass* demands."[35] As Dittmer nicely puts it, "the compatibility of these two objectives . . . was not entirely realistic." Quite naturally, the evolution of the Cultural Revolution provided ample evidence of the incompatibility between the will of the self-appointed representative of the masses and the spontaneous actions of various substrata of the same masses, defending, in Dittmer's words, "their own short-term particular interests." The latter groups were the real masses, as opposed to the ideal masses whose long-term interests the chairman was supposed to embody.

In other words, by ways different from those of Stalin, Mao did his best to make Rosa Luxemburg's forewarning that Bolshevism would lead to personal despotism come true.[36] But whereas Stalin succeeded in imposing his personal despotism, Mao failed.[37] To be sure, his failure can in great part be attributed precisely to the fact that his methods were more original, i.e., less classically expeditious, than those of Stalin. Mao's own efforts to counterbalance the enormous power of the party leadership did not infuse a substantial amount of genuine democracy into an extremely authoritarian system but amounted in the end only to tempering and at times overriding oligarchical rule by the personal will of the party chairman. The initiative in watching over, correcting, and purging the party was undertaken by none other than Mao himself. No procedure was laid down for the correction or the replacement of the supreme leader, who was reputedly infallible. Such was the case at least during the Cultural Revolution, when Mao's Thought came to represent the ultimate criterion of truth and goodness. By that time it had become a habit, as it remained for Mao's radical associates during the 1970s, to label as "antisocialist" everything from ideas to policies that diverged from Maoism or was at odds with Mao's most recent pronouncements, and to denounce as "antiparty" everyone who happened to disagree with Mao.

Conclusion

Many intellectuals in the West enthusiastically welcomed Maoist criticisms of bureaucracy and Mao's 1966 assault on the leadership of his own Communist party. They did so for the very reason that should have incited them to be skeptical, namely that Mao sat at the apex of the revolutionary (or in his eyes, no longer so revolutionary) hierarchy. That the Maoist criticisms were hardly new could not deter leftist intellectuals, who at least in my country had rarely bothered to listen to liberal criticisms of bureaucratic regimes, which they dismissed as anticommunist. It is precisely because Maoist criticisms and attacks did not come from liberal quarters that it was possible to attribute magical virtue to them. The rarely formulated but tenacious hope was that Mao could somehow go beyond Lenin's still imperfect model and make thirty years of Stalin's despotic rule look like a peculiar aberration, devoid of ominous implications for the future. As a true revolutionary and a victorious one at that—one who had displayed both insight and courage in criticizing and fighting the shortcomings of an established revolution—Mao found himself in the best position to advance beyond the extreme point once reached by Lenin. Mao's advances, or so the leftist intellectuals held, would be of universal significance for the whole of mankind.

The purpose of this paper was not to discuss the one-sided conception of progress implicit in the faith of such well-wishers of contemporary revolutions. Focusing more narrowly on the leader of the Chinese revolution, it has attempted to demonstrate that far from creating any practicable outlet from the impasses of the Leninist model, Mao Tse-tung fell victim to his own contradictions. As his successors now bluntly put it, what he attempted by launching the Cultural Revolution failed and could only fail: "the 'cultural revolution' was not and could in no way be a revolution, nor social progress."[38]

Such a sweeping statement would, in Mao's view, merely support what his successors are trying to do. They desperately want to further institutionalize the revolution (after so much precious time lost by Mao), in order to modernize the country. In such an endeavor the aim of achieving social progress, although not rejected, appears less fundamental than the basic economic and nationalistic goals, the yet-to-be-attained "fu-ch'iang" of late-Ch'ing patriots. With the apparent assumption that social progress, broadly conceived, will eventually follow economic modernization, the post-Mao leadership no longer assigns an urgent priority to the task of reducing current social inequalities. Mao was entirely right in that respect: institutionalizing the established revolution has led to giving up his own egalitarian, as well as his democratic, dreams.

Does institutionalization foreshadow, as Mao would have concluded, the end of the revolution? I would argue that by ending the revolutionary crisis, institutionalization makes revolutionary changes possible, although not certain. It opens the way to their realization. So far as these changes as now envisaged by the post-Mao leadership do not exactly coincide with each of the values explicitly proclaimed by the CCP during the last half-century, Mao would have some reason to castigate his successors as unfaithful to their ideals as well as to the most deprived part of the Chinese people, namely the peasant masses thanks to whom the Communist party achieved power.[39] Yet, as Tocqueville suggests, in the words of one contemporary commentator, "revolutionary periods are pre-eminently obscure historical periods, in which the cloak of ideology hides the true meaning of events from the very actors of the drama."[40] If, as I am inclined to consider probable, the true meaning of the Chinese revolution was and still is the modernization of a traditional society, coupled with nationalism (a meaning that Mao came to disregard),[41] then Mao's successors are more faithful to it than he himself was.

It is quite possible that the voice of the Great Teacher will still be heard long after the work of his opponent and successor, Teng Hsiao-p'ing, has been forgotten. Teng and his like are no more theoreticians than Mao was when he implemented his peasant strategy half a century ago. They content themselves to undertake in a serious manner the practical work that Mao belittled or suspected once it had proved to be too much for him.

Mao had once been up to his task, and therein lies his greatness. I will dispute not so much Gupta's formula ("the successful opportunism of a fiercely nationalistic Chinese") as the disparaging intent of his compliment. The successes obtained at the initiative and under the aegis of that steadfast and opportunistic nationalist leader remain a most impressive achievement and one that is congruent with the basic quest of the Chinese revolution. Should Gupta agree to go that far, I would myself agree that the pre-1956 Mao should be cut down to size. In the light of his post-1956 attitudes and performances, and pending the results of further research or revelations, one can already point out some striking continuities in Mao's unrestrained thought, proud and stubborn character,[42] and deviousness in dealing with political rivals,[43] as well as in the conscious building up of his image by the CCP leadership.[44] Unlike Moselwein or Burgundy, Mao did not become better by getting old, as illustrated by the change of stubbornness (which meant also will and determination) into obstinacy, of audaciousness into recklessness, and of pride into self-deception.

Notes

1. Krishna Prakash Gupta, "Mao's Uncertain Legacy," in ***Problems of Communism*** 31:1 (January-February 1982), pp. 45–50.
2. Ross Terrill, *Mao: A Biography* (New York: Harper and Row, 1980), p. 431.
3. Gupta, "Mao's Uncertain Legacy," p. 46.
4. Gupta, "Mao's Uncertain Legacy," p. 47.
5. See, for instance, Frederick C. Teiwes, "Chinese Politics 1949–1965: A changing Mao," in *Current Scene* 12:1 and 2 (January and February 1974).
6. Lucien Bianco, "La révolution fourvoyée," *Le Monde*, 10 September 1976. I concluded that given Mao's record during his last twenty years "the Chinese would not long be able to do without de-Maofication."
7. Gupta, "Mao's Uncertain Legacy," p. 47.
8. At the Sixth Plenum of the Eleventh Central Committee (CC) of the Chinese Communist Party (CCP) in June 1981. See "Resolution on Certain Questions in the History of Our Party Since the Founding of the People's Republic of China," *Beijing Review*, no. 27 (6 July 1981) and David Goodman's comments in *China Quarterly* (*CQ*), no. 87 (September 1981), pp. 518–527.
9. When reading recently the as-yet-unpublished memoirs of Mai Kang, a former Red Guard in Guangxi, who later escaped to Hong Kong to become a founder of *Huang-ho* (Yellow River) and a leading contributor to that magazine, I had at times the impression that I was listening to one of Lin Hsi-ling's speeches in May 1957: the same indignant mood, the same caustic or vigorous denunciations of power-holders, similar hopes and frustrations.
10. My refusal to separate the rectification campaign in the spring of 1957 from the antirightist campaign in the summer does not adequately solve the problem of when to begin an analysis centered on Mao's later years. One could just as well take as a starting point the initiation of radical economic policies in the autumn of 1957 or, on the contrary, go back to the July 1955 speech calling for the acceleration of agricultural collectivization. Or, if one chooses to center the analysis on the political process, one could just as well wait until the summer of 1959 and start with the decisive turning point at Lushan. Arguing against Gupta that Mao changed over time does not imply, of course, that one cannot find before the dividing line (1956 in the case of Gupta's review essay) some roots of certain of Mao's later policies, opinions, or attitudes; it would even be easy to detect some of them in Mao's writings, activities, and performance in the Yenan period. As a matter of pure convenience, this analysis will broadly encompass the last two decades (1955–1976) but consider the first four years (1955–1959) as a transition period, marked by the elaboration of the intellectual construction known as Maoism and the incipient erosion of Mao's confidence following the first unhappy experiments with various elements

of his new, incompletely built model. See "An incomplete list includes . . . " on text pages 30–31. Only after that confidence was badly shaken and Mao's former optimistic mood altered did the psychology of the rebel progressively override that of the revolutionary statesman. This paper will therefore devote fewer pages to the transition period than to the post-Lushan years. Rather than follow closely the political evolution during those seventeen years (1959–1976) it will concentrate on Mao's main impulses, which became more obvious during the Cultural Revolution.

11. Merle Goldman, *Literary Dissent in Communist China* (Cambridge, Mass.: Harvard University Press, 1967) and *China's Intellectuals: Advise and Dissent* (Cambridge, Mass.: Harvard University Press, 1981).

12. Benjamin I. Schwartz, "A Personal View of Some Thoughts of Mao Tse-tung," in *Ideology and Politics in Contemporary China,* ed. Chalmers Johnson (Seattle: University of Washington Press, 1973), pp. 367–368.

13. Leonard Schapiro, *The Communist Party of the Soviet Union* (London: Eyre and Spottiswoode, 1960).

14. Richard Curt Kraus, "The Limits of Maoist Egalitarianism," *Asian Survey* 16:11 (November 1976), pp. 1085–1086.

15. Kraus, "The Limits of Maoist Egalitarianism," pp. 1091 and 1096.

16. John Bryan Starr, *Continuing the Revolution: The Political Thought of Mao* (Princeton, N.J.: Princeton University Press, 1979), p. *ix*. Attempting to define Maoism in a colloquium devoted to Leninism (Paris, October 1977), I myself used the expression "tentation de la révolution permanente" in a report later published under the title "Essai de définition du maoïsme" in *Annales E.S.C.* (Paris, May 1979), pp. 1094–1108. Finally, Stuart Schram long ago pointed out the significance of the "permanent revolution" in Mao's Thought; see Stuart R. Schram, *La "Révolution permanente" en Chine* (Paris: Mouton, 1963) and "Mao Tse-tung and the Theory of the Permanent Revolution, 1958–1969," *CQ* 46 (April-June 1971), pp. 221–244. I shall not distinguish in this paper between the two concepts "permanent revolution" and "continuous revolution" but will use the former except when quoting Starr.

17. In order to prevent any confusion in the minds of readers familiar with the work of J. B. Starr, I must add that what I describe here as "the temptation of permanent revolution" is much less reminiscent of Mao's rather optimistic "theory of permanent revolution" than of his more pessimistic "theory of continuous revolution" as analyzed by Starr. See John Bryan Starr, "Conceptual Foundations of Mao Tse-tung's Theory of Continuous Revolution," in *Asian Survey* 11:6 (June 1971), pp. 615 and 621.

18. *Peking Review* 10:26 (23 June 1967), quoted in Starr, "Conceptual Foundations of Mao Tse-tung's Theory," p. 619.

19. To refer to the era of French classicism, Mao played the dual role of Descartes' God, who granted the initial spark, and of the deus ex machina of some of Moliere's plays, suddenly appearing and solving an otherwise inextricable mess.

20. One could argue, with Schapiro and others, that Lenin did not become a true statesman because he was unable to free himself of his dogma and therefore to compromise with his adversaries.

21. Noriyuki Tokuda, "The Impact of de-Stalinization on the Growth of Mao's Thought in 1956," paper presented at the *International Conference on the Analysis of Power and Policy in the PRC since 1949,* Saarbrücken, August 1982, pp. 7–8. The paper is reprinted as Chapter 3 of this book.

22. Tokuda, "The Impact of de-Stalinization," p. 9.

23. Allen S. Whiting, "New light on Mao: Quemoy 1958: Mao's Miscalculations," *CQ* 62 (June 1975), pp. 263–270.

24. For Mao's launching of the Hundred Flowers Campaign, see Roderick MacFarquhar, *The Origins of the Cultural Revolution,* vol. 1: *Contradictions Among the People,* 1956–1957 (New York: Oxford University Press, 1974). For the launching of the Great Leap Forward and sponsoring of the People's Communes, see Parris Chang, *Power and Policy in China* (University Park, Pa.: Pennsylvania State University Press, 1978), pp. 82–85. Mao's own admission of his responsibility in having "proposed," not "invented," the People's Com-

munes (in his 23 July 1959 speech at the Lushan conference) is translated in Stuart Schram, *Mao Tse-tung Unrehearsed* (Harmondsworth, U.K.: Penguin Books, 1974), p. 145.

25. See Lowell Dittmer, *Liu Shao-ch'i and the Chinese Cultural Revolution: The Politics of Mass Criticism* (Berkeley: University of California Press, 1974), p. 56; Teiwes, "Chinese Politics 1949–1965: A Changing Mao," part 1, p. 8.

26. Michel Oksenberg, "The Political Leader," in *Mao Tse-tung in the Scales of History,* ed. Dick Wilson (Cambridge, U.K.: Cambridge University Press, 1977), p. 113.

27. See, among others, Teiwes, *Politics and Purges in China: Rectification and the Decline of Party Norms, 1950–1965* (White Plains, N.Y.: Sharpe, 1979), ch. 9, especially pp. 423 and 437–439.

28. Byung-joon Ahn, "Adjustments in the Great Leap Forward and Their Ideological Legacy, 1959–1962," in *Ideology and Politics in Contemporary China,* pp. 287–288.

29. For Mao's post-Lushan self-criticism, see, among others, Ahn, "Adjustments in the Great Leap Forward," p. 282, and Teiwes, *Politics and Purges in China,* pp. 473–474 and 482. For Mao's counterattack and its effects on CCP leadership, see the same authors and sources (Ahn, pp. 292–294; Teiwes, pp. 441, 479–481, 493 ff) and Ellis Joffe, *Between Two Plenums: China's Intra-Leadership Conflict, 1959–1962* (Ann Arbor, Mich., 1975). The slight differences of emphasis and interpretation between these authors cannot be detailed here.

30. Parris H. Chang, "Mao's Last Stand?" in *Problems of Communism* 25:4 (July-August 1976), pp. 1–17.

31. As Benjamin Schwartz has observed, if, as is commonly assumed, one of the basic aims of the Hundred Flowers Campaign was to make the participation of intellectuals and professionals in economic and scientific development more efficient, then the experiment was not "given time to prove itself." The economic results that Mao had hoped to achieve had to be sacrificed to the overriding concern of maintaining his power. See "Modernisation and the Maoist Vision—Some Reflections on Chinese Communist Goals," *CQ* 21 (January-March 1965), p. 5, also reprinted in Benjamin I. Schwartz, *Communism and China: Ideology in Flux* (Cambridge, Mass.: Harvard University Press, 1968), p. 166.

32. I see no need to dwell on the distinction between Mao on the one hand and liberals and anarchists on the other. The reader can refer to the illuminating comments made long ago by Schwartz, "A Personal View of Some Thoughts of Mao Tse-tung," pp. 361–367.

33. Parris H. Chang, "Mao's Great Purge: A Political Balance Sheet," in *Problems of Communism* 18:2 (March-April 1969), p. 3.

34. These frustrations and grievances turned out to be deeper than Mao had expected, notwithstanding the lesson of his earlier underestimation of the resentment felt by the noncommunist intelligentsia against the party's rule in 1957.

35. Lowell Dittmer, "The Legacy of Mao Zedong," *Asian Survey* 20:5 (May 1980), p. 562. The emphasis is Dittmer's.

36. The Chinese Communist party was and is not, to be sure, the exact replica of the Bolshevik party, but it retains (and retained even more until 1959) many important characteristics of its model. Specifically, as Teiwes' study has detailed, before its conquest of the whole of the Chinese mainland it had integrated essential components of Leninist discipline and organizational norms. See *Politics and Purges in China,* chs. 1 and 3.

37. For an extremely stimulating interpretation of the Cultural Revolution as "a failed attempt at despotism," see Richard Lowenthal, "Different Stages on Different Roads: A Contribution to the Comparative Analysis of the Soviet and Chinese Political Systems," paper presented at a symposium on the Russian and Chinese revolutionary regimes organized by the CESES (Centro Studie ricerche su problemi economico-sociali), Milan, November 1976, 19 pp.

38. "Resolution on Certain Questions in the History of Our Party," (Art. 20, § 4).

39. As is well known, however, the majority of Chinese peasant families have in fact increased their income under the present leadership, especially since the adoption of the "responsibility system." If consulted, no doubt an overwhelming majority would be in favor of the current policies, in spite of the fact that their rationale would be primarily economic (to increase their productivity) rather than social (to reduce the gap between

rural and urban incomes). Similarly, they would have opposed Mao's egalitarian policies. This simply adds another argument to the commonly held assumption (which I share) that few Maoist policies were either popular or effective.

40. Francois Furet, *Penser la Révolution française* (Paris: Gallimard, 1978), p. 206.

41. Mao, to be sure, remained to the end a strongly nationalistic, or in Gupta's words, a "fiercely nationalistic" leader, devoted to China's strength and greatness. But the conflict between this goal and his broader ideological quest prevented him from pursuing the modernization of China with the same single-mindedness and efficiency (however limited) as his successors. Moreover, the peculiar brand of nationalism that he or his radical associates came to embody during the 1970s looks to me, as I have argued elsewhere, more traditional than that of his opponents at the time, now his successors (Lucien Bianco, "La Chine après Mao," *Revue des Travaux de l'Académie des Sciences Politiques,* Paris, second semester 1976, pp. 709–730).

42. See, for instance, the often-quoted sharp descriptions by Agnes Smedley of her first meeting with Mao, *Battle Hymn of China* (London, 1944), pp. 121–122. One could also recall Mao's 1953 outburst against Liang Shu-ming, which anticipated his 1959 anger at P'eng Te-huai. In both cases, Mao erupted so violently because he felt ill at ease or even insecure; he knew that many CCP leaders shared P'eng's opinion in 1959, and Liang's criticisms at the abandonment of the peasantry hit a sensitive point. Mao had furthermore long been impressed by Liang's personality and ideas. See Guy Alitto, *The Last Confucian* (Berkeley: University of California Press, 1979), pp. 1–3, 285, 290.

43. Chang Kuo-t'ao, *The Rise of the Chinese Communist Party,* 2 vols. (Lawrence: University of Kansas Press, 1971/72); see especially the last 200 pages of vol. 2. In spite of Chang's obvious biases and the reconstructed character of his reminiscences, one can no more dismiss everything he said about or against Mao than one can reject as unfair the celebrated description of B-52's tactics of "divide and rule" in the "Outline of Project 571"; see Michael Y. M. Kau, ed., *The Lin Piao Affair* (White Plains, N.Y.: International Arts and Sciences Press, 1975), p. 89.

44. See, for instance, William F. Dorrill, "Transfer of Legitimacy in the Chinese Community Party: Origins of the Maoist Myth," in *Party Leadership and Revolutionary Power in China,* ed. John Wilson Lewis (Cambridge, U.K.: Cambridge University Press, 1970), pp. 69–113; Liu's Report to the Seventh Party Congress (1945), as analyzed by Lowell Dittmer, *Liu Shao-ch'i,* p. 24; and finally the "Resolution on Certain Questions in the History of Our Party" adopted shortly before the Seventh Congress at the Seventh Plenum of the Sixth Central Committee, which was no doubt very much in the mind of Teng Hsiao-p'ing and other veterans when they gave a similar title to the June 1981 resolution that has been previously cited (see Notes 8 and 38).

3
The Impact of De-Stalinization on the Growth of Mao's Thought in 1956

Noriyuki Tokuda

Introduction

In considering the interaction between the formation of Maoism and the international environment, we must start from a simple but crucial fact: China's genuine challenge to the Soviet model of socialist construction took place *after* the death of Stalin in March 1953. China was unlike the East European countries that completed their conversion to socialism during the heyday of Stalinism, thereby experiencing a transplantation of Stalinism. China's revolutionary condition, too, was quite different from that of Eastern Europe. Nonetheless, Chinese socialist construction would have followed something of a different road if Stalin had been alive for ten more years. The "time lag" that allowed China to complete her conversion to socialism after Stalin's death was fateful indeed. Stalin's death, in R. Tucker's words, was a point of departure for de-Stalinization almost as a logical consequence of the nature of Stalinism.[1]

The centralized rule of a Stalinist USSR over the international Communist movement quickly passed away. The form of solidarity among Communist countries thereafter became pluralistic through the acceptance of their diversified characters. The imbalance of power relations between China and the USSR that had defined their alliance changed, too, to a form in striking contrast to that during the days of Stalin. The unstable leadership of the Soviet Communist party and the posture of Stalin's successors in seeking access to Mao after Stalin's death increased China's influence in the world and enhanced Mao's prestige in the international Communist movement. Thus, barriers to the independent way of China's socialist construction under the leadership of Mao disappeared one by one from the international scene. By 1955, Mao might have been almost "liberated"—to use his own word—from the psychological pressure of Stalin's authority.

In December 1955, when the prototype of the Maoist strategy was being formed, Mao declared that "no frequent comparison with the Soviet Union is needed at all";[2] he pointed out the more advantageous conditions of the Chinese revolution in comparison to the Soviet Union. In January 1956, immediately after this declaration, Mao made surprising remarks that later were considered to have indicated both a veiled "criticism of Stalin" and his own theoretical ambition: "We must also make a theoretical contribution and develop further what the elder generation has said. However, from the October Revolution up to the present, no distinguished new thing has been born."[3] Here we find Stalin's role left unmentioned, whereas in Mao's article "The Greatest Friendship" (9 March 1953), written on the occasion of Stalin's death, the Chinese leader had praised Stalin as a "great teacher" and spoken of his role in the "total and epoch-making development of Marxist-Leninist theory and in making new progress in Marxism."

By January 1956, therefore, Mao might already have been enthusiastic about building his own peculiar strategy, and so he tended to give a relatively low evaluation of the relevance of Stalinism to the socialist construction in China. Khrushchev's criticism of Stalin in the Twentieth Congress of the Soviet Communist party in the following month might not have been a cause for serious confusion and discouragement to Mao, unlike Communist leaders in Eastern Europe. According to his later testimony, Mao showed a quite ambivalent response to Khrushchev's criticism; he felt "awfully pleased" on the one hand and "afraid" on the other.[4] His fear was of disintegration of the authority system in the Communist world, but it also marked a decisive and "awfully pleasant" point of departure for the "liberation" of what came to be known as Mao Thought.

However, as would be illustrated by the dramatic dynamics of Chinese politics in the years 1956–1958, before the completion of his ideological "liberation" aimed in the direction of constructing his own socialist strategy, Mao had to make a temporary detour in order to get over the impact that criticism of Stalin had on Chinese politics. The new line of the Soviet Union of the Twentieth Congress of the Soviet Communist party and the subsequent political and military turmoil it gave rise to in Eastern Europe were linked in several ways with China's internal politics during 1956 and the first half of 1957. It should be noted, however, that the CCP leadership did not necessarily give a uniform response to such a great change in the international Communist movement and that Mao's own response to the new political trend generated in China by this change was not necessarily consistent.

Some groups of leaders within the CCP understood that the questions raised by the criticism of Stalin were closely related to China's internal affairs. The year 1956 was already a difficult period for China, which was handling simultaneously the task of a two-faceted transformation—both political and domestic (socioeconomic) changes inherent in conversion to socialism. At this very moment, the Soviet Union and East

European countries embarked on criticizing the "distorted elements" in the past Soviet model and in making efforts to build a more flexible system and establish socialist legitimacy. Thus, the fact that China's socialist construction was being implemented after Stalin's death marked the Chinese evolution of socialism as different in time from that in the Soviet Union and East Europe. Immediately after the opening of criticism of Stalin, this "time lag" was an advantage for Mao but was a disturbing element in China's domestic affairs and in CCP relations with the Soviet Union.

Chinese Communist Party Response to De-Stalinization

Chinese response to the Twentieth Congress of the Soviet Communist party was outlined by both official and unofficial documents during February and April of 1956. The contents of the documents largely explained the CCP's initial response as a whole, although they did not necessarily represent satisfactorily Mao's true intention, partly because of diplomatic considerations and partly because of compromises among a variety of opinions within the party.

After the Sino-Soviet conflict in 1960, the Twentieth Congress was often pointed out to be the turning point in their relationship.[5] We should note here, however, that in 1956 the CCP actually took a generally positive attitude toward the new line adopted in this congress. Judging from the past Sino-Soviet relationship, it was only natural that Mao's congratulatory telegram to this congress on February 15 commended Khrushchev's policy of giving priority to heavy industry and praised the Soviet Communist party as a "distinguished model." However, the editorial of the *People's Daily* on February 19 assumed separate importance; it praised Khrushchev's report to the Central Committee for "bringing about a creative development in Marxism-Leninism."[6]

In his "opening remarks" to the Eighth Congress of the CCP in September 1956, Mao again acclaimed the Soviet Twentieth Congress: "The Soviet Communist Party again promulgated many correct policies and also criticized shortcomings within the party at the Twentieth Party Congress which was recently convened." There is no doubt that Mao and the CCP did not officially change their positive response to the Twentieth Congress throughout 1956.[7] This fact is significant in that Khrushchev's criticism of Stalin was made in a secret forum attended exclusively by representatives of Soviet Communists, immediately before the end of the official schedule of the congress. When the text was later delivered to the CCP, one can imagine how deep the CCP's shock was. It was with no expectation of criticism of Stalin that Mao's congratulatory telegram had referred to Stalin's name, or the draft of Chu Teh's (chief of the delegation of the Central Committee of the CCP) speech had been prepared. The editorial of the *People's Daily* expressed the great embarrassment that such astounding criticism of Stalin created within the CCP. Although the *People's Daily* carried detailed reports of the congress, its editorial at the end of the sessions was unexpectedly simple in light of the significance of the criticism of Stalin. It made no reference to such questions as the personality cult and collective leadership, although it fully acclaimed the new line set by the congress.[8]

For a month from the end of February, the question of criticism of Stalin was perhaps discussed within the Politburo of the CCP, but no detailed information on the discussions is available. It is apparent, however, that this question entailed a dangerous logic that could possibly have been damaging to China and, therefore, that its appropriate handling seemed to be a crucial task for the party leadership as a whole. It raised two important issues, the first of which was the appraisal of Stalin's historical role. Given China's socialist construction, which was still in the "Stalinist stage," it was likely that criticism of Stalin's leadership would impair Chinese policies at that time. In the Soviet Union, criticism of Stalin was designed to institute prosecution against the past, to remove fetters upon "better" socialism in the future. However, in China, which was copying the past method of the Soviet Union, a rejection of the Soviet past would raise doubts about the legitimacy of the Chinese "present." The second issue was more concrete: There was concern that criticism of Stalin's personality cult possibly would turn into criticism of Mao's behavioral pattern as it had begun to emerge after 1955. In other words, the criticism of Stalin could have the impact of a "two-edged sword" on Mao and also reveal the fact that Chinese social development was lagging behind that of the Soviet Union. The CCP leadership thus had to stand for China's "national interests," and it saw dangerous implications in the criticism of Stalin.

On 5 April 1956, after a month of silence, a direct reply on the question of the criticism of Stalin was published in the form of a joint article of the Politburo of the CCP, entitled "On the Historical Experiences of the Dictatorship of the Proletariat." Basically, this article accepted Soviet criticism of Stalin as "courageous self-criticism" and also proposed to "make an overall and proper analysis" of "Stalin's great contributions and mistakes." At the same time, however, it addressed China's political difficulties with the situation by implicitly urging a more favorable appreciation of positive aspects of Stalin's achievements. Such an independent interpretation was undoubtedly made in order to reprove the Soviet Union for its *excessive* denunciation of Stalin. By approving of the basic principle of the Twentieth Party Congress as defined by Khrushchev, however, this article allowed the CCP to remain in collaboration with the new leadership of the Soviet Union. As for the second issue of opposition to personality cults, the CCP never admitted that its leadership was infected by the evils of personality cults, but supported the Soviet argument as a whole and urged continued struggle against personality cults in China. Furthermore, in this article the CCP tried to show the superiority of "China's way." In brief, the CCP's traditional principle of party organization, the "mass line" that had been formulated in "The Decision on Leadership Methods" in June 1943, was proposed as a prescription to the disease of Stalinism. In so doing, the CCP attempted to avoid one edge of the sword of Soviet criticism of Stalin.

The joint article of the Politburo made skillful use of the logic summarized above to defend China's position as much as possible from the external impacts of the criticism of Stalin. In terms of internal Chinese politics, however, the article appeared to have added implications. A group of leaders within the Politburo was inclined to limit Mao's style of leadership, which transcended institutions, and to secure the mass line and collective leadership of the party. This article gave them a chance to make skillful use of the question of criticism of Stalin for this purpose. Seen in this light, the article represented a compromise on the implicit "disagreements" within the Politburo. Mao probably felt that this article was a "two-edged sword" against Stalin and himself, and in recalling such a sword used against him within the party, he described in his speech of March 1958: "Khrushchev's clubbing Stalin to death with a single blow was a sort of pressure. The majority of the CCP did not agree to it. But some submitted tamely to this pressure and tried to overcome personality cult. *They are very much interested in opposing personality cult.*"[9] [my italics] An atmosphere of "opposing personality cults" clearly made Mao feel uncomfortable.

In summary, it seems evident that a delicate but significant gap in accord lay in the responses of the Politburo members to the trend of de-Stalinization. Beyond such a delicate gap, the responses among Chinese leaders projected the towering shadows of a distinctively Chinese way of perception in socialist politics. It was a logic contained in the experiences of the Chinese revolution. The Politburo members represented a fundamental view of the CCP beyond any *political* maneuver and hence marked both the peculiarity of Chinese Communism and its limitations in the international Communist movement as the latter entered the age of de-Stalinization.

Institutional Immaturity of the Chinese View

"China's way," to which the CCP tended to return, was in the words of the joint article to "have self-control and be moderate, keep in close touch with the masses, consult with the masses whenever necessary, investigate and study repeatedly actual conditions, and carry out constant criticism and self-criticism relevant to the realities." A combination of the leadership techniques and a sort of cultivation of personality among leaders and cadres was proposed in this "China's way."

Even in responding to the more complicated task of socialist construction, the past moralistic idea still remained strong within the CCP. In June 1956, Togliatti criticized the Soviet logic in denouncing Stalin: "If [criticism of Stalin] ends up with charging all mistakes to Stalin's personal defects, it would not go beyond the question of personality cult."[10] In examining the disease of political leadership, the CCP not only should have dealt with its relationship with the environment, but also should have introduced a more scientific and diversified perspective from which to consider its political culture, political structure, political line, and so forth. Although the CCP referred to a "certain system,"[11] it presented merely the Yenan tradition. The joint article certainly admitted officially for the first time the existence of contradictions in socialist society, but its disclosure of contradictory aspects was not full and its argument on the handling of contradictions was immature. The joint article made references to "good men and bad men" and "those whose ideas are correct and those whose ideas are wrong," but it searched for the reasons and justifications exclusively within a framework of moralistic self-criticism of leaders.

It was the comment on Stalin's purge that most vividly showed the CCP's insufficient understanding of the issue of personality cult, although the Politburo leaders affirmatively evaluated its significance. Stalin's personality cult was a prerequisite to the "eternal purge" in the Soviet Union. A denial of the personality cult would culminate in the reexamination and revision of the ruling methods in the Soviet Union. The joint article, however, simply described and separated these two issues, acknowledging that "The question of purging counterrevolutionaries has a tendency to be broadened." It failed to carry out an examination of this question, not even to the degree that the Soviet Union did. Perhaps the Soviet criticism of Stalin's thesis on class struggle preoccupied the CCP so much with difficult theoretical problems that it made only a simple reference to the purge. It is quite remarkable, however, that the CCP made no reference at all to the most fundamental questions the Soviet Communist party presented at this juncture in the new line. (Included in such questions were a denial of Stalin's thesis on the "intensification of class struggle" and an institutional proposal to "consolidate socialist legitimacy.") Instead, the ambiguity and maneuvering that characterized the assertions of the Chinese reply seem to have resulted from an inclination to minimize the political impact of the criticism of Stalin. The reply also indicated the limitations within which Mao and other leaders in the CCP understood the evolution of socialism.

Chinese official opinion during February and April, therefore, already showed in practice an implicit difference from the Khrushchev line, although reiterating basic support of the decisions made in the Twentieth Congress. This implicit difference apparently reflected a gap between Maoist ideas on socialist *transformation* and the Khrushchev line on the *developed* socialist system. Despite the fact that the political shock of the criticism of Stalin was tremendous, in the long run China's perception of socialism never shared any crucial point in common with the Soviet Union. The Chinese way of argument was, after all, for the benefit of her own position and interest. It appeared to be in direct opposition to Togliatti's painful but extremely analytical article searching for a new concept of socialism by criticizing Stalin.[12]

Mao's own personal response was also very different from the official one of the party. The criticisms of personality cult caused him some uneasiness[13] and led him to interpret the question of criticism of Stalin in the context of political relevancy to himself. In his speech in January 1957, he stated: "The surrounding conditions compelled our Soviet comrades to change step by step. Their old manner of governing would not work both at home and abroad. The Twentieth Soviet Party Congress may be utilized. Both imperialism and Tito have utilized the congress before and we can utilize it, too. We should help them."[14] His repeated use of "utilize" indicated that he perceived the Twentieth Congress as advantageous to his ideological liberation and to China's independence in the international Communist movement. In this light, one may make an ironic interpretation of Mao's appraisal of the "correct line of policy" of the Twentieth Congress, when he appeared before the Eighth Congress of the CCP. It was not the correctness of the content itself but its merits for his own purposes that made him appraise favorably the "correct line" of the Soviet Twentieth Congress. Early in 1956, Mao was already in the midst of building the prototype of Maoism. Whether or not Khrushchev's denunciations of Stalin were right, the Soviet model for socialist construction was increasingly becoming irrelevant to China. Thus, with some verbal advocacy of learning from the Soviet Union, China had to search for its own way at the time of its political and domestic transformation.

The Departure for China's Unique Way

Of pointed interest is a speech "On the Ten Major Relationships" that Mao made in April 1956, shortly after the Politburo's joint article was published. Almost two years later, Mao made the following remarks regarding this matter: "On impulse, I held a discussion with thirty-four ministers. When the ten major relationships were discussed, my head swelled and I 'boldly advanced.' "[15]

"On the Ten Major Relationships," a secret speech, was in effect Mao's indirect but systematic reply concerning the strategy for socialist construction in response to the impacts of the criticism of Stalin. As is well known, Mao attempted in this speech to apply his ideas on contradiction to ten contradictory relationships in socialist industrialization and nation-building. By comparison with his earlier philosophical arguments concerning mainly agricultural policies, class struggle, and social dynamics, his argument in this speech took into more concrete and systematic consideration problems that soon became extensively discussed. The first systematization of Mao's "line of construction" came about in this speech.

In his later remarks of March 1958, Mao further explained, "[We] have presented 'On the Ten Major Relationships.' We have started to propose our own line of construction. It is the same as the Soviet one in principle but has its own content."[16]

The joint article of the Politburo, which as noted had been published shortly before Mao's speech, referred largely to the facts of Chinese revolutionary history and did not formulate a strategy for socialist construction in dealing with the question of the "combination of the universal truth of Marxism-Leninism and the concrete situation of China." It briefly emphasized the necessity of "continuing [our] struggle against dogmatism." By contrast, "On the Ten Major Relationships" represented Mao's version of "Chinese Marxism" in the stage of socialism. It was undoubtedly this speech that was developed into "On the Correct Handling of Contradictions Among the People," which was presented in February 1957, about a year later, and published in June 1957. It should also be noted that the speech "On the Ten Major Relationships" already expressed not only the prototype of Mao's grand theory on social management but also his way of thinking, though in embryo form, in direct connection with the economic line during the Great Leap Forward.

Typical of Mao's thinking on the economy were parts of the first "relationship between industry and agriculture, heavy industry and light industry," the second "relationship between industry in the coastal regions and industry in the interior," and the fifth "relationship between the center and the localities." Though assuming that "heavy industry is the key sector which must be given priority," Mao presented a much broader image of the policy of industrialization as "walking on two legs": "We must put more emphasis on light industry and agriculture than in the past. We must make appropriate adjustments in the proportion of investment between heavy industry and light industry, and between industry and agriculture. We must make [an] appropriate increase in the proportion of investment in light industry and agriculture which is contained in the total industrial and agricultural investment."[17] The second and fifth relationships, too, were clearly in close association with the Great Leap Forward's policy of promoting the organization of small economic regions and stimulating the initiative and activism of the localities and basic units.

By elaborating his own "line of construction" as outlined in "On the Ten Major Relationships," Mao launched a systematic revision of the Soviet model for construction. Although in that private speech he had only generally referred to "mistakes of some socialist countries," "experiences of some socialist countries," or shortcomings in "the postrevolutionary conditions in some countries"—all of which apparently indicated the Soviet Union—these references emphasized the possible existence of some other way, distinct from the Soviet one. In asserting that "to learn the merits of foreign countries is of course not to learn their demerits," Mao attempted to reexamine—not with a "blind" but with an "analytic and critical attitude" in the context of "China's actual conditions"—the overall concept of the First Five-Year Plan, which had been heavily dependent on the Soviet model.

It is not known how Mao's secret speech "On the Ten Major Relationships" was accepted at first among the group of party leaders classified as pragmatic bureaucrats. According to Mao's remarks in May 1958, "Party secretaries of provinces and municipalities, too, attended the enlarged conference of the Politburo in April [1956]," and "This conference adopted no definite resolution but a simple gentlemen's agreement." Participants in this conference appeared hesitant to make any definite policy decision. In this context, Mao's "line of construction" might have been considered as just an individual experimental plan, although it gave important suggestions. As he stated in January 1957, "Since the latter half of last year [1956], the trend of right opportunism has pervaded everywhere and the reverse current of antisocialism has been present both inside and outside the party."[18] The entire party leadership as well as Mao, facing the tasks in this two-faceted transformation as earlier described, was in search of "China's unique way." They had not yet any established line to handle the new era, although they possessed an invaluable heritage of the past revolutionary war.

The CCP was unable to resist the overwhelming political trend of de-Stalinization in the international Communist movement in 1956, though it was able to make a double-faced response of approval and resistance. Mao temporarily withdrew his own strategy for socialist construction as represented in "On the Ten Major Relationships" and as party chairman officially approved the new "adaptive line," which was far removed from principles of his strategy and contrary to the revolutionism dominant in China in the year 1955. Underlying his response to the new line of the CCP's Eighth Congress were perhaps a concession to such an overwhelming political trend and also a recognition of the prevailing realities. This period was one of trial and error for Mao and the CCP. What the de-Stalinization policy and Khrushchev's new line meant to China, however, became clear in only a short period of time—in fact, in just a year. The response of the party *as a whole* to the political crisis of the struggle against rightists, from the summer of 1957 on, was to be the turning point leading to the rebirth and development of Maoism and to the establishment of its legitimacy in the spring of 1958.

Notes

1. Robert C. Tucker, *The Marxian Revolutionary Idea* (London: George Allen and Unwin, 1969), p. 46.

2. Mao Tse-tung, "Speech on Anti-Rightist Tendency and Anti-Conservatism," 6 December 1955, in *Mao Tse-tung Sixiang Wansui* [Long live the thought of Mao Tse-tung, hereinafter, Wansui], August 1969, p. 27.

3. Mao Tse-tung, "Speech at the Conference on the Question of Intellectuals Held by the Party Center," 20 January 1956, *Wansui,* p. 33.

4. Mao Tse-tung, "Speech at the Chentu Conference," March 1958, *Wansui,* p. 163. Here Mao also went on to say, "It is completely necessary to uncover the top, destroy superstition, eliminate pressure, and liberate ideology."

5. Donald S. Zagoria, *The Sino-Soviet Conflict, 1956–1961* (New York: Atheneum, 1964), p. 40. That the Twentieth Congress of the Soviet Communist party was a "turning point"

should not be necessarily understood as a starting point of the Sino-Soviet conflict. It is true that in "The Origins and Developments of Our Different Opinions from the Leadership of the Soviet Communist Party" on 6 September 1963, the editorial boards of the *People's Daily* and *Red Flag* insisted, "The differences in opinion [on the international Communist movement] took place in the Twentieth Congress of the Soviet Communist party of 1956." However, as is clear in this paper, this insistence on the Chinese side was inconsistent with its 1956 opinion.

6. "Commemorating Word of the Central Committee of the CCP" (Hsin-hua-she-shin-wen-kao, 16 February 1956); "Speech of Chu Teh, Chief of the Delegation of the Central Committee of the CCP," 15 February 1956; and "An Editorial: Document with Historical Significance" (*People's Daily,* 19 February 1956), Hsin-hua pan-yueh-kan, no. 6, 1956.

7. In the "Speech at the Supreme Soviet Conference of the Soviet Union in Commemoration of the Fortieth Anniversary of the October Socialist Revolution" on 6 November 1957, Mao also stated: "The Communist Party of the Soviet Union has creatively applied Marxist-Leninist theory in undertaking practical tasks and in winning consecutive victories in the construction projects of the people of the Soviet Union. The program of struggle which the Twentieth Party Congress of the Communist Party of the Soviet Union proposed for building Communism in the Soviet Union is a typical model for this." In so saying, Mao accepted the legitimacy of the Twentieth Congress.

8. "The Victorious Closing of the Twentieth Party Congress of the Soviet Communist Party," 28 February 1956, Hsin-hua pan-yueh-kan, no. 7, 1956.

9. *Wansui,* p. 162. Some important articles that set the political trend in 1956 were ignored or denounced after the Cultural Revolution. This indicates that Mao felt moderately strong but not total dissatisfaction with the political trend of de-Stalinization.

10. Palmiro Togliatti, "The Question of Socialist Democracy and the Development of Socialist Democracy: A Reply to the *Nuovi Argomenti,*" in *The Criticism of Stalin and Foreign Communist Parties,* trans. Shakaishugi Kenkyukai (Tokyo: Otsuki Shoten, 1956), p. 20.

11. In the joint article of the Politburo, the term "system" appeared: "For this, we have a certain system, guaranteeing to carry out the mass line and the collective leadership." The term "system" seems to mean a feedback system in the mass line, as a leadership method.

12. For Togliatti's articles in relation to the criticism of Stalin, see "The Struggle for the Italian Way to Socialism in the Changing Situation both in Italy and the World: Report of the Central Committee," "The Existence of Adversaries," and "Statement Concerning the Resolution of the Central Committee of the Communist Party of the Soviet Union" in *The Criticism of Stalin and Foreign Communist Parties.* His very sophisticated analysis impressively expresses the real agony of a Marxist. He never said, as Mao did in one sense, that the criticism of Stalin is "quite pleasant."

13. For Mao's argument supporting personality cult, see his speeches in January and March 1958 included in *Wansui.*

14. Mao Tse-tung, "The Conclusion of the Conference of Provincial and Municipal Secretaries," January 1957, *Wansui,* p. 84.

15. Mao Tse-tung, "Speech at the Nanning Conference," January 1958, *Wansui,* p. 151.

16. *Wansui,* p. 163.

17. *Wansui,* p. 41.

18. Mao Tse-tung, "An Episode at the Conference of Provincial and Municipal Secretaries," January 1957, *Wansui,* p. 73.

Part 2

Politics and Government in the People's Republic of China

4
The Evolution of the Chinese Communist Party Since 1949

Parris H. Chang

Introduction

With the establishment of the People's Republic of China (PRC) in 1949, the Chinese Communist Party (CCP) shifted from a revolutionary organization to a ruling party. For over thirty years since then, but with the exception of a few years during the Great Proletarian Cultural Revolution in the late 1960s, the CCP has been the most important structure of power, possessing ultimate authority and undisputed primacy and monopolizing the processes of policymaking in China.

During these three decades, despite continuity, the CCP has been undergoing significant transformations, not only internally but also in its relationships to other hierarchies of power and to the citizenry, and in its role in China's overall political system. This essay analyzes: (1) the evolution of the CCP as an institution (its membership and organizational structure); (2) the elite composition and leadership struggle of the party; (3) the relations between the CCP and other structures of power; and (4) the role of the CCP in China's overall political system and the CCP's relationship with the society at large.

Membership and Organizational Changes

Expansion of the Membership

In the past three decades, there has been an enormous growth in the human composition of the CCP (see Table 4.1). In 1949 (not shown in table), the party had a membership of 4.4 million, which accounted for less than 1 percent of China's population, but by 1977, at the time of the Eleventh CCP Congress, the membership had increased to 35 million, or 3.7 percent of the total population of 930 million. According to an official source, party membership was 39.6 million on the eve of the Twelfth Congress in September 1982; by now the membership should exceed 40 million.

Table 4.1 CCP Membership Growth Pattern

Party Congress	Year	Number of Members
First Congress	1921	57
Second Congress	1922	123
Third Congress	1923	432
Fourth Congress	1925	950
Fifth Congress	1927	57,967
Sixth Congress	1928	40,000
Seventh Congress	1945	1,211,128
Eighth Congress	1956	10,734,384
	1961	17,000,000
Ninth Congress	1969	20,000,000
Tenth Congress	1973	28,000,000
Eleventh Congress	1977	35,000,000
Twelfth Congress	1982	39,600,000

Sources: Figures from 1921 to 1961 are based on John W. Lewis, Leadership in Communist China (Ithaca, N.Y.: Cornell Univeristy Press, 1963), pp. 108-120. The 1969 party membership figure is an estimate calculated on the basis of about forty-percent increase in 1973 over 1969 given by Jürgen Domes, "A Rift in the New Course," Far Eastern Economic Review, 1 October 1973, p. 3. The 1973 total party membership figure is taken from Zhou Enlai's "Report to the Tenth National Congress of the CCP," Peking Review, nos. 35-36 (7 September 1973), p. 18. The 1977 party membership figure is based on Ye Jianying, "Report on the Revision of the Party Constitution to the Eleventh Party Congress, 13-18 August 1977," Peking Review 36 (2 September 1977), p. 36.

Table adapted from James C. F. Wang, Contemporary Chinese Politics: An Introduction (Englewood Cliffs, N.J.: Prentice-Hall, 1980), p. 82.

Several salient characteristics are discernible in the growth and change of the CCP membership. First, the policy and pattern of party recruitment has changed over the years, reflecting as well as responding to political, economic, and social developments outside the party. For example, there was a spurt in membership recruitment in the years 1949–1952, when the regime pushed for land reform in the rural areas and held its Five-Anti Campaign and other campaigns in the cities. The Five-Anti Campaign was a political drive against the bourgeois and capitalist elements in the cities; purported to oppose bribery, evasion of tax, fraud, theft of government property, and theft of government information, the campaign terrorized the businessmen and industrialists, resulting in the imprisonment and bankruptcy of many of them. Other great campaigns of agricultural collectivization, socialization of industrial and commercial enterprises, and of the Great Leap Forward demanded and produced

Table 4.2 Backgrounds of Party Members, 1956 and 1957

	Numbers			Percent of Total		
	1956	1957	Increase 1956-1957	1956	1957	Increase 1956-1957
	(Thousands)			(Percent)		
Workers	1,503	1,740	237	14.0	13.7	11.9
Peasants	7,417	8,500	1,083	69.1	66.8	54.5
Intellectuals	1,256	1,880	624	11.7	14.8	31.4
Others	558	600	42	5.2	4.7	2.1
Total	10,734	12,720	1,986	100.0	100.0	100.0

Source: Modified version of Franz Schurmann, Ideology and Organization in Communist China (Berkeley, Calif.: University of California Press, 1966), p. 132. By permission of publisher.

Table from James C. F. Wang, Contemporary Chinese Politics: An Introduction (Englewood Cliffs, N.J.: Prentice-Hall, 1980), p. 84.

millions of new party members; in fact, from 1954 to 1961, the CCP recruited over a million new members annually. However, in the second half of the 1960s, party membership recruitment virtually stopped as the Cultural Revolution generated serious political and social turmoil throughout China and most party organizations from the central to local levels became defunct or ceased to function. After the Ninth CCP Congress in April 1969, reconstruction of the party began and the number of party members increased again rapidly. With this massive recruitment of "fresh blood," membership rose to 28 million by 1973 and 35 million by 1977. Thus, according to an authoritative Chinese source, over half of the 35 million CCP members in 1977 had joined the party only after the Cultural Revolution began in 1966.[1]

Second, the social composition of the membership has changed over time, with a decline in the percentage of peasant members and an increase in the percentage of intellectuals. Such a trend was clearly discernible by the mid-1950s. A majority of the CCP members were of peasant origins, but the percentage of peasant members dropped from 69.1 percent in 1956 to 66.8 percent in 1957; over the same two years the percentage of intellectual members rose from 11.7 to 14.8 percent (see Table 4.2). Although we are unable to determine precisely the social backgrounds of the CCP members today (we do not possess detailed membership data), the representation of intellectual members may well have increased. The influx of intellectuals can be attributed to a specific policy to recruit more scientists and technicians needed for China's modernization programs.[2] If the Four Modernizations policies continue, the rapid admission of those with the needed technical skills can be expected to further increase the ratio of intellectuals to others in the

CCP membership and enhance the influence of "technocrats" in the party over the long haul.

Third, inasmuch as over half the 35 million CCP members in 1977 were recruited after 1966 (7 million of them during 1973–1977) and most of the 35 million were the post-1949 recruits, it seems correct to say that the CCP rank and file are rather young. This is especially true when compared with the party leadership personnel, although we do not have actual data on the age structure of CCP members after 1956. In that year, 24.83 percent were twenty-five years old or younger, 67.54 percent were between twenty-six and forty-five, and 7.63 percent were above the age of forty-six.[3] Given the massive influx of Red Guards and "revolutionary rebels" during the Cultural Revolution, the increase of young members in the CCP is understandable; however, a change in the recruitment policy since 1977 may have arrested or reversed this trend.[4]

In summary, party recruitment is closely tied to politics and the power struggle inside the CCP. During the Cultural Revolution, the radical leaders apparently sought to broaden their base of support and pack party rolls with their own followers. Hence they modified requirements for admission into the party, made it easier for their supporters to secure admission, and practiced what has been called crash admittance. In commenting on the need to tighten up membership requirements thenceforward, Marshal Ye Jianying said:

> There is the serious problem of impurity in ideology, organization and style of work among Party members as a result of the rather extensive confusion created by the "gang of four" who in recent years vitiated the Party's line, undermined the Party's organizational principle, set their own standards for Party membership, and practiced "crash admittance," and as a result some political speculators and bad types have sneaked into the Party.[5]

Thus, not surprisingly, the Constitution approved by the Eleventh CCP Congress of 1977 restored the one-year probation requirement and tightened considerably the admission standards and recruitment procedures. Moreover, there has been an ongoing campaign since 1977 to "purify" the ranks and "rectify" the party, i.e., to ferret out young party members suspected of radical ties. Without question, a large number of those who joined the CCP after 1966 have been supporters and beneficiaries of the Cultural Revolution and are not sympathetic to, or even oppose, many of the reform measures put forth by Deng Xiaoping and other victims of the Cultural Revolution who run China today. The rectification campaign thus represents an effort by Deng and his associates to overcome or remove opposition in the party. The question is whether young, radical party members can be purged en masse without causing new political disruptions and further polarizing the party ranks.

Changes in CCP Organizational Structure

In the past three decades the party as an institution has gone through a full cycle of expansion, eclipse, and comeback. I will analyze the changing fortunes of the party in a later section. Here the primary concern is with changes in party structures and mechanisms before, during, and after the Cultural Revolution. Of particular interest is how these changes help highlight broad, significant political problems or mirror elite conflict in the political system.

Take the case of six CCP Regional Bureaus that were set up in the late 1940s, abolished in 1954, reestablished in 1961, and discarded once again in 1967. At the time of Communist takeover in 1949, the regime instituted a highly decentralized administrative system. It divided the nation into six Great Administrative Areas covering North China, Northeast China, Northwest China, Southwest China, East China, and South-Central China. In each of these regions stood a Regional Bureau of the CCP, headed by top Communist leaders, which also controlled a Military and Administrative Committee as the highest local organ of state power. These regional organs wielded substantial power and directed the work of several provincial-level units within their areas on behalf of the national authorities.

However, in 1954 the six CCP Regional Bureaus were abolished, along with other regional military and government institutions. Many considerations underlay this organizational tinkering. Some were undoubtedly administrative and economic, presumably for the sake of improving efficiency and control from the center, as China was embarking on an essentially Stalinist model of economic development that necessitated tight centralized planning and execution of a major economic program. Another consideration was political. "Independent kingdoms" allegedly created by some powerful and ambitious regional leaders, notably Gao Kang and Rao Shushi, motivated Mao and his colleagues in the center who were wary of warlordism to do away with these regional bodies and centralize power in Peking.[6]

Centralization may solve some problems, but it easily generates others. China is so large and heterogeneous that it seems politically unfeasible, administratively inefficient, and economically counterproductive for the central authorities to administer the entire country directly. The Great Leap Forward of the late 1950s proved these points beyond doubt. In 1961, the party reversed itself and announced the reestablishment of six regional CCP bureaus (but not the parallel regional governmental or military organs) to coordinate and supervise the work of the provincial CCP committees within these regions. What had happened was an experience of sheer inability of the central authorities to coordinate, dissect, and cope with twenty-nine provincial-level units directly. Especially in the course of the Great Leap, provincial authorities had to set up these regional bodies to strengthen control on behalf of Peking.[7]

History repeated itself during the Cultural Revolution as these regional CCP organizations were abolished once again. As in the past, the regional bodies had been able to accumulate much political and economic power and functioned in some ways like "independent kingdoms." For instance, Tao Chu and Go Qingshi, respectively first secretary of the South-Central China CCP Bureau and first secretary of the East China CCP Bureau, apparently benefited from their regional bases (two of China's most resourceful areas) and acquired national offices as vice-premiers by 1965. In the summer of 1966, Tao was enlisted by Chairman Mao to help propel the Great Proletarian Cultural Revolution and for a few months ranked number four in the leadership hierarchy. But Tao displayed so much independence and showed so much solidarity with his colleagues in the regional and provincial party apparatus that he came into direct confrontation with the radical leaders; by December 1966 he was ousted. Moreover, during the Cultural Revolution, five of the six regional CCP bureau first secretaries were purged because they opposed Mao's policies and used all the power and resources vested in their party organizations to fight Mao.

To date, these regional party organizations have not been restored, despite the fact that other party organs that were done away with during the late sixties have been revived. Chinese Communist rulers, like their predecessors in Chinese history, have not been free from the problem of a proper division of power between central and regional or provincial authorities. If past history is any guide, the vacillation between the poles of excessive centralization and decentralization is likely to persist.

Additionally, several other more important party organs were adversely affected during the Cultural Revolution. For example, the CCP Secretariat ceased to function as a day-to-day administrative body of party headquarters soon after its general secretary, Deng Xiaoping, was ousted in the fall of 1966; the body itself was formally abolished in April 1969 when the Ninth CCP Congress approved a new Constitution. Most functions of the Secretariat were taken over by the Cultural Revolution Group (CRG), which had been set up in May 1966 under the Politburo Standing Committee to direct Mao's cultural crusade. This group was headed by two Maoist stalwarts, Chen Boda and Jiang Qing (Madame Mao). The existence of this group was disclosed by several sources inside China including Jiang Qing in her speech of April 1967. After the CRG was abolished in 1969, control over the daily decision making in the CCP high command shifted to the party General Office, which was headed then and until 1978 by Wang Dongxing, Mao's chief bodyguard.

During 1967–1969, the Politburo, in theory the party's topmost policymaking organ, was also in limbo although it did not disappear from the party's organization chart. This limbo came about because a large number of Politburo members were opposed to Chairman Mao's policies, and as a result he chose to bypass and ignore it for almost two years.[8] Instead the CCP witnessed the metamorphosis of a policymaking process whereby the deliberation of important decisions took place in an ad hoc body bearing the unconventional title of "proletarian headquarters." This entity, which consisted of twelve men and two women (many of them not even members of the Central Committee) headed by Chairman Mao Zedong and Vice-Chairman Lin Biao, made and issued decisions in the name of the CCP, although it had not been duly constituted through prescribed party procedures.

Frontal Assault on the Party and Its Revival

There can be no question that during the Cultural Revolution Chairman Mao and his supporters seriously violated the party's rule and norms and tinkered with its decision-making organs. Furthermore, they not only attacked and purged a large number of officials, from the central to the provincial and local party organizations, but also sought to destroy the source of these officials' power—the party organizations and the entire structure of authority in China.

This state of affairs began to be evident in early 1967 when the Maoist-controlled media called for the masses to seize power from the "capitalist powerholders" through a popular uprising from below, to smash thoroughly China's existing power structure and oust the "new class" that controlled the structure, and to construct a new political order and system of authority modeled on the 1871 Paris Commune.[9] Indeed, rebels in Shanghai led by Zhang Chunqiao (who was known subsequently as a member of the Gang of Four) launched what the Maoists called the "January Revolution" to seize power from the municipal party and governmental authorities and set up the Shanghai People's Commune. This event sparked and heralded a nationwide frontal assault on the party and its raison d'etre, rule, and authority, as rebels in other provinces emulated the Shanghai example and seized power from the party authorities and established new organs of power.

Consequently, although the party survived the assault and continued to exist in name, in reality it had ceased to function as an institution. Not only were the ranks of party leaders from the central to the local levels decimated, but also many party organizations were paralyzed or became defunct. At the center, the Politburo, the Secretariat, and various departments of the Central Committee (CC) suspended their activities, and in the provinces the party apparatus was replaced by the "revolutionary committee."

An equally if not more serious blow was administered to the party's role and authority during the Cultural Revolution as the Maoists elevated their "supreme leader," who would thenceforth bestow his mantle of authority on the party organization and legitimize its power, rather than vice versa. By placing Mao above the party, the Maoists promoted Chairman Mao as the source of legitimacy, ultimate authority, and all political power in China, contrary to what the Leninist orthodoxy preached. According to Benjamin Schwartz, Mao stood as the "fountainhead of all morality, standing high above all laws and institutions."[10] The supreme leader's "reign of virtue" manifested itself once again in 1976 when Mao, defying all rules and standards, drove Deng Xiaoping out of power, launched his last campaign against the rightists, and promoted Hua Guofeng to first vice-chairman and premier.

Since Mao's demise and, especially, since December 1978 when Deng and his supporters regained power, the party has stressed restoration of collective leadership and other party traditions and rules and has reestablished many pre-1966 organs that had been discarded during the Cultural Revolution. For example, the Dengists pushed for the restoration of the Secretariat and the appointment of Hu Yaobang as general secretary in February 1980, apparently in order to strip power from Chairman Hua Guofeng. A Central Commission for Inspecting Discipline, similar to the Central Control Commission that existed until 1966, has also been set up to strengthen discipline and rectify the party.

These restorative moves do not imply that the party has moved back completely to the pre-1966 pattern of organization and operation, although there are many similarities. Instead, the party's organization and rules continue to evolve in response to political considerations. One such major change in the party's high command came at the recent Twelfth Congress of the CCP. The posts of chairman and vice-chairmen of the Central Committee were abolished in order to remove such anti-Deng vice-chairmen as Ye Jianying, Li Xiannian, and Hua from positions of power and strengthen the hand of Deng's protégé, Hu Yaobang, who as the general secretary will remain the party's top leader. Similarly, the establishment of the party's Central Advisory Committee, a largely honorific entity, accommodates kicking "old guards" upstairs from other posts to weaken opposition to Deng's reforms and to enhance Hu's leadership status. Not altogether unlike the Maoists, the Dengists have also played with party organization and rules and, as a result, institutionalization continues to languish.

Changes in the Party Leadership

In an interview with "a man very high in the Party" in 1960, the journalist Edgar Snow learned that a group of approximately eight hundred leaders who had helped Mao seize power in 1949 were running China and would continue to do so for many years to come.[11] Many of these eight hundred were disgraced or purged during the Cultural Revolution, but other members of this elite group never lost their grip and continued to exercise effective control over China's ship of state. In the wake of Mao's demise and the ouster of the Gang of Four in the fall of 1976, virtually every top leader who was purged in the sixties and was still alive after 1976 was rehabilitated and has been appointed to a position of responsibility. These veteran leaders, about four hundred in number, who governed China prior to the Cultural Revolution, are still running China today. However, the rule of this take-over generation is approaching its end, as most of these surviving revolutionary leaders are quite advanced in age. Moreover, Deng Xiaoping has sought during and after the Twelfth

CCP Congress to step up the replacement of these "old guards" by a younger group of leaders, although his design has run into stiff opposition.

Elite Composition During and Since the Cultural Revolution

Despite a striking continuity of China's ruling elite before and since the Cultural Revolution, significant changes did take place during that upheaval. One such change was the extraordinary rise of radicals to the apex of power in the party. It was extraordinary because the Gang of Four—Jiang Qing, Zhang Chunqiao, Yao Wenyuan, and Wang Hongwen—began in 1965/1966 very much as "outsiders" to the power structure, being neither members of the CC nor incumbents in any major leadership posts at the center. By the standards used following the 1956 CCP Congress, Politburo membership would be based on party seniority and on contributions to the cause of Communist victory before 1949 and socialist construction after 1949. Yet three of these four radical leaders made the Politburo in the Ninth CCP Congress in 1969 without meeting these qualifications, but exclusively for their service to Chairman Mao. During 1965/1966, when most senior party officials had opposed or deserted Mao, the trio were among his most resolute backers and worked closely with him to launch and subsequently push his crusade in the Great Proletarian Cultural Revolution. Even more surprising, Wang Hongwen, who failed to make the Politburo in 1969, was elevated to party vice-chairman at the Tenth CCP Congress in 1973; still in his thirties, this young radical labor organizer from Shanghai officially ranked third in the party, behind only Chairman Mao and Vice-Chairman Zhou Enlai in the leadership hierarchy.

Another major change in leadership composition in 1969 was the predominance of military representation in the party councils. This had resulted from the extensive involvement of the People's Liberation Army (PLA) in the Cultural Revolution after 1966 and the enormous expansion of the PLA's political role in the wake of such involvement. Thus, in the newly elected CC in 1969 approximately 45 percent, or 127 of the 279 full and alternate members, were career soldiers, in stark contrast to the composition of the 1956 CC in which the PLA representatives constituted only 19 percent (see Table 4.3). In the 1969 Politburo, moreover, thirteen of the twenty-five members were PLA officers. Marshal Lin Biao greatly benefited from the Cultural Revolution as he was able to expand his base of power and place his supporters in the CC and the Politburo.

The political prominence of the PLA was even more conspicuous at the provincial level in organs of power during the late sixties and early seventies. In September 1968, when the new provincial organization, the revolutionary committee, was established in all of China's twenty-nine administrative units, twenty of these revolutionary committees were headed by PLA men. By the summer of 1971, when provincial party committees had been reconstructed throughout China, the PLA also dominated the provincial party apparatus. Thus of the 158 first secretaries,

Table 4.3 Changes in Composition of CCP Central Committee

	Eighth Central Committee (1956-1958)	Ninth Central Committee (1969)	Tenth Central Committee (1973)	Eleventh Central Committee (1977)
I. Number of members				
Full	97	170	195	201
Alternate	96[a]	109	124	132
Total	193	279	319	333
II. Turnover of members[b]				
Holdover from previous Central Committee	40%	19%	64%	56%
Newcomer	60%	81%	31%	38%
Returnee[c]	0%	0%	5%	6%
III. Occupational background[b]				
Civilian	81%	55%	63%	71%
Military	19%	45%	32%	29%
Unknown	0%	0%	5%	0%
IV. Occupational level[b]				
National	62%	33%	33%	35%
Provincial	38%	67%	62%	65%
Unknown	0%	0%	5%	0%
V. Average age of full members at election[d]	56.4	61.4	62.1	64.6

a. Twenty-five alternate members were added to the Eighth Central Committee at its second plenary session in 1958.

b. Figures in II, III, and IV represent percentages of total (full and alternate) Central Committee membership.

c. Returnees are those full and alternate members who were not elected to the immediately previous Central Committee but who were members of an earlier Central Committee.

d. Data for 1969 based on 162 of 170 full members; data for 1977 based on 163 of 201 full members.

Sources: For I and II: Who's Who in Communist China (Hong Kong: Union Research Institute, 1966), pp. 703-707; Donald W. Klein and Lois B. Hager, "The Ninth Central Committee," China Quarterly 43 (January-February 1971), pp. 37-56; Malcolm Lamb, Directory of Central Officials in the People's Republic of China, 1968-1975 (Canberra: Australian National University, 1976), pp. 5-16; K'ung Te-liang, "An Analysis of the CCP's Tenth National Congress," Issues and Studies 10:1 (October 1973), pp. 17-30; Central Intelligence Agency, China: A Look at the 11th Central Committee (Rp 77-10276, October 1977). For III and IV: China: A Look at the 11th Central Committee. For V: Jürgen Domes, "The Ninth CCP Central Committee in Statistical Perspective," Current Scene 9:2 (7 February 1971), pp. 5-14; Jürgen Domes, "China in 1977: A Reversal of the Verdict," Asian Survey 18:1 (January 1978), pp. 6-9.

Table from James R. Townsend, Politics in China, 2nd ed. (Boston: Little, Brown, 1980), pp. 264-265.

second secretaries, secretaries, and assistant secretaries, ninety-five (60 percent) were PLA representatives, fifty-three (33.5 percent) were civilian cadres and only ten (6.5 percent) were mass representatives. Of the twenty-nine first secretaries, twenty-one were military men.

Two other features worthy of note were the unusual turnover rates in the CC and the Politburo elected in 1969. In the CC, only 19 percent of the 279 members were reelected from the Eighth CC; the remaining 81 percent were newcomers, the beneficiaries of the political turmoil.

In the twenty-five–member Politburo, sixteen members were newcomers; only nine were holdovers. Moreover, of twenty-six full and alternate Politburo members elected in 1956 and 1958, three died before the Cultural Revolution and fourteen fell by the wayside as victims of Mao's purge. Thus the ruling elite as constituted in 1969 was a loose coalition of highly disparate forces: the victors—the upstarts and beneficiaries of the Cultural Revolution—and the survivors of political storm.

A realignment of political forces in the wake of the Lin Biao incident (ending in his death) and the Tenth CCP Congress in August 1973 produced a new leadership lineup. First, with the elimination of Lin Biao and his top aides, military representation was halved in the Politburo and reduced considerably in the CC (see Table 4.3). Second, first secretaries from eight provincial-level units were elevated to the Politburo, underlining the growing importance of a territorial base of power in Chinese politics. Third, the radicals greatly enhanced their political influence in the party as the radical group led by Jiang Qing placed several followers in the Politburo and promoted some fifty representatives of the mass organization to the CC.

Although Premier Zhou had emerged as Mao's top aide in the regime after Lin Biao's demise and had greatly enhanced his status at home and abroad through his management of Sino-U.S. rapprochement and Sino-Japanese normalization of relations, Mao was unwilling to designate Zhou his successor. Instead of making Zhou the sole party vice-chairman as Lin Biao was in 1969—by which action Mao would have publicly legitimized Zhou's number-two position in the party—Mao tacitly undercut Zhou by making him only one, albeit the first, of five vice-chairmen. Moreover, Mao proceeded to groom his own successor by personally promoting young Wang Hongwen to second vice-chairman and placing Zhang Chunqiao in the Politburo Standing Committee to checkmate Zhou.

However, the most far-reaching development of the Tenth CCP Congress may have been the party's public endorsement of the restoration of disgraced "capitalist powerholders" to positions of responsibility, a process that had been quietly in progress since Lin Biao's demise in September 1971.[12] The election of Deng Xiaoping and a dozen or so other prominent victims of the Cultural Revolution to the CC legitimated the policy and accelerated its pace. Deng's comeback was especially significant—it was requested initially by Zhou Enlai, but approved by Mao himself in 1972. Thus, Deng returned to a position of authority in a short time and made it to the Politburo by 1974.

The rehabilitation of these "capitalist powerholders" carried grave political implications. It not only called into question the legitimacy of the Cultural Revolution and eroded the radicals' base of support, but it also strengthened the positions of critics who sought to undo or soft-pedal Cultural Revolution innovations and, in general, refueled the clash between opponents and defenders of Mao's crusade. In this political atmosphere the years 1974–1976 witnessed fierce struggles by such leaders as Zhou and Deng against the Gang of Four. Zhou and Deng were in charge of the national economy and the day-to-day government operations and tried to stress stability even as the Gang of Four, supported by Mao, tried to hold to the radical policies of the Cultural Revolution and its socialist "newlyborn things." The clash was not just over policy and principles but was also a struggle for power.

Change in the Post-Mao Era

Since the death of Mao and the arrests of the radical leaders in the fall of 1976, China's political forces have regrouped once again. This realignment found clear expression in the Eleventh CCP Congress, which was held in August 1977 to approve a new leadership team and a new policy line. The composition of the new CC and the Politburo has in many respects reversed the trends of the 1969 and 1973 congresses.

One such indication has been the wholesale ouster of the Gang of Four and their followers from the Politburo and the CC. Especially in the CC, the bloc of young mass organization representatives patronized and recruited by the radical leaders was wiped out. Taking over their seats were the veteran officials of the party and government organizations. A heavy influx of veteran leaders was also discernable in the Politburo elected in 1977. Deng Xiaoping, who had clashed with Mao and the radicals over major policies and was sacked in April 1976, staged a second political comeback in the summer of 1977, epitomizing the resurgence of antiradical forces in the party.

Another striking feature of the leadership composition was that, in spite of the downfall of the Gang of Four, other Maoists remained strongly entrenched in the leadership councils. These Maoists, such as Hua Guofeng, who was confirmed as party chairman at the 1977 CCP Congress, and Wang Dongxing, who was elected one of the four party vice-chairmen, were beneficiaries of the Cultural Revolution and defenders of Mao's policies much as Jiang Qing and her cohorts were. However, unlike the Jiang Qing group, which consisted primarily of ideologues, Hua, Wang, and other leaders were professional bureaucrats in the party, army, or government and were less ideological and radical; furthermore, in October 1976 Hua and Wang helped stage the coup that deposed the Gang of Four.

Although Hua Guofeng succeeded Mao as party chairman, he had great difficulties consolidating his power. Despite his claim that he was Chairman Mao's hand-picked successor, his previous training was limited and his leadership performance after 1976 was undistinguished. Furthermore, his leadership had encountered a serious challenge from Deng Xiaoping and the many other veteran officials who were victimized by Mao's crusade; they strongly resented political upstarts like Hua who had benefited from Mao's purges. The rivalry and struggle between the groups allied with Hua and with Deng dominated Chinese politics.

The coalition under Hua consisted of two diverse elements. One was the Maoist "whatever" faction, whose members rose to political prominence during the Cultural Revolution and sought to defend *whatever* policy Mao favored; this faction has had numerous followers among the rank and file of the party. The other was the "petroleum" faction, a group of economists and technocrats who ran the Chinese economy under the late Premier Zhou's stewardship during 1966–1976. They were credited with the remarkable development of China's petroleum industry and have been strongly represented in the economic ministries of the State Council. Reportedly CCP Vice-Chairman Li Xiannian is this faction's behind-the-scenes leader. In addition, the Hua coalition has also drawn support from such elder statesman as Marshal Ye Jianying and from a few leaders of the PLA.

This coalition was in the ascendancy during 1976–1977 and largely controlled policy councils until the spring of 1978. Indeed, the political line of the Eleventh CCP Congress in August 1977 and the Ten-Year National Development Plan sanctioned by the National People's Congress in March 1978 bore the mark of the coalition's influence.

The coalition behind Deng, on the other hand, has consisted of several groups of veteran officials, great numbers of whom were victims of the Cultural Revolution. Many of them are long-time followers of Deng (e.g., Hu Yaobang and Wan Li), some are Deng's peers and political allies (e.g., Chen Yun and Peng Zhen), and some are co-optees into Deng's group (e.g., Zhao Ziyang and Yang Dezhi, PLA chief of staff since 1980).

The outcome of the political battle has been a most impressive victory on the part of the Dengists.[13] Since December 1978 Deng has become the chief architect of Chinese modernization programs and China's most prominent and powerful leader, although he has carried only the title of party vice-chairman. By the end of 1978, the Dengists had succeeded in removing most provincial leaders who were suspected of radical ties or were unsympathetic to the Deng reform. In February 1980, they ousted Wang Dongxing and three other leaders of the Maoist "whatever" faction from the Politburo, thereby substantially weakening Chairman Hua's position. Finally, in June 1981, they formally deposed Hua as party chairman and replaced him with Deng's protégé Hu Yaobang.

Although Deng and his supporters accomplished much of what they sought, they did not win every fight. Despite the vigorous campaign by Deng and his followers to remove the "old guards" from the levers of power and promote younger cadres of greater professional competence into leadership positions, their efforts have only been partially successful. True, at the Twelfth CCP Congress in September 1982, 172 veteran officials (both Deng's supporters and his opponents) stepped down willy-nilly from the Politburo, the Central Committee, and other front line positions of leadership to take a back seat in the newly established Central Advisory Committee, which will have only advisory functions. However, numerous other leaders have stayed on in the party's top policymaking councils, Deng's pressure notwithstanding.

As of 1985, out of the twenty-five Politburo members, eighteen are holdovers, and of these eighteen, seven are in their eighties and five more are in their late seventies. The seven newly elected members are not much younger, with six of them over seventy years old and one sixty-nine (see Table 4.4). All six members of the Politburo Standing Committee, the party's topmost decision-making body, have also been reelected, despite Deng's earlier maneuver to kick upstairs Marshall Ye Jianying (88 years old) and Li Xiannian (76 years old), who have opposed Deng's policies.

Deng and his supporters did succeed in removing from the Politburo ex-Party Chairman Hua Guofeng and several other leaders who were antagonistic to Deng's reforms. Although unable to force the party elders to retire from the Politburo, Deng elevated seven of his staunch supporters to the Politburo, thereby diluting the strength of the opposition and ensuring the control of his backers and allies over this key policymaking body.[14]

Furthermore, as a result of the recent reshuffling the Dengists have greatly strengthened their control over the central Secretariat, the strategic day-to-day decision-making organ.[15] The Secretariat is headed by Deng's confidant and protégé, General Secretary Hu Yaobang, officially the party's ranking leader. Although Hu replaced Hua as party chairman in June 1981, that post, which Mao created and assumed in 1945, was abolished at the Twelfth CCP Congress, thus erasing this vestige of Mao's era in CCP history.

Likewise, the Dengists dominate the new Central Committee (CC), which consists of 210 members and 138 alternates. Several salient characteristics of the new CC deserve attention. First, a total of 210 members, 96 full and 114 alternate members, or slightly more than 60 percent of the Twelfth CC, are newly elected. The large number of the new recruits, especially among the alternate CC members, are relatively young and followers of Deng. Hu has also elevated many of his cohorts to the CC. Second, 75 (50 full and 25 alternate) members, or about 21 percent of the CC, are from the PLA; by comparison with the makeup of the Eleventh CC, military representation has declined. This trend seems to underscore Deng's apparent desire to curtail the influence of the army, which has become a center for opposition to his reforms in recent years. Third, aside from the transfer of 64 former CC members to the Central Advisory Committee, an additional 53 members and 80 alternate members of the Eleventh CC have been dropped. Thus, almost all of the supporters of the Gang of Four and Hua are out.[16]

With their overall position strengthened, the Dengists began soon after the Twelfth CCP Congress to reorganize the leadership bodies at the provincial level, with a view to tightening control. The reshuffle is still going on as of this writing, but several features are worthy of note in more than a score of provinces where the new party leadership has been installed. First, the reorganization has rid these provinces of five "kinds" of cadres,[17] among them leftists and those who resisted current

Table 4.4 Reshuffled Leadership Lineup at Twelfth CCP Congress

Party Organ and Membership	Member's Age (as of 1985)	Concurrent Post
1. Politburo (25 members and 3 alternate members)		
a. Standing Committee members		
Hu Yaobang	70	General Secretary
Ye Jianying	88	Vice-chmn, Military Affairs Committee
Deng Xiaoping	81	Chmn, Central Advisory Committee; Chmn, Military Affairs Committee
Zhao Ziyang	66	Premier
Li Xiannian	76	Chmn, People's Republic of China (PRC)
Chen Yun	80	First secretary, Central Commission for Inspecting Discipline
b. Members[a]		
Wan Li	69	Vice-premier
Xi Zhongxun	72	Vice-chmn, National People's Congress (NPC)
Wang Chen	77	President, Higher Party School
Wei Guoqing	79	Vice-chmn, NPC
Ulanfu	82	Vice-chmn, PRC
Fang Yi	69	Councilor of State Council
Deng Yingchao	82	Chmn, Chinese People's Political Consultative Conference
Li Desheng	69	Commander, Shenyang Military Region
Yang Shangkun	78	Permanent vice-chmn, Military Affairs
Yang Dezhi	73	Chief of staff, PLA
Yu Qiuli	71	Director, PLA General Political Department
Song Renqiong	76	
Zhang Tingfa	70	Commander, Air Force
Hu Qiaomu	73	
Nie Rongzhen	86	Vice-chmn, Military Affairs Committee
Ni Zhifu	59	Director, All-China Federation of Trade Unions
Xu Xiangqian	83	Vice-chmn, Military Affairs Committee
Peng Zhen	83	Chmn, NPC
Liao Chengzhi		Deceased in June 1983 at age 77
c. Alternate members[b]		
Yao Yilin	68	Vice-premier
Qin Jiwei	73	Commander, Peking Military Region
Chen Muhua	64	Minister, External Economics and Trade
2. Secretariat (10 members and 2 alternate members)		
a. General secretary		
Hu Yaobang	70	
b. Members[a]		
Wan Li	67	Vice-premier
Xi Zhongxun	72	Vice-chmn, NPC
Deng Liaun	70	Director, CCP Propaganda Department
Yang Yong		Deceased in early 1983 at age 71
Yu Qiuli	71	Director, PLA General Political Department; deputy secretary-general, Military Affairs Committee
Gu Mu	71	Councilor of State Council
Chen Pixian	69	Vice-chmn, NPC
Hu Qili	56	Director, CCPCC Staff Office
Yao Yilin	68	Vice-premier
c. Alternate members[b]		
Qiao Shi	61	
Hao Jianxiu	50	

Table 4.4, continued

3. Military Affairs Commission of CCP Central Committee		
a. Chairman		
Deng Xiaoping	81	
b. Vice-chairmen		
Ye Jianying	88	
Xu Xiangqian	83	
Nie Rongzhen	86	
c. Permanent vice-chairman and secretary-general		
Yang Shangkun	78	
d. Deputy secretary-generals		
Yu Qiuli	71	
Yang Dezhi	73	
Zhang Aiping	75	Minister of defense

a. Members are listed in order of the number of strokes in their surnames.
b. Alternate members are listed in order of declining number of votes.

reform programs. Second, there is a discernible tendency to retire the old and promote the "young"; thus, in a few provinces like Sichuan, Heilongjiang, Hubei, and Gansu, the first party secretaries are in their fifties, and in virtually every province there are two or three secretaries or assistant secretaries who are in their fifties. Third, under a policy to trim the bureaucracy, the number of provincial secretaries or assistant secretaries has been cut by as much as 60 percent, to only four or five per province.

Another significant development is the rapid promotion of Hu Yaobang's cohorts to positions of leadership both at the center and in the provinces. From 1952 to 1966 Hu was head of the Youth League, an auxiliary organization to the CCP, and he must have known a large number of cadres of the league (which had more than 20 million members in 1966). Undoubtedly Hu is in a good position to build an organized following. So far, he has done a lot to patronize his former associates at the league and has placed them in important positions of responsibility. The outstanding examples at the center are Hu Qiuli, director of the CC General Political Office; Deng Liqun, director of the CC Propaganda Department; Qiao Shi, director of the CC International Liaison Department; and Foreign Minister Wu Xuequian. (The first three are also newly elected secretaries of the CC Secretariat.) At the provincial level, Hu's associate Xiang Nan already heads the CCP committee in Fujian, and another, Liang Buting, heads the committee in Shandong. Li Ruihwan may soon take over control in Tianjin, and Li Qingwei in Shaanxi. Other associates of Hu serve as party secretaries or assistant secretaries in numerous other provinces.

Despite all this change and an emphasis on younger personnel, it should be pointed out that old leaders continue to dominate China's decision-making councils. In the Politburo, for example, the average age is over seventy-five (see Table 4.4). Although the members of the Secretariat are slightly younger, their average age is still above the mid-sixties. This means that within five to seven years, the Peking regime will face a critical generational transition in leadership. Also, despite the predominance of Deng and his associates, leadership factionalism continues, and conflicting viewpoints on major issues persist. Thus, different approaches to economic construction are represented by Deng, Hu Yaobang, Chen Yun, and Zhao Ziyang on the one hand, and by Li Xiannian and the "petroleum" faction on the other. Even among the Dengists, differences also exist, with Chen stressing readjustment of policy priorities as Hu and Zhao place heavy emphasis on reform of the economic system and institutions. In the government, the "petroleum" faction is strongly entrenched, as its members control many of the economic and industrial ministries; they have resisted any changes in economic priorities (the tilt toward agriculture and light industry) and any economic cutbacks and are strongly against structural reform.

Changes in the Norms of Elite Conflict

The elite conflict in post-Mao China has, in many respects, become more "routinized" and less volatile and violent. Whereas struggle for personal power goes on and Chinese leaders continue to clash over a wide range of domestic and foreign policy issues, their cleavages are no longer a "struggle between the two lines" as they were during the decade of the Cultural Revolution, when the Maoists and the "capitalist powerholders" were so polarized and deeply divided over the direction of Chinese revolution and basic national priorities.

If the issues of contention have become less significant, the arena of conflict has also been contracted and the techniques used have become more selective. During the Great Proletarian Cultural Revolution the Chinese people witnessed an enormous expansion of the arena of conflict as Mao went outside the party to mobilize the support of the Red Guard and the masses. At the height of this conflict, antagonists used political assassination. Likewise, the Gang of Four resorted to a set of "campaign" tactics during 1973–1976 and went "public" to enlist support of labor, women, and youth groups in attacking the establishment.[18] Consequently, leadership conflict infected the society and generated widespread violence. In the post-Mao years, there has been a tendency to confine leadership conflict inside the prescribed channels; the decision to outlaw strikes and the Four Big Freedoms (including freedom to put up big-character posters) is highly indicative.

Basically the post-Mao leaders, in line with their emphasis on the socialist legal system, have strived to establish and follow the rules of the game. Chairman Hua's "resignation" provides a good illustration. For the first time since 1949, the party chairman has been toppled in accordance with some procedures, and his exit accorded some "courtesy" inasmuch as Hua was allowed to "resign" but to stay in the Politburo as a party vice-chairman. In fact, for several years it has been fairly common practice for the leadership not to totally disgrace the defeated elite—the victors now have the grace to reassign the vanquished to lesser posts rather than confine them to jail. The last exceptional purge was the trial and imprisonment of the Gang of Four, their hardcore supporters, and Lin Biao's top aides.

The current trend contrasts distinctly with the practices of the Red Guards and "revolutionary rebels" during the Cultural Revolution. At the height of political turmoil they carried out "seizure of power" and sought to oust the "capitalist powerholders" en masse. Moreover, the purge victims suffered from severe mistreatment. Almost all of them were subjected to a harsh ordeal of public "self-criticism" and struggle meetings, and not a few were "tried" by self-appointed kangaroo courts and paraded through the streets with dunce caps on. Some died of physical torture and psychological persecution. Rightly or wrongly, the Gang of Four and the Lin Biao group were blamed for the excesses of their followers and have incurred the deep hatred of the victims. All of this may partly explain the humiliation and treatment they received after their downfall.

The Red Guard observed at least one long-standing norm, namely, that rarely if ever are defeated political leaders physically liquidated. Unlike Stalin, who had his rivals and even many of his supporters executed, Mao avoided this type of terror against his former comrades. Reportedly the CCP passed a resolution in 1942 to ban the use of physical liquidation against its disgraced leaders, especially those with the rank of CC members or higher. If this is true, then such a rule has been rather closely observed, even during the Cultural Revolution.

Another interesting tradition has been political rehabilitation—and not always posthumously. While Mao was still alive, he permitted many erring former leaders, including Deng Xiaoping, to return to active political life and major leadership posts. This practice has been continued in recent years. Whatever merits these modes of management of the opposition may have, they also have interesting consequences. For example, inasmuch as the punishment for those who oppose the leadership is a brief retirement, and not a matter of life or death, they may be less inhibited in asserting themselves. Another consequence may be the creation of a "counterelite"—for example, the "capitalist powerholders" of the 1960s—who place great constraints on the incumbent and can plot their own comeback.

The Roles of the Party

Prior to the Cultural Revolution, the CCP was the source of legitimacy and all political power in China both in theory and in practice. It alone determined the social, political, and economic goals for the society and guided and directed the entire machinery of state, the PLA, and every mass organization. However, the CCP has experienced vicissitudes in this regard during and since the Cultural Revolution. The sharp leadership conflict and the immense political turmoil it generated seriously eroded the CCP's leading role. Other social, economic, and political changes since the 1960s have also exposed many problems and defects of the CCP leadership and its operation and have raised fundamental questions concerning its legitimacy as well as its ability to lead China toward modernization.

The Party and the PLA

As a result of the Cultural Revolution, the PLA has been drawn into the vortex of Chinese politics. During the second half of the 1960s, the PLA took part in the resolution of leadership conflict at the highest level, displacing political leaders, supplanting party and government institutions, and enormously expanding its political role.

It should be noted that the *initial* (1965–1966) expansion of the PLA's political power falls into the category of what Morris Janowitz calls "reactive militarism."[19] That is, the PLA gained new political power not through a premeditated coup ("designed militarism" by Janowitz's definition), as the military has done in many other political systems, but through circumstances largely not of its own making. In this case, it was Mao Tse-tung, chairman of the CCP, who engineered the intervention of the PLA in leadership conflict so as to redress the balance of power in his favor. For in the wake of the severe setback in his own utopian Great Leap Forward and commune programs in the early sixties, Mao incurred strong criticism and opposition and was politically eclipsed by other party leaders who controlled the party machinery. To overcome the opposition within the party and to recapture the direction of the Chinese revolution, Mao was compelled to go outside the party organizations to recruit support from other groups. Hence, he turned to the PLA, co-opted its leaders, particularly Marshal Lin Biao, and changed its political role in the system.

The PLA's direct, extensive involvement in the Cultural Revolution after January 1967 soon led it to supplant civilian party/government authorities in most provinces and take over various political and economic functions previously performed by party and governmental organizations. From the spring of 1967 onward, and for more than a year, a military government existed in most provinces as local PLA leaders enforced a direct military rule through the mechanism of their local Military Control Committees. The assumption of such important political functions by the PLA, it should be pointed out again, was not the result of the PLA's own initiative. What happened was that the leftists' assaults on the provincial authorities in their attempts at "seizure of power from below" (in emulation of the 1871 Paris Commune) paralyzed the party and government machinery and severely disrupted public order, and the Maoist leadership was compelled to move the PLA into the power vacuum to maintain law and order. Hence political power devolved into the hands of local PLA leaders.

Strictly speaking, the PLA intervention in Chinese politics from late 1965 to the beginning of 1967 did not really contravene the principle of civilian supremacy and control, in that the expansion of its political roles was explicitly sanctioned by the party leadership headed by Mao. Not a few PLA leaders actually had misgivings about the PLA involvement in what they considered a purely intraparty conflict (not class struggle as Mao had claimed); some reluctantly went along, but others abstained and were consequently purged, which gave rise to dissension in the PLA ranks. Once the floodgate to military intervention was opened, however, the involvement of the PLA in Chinese politics was not easily limited or controlled by the party leadership. In part this was due to the PLA's disapproval of the radical goals of the Cultural Revolution and the different perceptions held by Mao and by most of the PLA leaders with regard to the proper mission, particularly the political roles, of the PLA during the turmoil. For Mao, the Great Proletarian Cultural Revolution was a genuine revolution launched to smash China's existing power structure, to oust en masse the "new class" (the capitalist power-holders) that controlled the structure, and to institute a new system of authority modeled on the Paris Commune. However, many PLA leaders (except for Lin Biao and his followers) disagreed with Mao's vision and displayed serious misgivings about the extraordinary political roles imposed on the PLA. For them, as already noted, the *real* conflict was an intraparty conflict; they believed that the PLA should not become involved, let alone used by Mao as his own political instrument to purge his opponents (whom Mao labeled as "capitalist power-holders").

Moreover, most PLA leaders considered themselves "the pillar of proletarian dictatorship," that is, as defenders of the Communist system; they had assumed their responsibility primarily to maintain order and stability in the system and protect it from radical changes. Therefore, they strongly resented the task assigned to them by the Maoist leadership—to support the leftists' revolutionary crusade. Instead they viewed with deep hostility the riotous Red Guards and leftists who attempted to restructure the political order. The perception of their guardian role inevitably led these PLA leaders to restrain the leftists and intervene against Mao's crusade.

The weakening of the civil institutions completed the disorder. In the wake of attacks launched by Mao and his Red Guard supporters upon the party organizations after the fall of 1966, the image and legitimacy of the party was severely tarnished.[20] This fact, coupled with a divided leadership in the party and Mao's waning influence in it, tended to embolden the PLA leaders to defy the party leadership. Moreover, as both the Maoist faction and its opponents vied for the support of the PLA, some of the PLA leaders were able to play the two groups against each other to exact political concessions.

The virtual destruction of civilian party and government authority after January 1967 left the system with only one organizational hierarchy capable of exercising effective control—the PLA. Not even the party's mechanisms of control over the military were left intact; hence, the PLA stepped in. Previously, civilian party officials had headed provincial institutions (except in outlying border regions like Sinkiang and Tibet), and there was a system of separation of powers, with checks and balances, between civilian-party and PLA officials. Now, however, local PLA commanders or professional political commissars headed the party and government apparatus in most provinces; in fact, PLA personnel comprised the core of the leadership in virtually every province.

Against such a background, it is even more striking that after the mid-seventies the PLA largely disengaged again from the political role it assumed during the Cultural Revolution, and has since maintained a generally low political profile. Yet some PLA involvement in politics has continued. Certain leaders and troop units of the PLA took part in the October 1976 coup that deposed the radical leaders, and they backed Hua Guofeng's succession to party chairmanship. During 1977/1978 several PLA leaders also provided strong support for Deng's drive to capture control of power and policy from Hua.

Although Deng seems remarkably successful in returning the PLA "to the barracks," he does have some serious residual problems. His reform programs are highly unpopular inside military ranks. Furthermore, many PLA leaders are strongly antagonistic to Deng's protégé Hu Yaobang, who succeeded Hua as party chairman in June 1981. Inasmuch as Hu is not too popular with the PLA, Deng took over the chairmanship of the Military Affairs Committee, a post formerly held concurrently by the party chairman. Deng's success in keeping the PLA's discontent and opposition in check may be due mostly to personal factors—his ability, towering stature, and personal ties. Thus his feat may be difficult for others to duplicate.

Deng is quite advanced in age, eighty-one in 1985. How long will he be around to keep things under control? Can Hu Yaobang survive politically after his mentor is gone? How will Hu perform as the top party leader? Can he in time develop his own political strength and convincingly demonstrate his stewardship, thereby proving to his allies and critics that he deserves to be China's supreme leader? These are crucial questions that will have a bearing on Chinese politics. If Hu fails to perform, he, too, may suffer Hua Guofeng's fate.

An Overview of the CCP's Future Role, Leadership, and Problems

At present, China stands on the threshold of an important leadership transition. In a few more years, leaders like Deng who have dominated China's politics since 1949, and even the second-generation leaders like Hu, will be out of the political picture. In the past several years they have placed great emphasis on China's modernization and have strived to carry out reforms and implement policies to that end.

Will these reforms and policies last? Will the newcomers to the leadership discard these innovations and measures, as the Dengists have done to Mao's? Do the present leaders and their hand-picked successors possess the necessary ability and training to lead China into modernization? These questions cannot be answered with certainty now, but they will have an important bearing on the legitimacy and relevance of party leadership and the future of China.

It is true that Deng and Hu have made much effort to recruit and to promote people of greater professional competence into leadership positions in order to implement the program of Four Modernizations. Their policy has been manifested in new government appointments in which experts—scientists and cadres who have strong professional backgrounds—have been promoted to provincial vice-governors, vice-mayors, department chiefs, and even to vice-ministers and a few posts as ministers at the central government level. What has been done is unquestionably a step in the right direction, but it is still too slow and too little. To modernize China, the Chinese leadership needs a vast number of experts and technocrats in major positions of responsibility in the government *and* in the party councils. As pointed out before, many veterans who are more "Red" than "expert" are reluctant to step down and have fought against the Deng-Hu efforts to make changes in personnel and policy.

Like Mao, the "old guards" who are running China were master strategists and organizers of revolution. Whereas they excelled in the battlefield and were experts at creating organizations, conducting political campaigns, and manipulating human relations, their subsequent records and writings betray little genuine understanding of the requirements for China's industrialization and modernization. These revolutionary leaders were probably indispensable at the initial stages of postrevolutionary consolidation of power, but they have been wholly inadequate and deficient in providing leadership for China's modernization drive since then. With industrialization and its concomitants of higher educational attainment and increasing differentiation and specialization of function in the economy and the state administration, it will be necessary to bring into the party leadership more and more of the new functional specialists. So far this has not happened to a significant extent. In addition to the aforementioned reasons that hamper the upward political mobility of the junior members in the elite circles, the emphasis on "Red" over "expert" and even the antiintellectual biases of many of the veterans have operated against the recruitment of elite from the society at large. The failure of the power elite to co-opt the talented members of the better educated and technical intelligentsia into its ranks is likely to retard China's modernization efforts.

In many important ways, the Cultural Revolution was a major watershed in Chinese politics and polity since 1949. Mao's last crusade shaped the course of events in China for more than a decade and left a legacy that will continue to affect the Chinese political system. One such effect is factionalism. Factions and cliques have long existed in the CCP leadership in the course of the Communist movement. During the fifties the impact of personal animosities and of factional conflict on policy was less salient, as the leadership was able to maintain a high degree of discipline and coherence. However, Mao's drive to recapture leadership control in his fateful last decade exploited the tactics of "divide and rule, check and balance," while permitting him to maximize control. Such tactics have aggravated and intensified factional cleavages. The leadership division and rivalry encouraged by Mao's manipulative approach appears to have outlived Mao and is likely to plague his successors for years to come.

Another debilitating development in China's political system in the past decade has been the fragmentation of leadership power. The trend was already evident in the final years of Mao's life but has advanced further in recent years. It is quite obvious that today Deng, not to mention Hu, lacks the authority of Mao to generate personal power or the power of Mao to create personal authority. Mao was both the ruler and the high priest (chief ideologist) of Communist China—performing several important leadership roles (policy initiation, policy legitimization, conflict resolution, and political integration) and the paramount function of "law giver."

By contrast, neither Deng nor Hu is an established ideologist, and no one in China today can combine all of Mao's roles. Unquestionably, there is a discernible decline in power and leadership status for Mao's successors. However prominent Deng may have appeared since 1978, he has been only first among the equals and has had to share his leadership roles with, and in turn be constrained by, such leaders as Ye Jianying, Chen Yun, Li Xiannian, and, to a lesser extent, Peng Zhen. Deng has to rest his power on persuasion rather than on fiat (as Mao did) and his style of leadership is one of consultation and consensus building. Unlike Mao, Deng has sought to exercise leadership *through* the party councils.

Hu wields even less power under Deng's shadow and, making virtue out of necessity, has preached collective leadership on many occasions. The fact that Chairman Hu no longer holds the position of chairman of the Military Affairs Committee seems to attest to increasing differentiation of leadership roles and fragmentation of power among the Chinese elite.

Fragmentation of power can lead to many adverse consequences. It tends to breed leadership disunity and limits the capacity to map out and implement forcefully strong reform measures needed for many of China's deep-seated problems. The need to accommodate all factions and to compromise on divisive issues on personnel and policy has forced the Chinese leaders to "muddle through" without really taking necessary measures to solve problems. This in turn has adversely affected the ability of the regime to perform services and deliver goods to the society, thereby generating greater popular discontent.

Since the second half of the 1960s, the Chinese leadership has had a continuing crisis of authority that seems to have deepened in the past few years. The wild charges, both political and personal, leveled against large numbers of disgraced officials during the Cultural Revolution in 1966–1969, during the anti-Lin Biao campaign in 1972–1974, and against the radicals since October 1976 must have severely tarnished the image of Communist leadership and undermined the Chinese people's respect for and confidence in "leaders." The changing leadership has rewritten history and changed the official line so frequently and so blatantly that it cannot but suffer from a severe credibility gap; consequently, its authority and power to persuade have been eroded.

More important, Mao's exhortation that "rebellion is justified" and his mobilization of the Red Guards in 1966–1967 to attack the party organizations, as well as the radicals' open instigation of the revolutionaries "to go against the tide" (i.e., to fight the Establishment)—a sanction explicitly inscribed in the 1973 Constitution as a Marxist principle—have had the effect of breeding defiance against and contempt for authority in China. The numerous reports of breakdowns in law and order, bank robberies, crimes, labor strikes, lax labor discipline, and widespread executions of criminals, not to mention the riots in Peking and other Chinese cities in 1976, have been indicative of the deepening authority crisis and erosion of discipline and order in Chinese society.

All of these examples plus the widespread corruption practiced by high-ranking as well as low-level cadres in the party, government, and the army have generated severe crises of belief, confidence, and trust. These crises in turn have raised questions about the legitimacy of the system. Authority crises may eventually force the regime to rely more and more on coercive means of control to secure compliance from society. Otherwise, if the Chinese leadership fails to arrest these crises, China's PLA leaders can again be expected to play more active roles in the polity, especially in times of intense leadership conflict.

Notes

1. Ye Jianying, "Report on the Revision of the Party Constitution," *Peking Review* (*PR*), no. 36 (2 September 1977), p. 36.
2. "More Scientists and Technicians Join the Party," *PR*, no. 30 (28 July 1978), pp. 21–22.
3. John W. Lewis, *Leadership in Communist China* (Ithaca, N.Y.: Cornell University Press, 1963), pp. 108–109.
4. For example, the CCP Constitutions adopted at the 1969 Ninth CCP Congress and the 1973 Tenth CCP Congress dropped the one-year probation requirement and added a stipulation (Article 2) requiring the "opinions of the broad masses inside and outside the Party" be sought to assess a candidate. A Chinese book published by the Shanghai People's Press in 1974, which was aimed at young activists who sought to join the CCP, is highly indicative of the radicals' design to recruit and seek support among the young intellectuals; the book is available in English translation in Pierre M. Perrolle, ed., *Fundamentals of the Chinese Communist Party* (White Plains, N.Y.: International Arts and Sciences Press, 1976).
5. Ye Jianying, "Report on Revision," p. 36.
6. For a more detailed analysis of the issue, see Parris H. Chang, *Power and Policy in China,* 2nd & enlarged ed. (University Park, Pa.: Pennsylvania State University Press, 1978), pp. 47–49.

7. Ibid., pp. 129–130.

8. See *Zhongyuo Gongchandang Lishi Jiangyi* [History of the Chinese Communist Party], vol. 2 (Shanghai: Shanghai People's Press, 1981), p. 126.

9. For a fuller analysis, see Parris H. Chang, *Radicals and Radical Ideology in China's Cultural Revolution* (New York: Research Institute on Communist Affairs, Columbia University, 1963), pp. 23–26.

10. Benjamin I. Schwartz, "The Reign of Virtue: Some Broad Perspectives on Leader and Party in the Cultural Revolution," in *Party Leadership and Revolutionary Power in China,* ed. John W. Lewis (New York: Cambridge University Press, 1970), p. 168.

11. Edgar Snow, *The Other Side of the River* (New York: Random House, 1962), p. 331.

12. See Parris Chang, "Political Rehabilitation of Cadres in China," *China Quarterly,* no. 54 (April-June 1973), pp. 331–340.

13. For a fuller analysis of these events, see Parris H. Chang, "Chinese Politics: Deng's Turbulent Quest," *Problems of Communism,* January-February 1981, pp. 1–21.

14. The seven additions are Wan Li, Xi Zhongxun, Yang Shangkun, Yang Dezhi, Hu Qiaomu, Song Renquiong, and Liao Chengzhi; those dropped from the Politburo are Hua Guofeng, Geng Biao, Peng Chong, Xu Shiyou, Chen Yonggui, and Liu Bocheng, who is over 85 and asked to be relieved. Furthermore, Yao Yilin, who is one of the two vice-premiers in the State Council and heads the State Planning Commission, and Qin Jiwei, commander of the Peking Military Region, have been elected alternate Politburo members.

15. Six members of the Secretariat have been dropped—they are Xi Zhongxun, Yang Dezhi, Hu Qiaomu, and Fang Yi, all of whom won seats at the Politburo, and Peng Chong and Wang Renzhong, who have suffered political eclipse. Added to the Secretariat are four secretaries, Yang Yong, Deng Liqun, Chen Pixian, and Hu Qili, and two alternate secretaries, Qiao Shi and Hao Jianxiu.

16. Not every radical or Maoist supporter has been ousted—Hua Guofeng is still a member of the CC, Wang Dongxing an alternate member of the CC, and Mao Zhiyong (a Hua appointee and Mao's relative) a CC member and first secretary of the CCP Human Committee.

17. At the Twelfth CCP Congress, the Chinese leadership declared purges of: (1) followers of Lin Biao and the Gang of Four; (2) cadres heavily imbued with factional tendency; (3) cadres who were "beaters, smashers, and looters" during the Cultural Revolution; (4) cadres who opposed the new line established since the Third Plenum of the CC in December 1978; and (5) cadres who committed serious economic crimes.

18. Parris Chang, *Power and Policy in China,* postscript 2.

19. Morris Janowitz, *The Military in the Political Development of New Nations: An Essay in Comparative Analysis* (Chicago: University of Chicago Press, 1964), p. 16.

20. See Schwartz, "The Reign of Virtue," pp. 149–150 and 156–157, and Leonard Schapiro and John W. Lewis, "The Role of the Monolithic Party Under the Totalitarian Leader," in *Party Leadership and Revolutionary Power in China,* pp. 137–142.

5
The Structure of the Chinese State

Lowell Dittmer

Before adumbrating the structure of Chinese politics, it behooves us to define our terms. "Structure" refers to those aspects of politics that are relatively institutionalized and impersonal, whether formal or informal. By "politics" I understand the struggle over national power and policy. This struggle takes place within the framework of government, in somewhat the same way that the struggle to capture a city utilizes the constituent buildings. Although the structure of politics is admittedly more easily modified by interested participants than the landscape of a battleground, it is as implausible to conceive of a politics without structure—a highly personal, factionalized melée in which "power" is the only fixed value—as it is to imagine a battle taking place without any terrain.

In the first part of this essay I attempt to place the study of the structure of the Chinese Communist State in a comparative theoretical perspective. This is followed by a brief chronological survey of the historical origins and development of the PRC over the past thirty years. Perhaps the most analytical section of the paper is the ensuing examination of the organizational principles of Chinese Communist state-building. In the concluding section I review the thrust and direction of the various Communist efforts at structural reform, culminating in the reorganization under way at the time of writing.

Definition of the State

The rise of "behavioralism" in the study of the post-World War II era has been marked by the neglect of the state and a consequent depoliticization of the study of politics. Politics have tended to be viewed as a derivative form of activity, the understanding of which is based upon an investigation of "environmental" or contextual factors such as sociology, economics, culture, and individual psychology rather than political factors themselves; political explanation hence consists of the "reduction" of political explicanda to other disciplines. Political institutions and ideologies are analyzed by referring to the "underlying" social and economic processes. Political science consequently becomes a science without politics.[1]

According to Sheldon Wolin, the development of political theory, especially liberalism in the modern era, anticipated this development: the eclipse of political authority and the discovery of society can be traced back all the way to the period immediately following Thomas Hobbes. Since that time, developments in the British-U.S. political tradition hardly seemed to warrant attributing greater significance to the state.[2] According to J. P. Nettl, Great Britain and the United States were largely "stateless societies," in which functional equivalents to the state arose in the form of political parties in the former and Law in the latter.[3]

Although these strains in the liberal tradition were reinforced by the advent of behavioralism and not allayed by the rise of comparative politics in the post-World War II era, there was a recognition that the state, and political factors generally, could play a much more determinative role in the political system through the theory of "totalitarianism." As the predominantly negative evaluation of totalitarian systems confirmed the liberal notion of the corruption of power and the demonic nature of the state (the omnipotence of the state was perhaps overstated), the tendency to relegate politics to the status of a dependent variable was overcome. In the case of Communist China, even the negative evaluative presuppositions were to some degree discounted, partly because of the state's forthright intentions and fairly successful actions toward promoting economic development and distributive equity, and partly because, despite excesses in the Great Leap Forward and the Cultural Revolution, the state at least avoided such outright barbarities as the anti-Semitic holocaust in Nazi Germany or Stalin's great purge.[4]

This paper thus begins with the assumption that the state plays a central role in Chinese politics. Although the state may also be seen as a dependent variable, changing its internal structure in response to various environmental determinants, it is undoubtedly more importantly considered as the greatest independent variable in the contemporary Chinese political system. Every important policy to be initiated since liberation in 1949 has arisen as a direct consequence of decisions by leaders of the state. Although there is no perfect correlation between formal position and actual political power (the best recent example is given by Deng Xiaoping, whose primacy remains undisputed despite his formally subordinate role), it has been impossible for anyone to accumulate political capital from a position outside of the formal political structure or for any politician to grasp power without going through his bureaucratic paces.

The foregoing assertions, however, beg the question of the relationship between party and state. According to Marxist-Leninists, the state is merely a tool of the ruling classes, and the Communist party is the vanguard of the workers and peasants who have allegedly gained power as a result of the Communist revolution. As a result, the party would seem to be the actual ruling apparatus in the Communist political system, relegating the state to a subordinate role as an implementer of the party's commands. The only problem with this thesis, which otherwise seems admirably suited to the realities of power in Communist China, is that it has become difficult to distinguish between party and state. This is perhaps even more true in China than in other Communist systems because of the legacy of the guerrilla war, which dragged out the involvement of the military in the political system.[5]

In Western pluralist systems, the party distinguishes itself from the state in many respects: the state is the permanent fountainhead of power and authority, the party a contestant for power that alternates with at least one other party in holding office. The party thus tends to be a loosely organized mobilizational organ in a state that is a permanent and highly stable bureaucratic organization. I would argue that in Communist systems—and perhaps in *all* one-party systems—the party and the state become so thoroughly assimilated that a distinction loses meaning. This is so despite the fact that the party does not simply collapse when it gains command of the state, leaving behind, as in the U.S. system, a skeletal organization for the purpose of regenerating power during the next election. Indeed, the Communist party has remained an unusually well-articulated and comprehensive organization even after gaining command of the state, duplicating so many state functions and structures that it results in the phenomenon that organization theorists refer to as "dual rule."[6] But the party becomes "established" as a result of the fact that it no longer has to compete for power.[7] It acquires its own permanent structure and inevitably becomes "bureaucratized": party members come to identify their interests with the nation-state and with their superiors rather than with their constituents, to whom they are no longer practically responsible. Although the party-government distinction retains a certain significance for the Chinese and cannot be dismissed outright, the party has become part of the established state structure and must be included in any meaningful analysis of that structure.

Historical Origins and Development of the State

Although the Chinese Communist party (CCP) was unable to establish a "state" in the sense of a monopoly of force over the Chinese territorial domain until it had won control of the mainland and chased the Kuomintang to the island of Taiwan, the first prototypes of the CCP state organization were set up in the soviets in the 1920s and 1930s. They were of some importance not only for historical reasons, but also because of the organizational principles and intraorganizational relationships first worked out at this time. There were at least 300 of these soviets in existence at one time or another from the time of the founding of the CCP in 1921 to the proclamation of the PRC in 1949; they lasted for varying periods of time and ranged in nature from primitive hideouts to functioning political entities.

Certainly the most advanced of these organizations was the Jiangxi Soviet, which lasted from the spring of 1929 to the fall of 1934 when Jiang Jieshi drove the Communists out of south-central China. Establishment of this soviet followed what has become familiar as a sort of standard operating procedure; it began with the creation of a Central Bureau of the Soviet Areas—which included minority representation of the various ethnic and religious groups in the area—and proceeded to class categorization of the population, arrangement of elections, and the initiation of land redistribution programs. Class categorization preceded elections because only those citizens who were not landlords, gentry, capitalists, rich peasants, or members of other ideologically pejorative categories were permitted to participate. However, regarding the election campaign of the summer and fall of 1931, Waller has found evidence indicating that these elections were either not conducted at all or that they were carried out in a manner bearing little relationship to the formal system of organization. Apparently Mao's operatives kept a tight grip on the electoral machinery to ensure the election of those delegates with views sympathetic to their own.[8] (Some thirty years later, during the Great Proletarian Cultural Revolution, Mao again denigrated elections.)

The governmental organization for the soviets followed a pattern that was to become standard: each lower-level soviet sent delegates to form the next higher-level soviet's delegate conference, from the "xiang" and the "shi" up to the provincial and central levels. Each of these delegate conferences then elected an executive committee, which in turn elected a presidium and a chairman of the presidium. Underneath each presidium were established the various departments for land, finance, labor, military affairs, culture, and so forth; these departments were accountable not only to the "line" offices directly above them (i.e., the presidium) but also to the superior staff offices. In general, from the lower to the higher levels, there was a progressive increase in the total number of delegates assembled, as a result of which the plenums met infrequently. Thus, the lower the legislative assembly in the hierarchy of such assemblies, the stronger the chances for it to retain actual deliberative functions. The structure also tended to be simpler at the lower levels, with less delegation of power to standing committees: a shi soviet had a presidium, which met once a week, but no executive committee; a xiang soviet had neither an executive committee nor a presidium.

At the top level, on the other hand, there was delegation of power to a Central Executive Committee (CEC), the counterpart of the party's Central Committee, and the CEC in turn appointed a Council of People's Commissars (renmin weiyuan hui) as the highest administrative organ of the state (corresponding to what was later to become the State Council). When the first National Soviet Congress convened in Ruijin on 7 November 1931 the delegates announced their support of "democracy," including freedom of speech, assembly, and the press (but only for the "people" and not for landlords and bourgeoisie, who were to be deprived of all political freedom). The congress approved a political program, a constitution, and land and labor laws, and it endorsed proclamations espousing the liberation of women and free and universal education for the worker and peasant masses.

It appears that Mao Zedong, who at this time was somewhat disgruntled with the party leadership, availed himself of the establishment of the soviet government to build an independent organizational base for himself. It was possible for him to get away with this at the time for two reasons: the soviet headquarters in Ruijin was physically removed from the party headquarters in Shanghai, and the organizational mechanisms of party control had not yet been perfected. Thus Mao succeeded in having himself made the first chairman of the Council of People's Commissars as well as the first chairman of the CEC (and thereby presumably first chairman of the People's Republic), combining in his own hands both organizational and ideological authority. The policies adopted by the first National Soviet Congress convened by Mao had distinguishable differences from those endorsed by the Returned Student leadership in Shanghai, with regard to both military and agrarian policy. Not until 1933 did the Returned Student leadership succeed in reasserting its authority. It did so by taking charge of the electoral machinery and, more importantly, by controlling the party factions that were placed in command of each delegation to the National Soviet Congress. As a result, at the second congress a new presidium of the CEC was formed in which Mao's supporters were outnumbered. Mao was not only dropped from his chairmanship of the Council of People's Commissars but removed from that body altogether.

Since the establishment of the People's Republic in 1949, the Chinese Communist State has periodically redefined its historical function in its progress toward the Communist utopia. The theoretical underpinnings of the Common Program and Organic Law of the Chinese People's Political Consultative Conference (CPPCC) and the Organic Law of the Chinese People's Government were provided by Mao Zedong's concept of New Democracy, or People's Democratic Dictatorship. As Benjamin Schwartz has shown, the Chinese subtly differentiated this from the concept of "People's Democracy" used in the Eastern European states.[9] Like the "united front" on which it was modeled, New Democracy allowed maximal latitude for representation of the petty bourgeoisie and national bourgeoisie as well as the peasantry and the proletariat, foreseeing, however, that these nonproletarian classes would eventually need to undergo "reeducation" in order to facilitate peaceful transition to socialism. Mao later expressed regret about this relatively liberal period, opining that it had allowed "bourgeois democratic" opposition to socialism to become firmly entrenched. But in the view of most Western observers at the time, it did permit a more cooperative and less violent transition than had characterized the Stalinist revolution of the 1930s.[10]

The highest organ of state in the 1949–1954 period was the CPPCC, which was first convened in Beijing on 21–30 September 1949. The CPPCC was formed at the initiative and under the direction of the CCP; there was no election, representatives of the various parties, groups, sectors, and interests having apparently been appointed. The CPPCC in turn formed a "standing" governmental structure consisting of three great branches: the Government Administrative Council, forerunner of the State Council; the People's Revolutionary Military Council, which anticipated the National Defense Council; and the court system, consisting of the procuratorate, the Supreme Court, and their inferior organs. Despite its provisional status, the CPPCC did pass some of the most important legislation to be implemented in the history of the People's Republic, the Land Reform Law and the Marriage Law, both of which were enacted in the spring of 1950. But, presumably because government organs had not yet been articulated at lower levels, these laws were implemented by party committees and by party work teams dispatched from higher levels.

During these early years, provincial and local governmental functions were generally executed by the People's Liberation Army (PLA), acting through its local Military Control Committees. Military rule was only gradually replaced in rural areas by people's congresses and frequently involved the transfer of local military commanders from military to civilian political status (an interesting parallel process was to recur in the wake of the Cultural Revolution in 1968–1971). After civilian authority had been firmly established (on an appointive basis) by the PLA and the party, the first local elections were held in accordance with the Electoral Law of 1953.

The primary function of the state during the New Democratic era was to eliminate the economic and political basis for "feudal and semifeudal" resistance to the new regime and to create the prerequisites for industrialization of the country. The early priorities of the regime seemed well suited to this objective. Although the Marriage Law did not altogether succeed in modernizing the Chinese family system, particularly in rural areas, it has appeared to achieve its political goal of breaking up the clans that had formed the bulwark of local resistance to CCP innovations. The Land Reform Law eliminated the power of the landlord class to the chief benefit of the middle peasantry, coincidentally resulting in the classification of the rural populace into classes and the introduction of a comprehensive dossier (dangan) system for purposes of control.[11] In the cities, the Three-Anti Campaigns and Five-Anti Campaigns were mobilized to intimidate any opposition from the national bourgeoisie and to rectify a state bureaucracy that had been compromised by the rapid absorption of officials from the old regime. The primary tasks of the state during this period avowedly were completed by the time of the first National People's Congress in 1954.

The 1954 Constitution was heralded by the announcement that China was now in a period of "transition to socialism," involving the transformation of private property to collective or state ownership. Given the relatively enormous size of the agricultural sector, the socialist transformation of agriculture was the major task facing the regime, and although contrast with the experience of the Soviet Union may have prompted some observers to overstate somewhat the smoothness of the transition, the unity and efficiency of the leadership and its organizational apparatus was not to be seen again.[12] By 1957, peasants farming individually comprised only 2 percent of the population; the remainder had been organized into advanced collectives. In January 1956, socialist transformation was also accelerated in the cities, so that by late 1957, 99.4 percent of the value of industrial output and 95.7 percent of trade turnover was under state, joint public-private, or cooperative ownership in the representative city of Guangzhou.[13]

Although this transition was achieved under the auspices of the continuing New Democratic Dictatorship, its inception justified the introduction of major structural changes as well as substantive policy innovations. The National People's Congress (NPC) was established on 20 September 1954 as the "highest organ of state power" to replace the makeshift CPPCC—which was nonetheless permitted to survive as a symbol of the united front. Although most of the legislation introduced by the NPC originated externally, as in most parliamentary systems (e.g., from the State Council, the NPC's own Standing Committee, or the CCP Central Committee), and was then perfunctorily and unanimously endorsed, the NPC cannot be dismissed entirely as a "rubber stamp." Important legislation was passed by the first NPC, some of it initiated from the floor.[14] Under the chairmanship of Liu Shaoqi (1954–1964), the NPC did at times scrutinize proposals on economic development programs before giving its approval, and at least on one occasion (the Fourth Session of the first NPC in June 1957), NPC delegates criticized Mao in relation to the antirightist campaign and the party's handling of the affairs of Shanghai University.[15]

Delegates to the NPC are elected indirectly: the local people's congresses elect delegates, and these delegates in turn elect delegates to the provinces, municipalities, and autonomous regions, and so on up to the national congress. NPC delegates are elected for a term of five years (four years before 1958), and their chief duties are to convene once annually (under the valiant assumption that the schedule is kept) for a session lasting from ten to seventeen days. Nonparty members still occupied roughly a third of the seats at the 1962 and 1963 sessions of the Second NPC, but only 15 percent of the seats at the Third NPC in December 1964; more recent figures are not available. Election is considered an honor for which no financial recompense is provided, and delegates must continue to work at their regular jobs for their livelihoods. A large proportion of delegates are model workers, model peasants, or militia heroes whose election is considered a form of commendation, and the repeated re-election of delegates has been surprisingly common despite the political vicissitudes of the past twenty years.[16] Voting was originally based on a single list prepared by the CCP, but since the spring of 1979, provision has been introduced for competition between at least two candidates for each post, with somewhat greater opportunity for mass participation in the nominating process. This is an interesting but not unprecedented development, resembling electoral arrangements made as long ago as during the operation of the Jiangxi Soviet.

The main executive organs of the NPC are its Standing Committee, the State Council, and the chief of state, a position restored in the most recent (1982) draft Constitution after a period of vacancy dating from the purge of Liu Shaoqi in 1978. The Standing Committee of the NPC, the Chinese counterpart of the Presidium of the Supreme Soviet, has the power to interpret laws (falu) and to enact decrees (faling), in addition to handling certain ceremonial aspects of diplomacy (particularly during the period of vacancy of the chairmanship of state). The 1982 draft Constitution for the first time introduced other functionally specialized permanent committees to operate under the supervision of the Standing Committee, on the model of the departments of the CCP Central Committee or the ministries of the State Council.[17]

Although no meetings of the Standing Committee were reported from the beginning of the Cultural Revolution until well after the death of Mao, it has reemerged as a vigorously active organ under the chairmanship of Ye Jianying. Contrary to widespread opinion, the position of chief of state was constitutionally very strong from the outset, possibly because it was tailored for its first incumbent, Mao Zedong; however, the prerogatives of the recently rehabilitated position have been curtailed. Originally the chief of state could convene and chair the National Defense Council (however, the Central Military Affairs Committee in the 1982 draft is accountable only to the NPC or its Standing Committee) and the Supreme State Conference (an ad hoc assemblage that was not revived in the 1982 draft), and he is still formally empowered to appoint or remove the premier, vice-premiers, and other members of the State Council and to proclaim a state of war or promulgate other laws and decrees.[18] The State Council has day-to-day control of the preparation of economic plans, management of the financial and economic systems, and the implementation of foreign policy, and is generally recognized to be the most powerful governmental executive organ.

To honor and endow theoretical significance to the successful completion of socialist transformation, the Chinese State began to redefine itself as a "socialist state of the dictatorship of the proletariat" rather than a "New Democracy" or "People's Democratic State." Though this appellation began to appear as early as 1957, the second and third NPCs did not introduce new constitutions and the new designation was hence first constitutionally enshrined in the party Constitution of the Ninth CCP Congress, then—more appropriately—in the state Constitution of the Fourth NPC in 1975. Consistent with progress toward the Communist utopia that this change in designations betokens was continuing pressure for more egalitarian and communitarian ideals, particularly during the

Great Leap Forward and the Cultural Revolution, and corresponding pressure for decentralization to the village level or its urban equivalent[19] and the "withering away of the State" with its replacement by the vanguard party. Accordingly, the NPC was omitted almost entirely from the legislative process: No laws were enacted from 1966 to 1976, authoritative commands usually originating rather as "central documents" (zhongfa) issued by an assortment of leadership organs supervised by the CC Politburo;[20] the CPPCC did not meet during the entire 1965–1978 period, and the NPC met only once, to draft a Constitution that was brief and singularly self-abnegating.

This trend was reversed with the Fifth NPC in February 1978, primarily because the tendency toward decentralization resulted in the destruction of the united front and led to a "dictatorship of the proletariat" in which the latter class was ideologically rather than empirically defined, resulting in dictatorship by a determined radical minority. The Fifth NPC Constitution therefore expanded the powers of the state structure and reconvened the somnolent CPPCC, and the draft Constitution of the Sixth NPC artfully defined the state as "the people's democratic dictatorship led by the working class and based on the alliance of workers and peasants, that is, the dictatorship of the proletariat,"[21] thereby serving the ambiguous function of affirming both the old People's Democratic State and the theoretically more advanced (but economically inconvenient) Dictatorship of the Proletariat.

Although the judiciary in some Western states constitutes a third branch of government exercising judicial review over legislation to ensure that it does not gainsay constitutional provisions, the judiciary has never been empowered to review legislation in the Chinese State, despite the renewed emphasis being placed on the importance of the law. The political significance of the codification of law introduced at the second session of the Fifth NPC in June 1979 appears to be to provide a functional equivalent for Marxist-Leninist-Maoist ideology (the party "line") as a basis for demanding popular conformity with regime policies, rather than to establish a fixed set of principles to regulate elite behavior. This conclusion appears true despite the provision in the 1982 draft for "equality before the law" (Chapter 2, Article 32) for the reasons that no organ is empowered to enforce the Constitution within the government and the Constitution itself can easily be amended or completely rewritten. According to my conversation with Chinese constitutional law specialists in the spring of 1982, the need for an organ empowered to protect the Constitution has been acknowledged but not yet resolved.

The absence of a political culture of obedience to the law has in the past led to flagrant abuses by leaders as well as masses, including not only Lin Biao's alleged coup attempt but also numerous instances of direct or indirect slander and the bypassing of regular procedures in the policymaking process. If the current very strong emphasis on legal education for future cadres is sustained, then some of these abuses may be mitigated. The court process in the trial of the Gang of Four was already a vast improvement over the mass struggle meetings launched against the targets (duixiang) of the Cultural Revolution, though of course it cannot compare favorably with the Western judicial process.

It would be misleading to suggest that all conceptual obstacles to a rational-legal political culture have been cleared. Although party ideology has been in disarray since the fall of the Gang of Four, the CCP has by no means forfeited fealty to the snakelike historical undulations of the party line in favor of the more rigid rule of law.[22] The importance of political "weather," even in the pall of the mass movement's demise, is one testimonial to the surviving influence of the "line" mentality. So long as the Chinese remain so responsive to meteorological vicissitudes the rule of law will remain a paper tiger.

Organizational Principles

The first principle of leadership is that of "democratic centralism," correctly perceived by Schurmann to be an inherently contradictory fusion of organizational imperatives. Centralism means that once a decision has been reached, the minority must obey the majority, the lower level must obey the higher level, and everyone must obey the central leadership. Decisions are disseminated through "a web of organization with vertical chains of command which ultimately merge, like the apex of a pyramid, at the very top."[23] Democracy means that each authorized participant in a policy or decision-making process should participate with "activism" and "creativity" rather than passively wait for decisions to be handed down and then blindly obey them, and that the activism and creativity of the masses should be mobilized in the process of implementation.

To the amazement of most Westerners, there seems to be no expectation that democracy could conceivably result in the emergence of opposition, and whenever it does result in the public expression of contrary opinions the CCP leadership is apt to evince surprise and dismay. For example, when the Democracy Wall activists in the fall and winter of 1978 transgressed what the authorities considered a creative and activist realization of democracy (by leading demobilized soldiers and sent-down urban youth and other disprivileged groups in urban protest marches and by utilizing big-character posters to criticize not only the Gang of Four but also Mao Zedong, Deng Xiaoping, and the theoretical fundamentals of the Communist party-state), the leadership began taking a much more censorious perspective of their activities. The same transformation of elite attitudes followed in the wake of certain untoward developments that occurred in the local electoral campaigns conducted in Changsha and Beijing in 1980. Many observers inferred that the opening to democratic expression must have been cynical from the outset; they failed to take into account the possibility that it was sincere but simply did not entertain the possibility of sustained, even proliferating dissidence. Any opposition within a "democratic" framework was expected to be polite, "constructive" to the degree that most Westerners might consider it sycophantic, and disposed to capitulate fully if outvoted; preferably, dissenting opinions were even hoped to pleasantly surprise the leadership by making new and original contributions to the implementation of the preferred alternative. Dissent in excess of these rather narrow bounds would be "uncultivated" and demonstrate the dissenters' lack of the necessary maturity to practice democracy—meaning that they must be suppressed for their own good and that of the collective. In brief, there appeared to be a feeling that any group discussion in which consensus had not been painstakingly arranged well in advance could lead to some chaotic, disastrous outcome.[24]

A second characteristic of Chinese Communist organization building has been a marked secular trend toward bureaucratic accretion. This generalization is true of all bureaucracies, as Northcote Parkinson pointed out long ago, but there are reasons to assume that the trend is even more pronounced in the PRC than elsewhere.[25] An example is the traditional aversion to fire or retire senior political officials, who tend to acquire prestige with seniority and thus become increasingly invulnerable. This aversion was probably reinforced by the post-Mao repudiation of dangerous radicalism by a conservative coalition of veteran cadres, as a result of which the outlook for the most recent reforms designed to retire senior people on behalf of professionally educated younger officials seems fairly bleak. Another example is the analogous aversion to "retire" organizational entities. Once established, any given organization is found to serve *some* function, as a result of which it cannot be rescinded even if it becomes functionally superfluous; the source of organizational innovation is the creation of new organs, a recourse that may be tapped liberally without much concern for organizational "costs" in terms of the redundancy of old organs. Such proliferation seems to be particularly true for legislative organs and line agencies. Thus, the size of the National Party Congress increased from 544 delegates at the Seventh Congress in 1945 to 1,510 delegates at the Eleventh Congress in 1977, and the size of the NPC has grown even more dramatically, in part because of a 1963 decision to double the representation allowed a given population unit. When the NPC was introduced as the chief legislative body of the state, the CPPCC was neither suspended nor incorporated into the NPC, but allowed to survive as an "advisory" body, which in practice means that it convenes following NPC sessions to examine and approve proposals first submitted to and approved by the NPC. Staff organizations have been contracted in number or size with greater flexibility. But as long as the "parent" line organization has survived and retained its original functions, historical experience indicates that what has been retrenched may later be reexpanded.

Because of the tendency of organizations to grow, they are apt to become too large to deliberate or indeed to do anything but convene and listen to reports. Thus another basic organizational principle is the "standing office" system for the delegation of authority. This means that elections need not be held for each plenary session, but that delegates may be chosen to function on behalf of the larger body. The result in effect is that only those top leaders who have been selected to function full time in a leadership capacity have real power. As organizations grow, power is successively delegated from one to another, resulting in the creation of "chains" of organizations in which the larger, original organizations are progressively more removed from the locus of power.[26] For example, in the twenties the CCP Congress was still an important deliberative and decision-making body, in the thirties its power was effectively usurped by the Central Committee (CC), by the forties the Politburo became the standing locus of power, and finally in the late fifties the Politburo Standing Committee emerged as the elite within the elite. Power is also functionally divided among various departments of the CC and among commissions and ministries of the State Council that are also "standing." The political implications of the "standing office" system are that the delegation of power is the abdication of power, and that any attempt to build a broader consensus by inclusion of new representatives of the public takes place at the expense of the dilution of the decision-making power of all participants. The tugging and hauling of politics must occur behind the scenes; the more public organizations serve acclamatory and legitimating functions and therefore require a display of consensus.

The delegation of power leads to a predictable sequence in the revelation of decisions, as these decisions proceed from the smaller and more informal meetings of standing committees to the larger and more formal legislative assemblies. There is an operating assumption that a new policy initiative must be approved by some major legislative assembly to stand any chance of implementation, although legislative approval is not formally required. In the past the choice of a specific assembly of approval has not even followed a discernible pattern: sometimes the NPC would give its endorsement, sometimes the National CCP Congress, sometimes the Supreme State Council. Perhaps the selection of an assembly to consider a new legislative proposal depends not so much on which assembly is functionally appropriate to the proposal as on which is slated to convene next; usually approval of the proposal may be assumed, but the convention of meetings follows its own logic.

In principle there is expected to be a proper sequence in the holding of meetings, as each meeting approves the proceedings of the previous smaller meeting. The Politburo Standing Committee presumably meets on a daily basis, the Politburo itself slightly less frequently, and they then report to the CC in a plenary meeting, which is followed by a CCP Congress, and finally by a convention of the NPC; the direction of movement is from private power to public ceremony. This "normal" sequence may be upset by special circumstances, however. For example, the Ninth CCP Congress "should" have been followed by the Fourth NPC, and in fact a draft of the state Constitution for the Fourth NPC was circulated at the Second Plenum of the Ninth Congress in August-September 1970. But the dispute between Lin and Mao, culminating in Lin's death in September 1971, made it necessary first to hold a Tenth CCP Congress to rescind some of the decisions adopted at the Ninth Congress, before holding a Fourth NPC.

Given the predictable direction of flow and sequence in meetings or forums, it is thus possible to make inferences about the content of the often quite secretive policy discussions under way. Sufficient institutionalization has taken place to facilitate similar inferences on the basis of the intervals between meetings of the same forum or the duration of the sessions. Thus the normal interval between CC Plena is no more than one year; a longer interval reflects the inability of the party to reach consensus on the party line. There was a lengthy hiatus between CCP Plena preceding the Cultural Revolution (the Tenth Plenum of the Eighth CC was in September 1962, the Eleventh not until August 1966), and another following the purge of Lin Biao (the Second Plenum of the Ninth CC was in August 1970, the First Plenum of the Tenth CC in August 1973), due to deep cleavage within the party during those periods.

The upheavals of the 1966–1968 period precluded large formal meetings and indeed the entire Cultural Revolution decade (1966–1976) was marked by unusually lengthy intervals between both party and state meetings. The normal interval between CCP Congresses or NPCs is not more than five years; thus the long interval between the Eighth and Ninth CCP Congresses (from the second session of the Eighth Congress in 1958 to the Ninth in 1969) or between the Third and Fourth NPCs (from the Third in 1964 to the Fourth in 1975) reflected difficulty in the party's attaining a consensus.

On the other hand, an abnormally brief interval between meetings leads one to infer that decisions are being accelerated for some reason. Thus the brief time span between the Second Plenum of the Tenth CC (8–10 January 1975) and the opening session of the Fourth NPC (13–17 January 1975) led to the impression that these meetings were convoked with unseemly haste, perhaps in order to take advantage of Mao's absence from the capital to achieve a fait accompli.

The significance of the duration of a meeting is not entirely clear, but the usual inference is that a meeting of long duration must have occasioned a great deal of discussion and debate, whether because of deep cleavages riving the participants or because of the inherent complexity of the issues involved. A meeting of unusually short duration must have occasioned little deliberation, but functioned more or less as a rubber stamp. The normal duration of a CCP Congress or NPC is ten days, of a CC Plenum around two weeks. Any prolongation suggests unanticipated discord. For example, the Central Work Conference of October 1966, which discussed implementation of the Cultural Revolution, lasted nearly a month, probably because of divisions among participants; and the Ninth CCP Congress lasted twenty-four days, apparently because of debate about Lin Biao's report (which had to be revised before being approved). The Tenth CCP Congress, on the other hand, lasted only four days (24–28 August 1973), indicating that it deliberated virtually nothing.

Another facet of the Chinese pursuit of organizational innovation—and one that ignores organizational immortality—is the problem of structural duplication. As old organs grow too large and public to be vested with power and become increasingly ceremonial, new and supposedly autonomous organizations will be introduced to serve identical or overlapping functions. The clearest and most archetypal example of this is the complete structural duplication between governmental and party organs at every level of the hierarchy. The functional distinction that is sometimes claimed, citing the governmental hierarchy as an implementing agency and the party hierarchy as a policymaking body—a distinction analogous to the Western distinction between executive and legislative branches of government—is belied by the fact that both government and party hierarchies are replete with both executive and legislative organs at every level. Organizational logic would have dictated that the party relinquish some of its functionally redundant structures upon the introduction of the government hierarchy in the fifties, but following the CPSU precedent it refused to do so. For apparently similar reasons, the CPPCC survived introduction of the NPC. Thus the state structure can currently boast no less than three legislative organs: the NPC, the National CCP Congress, and the CPPCC. (The Supreme State Conference was wisely retired during the vacancy of its chairman, the chief of state.) Each has its own constitution, and each seems fully equipped to consider any proposed legislation. At latest count, there would seem to be no less than five executive organs: the CCP Politburo, the CC Secretariat, the premier (and State Council), the chairman (and Standing Committee) of the NPC, and the recently resurrected chief of state. The division of functions among these duplicate structures remains unclear.

Structural duplication and incremental growth tend to result in an unwieldy and complex structure, increasing the requirements for coordination and control. The introduction of structurally distinct organs fosters the suspicion that they will become politically autonomous ("independent kingdoms"). The mechanism most frequently used to forestall this possibility is bureaucratic interpenetration. Again the classic paradigm is the CCP's penetration of the governmental hierarchy. The specific means of interpenetration are numerous, including overlapping memberships in the two organizations, a party committee and "leading party group" (dangzu) or party fraction within the host organization. Thus we find that of the thirteen vice-premiers of the State Council elected by the Fifth NPC, nine were also members of the Politburo and all were CC members; of the thirty-six ministers, twenty-nine (81 percent) were also CC members. All major economic ministries (e.g., economic planning, capital construction, research and development, foreign trade, and heavy and light industry) were under the control of ministers who were also members of the Politburo or the CC. The party similarly penetrates the various auxiliary organizations (for youth, women, and trade unions).

In the mid-sixties the PLA under Lin Biao used the same organizational paradigm to penetrate governmental and auxiliary organizations. Beginning in 1964, the PLA began to set up political departments parallel to established party organs to ensure that Maoist values would be duly honored. During the Cultural Revolution period, there is some indication that the Jiang Qing group inserted political departments into the provincial revolutionary committees for the purpose of supervising the reestablishment of mass organizations in 1973, propagating the films of Jiang Qing's revolutionary model operas, and so forth.[27] The Gang of Four reportedly also attempted to penetrate the trade union movement, the military, and other organizations in order to collect incriminating information about their rivals within the leadership.[28]

The chief advantage of bureaucratic interpenetration is that it facilitates extensive consultation and coordination among parallel organizations. The drawback is that it tends to moot the putative advantages for the sake of which a distinct organization was introduced in the first place. Among these is the desirability of having an independent outside monitoring agency to control corruption. The Central Control Commission was created for this purpose in the fifties, and the Central Commission for Inspecting Discipline was introduced at the Third Plenum of the Eleventh CC in December 1973 for the same purpose. Yet fear of the power a truly autonomous control hierarchy might wield (one Beijing University professor, in a recent interview, invoked the specter of Beria) has led the party to penetrate the commissions for inspecting discipline: the party committee at each level elects members of the corresponding level's Commission for Inspecting Discipline, and the latter remains accountable to the party committee as well as to the superior Commission for Inspecting Discipline; membership in the two organs is not mutually exclusive. The most likely consequence is that the Commissions for Inspecting Discipline will not inspect the discipline of the corresponding party committees as rigorously as they will inspect the party committees subordinate to them, so that the entire control hierarchy will tend to become a means whereby higher authorities exert their authority over their subordinates without, in turn, being held any more accountable than before.

Another of the theoretical benefits of introducing distinct organizations is that of providing a more rational allocation of functional responsibilities, thereby also making more adequate provision for the integration of professional expertise into the leadership based on functional specialization. This is the most frequently adduced reason for the attempt to differentiate between party and government hierarchies, at least since the repudiation of the relevance of the theory of "checks and balances" to the Chinese state structure in late 1981.[29] Thus it has been stipulated that although overlapping memberships might continue, a leading official in a party (or government) organ may not hold a leading position in the corresponding governmental (party) organ. Whether this latest reform manages to provide a more distinct locus of accountability remains to be seen, but hitherto ubiquitous bureaucratic interpenetration has functioned to disperse responsibility. Did Marshall Peng Dehuai, erstwhile defense minister (and Politburo member), represent the interests of the military when he criticized Mao Zedong's agricultural policies in 1959? Did Zhou Enlai or Liu Shaoqi represent the interests of the government or the party in the early sixties when both men held high posts in both organizations? Of course the ideologically orthodox Chinese answer is that an official should not represent an organizational or any other specific vested interest, but rather the interests of the people as a whole. But the organizational logic of this is bewildering, tending to obfuscate accountability.

When a policy works out successfully this system ensures all-round consultation and consensus, but if a major policy for any reason fails, who is to blame? No one is really certain, because almost everyone was involved in making and implementing the policy. Thus acknowledgment of a policy failure automatically triggers a "reckoning of accounts" or post mortem. Whoever is finally selected as the target of criticism is apt to feel quite bitter about it, finding that a responsibility that was generously diffused during the policymaking and policy-implementing phases has suddenly become quite narrowly focused. And to a considerable extent this "summary of experience" is indeed necessarily a scapegoat process, given the almost universal consultation that preceded the alleged policy error.

The final disadvantage of extensive structural duplication is that actual power tends to meander from one structure to another, depending on the prestige and political resources of the individuals holding positions in those structures. The most obvious example is of course the position of chief of state, which was considered essentially ceremonial before 1959 but came to be deemed so powerful during the subsequent incumbency of Liu Shaoqi that the chairman of the party apparently felt it posed a threat to him and had it eliminated for that reason. Based on the frequency of their meetings it would seem that power wandered from the CPPCC to the NPC and the various other organs of state in 1954 and from there to the party in 1965, though there appears to have been a shift since 1977 back toward the organs of state, particularly the Standing Committee of the NPC and the State Council.[30]

"Collective leadership" is actually a form of structural duplication in the sense that all full members of the Politburo Standing Committee (as well as all members of structurally analogous subordinate executive boards) have full voting rights and are organizationally equal, with the result that power may also wander freely among them depending on the cogency of their arguments or the strength of their political bases. The "cult of personality" entails among other things an attempt by the formal chairman to parlay his greater public visibility into greater de facto power over other members of the board. Thus there is really little wonder that Vice-Chairman Deng Xiaoping's rise to hegemony within the Politburo was accompanied by a litany on the virtues of collective leadership and the folly of the personality cult.

Structural Reform

The two types of structural reform that have received the most attention since 1949 have concerned the retrenchment of the bureaucracy and the revitalization of the legislature. The first of these projects has been recurringly attempted without lasting success. The second has remained on the drawing boards until recently, when limited aspects of a far more ambitious reform platform were put into effect.

As noted above, retrenchment of the bureaucracy, an endeavor that has been close to the hearts of the CCP leadership for a long time due to nostalgic memories of a much less bureaucratic society in Yenan, has in practice consisted of the rescission of administrative staff and secretarial personnel while leaving most line agencies largely intact. Thus during the Great Leap Forward there was a "structural simplification" of the State Council involving decentralization and a "xiafang" campaign that emptied ministries of administrative personnel. The main result was the amalgamation of ministries, bureaus, and other agencies with similar functions into unitary bodies; the number of ministries and commissions was reduced from forty-one in 1956 to thirty in 1958. Then the number increased again, reaching a peak of forty-nine just before the Cultural Revolution; this time the number of ministries and commissions was reduced to twenty-nine by the time of the Fourth NPC in 1975. In May of 1982 a new retrenchment resulted in cutting the number of vice-premiers from thirteen to two, and of ministries and commissions from fifty-two to forty-one. Many veteran ministers have been retired, and a large number of younger ministers appointed.

The chief distinguishing characteristic of the most recent bureaucratic retrenchment has been the attempt to ease the retirement of veteran cadres by creating advisory panels to which they may be "promoted." For example, of the eleven vice-premiers removed in the recent State Council reorganization, nine have been appointed to the post of "state councilor." One aspect of the reform plan (geng shen gai geng) proposed by Deng Xiaoping in a speech to an enlarged meeting of the Politburo on 18 August 1980 was for the party's CC also to establish an "advisory committee" to which senior party officials (including Deng himself) could be retired. Thus the CC would consist of three parallel committees: the CC would become the Central Executive Committee, joined by the Central Commission for Inspecting Discipline (already established) and the advisory or oversight committee, all mutually checked, balanced, and supervised.[31]

The roles of the state and party advisory committees remain to be clarified. Will they compose a kind of inner cabinet, analogous to the Japanese *genros?* If so, their function in the retirement of senior officials would be vitiated and the advisory committees would be dominant by dint of seniority, prestige, and experience. Some of the state councilors concurrently hold important ministerial assignments—Huang Hua as foreign minister, Geng Biao as defense minister, Chen Muhua as minister of foreign economic relations and trade, and Fang Yi as minister in charge of the scientific and technological commissions—but others (Yu Qiuli, Gu Mu, Kang Shien, Ji Pengfei) have no ministerial responsibilities.

The first proposals for revitalization of the legislature were made by representatives of the bourgeois democratic parties during the abortive Hundred Flowers Campaign. They suggested that the bourgeois democratic parties be permitted to compete electorally with the CCP and possibly even alternate in positions of power, and that the CPPCC become a "senate of political planning" (zhengzhi shezhiyuan). These proposals were indignantly rejected during the antirightist campaign as evidence that unreconstructed capitalist thinking was still extant in China.[32] Amid the subsequent radicalization of the Chinese political climate no similar proposals were made until well after the death of Mao Zedong, but in 1980 the reform thrust resurfaced with considerable éclat in Chinese intellectual circles. Deng's "geng shen" reforms proposed that the NPC be reduced in size to about 1,000 members and split into two chambers, one as a regional chamber (with about 300 members) representing regions and minorities on a federal basis, the other as a social chamber (with about 700 members) representing various strata and enterprises on a corporate basis. Both chambers would share initiative and legislative power, oversee the government's executive organs, and otherwise assume the supreme power of the state; each would check and balance the other. The NPC would convene twice a year (rather than once), with longer sessions than in the past, thereby giving delegates more adequate time to examine the materials presented to them and actively discuss them.[33] The Standing Committee of the NPC would be reduced in size in keeping with the retrenchment of the NPC itself, from 300 members to sixty or seventy. Both chambers would also establish various specialized committees that would meet on a standing basis with the help of scholars and experts as advisors. The party would be retracted from its direct supervisory role vis-à-vis subordinate governmental agencies, which should be bound to obey only directives and decisions issued under jurisdiction of the State Council and other governmental organs.

The general thrust of the reform proposals is toward the "institutionalization and legalization of socialist democracy" (shehui zhuyi minzhu zhiduhua faluhua); that is, with the historical enfeeblement of the reactionary classes, the scope of dictatorship may shrink as the scope of democracy expands concomitantly.[34] The specter haunting the reformers is a recurrence of the Cultural Revolution, but they are operating on the premise that it was caused by the excessive concentration of power in the hands of the Gang of Four (and their unmentioned patron). Thus power should be dispersed among various institutions designed to check and balance one another—their integrity assured by various guarantees and by a political culture thoroughly inculcated with the rule of law.

The ultimate fate of the "geng shen" package—perhaps the most sweeping set of reforms to be bruited since the Hundred Day reform of Kang Yuwei and Liang Qiqiao—remains unclear. But preliminary indications are that the more ambitious proposals will die aborning. The 1982 draft Constitution adopted a few reform proposals, such as specialized permanent NPC committees, a fixed term of office for certain government positions, greater autonomy for governmental (and auxiliary) organizations, and greater emphasis on due process under law. But the other proposals disappeared, and the overall political climate since the fall of 1980 has become increasingly inhospitable to reform proposals.

It is entirely possible that the "geng shen" reforms are not dead but sleeping, destined to be reawakened at some more propitious time. If so, it seems to me that it would be helpful in expediting the progress of reform for Chinese intellectuals to work out the answers to two conceptual quandaries that in the past have frustrated their best-intended efforts. First, what is the proper role of conflict in the political system? Given the late Mao Zedong's penchant for defining politics purely in terms of conflict, the current disenchantment with its incorporation into the political structure is perhaps understandable. However, one searches in vain amid the reform proposals for any notion that politicians could seriously disagree. Even the republication of Liu Shaoqi's classic, *On Inner-Party Struggle* (*lun dangnei douzheng*), was accompanied by interpretation that would have confirmed radical criticisms of the original. The concept of checks and balances seems to have been dropped in favor of a functional division of labor, still governed by norms of all-round consultation. The problem with this view is that as long as conflict is denied or ignored in the structure of an organization, it will impair that structure when it surfaces. By officially ignoring conflict, the Chinese Communists, in effect, drive it underground where it takes the form of clandestine factional organizations.[35] These factions do not operate according to "principle" for the excellent reason that no principles have been laid down for them, and past experience has shown that their activities may become quite disruptive.

Second, what is "socialist democracy" and exactly how does it differ from "bourgeois democracy"? In the past, the answer has been that socialist democracy is a means rather than an end and that it is based on substantive rather than mere procedural justice. This answer has in effect nullified democratization by stipulating that the substantive ends of democracy are decreed by the dialectic of history, known only to the vanguard of the proletariat, and that if the people are not spontaneously aware of historical necessity they must be educated and guided to their salvation. The reformers have attempted to compromise this issue by contending that democracy is both end *and* means, procedure as well as substance. This contention is unfortunately no solution, either conceptually or politically. Conceptually, it begs the question of what is to be done when procedure and substance conflict, when the necessity for socialist ends negates democratic means. Politically, it leaves that question to be decided by the actors who have most power to decide it in the existing system—and the latter are likely to have a vested interest in the status quo.

Acknowledgments

I am grateful to the Center for Chinese Studies of the University of California at Berkeley for research support and to the Department of International Politics of Beijing University for research assistance contributing to this study. I also thank Tun-jen Cheng for his assistance on the final section of the paper.

Notes

1. Charles A. McCoy and John Playford, eds., *Apolitical Politics: A Critique of Behavioralism* (New York: Crowell, 1968).
2. Sheldon Wolin, *Politics and Vision* (Boston: Little, Brown, 1960), pp. 286–351; see also Charles Tilly, ed., *The Formation of National States in Western Europe* (Princeton, N.J.: Princeton University Press, 1975), pp. 70–73.
3. J. P. Nettl, "The State as a Conceptual Variable," in *World Politics,* July 1968, p. 69.
4. Among the best recent texts to utilize the concept of totalitarianism in the study of the People's Republic of China is James Townsend, *Politics in China* (Boston: Little, Brown, 1974).
5. Tony Saich, *China: Politics and Government* (New York: St. Martin's Press, 1981), pp. 92–93.
6. Franz Schurmann, *Ideology and Organization in Communist China* (Berkeley: University of California Press, 1968 ed.), pp. 188 ff.
7. See Harry Harding, *Organizing China: The Problem of Bureaucracy, 1949–1976* (Stanford, Calif.: Stanford University Press, 1981) for the most recent and extended discussion of the leadership's reaction to this problem.
8. Derek J. Waller, *The Kiangsi Soviet Republic: Mao and the National Congresses of 1931 and 1934* (Berkeley, Calif.: Center for Chinese Studies, 1973).
9. Benjamin Schwartz, *Communism and China: Ideology in Flux* (Cambridge, Mass.: Harvard University Press, 1968).
10. Thomas Bernstein, "Keeping the Revolution Going: Problems of Village Leadership After Land Reform," in *Party Leadership and Revolutionary Power in China,* ed. John W. Lewis (Cambridge, U.K.: Cambridge University Press, 1970); and Bernstein, "Leadership and Mass Mobilization in the Soviet and Chinese Collectivization Campaigns of 1929–30 and 1955–56: A Comparison," *China Quarterly* 31 (July-September 1967), pp. 1–47.
11. Richard Curt Kraus, *Class Conflict in Chinese Socialism* (New York: Columbia University Press, 1981), pp. 39–63.
12. See Chalmers Johnson, "The Changing Nature and Locus of Authority in Communist China," in John M. H. Lindbeck, *China: Management of a Revolutionary Society* (Seattle: University of Washington Press, 1971), pp. 34–79.
13. Ezra Vogel, *Canton Under Communism: Programs and Politics in a Provincial Capital, 1949–1968* (Cambridge, Mass.: Harvard University Press, 1969).
14. In the first session of the NPC, thirty-nine members' private bills made their appearance. Seven of these bills dealt with industry, mining, and labor; three with agriculture;

eight with water conservation; four with communication and transportation; three with cultural and educational affairs; seven with medicine and pharmacy; four with the administrative system; and another three with weights and measures, construction of the capitol, and proclamation of a martyr day, respectively. No oral or written questions were addressed to the government ministers, however. See *China Daily,* 9 October 1954, as cited in Franklin W. Houn, "Communist China's New Constitution," in *Government of Communist China,* ed. George P. Jan (San Francisco: Chandler, 1966), pp. 213–251.

15. Union Research Institute, *Communist China, 1949–1959* (Hong Kong: Union Research Press, 1960), p. 60.

16. Li Yuan, "Bring into Full Play the Role of the National People's Congress," *Guangming Ribao,* 14 April 1981, p. 3.

17. "Draft of the Revised Constitution of the People's Republic of China" (hereinafter "Revised Draft"), Ch. 3, Sect. 1, Art. 69, as published in *China Daily* (Beijing), 28 April 1982, pp. 4–6. Provision is also made in Art. 70 for the Standing Committee to appoint temporary commissions of inquiry to investigate specific questions when this is deemed necessary.

18. "Revised Draft," Ch. 3, Sect. 2.

19. The Great Leap Forward resulted in the temporary elimination of private plots, rural markets, and sideline industries; bureaucrats began to be removed from their offices at national and provincial levels and sent down to county levels. There was also a marked tendency toward decentralization. Up to 20 percent of the profits in industry could be retained locally during the Great Leap, local adjustments of budgets were permitted, and reporting was simplified; from 1957 to 1959 the percentage of industries under central control fell from 46 to 26 percent. The Cultural Revolution followed suit, resulting in the devolution of responsibility for health, education, and various other functional areas from higher to lower levels, with an emphasis on local self-reliance.

20. See Kenneth Lieberthal, *Central Documents and Politburo Politics in China* (Ann Arbor: University of Michigan, Center for Chinese Studies, 1978).

21. "Revised Draft," Preamble.

22. See Gua Hua, "Some Remarks on the 'Rule of Men' and 'Rule of Law'," *Xueshu Yanjiu,* no. 1 (January 1981), pp. 87–90.

23. H. F. Schurmann, "Organizational Principles of the Chinese Communists," *China Quarterly,* April-June 1960, pp. 47–59.

24. On the Chinese presumption that action must be preceded by elaborate preparation, see John H. Weakland, "The Organization of Action in Chinese Culture," *Psychiatry,* no. 13 (1950), pp. 361–370; on Chinese attitudes toward chaos, see Richard Solomon, "Mao's Effort to Reintegrate the Chinese Policy: Problems of Authority and Conflict in the Chinese Social Process," in *Chinese Communist Politics in Action,* ed. Doak Barnett (Seattle: University of Washington Press, 1969), pp. 271–365.

25. C. Northcote Parkinson, *Parkinson's Law, and Other Studies in Administration* (New York, 1964).

26. See Lowell Dittmer, "The Formal Structure of Central Chinese Political Institutions," in *Organizational Behavior in Chinese Society,* ed. Sidney L. Greenblatt et al. (New York: Praeger, 1980), pp. 47–76.

27. Lieberthal, *Central Documents.*

28. See Guo Yongxian and Yan Qimin, "How to Understand the Bourgeois 'Two-Party System'," *Hongqi,* no. 11 (November 1981), pp. 33–37.

29. Jürgen Domes has demonstrated the utility of correlating meeting frequency with decision-making power in his entry, "Politscher Entscheidungsprozess," in *China Handbuch,* ed. Wolfgang Franke (Duesseldorf: Bertelsmann Universitaetsverlag, 1974), pp. 1046–1050.

30. Liao Gailong, "The Reform Plans of the Chinese Communists in 1980," *The Seventies,* no. 3 (March 1981), pp. 38–48. For a translation of the original address, see Teng Hsiao-p'ing, "A Speech at the Enlarged Meeting of the Politburo of the CC (delivered on August 18; passed after discussion by the Politburo of the CC on August 31)," in *Issues and Studies* 17:3 (March 1981), pp. 81–103. For a perceptive analysis, see Shen Si,

"Restoration, not Reform: On the PRC's Geng Shen Reform," *Zhong Bao Yuekan* (Hong Kong), no. 18 (July 1981), pp. 19–22.

31. Yu Gang, "Further Strengthen Cooperation Between Party and Non-Party," *Hongqi*, no. 8 (August 1981), pp. 24–28.

32. Li Yuan, "Bring into Full Play," p. 3.

33. Wang Jingrong, "Rousseau and His Theory of Civil Rights," *Liaoning University Xue Bao,* no. 1 (January 1980), pp. 36–42.

34. One of the more subtle and provocative analyses of factionalism is Lucian Pye, *The Dynamics of Chinese Politics* (Cambridge, Mass.: Oelgeschlager, Gunn and Hain, 1981).

35. See Sun Bokui, "Concerning Socialist Democracy," *Zhexue yu shehui koxue* (Nanjing University), no. 2 (February 1979), pp. 17–24; Li Qianheng, "On Socialist Democracy and Legal System," ibid., pp. 24–29; and Ko Muhua, "Concerning Some Questions on Socialist Democracy," *Zhueshu Yanjiu,* no. 2 (February 1979), pp. 23–26.

6
The Redefinition of Politics: Communist China's Movement to a Postrevolutionary Polity

Teh-hou Jen

For contemporary political scientists, the most familiar definition of politics is probably David Easton's: Politics is "the authoritative allocation of values for a society."[1] There are three essential issues concerning politics: (1) What are the values—political affairs—that need to be allocated? (2) Through what channels are these values to be allocated? (3) How do decisions concerning allocations of values acquire their authoritativeness? The different answers provided to these three questions in different societies are interpreted in contemporary political science in terms of those variables related to the structure of the particular political system and in terms of the relations between the system and its environment.

The set of terms and concepts connected with Easton's definition has proved useful in comparing the politics of different societies. For example, when a political system remains stable for a long time, the system has probably acquired the capacity to regulate its activities so as to adjust to pressures and be able to seek other goals. When a political system is unstable, it most likely has failed to respond effectively to change. Furthermore, revolution can often be explained in terms of input overload created by a drastic change of environment. When environmental change causes the breakdown of a political system, it means that the sphere of politics, the sources of political authority, and the manner according to which political decisions are made should have undergone considerable readjustment. Because politics not only responds to environmental conditions but also aims to modify them, once a revolution is completed the abovementioned questions will presumably have been settled.

I

The above introduction is highly relevant to our understanding of the modern Chinese experience, because what happened in China could be defined briefly as the result of both high hopes and deep frustration that resulted from the persistent effort to attain values and goals through revolutions and other political means. It is well known that the tremendous pressures that accumulated during the pre-1949 period led to the Nationalist debacle and the Communist takeover of the China mainland, but exactly what happened in China during the following three decades still constitutes a great puzzle for many, despite journalistic reports and scholarly analyses. It is for this reason that China scholars have lately become quite conscious of their field's appropriate theoretical orientation. Although the issue is still being debated, it is my belief that the political experience of the entire period probably could be perceived best in terms of the PRC's movement from the revolutionary stage to the postrevolutionary stage.[2]

In order to understand such a development, the most important aspect to consider is the Communist view of the nature and function of politics. First of all, the Communist view of politics is both instrumental and all-encompassing. Ideologically committed to the goal of building a classless society on a world scale, the Communists believe such a goal can be achieved through an overall socioeconomic and cultural transformation brought about by the use of political power. Second, the Communists believe in the moral foundation of political authorities. The Marxist ideology is essentially a revolutionary ideology; its believers do not accept the claims of any legal-rational authorities without first considering their class nature. Marxists' claims of power are derived instead from the belief that they stand for both the moral and the scientific truth concerning human existence. Even in the established Communist political system, a sophisticated form of socialist legality could never supersede the position just cited, which supposedly is in harmony with the principle of the consent of the governed. A closely related third aspect is the Communists' belief in the proper manner for making political decisions. Despite their stress on the democratic nature of the decision-making process in the Communist system, the Marxist-Leninists essentially rely upon a tightly organized leadership core to reach decisions and to direct their political affairs.[3]

The Communists believe that, under the guidance of their ideology, they have acquired the ability to find correct answers for every question they encounter. The only condition is that their understanding of those ideological principles should be correct. Many analysts have pointed out, however, that the various aspects of the Communist view of politics are not always in harmony with one another. For example, Richard Lowenthal believes that the very tendency of the Communist regime to seek rapid socioeconomic changes, particularly industrialization, through political means creates a highly undesirable situation in relation to the building of a classless society as the ultimate moral imperative. The conflict between the Communists' immediate goal and their ultimate goal is described as development versus utopia. Lowenthal believes that although the Communist rulers tend to take various measures to prevent the emergence of the "economic man" and the "bureaucratic man" during the initial period, they must live with the trend in the long run. In other words, those in power will have to put concrete socioeconomic achievement as well as their own political positions in first place, leaving the commitment to a classless society in the Marxist sense to be transformed into slogans and symbols that serve the purpose of legitimizing the existing order.[4]

In terms of a Communist regime's movement to the postrevolutionary stage, Lowenthal's thesis could be put in a broader perspective. In other words, there would always be a wide gap between the political system and its environment at the beginning of the Communist rule. Such a gap indicates both the radicalness of the Communist policies and the resistance that they generate as a result. It is not completely inconceivable, however, that the gap would become somewhat narrower over time. The narrowing of the gap between the political system and its environment—or the lessening of tension between the state and the society—could come about by several means. If the increase in the regime's extractive ability leads to an increase in its distributive ability, then compliance could be induced on utilitarian grounds. If the regime and the general population deem it necessary to create certain mutual predictability in their dealings with one another, then the revival of a certain sense of legality could also be expected. In addition, as the elite grow more and more burdened with the duty of governing the country on a daily basis, their perception of political realities as well as their ideological concerns would likely undergo further change. With the Communist elite taking a more nationalist outlook, the stabilization of the sociopolitical order could encounter a more favorable situation.[5]

The stabilization of any Communist revolutionary regime, not completely unlike the stabilization of a nationalist regime, could be affected by many variables beyond its own control. One issue that distinguishes these two types of political systems is their ability to influence or control the various environmental factors during the postrevolutionary stage. The nationalist regime could be considered postrevolutionary as soon as the country acquires independence, because its definition of revolution does not go much further than that. The more receptive attitude of the regime toward demands coming from the society could mean that the political system has a better chance to democratize itself, but it could also mean that the political system would be easily challenged by qualitative or quantitative input overload. The Communist regime, on the other hand, would remain revolutionary much longer under the influence of its ideology. Even after it is transformed into a postrevolutionary polity, its political machines and powers that have been built and accumulated would remain. The concrete result of this situation would be twofold: The regime would continue to have a stronger ability to mobilize resources and thus a stronger ability to fulfill various goals and expectations, but the vested interests of the governing elite would motivate them to refuse any fundamental change that could endanger their position. Tension between the state and the society would thus be lasting or even permanent.[6]

Students of comparative politics have long noticed these two contrasting characteristics of a revolutionary regime's evolution. On the one hand, there are those within the regime who favor the acceptance of changes such as value secularization and structural differentiation in the belief that such changes are inevitable. On the other hand, there are those who are determined to resist, perceiving new trends as degenerative. The conflict can become quite acute as differences in opinion are transformed into struggle over power or political offices. Competition and maneuvering in a series of waves and counterwaves reflects the fluctuation of the regime's policy orientations.

With gradual sociopolitical stabilization, established Communist political systems have generally accepted the fact that in any policy issue a realistic assessment of various environmental factors is necessary. The Maoist faction in politics in China nevertheless made all-out efforts to emphasize the need to combat trends considered detrimental to Marxism with its utopian goals. Such an experience deserves close scrutiny because it can help us understand the dynamics of the Communist revolution and even the dynamics of revolutions in general.

II

China scholars have for years talked about the policy oscillation or the repetition of certain patterns in the Communist regime's initiation, implementation, and conclusion of various policies.[7] G. William Skinner has noticed, for example, that Communist policy toward the village has gone through a set of cycles, and each cycle can further be divided into five stages, including mobilization, the "big push," crisis, retrenchment, and respite or "normalcy."[8] Looking at the issue in the 1980s, observers have sensed that the pattern of repetition involved exhibits a much larger variation among different cases. There seems no question, however, concerning the fact that each cycle represents the outcome of a series of waves and counterwaves. If we put these cycles together, it is highly possible that we will see a curve emerge, indicating that the forces advocating revolutionary mobilization played a more and more influential role in policy decisions during the first two decades of the Communist rule. This trend reached its highest point during the late sixties and early seventies, as indicated by the Great Proletarian Cultural Revolution. After the death of Lin Piao and the reemergence of Chou En-lai as the undisputed number-two man, the trend seemed largely to be reversed. Although the radicals continued to play an active and significant role in political affairs and were even able to stage the second fall of Teng Hsiao-p'ing, their relative influence was clearly in decline. Even after the purge of the so-called Gang of Four, the continuing interactions between the two schools of thought, as well as the interactions between forces behind these two schools of thought, could still be detected. In contrast to the earlier pattern, the force taking a more receptive attitude toward environmental demands acquired a clear upper hand.[9]

The course of the Communist revolution in China has been partly similar and partly dissimilar to the course of evolution in the other established Communist regimes. It has a similar aspect if the waves and the counterwaves are recognized, but the stormy crests have been higher in China. Few other Communist countries have gone through such a period of radicalization and political upheaval as that created by what some people called Maoism. How and why did this happen? The key to understanding such a development is that the Chinese Communist elite, under the influence of Mao, interpreted their situation in a way that led them to adopt a series of policies having the effect of widening the gap between the revolutionary regime and its overall environment. It was rather clear, for example, that a sequence of political campaigns as well as other measures resulted in alienating village and other people on whom the regime originally based its support. Simultaneously, the increasingly radical posture that the regime took in domestic affairs also tended to make it more and more antagonistic to the outside world. The causes of this situation had a great deal to do with the role that ideology played in Chinese politics.[10]

Analytically speaking, ideology is at once a cognition map, a hierarchy of moral values, an image of the future, and a program of action. Ideology is thus a body of knowledge intended to provide its believers with a complete and comprehensive understanding of human experience and therefore to enable them to act in a way that can make the ideal state of human existence a reality. As ideology is rooted in the experience of a society's own past and is oriented toward the creation of an ideal future, its content consists of both empirical knowledge and value judgment, along with other tenets and claims that are probably unverifiable. Although its appeal to members of a society could be based on any of these characteristics, its rise and fall seems to be largely a matter determined by sociopsychological factors. Broadly speaking, the function that the ideology has fulfilled in the Chinese Communist movement can be divided according to two major periods. Before coming to power, the Chinese Communist party's ideology served it well in the sense that this ideology provided its followers with a clear sense of direction, an effective form of organization, and a set of strategic principles and political tactics that had proved workable. With the founding of the People's Republic, the question of how the ideology should guide the thinking of the Communist decision makers became a far more complicated matter.

What distinguished the pre-1949 period from the post-1949 period in the Communist elite's relations with its party ideology can be found in several aspects. First of all, the ideological concerns of the Chinese Communists during the pre-1949 period centered primarily on issues of a strategic and tactical nature. In other words, although Mao's contribution to the "Sinocization" of Marxism-Leninism has been praised by many, the most effective elements of his work were to enhance the Communist party's own organizational strength, to strengthen its basis of popular sympathy or support, and to undermine the moral claims of the Nationalist government. It was not until the post-1949 period that the task of building a socialist or even Communist society became a second aspect.

As many observers have pointed out, the Chinese Communists' knowledge of Marxism-Leninism remained marginal for a considerable period of time. However, the success they scored in 1949 greatly heightened their belief or faith in ideology and subsequently made the "correct application" of the ideology a much more sensitive and difficult problem. A related third aspect of the pre- and post-1949 difference was the role of Mao Tse-tung in his relations with the ideology and the party. Although Mao had achieved a dominant political position within the Chinese Communist party as early as the 1930s, it was the 1949 victory that brought him the great recognition from home and abroad. As the Communist victory was attributed to a large extent to the correct handling of ideology by Mao, thereafter the Communist party's self-identity, Mao's historical status, and the faith in or even the worship of ideology became closely intertwined.[11] It was for this reason that the ideological and political struggles that have occurred since 1949 have had so strong a personality factor.

The growing radicalization of PRC politics as the political system's particular form of response to environmental pressures can therefore be understood on an additional two levels. On the one level there was the problem of political control over government affairs. In an established democracy, issues of a political nature are decided through parliamentary politics, the electoral process, or public opinion. With a strong infrastructure supporting each process, the political decisions have a high, though limited, binding effect on those whose responsibility it is to carry out the decisions. In a revolutionary Communist polity such as the People's Republic of China, no clear distinction existed between political and administrative affairs in the beginning. As certain governmental activities or working styles were routinized over time, the question of how to guide and control them posed a problem for the top leaders. Without certain institutional channels to determine and articulate popular will, the top leadership's natural answer was to seek from ideology the criteria for judgment and criticisms of administrative performance. Tension and conflict between ideology and administrative performance thus became inevitable. Such a dilemma was made more serious as it was largely intertwined with another level of the problem, i.e., Mao's roles within the Communist party, the Chinese political system, and the world Communist movement. Analytically speaking, Mao played dual roles in each of the three arenas. In the Communist party, he was both the ideological authority and a power player. In Communist China's political system, he was both the leader of the governing elite and the founder of the state. And in the world revolutionary movement, he was both the spokesman for the Chinese Communist party and a senior statesman-theoretician.[12] How were these three sets of dual roles linked to the radicalization of Chinese politics? To answer the question simply, the ideological posture Mao consciously or unconsciously chose to take had the effect of reinforcing his ability to play and enlarge upon these roles in a particular way. For example, Mao was able to expand his political power by expanding the sphere of socioeconomic affairs in which the ideology had a legitimate concern. With the expansion of his political power, the ideological position he took was thus less likely to be challenged by others within the party. Similarly, Chairman Mao's identification with the somewhat mystical "masses" also had a mutual reinforcing effect on his roles within the party and within the political system. The same could also be found in terms of his position in the world Communist movement.

What constituted Mao's radicalization was symbolized by one of his favorite slogans, "politics in command." As first applied during the Great Leap Forward, it meant the party's direct involvement in productive activities but with emphasis on the use of nonmaterial incentives.[13] Over time, however, "politics in command" acquired a set of meanings that were also to become the basic characteristics of Maoist politics: first, that politics was present in each and every aspect of human and social existence, and the true nature and value of these activities were only to be found at the political level; second, that the proper way to resolve political issues was through struggle, especially through struggle between two lines; and third, that the moral justification of political authority had to be determined in terms of its contribution to the task of continuing the revolution. In contrast to reformist politics, whose first principle is to reduce any political issue into administrative or technical considerations, the Maoist approach inclined to make any minor dispute into a question of ideological purity or individual motivations. Reflecting his sharp rejection of the Soviet notion on the "state of all people," Mao had, in fact, provided a prescription according to which class struggle and revolution would proceed indefinitely by their very definitions.[14]

The effectiveness of an ideology is, as mentioned earlier, largely determined by certain sociopsychological factors. In other words, whether an ideology can appeal to those it is addressed to will be basically decided by whether the content of this ideology is in accord with the experience and expectations of its audience individually and collectively. One of Mao's great strengths that he demonstrated fully during the pre-1949 period was his language and theorizing ability, and his impact on the outcome of events through the use of this ability was well recognized. However, although this extraordinary gift with words remained with Mao during the post-1949 period, his growing concern with utopian values may have lessened the appeal of the ideological formulations he presented, as the content of these formulations became less and less relevant to concerns in ordinary men's lives. Although the instructions Mao issued during his last years, sometimes in quite obscure forms, still carried tremendous political weight, the difference between the ideology and the sociopolitical situation became more and more widely sensed. The dissonance was to be found between words and deeds, between theory and reality, and between the moral claims of the ideology and the judgment people made from their own experience. It took the dramatic events of the T'angshan earthquake and the T'ien An Men incident, however, to make such feelings a communicable fact. With the purge of the Gang of Four and other drastic changes, the curious question of whether human nature is infinitely malleable, permitting man to be politicized-socialized into believing anything, was thus answered.[15]

III

What happened in China between the emergence and demise of the Maoist political order could be described as a period of prolonged revolutionary upheaval, created artificially through the manipulation of the symbols and content of ideology. As Communist China now moves away from Maoist politics, even more interesting questions would include: What kind of legacy has the post-Mao regime inherited from earlier experience? How has China arrived at its current political state? And what form of sociopolitical order will eventually emerge in postrevolutionary China? To answer these questions, it is necessary for us to examine first a situation that could be seen as a particular form of political decay.

When Samuel P. Huntington talked about political decay, what he meant was a situation in which political institutions failed to contain or regulate the various forms of political participation that resulted from social mobilization.[16] Although the Red Guard activities and the military's role during the Cultural Revolution bore some similarities to praetorianism, the exact situation described by Huntington did not appear—and indeed would be rather unlikely to appear—whenever a country's governing and organizational principles are Leninist. What we mean by political decay in China during the seventies therefore has a somewhat different and broader connotation. More specifically, one aspect of political decay to be found in China was the blurring or disappearance of the distinction between political and nonpolitical, or between public and private. As the Maoists believed that the only meaningful criteria by which to judge things were ideological criteria, the sphere of warranted political concern became expanded infinitely. It came to be a common rule in Maoist China that private acts could be explained politically, and that political acts were partly to be understood in terms of private motivations. What result was an expected loss of meaning in public affairs, a situation closely related to the second aspect of China's political decay: intensified factionalism and power struggle.

Factionalism is a term referring to differences that come to exist among informal groups within a larger, often formal organization. It is a familiar fact to students of organizational behavior that in any formal organization people tend to form informal relations through their interactions with one another. Consequently they may work toward public or private goals through either formal or informal channels. It is believed that to the extent that groups formed by informal relations do not hinder the organizational functions, their existence is to be tolerated or even encouraged. The Chinese Communist party, however, has never recognized any informal groups, despite the fact that factionalism is almost a ubiquitous phenomenon.[17] Factionalism in the Communist party has been linked to two interesting concepts: intraparty democracy and struggle between the two lines.[18] The Chinese Communists stress that intraparty democracy should be practiced. Yet in this practice it is inevitable that different people will compete to mobilize political resources, so that they can influence the outcome of value allocation. Based on political or many other considerations, factionalism would result over time from such efforts. Intraparty democracy has never been a well-institutionalized thing. When policy issues related to ideology are perceived to be life-or-death matters, participants in decision-making processes can become tempted to defeat their opponents by trying to shift the criteria of value judgment—or even destroy their opponents by nullifying the rules of the game. When the tactics are successful, the outcome is explained in absolute terms so that it can be justified, and centralism is then restored.

Factionalism, theoretically speaking, is not completely unlike the so-called second economy, in that both can help maintain the formal system by providing services the latter fails to provide. In the meantime, they can also pose a serious threat to the formal system if they acquire a prestige and claims of their own, or if the formal system fails to strengthen its position vis-à-vis these competitors in due time. In the case of the Chinese Communist party, it was able to maintain itself as a unified force during the pre-1949 period despite serious open breaks and factional struggles. The intraparty unity was probably due to the effectiveness of the party ideology, as well as to heavy pressures from outside. Another relevant factor may have been that during the earlier period of its existence, the party had yet to complete its organizational form and sense of identity. When a break occurred, the still-maturing party probably had a better chance to heal itself.[19] These factors disappeared one by one, however, during the post-1949 period. As the Communists now admit, they were contented with their achievements and thus became arrogant. This change of attitude meant a lessening of their ability to pragmatically perceive reality and a lessening of their willingness to restrain themselves in political infighting. During the Hundred Flowers Campaign, for example, Mao attempted to introduce extra-elite factors into the intra-elite rectification. And during the late fifties, he defeated his critics by making party unity and his leadership the issue. But it was during the Cultural Revolution that formal party organizations were destroyed and the intraparty dissenters were turned into class enemies. It was at this point that factional politics in China made a significant turn.[20]

With the extreme personalization of political authority during the Cultural Revolution, both personal security and policymaking became highly unpredictable. In order to secure personal values or to influence political affairs, one had to rely to a considerable extent upon maneuvering tactics such as "ritualistic compliance" or manipulation and counter-manipulation of symbols and information.[21] Although the maneuvers were carried out mostly in bureaucratic hierarchies and other forms of organizational networks, the aims of the maneuvers were closely related to the formal decision of these organizations; any successful use of such tactics would invariably demand certain conditions, including implicit mutual understandings, informal rules governing the exchange of values, and alternative communication channels to transmit messages. Needless to say, these conditions could be found or established only in the form of factions.[22]

If we accept Abraham Maslow's hierarchy of needs, a reason for the intensification of factional activities during the Cultural Revolution can easily be found.[23] In other words, although any one or more of the values included in his hierarchy could be the basis of factional links, the more basic the values involved, the more likely people would be to make efforts to secure them. Moreover, the pursuit of values is not the only reason for the formation of factional links. Other efforts to form factions could be a response to the threats created by the activities of other groups. The very concept of factionalism therefore presupposes the existence of a multiple number of factions within a certain political system. With the formal organizational norms losing their effectiveness, a political process that is dominated by factional interactions has to be a highly complicated one. With each faction attempting to put itself in a more favorable position, the most outstanding feature of the factional conflicts could thus be described as "power struggle."

Power struggle constitutes a most important and obvious aspect of politics when the meaningfulness of political life is in serious question and when value allocations cannot be explained in any way other than their effects on individuals and groups in politics.[24] It is not, however, the only content that the concept of factional politics would entail, particularly when the political arena in which factional politics has been played is to undergo fundamental transformations. When such a case occurs, the factions must consider issues beyond power distribution, as the change could make power plays in the original form no longer possible. Idealistically or realistically, each faction—and the factions as a whole—would therefore have a common concern over the future of the political system.[25]

IV

What happened between the mid-seventies and the early eighties in Communist Chinese politics is an ideal example in case. One of the first acts that a new coalition of major members in the Communist elite took, following the death of Chairman Mao, was the smashing of the Gang of Four. With the Gang's major supporter gone from the scene, the political strength that Chiang Ch'ing and others had built was in no way comparable to the factional and institutional powers that could have been mobilized by their opponents. What Chiang Ch'ing and her followers had originally intended was to claim a dominating position during the post-Mao era by virtue of their close association and strong identification with the legitimizing symbols. The purge was probably the right thing for others to undertake because it provided the opportunity for them and the factional interests they represented to seek rewards and even to establish a more stable order through more flexible mutual adjustments and political realignments.[26] What the participants of the purge did not fully realize was that by undertaking their act they were decisively shattering the all-embracing ideological net created by Mao and thus reopening more issues than they had intended.

The first erosion of the sociopsychological basis for the Maoist approach can in fact be traced back to the moment when Mao recommitted himself to the restoration of a certain sense of order. The trend was probably also strengthened by the shift in the Chinese Communist foreign policy and the subsequent inflow of new information from the outside world. The change of perceptions of political realities triggered a series of events that at once involved intra-elite relations, elite-mass relations, and relations between the political system and its environment. As a later result of the purge of the Gang of Four and the indirect de-Maoization that followed, the status of the purge's leaders and the relative positions of various groups within the Communist elite were put under a different light. The Communist elite became more vulnerable to pressures, especially pressures from the population it was governing, as the latter became less inclined to accept authority.[27]

Subsequent interactions between the elite and the masses could be observed from three perspectives. One involved factional use of the masses; certain forms of popular participation in political affairs were exploited to undermine the position of rival leaders or to gain support for policy favored by the sponsoring factions.[28] A second perspective on the interactions was the elite's response to popular pressures. The popular mood remained fairly clear during the period, so that both the relative unity to be found in the elite and the steady shift of policy priorities could be attributed partly to the impact of popular pressures as the elite perceived them to be. The third perspective was on the elite's delayed use of coercive power. During the few years immediately following the purge, mass criticisms as a form of political participation were encouraged. Such an attitude did not last for too long, as the Four Big Freedoms were abolished and state power was used more and more to suppress such criticisms.[29]

The return to the use of coercion reflected one basic nature of the post-Mao regime: it was essentially built by those forces rooted in Communist China's bureaucratic and organizational traditions, and it did not yet have an effective ideological system to fully legitimize the order or to guide the regime's course of action. In other words, the post-Mao leadership took its shape as a forceful reaction to the Cultural Revolution experience. After the initial optimism created by the promise of the Four Modernizations faded, Teng and his associates were forced to take a deeper look into those principles and assumptions of the Communist political system, and a new reform was promised.

If one needs to pinpoint the basic character of Teng Hsiao-p'ing's reform efforts, there is no better statement that his famous catch phrase "practice is the sole criterion for truth." Despite the fact that the phrase was coined from Mao's own writings, Teng used it for the explicit purpose of repudiating the belief of "politics in command" and to further dismantle the dogmas that emerged during the Cultural Revolution.[30] To pave the way for policy changes, one of the first things that "practice as the sole criterion" has done is to provide the Communist cadres and the masses with a new frame of reference. For years the Communists have relied upon such simple tactics as catch phrases to help mold the thinking of the average people. "Recalling the bitterness" had been a ritualized practice, and the recent socioeconomic situation was compared vaguely with the pre-1949 period. Although these approaches were aimed at inducing the masses to believe that they were enjoying a much better life than before, the new stress on practice and truth essentially told people that this was not the case. In fact, it has been explicitly admitted that in socioeconomic achievements, Communist China is far behind such places as the Republic of China on Taiwan or Hong Kong.[31] This admission on the part of the Communist leadership was not without domestic repercussions—although what Teng and his associates wanted was probably to create only a limited sense of dissatisfaction with the state of affairs and thus provide the necessary impetus for change.

With public attention diverted to improvement of living conditions, a bold ideological reinterpretation was introduced. This argument held that although class struggles still existed, they were no longer that important. Consequently, the major contradiction to be found in the Chinese society was not contradiction between classes, but rather contradiction between "the people's need for rapid economic and cultural development and the current economic and cultural conditions that failed to satisfy the people's needs." What this thesis meant was that the most prominent issue that the Communist political system had failed to resolve was the significant gap between expectations and performance.[32] In order to improve their output capacity, the new regime obviously sensed the need to find channels other than the Maoist ones, so that mobilizations of support and human resources could be achieved. With great emphasis on internal unity, another whole level of ideological modification was undertaken, involving both the redefinition of the political community and the redelineation of the line between politics and other forms of human activities. In other words, the black labels attached to certain categories of people were largely removed, and the dictatorship of the proletariat was renamed the People's Democratic

Dictatorship. In the meantime, the relatively autonomous status of various social activities, especially the economy, was recognized within those limits set by the so-called four unchangeables.[33]

What the new leadership team in Peking has tried to do, to put the matter quite simply, is to rationalize public affairs through the expansion of the regime's political base, as well as the narrowing of the sphere of ideological concerns. As a Western observer put it, what they want is "socialism without revolution."[34] And so as Communist China enters into the postrevolutionary stage, the ultimate issue is really what kind of postrevolutionary polity will emerge and whether this postrevolutionary polity in China indeed has the capacity to fulfill goals such as economic modernization, social justice, or even the promised "high level of spiritual civilization."[35] If revolutionary politics lead to postrevolutionary politics, such movement could reflect either the successful change of the society by the state or the reemergence of the society over the state—or it could reflect a certain form of reconciliation in between. Although Mao made a deadly effort to ensure that China would follow the first path, the trend now seems to be toward the second one. This is well indicated by the fact that in the latest round of the rewriting of history, the noncommunist past has been given a stronger recognition. Could a certain sense of continuity be restored in the midst of historical discontinuity?[36]

Having been deprived of what Robert McIver called the "central myth," the Communist Chinese political system is now anxious to push its institution-building efforts forward in a pattern very similar to the one experienced during the mid-fifties. With both the self-confidence and the popular goodwill gone, the prospect that these actions will be successful cannot be judged solely by policy goals. In other words, the success or failure of the new round of institution-building will invariably be related to the question of whether the system can induce compliance on utilitarian grounds or must resort to coercion. With a relatively low level of symbolic capability, the regime will probably face increased demands for immediate material satisfactions rather than tolerance for the status quo, or still less a decrease in such demands.[37] Thus any commitment to material improvement will probably be accompanied by the increased use of coercive and suppressive measures. In the long run, the issues involved can be broken down as follows: How is the political system to generate a minimal but necessary level of legitimacy in the midst of continuing changes? Through what strategy will the mobilization of support and human resources be conducted, without excessive reliance upon the use of coercion on the one hand or the danger of political instability on the other? And furthermore, how can the system maintain a relative balance between various policy goals, or a balance between its ambitions and the resources available, so that the danger of reverting to the Maoist approach will be avoided?[38]

The final choices will certainly have to be made by the post-Mao leadership and its successors. As the secularization of values advances, one can expect that the Chinese people at large will also be able to exercise a stronger influence over the future of China. As with every political system, the Communist Chinese system cannot avoid responding to input from its external environment. Thus it is not far-fetched to say that the outside world will not definitely be limited to the role of a detached observer, and if not, then new chapters of modern Chinese politics are yet to be written.

Notes

1. David Easton, *A Framework for Political Analysis* (Englewood Cliffs, N.J.: Prentice-Hall, 1965), and Gabriel A. Almond and G. Bingham Powell, Jr., *Comparative Politics: System, Process and Policy* (Boston: Little, Brown, 1978).

2. For studies on the established Communist systems, see Chalmers Johnson, ed., *Change in Communist Systems* (Stanford, Calif.: Stanford University Press, 1970); David Lane, *The Socialist Industrial State: Toward a Political Sociology of State Socialism* (London: George Allen and Unwin, 1976); and Robert C. Tucker, "The Deradicalization of Marxist Movements," in *Marxian Revolutionary Ideas,* ed. Robert C. Tucker (New York: Norton, 1969), pp. 172–215.

3. See, for example, Shlomo Avineri, *The Social and Political Thought of Karl Marx* (Cambridge, U.K.: Cambridge University Press, 1969).

4. Richard Lowenthal, "Development vs. Utopia in Communist Policy," in *Change in Communist Systems,* pp. 33–116.

5. See, for example, the survey reported in Alex Inkeles and Raymond A. Buer, *The Soviet Citizen* (Cambridge, Mass.: Harvard University Press, 1959), p. 236.

6. The fact has been explicitly or implicitly acknowledged in discussions on the politics in established Communist systems. See Samuel P. Huntington, "Social and Institutional Dynamics of One-party Systems," in *Authoritarian Politics in Modern Society,* ed. Samuel P. Huntington and Clement H. Moore (New York: Basic Books, 1970), pp. 3–48. See also Kenneth Jowitt, "Inclusiveness and Mobilization in European Leninist Regimes," *World Politics* 28: 1 (October 1975).

7. Such a view has been expressed by many authors. For a debate on its merit, see Andrew J. Nathan, "Policy Oscillation in the People's Republic of China: A Critique" and Edwin A. Winckler, "Policy Oscillations in the People's Republic of China," *China Quarterly,* no. 68 (1976), pp. 720–750.

8. G. William Skinner and Edwin A. Winckler, "Compliance Succession in Rural Communist China: A Cyclical Theory," in *A Sociological Reader in Complex Organizations,* ed. Amitai Etzioni, 2nd ed. (New York: Holt, Rinehart and Winston, 1969), pp. 410, 424–426.

9. The factional conflicts during the post-Mao era were more mobile and subdued than before, and many believed there was a significant third line, led by Yeh Chien-ying, which hoped to function as a balancing force.

10. It has been pertinently pointed out that ideology under Mao actually took precedence: "Ideology is the central purpose, organization is the means to effect it." See James Chieh Hsiung, *Ideology and Practice: The Evolution of Chinese Communism* (New York: Praeger, 1970), pp. 6–7.

11. See, for example, Franz Schurmann, *Ideology and Organization in Communist China* (Berkeley: University of California Press, 1966), and Robert Jay Lifton, *Revolutionary Immortality* (New York: Random House, 1968).

12. Mao's roles could, of course, be defined in other terms. Dick Wilson edited a book on Mao that attempted to evaluate him as a soldier, philosopher, teacher, etc.; see *Mao Tse-tung in the Scale of History,* ed. Dick Wilson (Cambridge, U.K.: Cambridge University Press, 1977).

13. Schurmann, *Ideology and Organization in Communist China,* pp. 154–156, 206–209.

14. Richard Curt Kraus, "Class Conflict and the Vocabulary of Social Analysis in China," *China Quarterly,* no. 69 (1977), pp. 54–74. For a scalding criticism of Mao's theory of permanent revolution by a contemporary Chinese Communist theorist, see Liao Kai-lung, "The Experience from History Provides Us with Road for Development," *Fei-ching Yueh-pao* (*FCYP*) [*Communists Affairs Monthly*] 24:3 (1981), pp. 93–104.

15. Robert Lifton observed that the thought of Mao was built on the basis of several psychological assumptions, including that the human mind is infinitely malleable and capable of being reformed spiritually beyond the world of common man; see Lifton, *Revolutionary Immortality,* p. 70. See also Donald J. Munro, "Malleability of Man in Chinese Marxism," *China Quarterly,* no. 48 (1971), pp. 609–640.

16. Samuel P. Huntington, *Political Order in Changing Societies* (New Haven, Conn.: Yale University Press, 1968), ch. 1.

17. Franz Schurmann suggested that a distinction can be made between "opinion groups" and "factions." An opinion group is an "aggregate of individuals" who have in common a likeness of individual opinions but no organizational basis for action. A faction is an "opinion group with organized force behind it." Schurmann, *Ideology and Organization in Communist China,* pp. 55–56. Jürgen Domes suggests, on the other hand, that the intraparty conflict could be divided into two different stages: factionalization and factionalism. See Domes, "The 'Gang of Four'—and Hua Kuo-feng: An Analysis of Political Events in 1975–76," *China Quarterly,* no. 71 (1977), pp. 473–497.

18. See, for example, Lowell Dittmer, "The Structural Evolution of Criticism and Self-Criticism," *China Quarterly,* no. 56 (1973), pp. 708–729.

19. For an analysis of developments that eventually led to the Cultural Revolution, see Tang Tsou, "Revolution, Reintegration, and Crisis in Communist China," in *China in Crisis,* ed. Tang Tsou et al., vol. 1, book 1 (Chicago: University of Chicago Press, 1968), pp. 277–356.

20. For an analytical study of the Cultural Revolution from the perspective of political development, see Hong Yung Lee, "Mao's Strategy for Revolutionary Change: A Case Study of the Cultural Revolution," *China Quarterly,* no. 77 (1979), pp. 50–74.

21. Ibid. See also Jean Chesneaux, *China: the People's Republic, 1949–1976* (New York: Pantheon Books, 1979), and Richard Baum, ed., *China in Ferment: Perspectives on the Cultural Revolution* (Englewood Cliffs, N.J.: Prentice-Hall, 1971).

22. For discussions on this factionalism, see Andrew Nathan, "A Factionalism Model for CCP Politics," *China Quarterly*, no. 53 (1973), pp. 34–66, and Tsou Tang, "Prolegomenon to the Study of Informal Groups in CCP Politics," *China Quarterly,* no. 65 (1976), pp. 98–113.

23. Abraham H. Maslow et al., "A Clinically Derived Test for Measuring Psychological Security-Insecurity," *Journal of General Psychology* 33 (1945), pp. 21–41, and Maslow, *Motivation and Personality,* 2nd ed. (New York: Harper and Row, 1970).

24. In his defense of politics, Bernard Crick stated, "Politics should be praised for doing what it can do, but also praised for not attempting what it cannot do." See Bernard Crick, *In Defense of Politics,* 2nd ed. (Chicago: University of Chicago Press, 1972), p. 156, and Christian Bay, *The Structure of Freedom* (Stanford, Calif.: Stanford University Press, 1965).

25. Such a sentiment was well expressed by Chen Yun in "Talks on the Central Working Conference," *FCYP* 22:10 (1980), pp. 9–95, 79.

26. Andres D. Onate, "Hua Kuo-feng and the Arrest of the Gang of Four," *China Quarterly,* no. 75 (1978), pp. 546–565.

27. Chen Yun, "Talks on the Central Working Conference."

28. See, for example, Dorothy Grouse Fontana, "Background to the Fall of Hua Guofeng," *Asian Survey* 22:3 (1982), pp. 237–259.

29. The Four Big Freedoms, including the right to write wall posters, were formally abolished by the National People's Congress on 10 September 1980.

30. For an analysis of the epistemological aspect of the change, see Brantly Womack, "Politics and Epistemology in China since Mao," *China Quarterly,* no. 80 (1979), pp. 768–792.

31. For an analysis of the political significance of the Four Modernizations program, see Teh-hou Jen, "Institutionalization, Political Development, and Communist China's Four-Modernization Program," *Cheng-chi Hsueh-pao [Annal of the Chinese Politi-Science Association]*, no. 7 (1968), pp. 399–412.

32. Wei Ching-lin and Chia Chun-feng, "On the Transformation of the Principal Contradiction," *Jen-min Jih-pao,* 28 August 1979, and *Hung-chi* 12 (1982), pp. 11–12.

33. See Heng Kuo-chiang, "The New Moves in the Domestic United Front of the Chinese Communists," *FCYP* 22:6 (1979), pp. 39–39, and Yu Chiu-li, "Relations between Politics and Economy," *FCYP* 22:7 (1979), pp. 84 and 93.

34. Arif Dirlik, "Socialism without Revolution," *Pacific Affairs* 54:4 (1981–1982).

35. Liao Kai-lung claimed that "high level civilization means a spiritual civilization more advanced than those developed by capitalism." See Liao, "The Experience from History Provides Us with Road for Development," pp. 89–90.

36. The great emphasis that has been given to the commemoration of the 1911 revolution and Dr. Sun Yat-sen's birthday clearly had united front purposes. It could not be denied, however, that these acts also reflected the Communists' desire to strengthen their own claim as being the true successor of the "revolutionary tradition" of modern China.

37. For the issue of the legitimacy crisis, see Alan P. L. Liu, "Political Decay on Mainland China: On Crisis of Faith, Confidence and Truth," paper presented to the Sino-American Conference on Mainland China, Taipei, Taiwan, ROC, and also Kjeld Erik Brodsgaard, "The Democracy Movement in China, 1978–1979: Opposition Movements, Wall Poster Campaign, and Underground Journals," *Asian Survey* 21:7, pp. 747–774.

38. It is interesting to note that in the Communist theorist Liao Kai-lung's essay, he not only repeated the theme of separating the party from the government, but also suggested that independent functional groups be formed under the party's guidance in order to represent various interests of the society. See Liao, "The Experience from History Provides Us with Road for Development"; see also Maria Chan Morgan, "Controlling the Bureaucracy in Modern China," *Asian Survey* 21:12 (1981), pp. 1223–1236.

Part 3

Foreign Policy and National Defense

7
In Quest of National Interest—The Foreign Policy of the People's Republic of China

Robert A. Scalapino

Over the past thirty-three years, the foreign policy of the People's Republic of China has passed through three broad stages, each with quite separate general features, but all aiming to enhance the security and development of this massive, yet fragile society. The first stage, lasting from the PRC inauguration in 1949 to the late 1950s, can be labeled the era of reliance upon the Soviet Union.

When Mao Zedong proclaimed, "We lean to one side," he signaled China's commitment to what Beijing then regarded as the indestructable socialist camp, and even though this commitment lasted less than a decade, it was to have far-reaching repercussions on Chinese domestic as well as foreign policies. Indeed, despite the later PRC break with the USSR, the Soviet imprimatur remains on many facets of contemporary China—from education to economics, and not excluding politics.

Prior to examining the central features of the first stage, however, let me comment briefly on a question that has intrigued many scholars. Had the United States pursued different policies toward the Chinese Communists in the 1940s, might the PRC alignment with the USSR have been prevented or, at a minimum, significantly diluted? The "what if" issues of history can rarely be definitively resolved, but there are several reasons for rejecting an affirmative answer to this question. Whatever private reservations certain Chinese Communists may have had about the correctness of past Soviet policies toward China or the USSR's knowledge about their society (and both of these reservations did exist), the key Chinese Communist leaders all regarded themselves as members of an international socialist movement headed by the Soviet Union. Their loyalty to Stalin and the USSR had been amply demonstrated for nearly thirty years. In this era, prior to any experience with national power or with the Soviet Union as an ally, a conjecture that they would suddenly desert the socialist camp for an alignment with the world's "foremost capitalist-imperialist power"—or even seek in some sophisticated fashion to play Washington off against Moscow—requires extraordinary credulity. If the seeds of such Machiavellian tactics lay embedded in Chinese culture, they could not possibly have sprouted under the conditions prevailing in the 1940s.

Individuals like Mao, having been tested by guerrilla warfare for several decades, were realists. They knew where power lay in continental northeast Asia at the close of World War II. Indeed, they benefited greatly from the Soviet presence there during the post-1945 civil war. And unlike Yugoslavia, which fronted on Western as well as Eastern Europe and had no common border with the USSR, China was far from a meaningful Western power base and had a 4,500-mile border with the Soviet Union.

Tito, it will be recalled, quarreled with Stalin before there was any sign of Western assistance, gambling in considerable part on his geographic position. The Chinese Communists would not have been likely to have taken such a gamble. Stalin did worry about Mao after the Tito defection, and Anastas Mikoyan was sent secretly to China just before the final Chinese Communist victory to ascertain Chinese views.[1] Mao gave full assurances of loyalty verbally, and Liu Shaoqi did so via a written attack upon Titoism, the very sizable quotient of nationalism existent in Chinese Communism notwithstanding.

Had Mao and his close associates acted otherwise, there would have been trouble, as they no doubt realized. Soviet scholars have indicated privately that "We would never have permitted Mao to have taken the Party toward the United States, and we had the means—both in terms of friends within the CCP that would have adamantly opposed any such trend and in terms of *our* material resources in the area—to prevent this."[2]

It is equally unthinkable that any U.S. administration would have given sustained support to the Chinese Communists against the Nationalists in the 1940s or, as Barbara Tuchman suggested in retrospect, would have invited Mao to Washington. Naturally, as a shrewd politician, Mao lobbied for U.S. aid with the U.S. Yan'an team and, at the same time, played his role well as the champion of New Democracy, thus presenting a political visage significantly different from the one that had preceded and the one that would follow. Because Washington had been brought into the war primarily over the China issue, however, and had high hopes that a postwar China practicing Western-style parliamentarism would take Japan's place as the major Asian power, it is fanciful to believe that the United States would invite to the U.S. capital the guerrilla leader opposing the Chongqing government that Washington and all other allied governments recognized. Even to give the Communists significant assistance would have created a political earthquake in China, in the United States, and throughout the world. No U.S. administration could conceivably have taken the risk, especially when it would have produced no quick payoff in terms of U.S. national interests.

When the cleavage between China and the Soviet Union arrived, it was the product of complex issues developed over a decade of intimate interaction. Each step in the break came in arduous, painful manner, with evidence of substantial doubts on the part of certain Chinese leaders concerning the wisdom of Mao's decisions.

If the argument that a different U.S. policy toward the Communists between 1944 and 1949 could have altered basic Chinese Communist foreign policies has little data or logic to support it, a more substantial case can be made for another "what if" relating to the opening era of Chinese foreign policy. What if the Chinese Communist leaders had been willing to set aside their deep grievances against the United States in 1949 and cultivate U.S. diplomatic recognition of the new government? The records make it clear that Washington was willing. The United States openly stated that it regarded the Chinese civil war as having ended, with the Communists victorious. Firm indications were given that the United States did not view Taiwan as important from a strategic standpoint and had no intention of assisting the Nationalists who had now retreated to that island. Indeed, various U.S. officials including Secretary of State Dean Acheson intimated that after a decent interval, the United States intended to recognize the PRC, and U.S. consuls were left at their posts in several key cities.

Various incidents, however, signaled the fact that the new Communist officials were not especially interested in immediate U.S. recognition, preferring to see the West in general and the United States in particular punished for its past behavior toward China. However understandable such a position was from the Communist perspective, it had fateful consequences. The decision to cast the United States in the role of "the greatest enemy of the world's people," followed by the Korean War, brought the PRC and the United States into a series of conflicts and crises stretching over more than twenty years.

It is difficult to imagine what might have occurred in Sino-U.S. relations, or in PRC foreign policy in general, had a U.S. presence in China continued. Perhaps events would have unfolded much as they did, with the Korean War the catalyst for direct conflict. The British experience in the opening era of the PRC suggests that the establishment of even minimal PRC-U.S. relations would have been difficult. Yet if a U.S. presence *had* been maintained and gradually expanded, certain basic aspects of Chinese foreign policy might have been different. Indeed, one can argue that under such conditions the Sino-Soviet split would *not* have occurred—or at least it would not have occurred at the time and over the issues that produced it, because the dispute over how to handle the United States was one central cause of that cleavage. In sum, initial PRC hostility toward the United States and the U.S. effort to contain China through maximum isolation (thereby forcing the PRC to be heavily dependent upon the USSR) had entirely unintended and far-reaching results at a later point.

It is also possible that the Sino-U.S. conflict in Korea could have been avoided. Thus, the effects of Sino-U.S. estrangement during the 1950s were both positive and negative from the U.S. perspective.

Alliance with the Soviet Union

Turning to the actual developments during the first decade of PRC foreign policy, one can discern three broad factors in operation. The first was complete fidelity to the Soviet Union. As noted, this represented a continuance of the pre-1949 CCP stance. To be sure, it was indicated that differences in the nature of Chinese circumstances and development made it imperative that the PRC pursue certain policies at variance from those pioneered by the Soviet Union. But even this was justified by citing from the works of Marx, Engels, Lenin, and Stalin. The thrust of Chinese writings, speeches, and resolutions, moreover, was toward learning from the Soviet Union; acknowledging the USSR as the leader of the forces of peace and democracy; rewriting the history of World War II to feature Soviet and Chinese (Communist) exploits exclusively; depicting the Soviet Union as advanced in science and technology as well as in its social system, hence, the most important model for China in its modernization drive; and paying homage to Stalin as a great theorist as well as policymaker.[3]

It is asserted by some observers and scholars, including those of different ideological persuasions, that the public tribute paid by Chinese leaders to the Soviet Union masked private reservations and doubts. Mao in particular is depicted as not trusting the Soviet Communists in general—and Stalin in particular—waiting his chance to strike out on an independent course. The lengthy, sometimes tough negotiations of the winter of 1949/1950, resulting in the treaty of friendship and various aid agreements, are cited as evidence. Soviet imperialist demands upon China at the close of World War II, the misbehavior of Soviet troops in Manchuria, instances of Soviet arrogance in connection with aid projects, and the imbalance of sacrifices and costs stemming from the Korean War are added to the list of grievances.

That these latter issues affected a number of Chinese, including some high-ranking cadres, is unquestionably true, as interviews have revealed.[4] It is quite possible, moreover, that Mao harbored resentment over his earlier treatment by Comintern sources. He was surely aware of the fact that he was not Stalin's favorite Chinese Communist, and that various Soviet Communists had questions concerning his internationalist (versus nationalist) credentials. The later Soviet charge that Mao always harbored a provincial mistrust of all forces external to his environment, coupled with a deep suspicion of anyone who might challenge his power, has a strong element of validity. Notwithstanding these considerations, however, the thesis that the Sino-Soviet alliance was interlaced with deep mutual doubts and suspicions from the beginning is an exaggeration, at least on the Chinese side. Not only the documentary evidence but interviews with both Soviet and Chinese figures intimately involved in the relationship make it clear that the great majority of the Chinese cadres, Mao included, committed themselves sincerely to the alliance. It was not merely that they believed in the type of socialism pioneered by the Soviets. It was also that they saw this alliance and the form of internationalism preached in Moscow as in the Chinese national interest.

When, then, did the first serious, sustained problems emerge? They did not arise during the lifetime of Stalin, nor in the first two Khrushchev years, although Mao and his colleagues must have watched the post-Stalin succession struggle with apprehension. In his opening moves Khrushchev pleased the Chinese by agreeing to relinquish certain traditional USSR privileges such as that with respect to Dalian which Stalin had insisted upon regaining. Khrushchev's personal style, however, was not an asset. The Chinese came to regard the new Soviet leader as crude, uncouth, and, worst of all, unpredictable. The attack on Stalin delivered at the Twentieth CPSU Congress early in 1956 shocked and embarrassed the Chinese leaders, both because a man whom they had repeatedly praised in written and spoken word had been denigrated and because this momentous act had been taken without consultation or even warning. It was also an action that drew attention to the cult of Mao, which was now reaching full bloom. The conventional wisdom that this was the true beginning of serious problems between the PRC and the USSR is essentially correct, although the Chinese made suitable adjustments for the moment.[5] If the rumor that Mao felt insulted in the course of his second visit to Moscow at this time is valid, fuel was added to a smoldering pile about to burst into flame.

De-Stalinization, it must be realized, raised a much broader issue—namely, what were the international obligations of the Soviet Union, and were these being properly fulfilled? If Stalin was a national figure, he was also the leader of an international movement. Thus, his posthumous purge could drastically affect that movement, and unilateral decisions taken in Moscow were impermissible. The signal first sent forth by Tito, in his defiance of the imperious Soviet behavior, would soon be advanced by others.

For the time being, however, Beijing was precluded from empathizing with Belgrade by the fear that if the "socialist camp" were seriously weakened, the "capitalist camp" would become entrenched or even score gains, and because the PRC was profoundly dissatisfied with the status quo, this outcome too was impermissible. Hence, when events in Eastern Europe threatened to get out of hand during the following year, Beijing ultimately took a hard line, backing Moscow in insisting that any new form of Titoism or retreat from Soviet-style socialism had to be smashed. Two contradictory forces were now competing for PRC support: *independence* from the dictation of any external force and *solidarity* so as to strengthen the socialist bloc against its enemies.

Meanwhile, another pillar supporting the Sino-Soviet alliance was weakening—namely, the acceptance of the Soviet economic model in its major outlines. When Mao introduced the commune system, he did so contrary to Soviet advice. More importantly, Mao's economic programs, from a Soviet viewpoint, were based upon a naive romanticism and could only fail, bringing down with them the USSR's sacrifices on behalf of China during recent years. The Great Leap Forward with its efforts to give equal emphasis to agriculture and industry—and hinged to the tactics of political mobilization and exhortation rather than a rational allocation of resources—was correctly perceived by Soviet specialists as doomed. The Chinese revolution had gotten out of hand.

The climactic act in the Sino-Soviet drama of this era opened in 1958, with the issue in Chinese eyes being nothing less than the credibility of the Soviet Union as an ally in the struggle against China's current enemy, the United States. The details have often been presented.[6] The Chinese decided to launch an assault against the off-shore islands with the presumed objective being the "liberation" of Taiwan. This threatened confrontation with the United States ran directly counter to Khrushchev's hope for a USSR-U.S. détente that would enable the Soviet Union to concentrate upon domestic economic problems. In the emerging controversy, contrary perceptions of national interests gave rise to growing fears and antagonisms. The Soviet Union decided that the Chinese were recklessly prepared to see a global war ensue, believing that they (if not the USSR) would survive. According to a Soviet version, moreover, Beijing had an entirely unrealistic idea of Soviet capacities to furnish China with additional submarines and other military equipment; as a counterproposal, joint Sino-Soviet use of existing ships (and Chinese bases) was offered. Under the circumstances, however, an earlier pledge to aid in the development of nuclear facilities was withdrawn.

Chinese perceptions of the situation were naturally different. Khrushchev and his colleagues were seen as more interested in collusion with the enemy than in maintaining the Sino-Soviet alliance. In addition, the Soviet Union was charged with seeking to return to the imperialist path of the past by attempting to secure bases on Chinese soil and in other respects demanding that the Chinese march to their baton. Then came the "Great Betrayal." With disagreement having turned acrimonious, the Soviet Union withdrew its technicians; took home its blueprints, leaving unfinished monuments to the period of Soviet aid; and denounced the Chinese leadership and party before other Communists as having become "Great Han Chauvinists." By 1960, the alliance had wholly ended, although sporadic attempts to resurrect it took place during the next four years. With the Chinese having decided that the USSR was no longer credible as an ally, the basic raison d'etre of the Sino-Soviet alliance had disappeared.

A second factor in Chinese foreign policy in this first period related to attitudes and policies directed toward the West in general, and toward the United States specifically. At the beginning, as indicated, PRC officials showed little concern for an expansion of ties with the West except on China's terms. Thus, relations with nations like Great Britain—prepared to recognize the PRC—were kept in the negotiatory stage because these nations would not vote to oust the Nationalists from the United Nations. The core group of U.S. allies was regarded with great suspicion because of these countries' past and present actions; this was the only position compatible with Soviet views in any case. For such reasons, Beijing took no interest in tapping these sources for purposes of its economic development, accepting the Soviet connection as sufficient. This attitude was also applied to Japan, a nation seen as a pawn of U.S. militarism, although some trade between China and Japan commenced. The Western European nations with which the PRC first opened full-fledged relations were several Scandinavian states and Switzerland—nations regarded as untainted by past imperialism or current alliance with the United States.

As was to be expected, the verbal attack upon the United States was unrelenting, and it revealed much about both PRC methods of assault and certain inner PRC concerns. At the outset, the Communist leaders realized that the task of undermining and destroying the U.S. image would be a formidable one, given the lengthy history of American interaction with China and the significant portion of the Chinese elite with close past ties with the United States through education, religion, or wartime cooperation. Thus, it appeared necessary to demonstrate that the United States as a government had *always* been an evil imperialist predator. Events—starting with the Taiping rebellion—were interpreted in this vein, and a stark picture of U.S. officials, missionaries, and businessmen was drawn, with no shadings permitted.[7] This approach blended well with general Communist techniques pioneered by the Soviet Union: when a nation or an individual is adjudged an "enemy," it or he must be thoroughly discredited, meaning that the object of attack must be demonstrated as evil and *only* evil from the outset. No redeeming features are allowed to sneak in at any point; complexity is only confusing to the audience.

Yet in keeping with the rather substantial quotient of ideological commitment that accompanied this first period of Communist rule, PRC spokesmen regularly sought to differentiate between the U.S. government and "the American people," making it clear that friendship between the two peoples was eternal, blocked only by the machinations of Washington.

A second aspect of the approach to the United States revealed the strongly defensive mentality of those who now ruled China. Apprehension about U.S. power and its possible use against the PRC ran high in the early years of Communist rule. Although the Korean War had ended in a stalemate, the Chinese had suffered enormous losses and, in the process, discovered that modern weapons could wreak havoc on their ill-equipped forces. They were also aware of the military imbalance between the United States and the Soviet Union during this period, although at its conclusion, Beijing leaders were taking the position that with its newly developed nuclear arsenal, Moscow could stand up to the United States.

Thus, it now had to be demonstrated that despite appearances, the United States was a paper tiger.

Such a feat was attempted by playing upon internal U.S. problems from race relations to economic inequities. In addition, points of difference or friction within the Western alliance were emphasized, but the solidarity of the socialist bloc heralded. The basic message was that the East wind was prevailing over the West wind. Yet reading between the lines, one could discern a very healthy respect for U.S. power and a sensible desire to avoid any repetition of direct conflict with the United States *alone*—a fact that irked Soviet leaders, who came to feel that Beijing's provocative actions were intended to induce a U.S.-USSR confrontation, with the Chinese standing on the mountain top watching two tigers fight.

The manifestation of a third factor in Chinese foreign policy during this period was to be found in the somewhat contradictory approaches taken toward the emerging nations of Asia, Africa, and Latin America—later to be labeled the Third World. The dominant theme was that the New China shared the problems and supported the aspirations of the world's poor, underprivileged, and exploited peoples. Ideology and national interest combined in promoting these themes. China's closer affiliation with the ex-colonial world advanced the global revolution and weakened the imperialist bloc. China's interest thus lay in developing united front policies on a global scale. In this respect, Zhou Enlai's performance at the time of the 1955 Bandung Conference was a sterling presentation of the New China as moderate, understanding, and prepared to cross ideological lines in an effort to achieve peaceful coexistence with all reasonable states.[8]

On the other hand, ideology and national interests could also be interpreted as dictating or encouraging different, more exclusivist policies. In this period, Chinese leaders insisted that there was no "third way." One must either stand with the forces of "democracy and peace" or the forces of imperialism. Neutralism as preached by Nehru and others was a myth—indeed, a dangerous myth. Thus, despite interludes like Bandung, Chinese attention to cultivating the emerging states was limited, with more attention being paid to pursuing the Soviet path at home and abroad. It is ironic that in this era, the moral-political leadership of the "Third World" rested with India, while China's ties were rather exclusively with the Soviet bloc, Bandung notwithstanding. Some years later, this pattern would be partly reversed.

National interest or pure nationalist considerations also interfered with united front policies on occasion. Chinese traditional attitudes toward border peoples and commitments with respect to boundaries did not suddenly change as a result of the Communist victory. On the contrary, attitudes of racial-cultural superiority combined with the renewed spirit of nationalism that accompanied the successful removal of Western power to promote a series of policies and attitudes remarkably similar to those advanced by China historically when the nation was strong. Thus, at the outset of Communist rule the PRC exchanged sharp words with India over the issue of "liberating" Tibet and, more interestingly, deferred a formal exchange of diplomatic representatives with Outer Mongolia until after the outbreak of the Korean War. Ties were retained with overseas Chinese, especially those in Southeast Asia, as the Communists sought to wrest these compatriots away from Nationalist influence. And at least moral support was given to various Communist guerrilla movements in Southeast Asia that flew Maoist banners and, in some cases, were composed primarily of ethnic Chinese. To certain governments on or near China's borders, therefore, even a weak China loomed up as a neighboring state of massive proportions that had always been intent upon asserting itself in a region it considered a legitimate sphere of influence.

In the various facets of Chinese foreign policy set forth above, one can see the primary forces and elemental techniques involved in fashioning initial PRC approaches to the external world. A combination of three basic elements shaped the broadest contours of PRC foreign policy: tradition, ideology, and nationalism.

As has been suggested, the attitudes of the new Chinese leaders toward the outside world retained sentiments of superiority, exclusiveness, and xenophobia, notwithstanding the internationalist, egalitarian creed to which they subscribed. How to manage barbarians was still a central concern, as demonstrated even in the techniques employed: colorful pageantry to entertain visitors to the Celestial Kingdom; exchanges of gifts (massive quantities of pottery, salt, and cloth upon the conclusion of the Burmese-Chinese border agreement); and for the truly privileged, a visit to the Emperor in the Forbidden City. The concept of rewarding good barbarians and punishing bad barbarians reflected a traditional attitude deeply implanted in this ancient, prestigious land now governed largely by military men of peasant stock, hence, harboring very traditional values on some matters despite their revolutionary commitments.

As for ideology, the second element, Chinese acceptance of an overarching, commanding ideology did not begin with Marxism-Leninism. In certain respects, Chinese politics have been governed by a dominant ideology since ancient times. Only in its intensity and in the foreign character of some of its messages was Marxism-Leninism-Maoism (MLM) revolutionary. As in other settings, Chinese Marxism served partly to shape the content of Beijing's foreign policies and even more conclusively to rationalize those policies, once determined. MLM in effect created a new language for both the domestic and international fronts and, in the process, sought to bind all citizens to the decisions of party and state. It is true that only leaders who espoused Marxism-Leninism would have tied their nation to the Soviet Union; in most other respects, however, such as the drive for international recognition combined with the desire to be accepted not just as another state but as a major power, China was behaving in an orthodox manner. Equally natural was the concern over security, together with the determination to reestablish authority over the classical Chinese empire, or the major portion of it.

The unique feature lay in the rationalizations that MLM gave to such policies. Proletarian states stood against capitalist ones. Victory for the socialist bloc was inevitable since the course of history was inexorable. Ideology not only provided an absolutistic quality to Chinese foreign policy expressions, but also clothed them in a self-righteousness that seemed to brook no compromise. China's case was invariably put in moral as well as political terms, thereby defining the opponent as not merely wrong but evil. In this first era, it was easier to utilize MLM because there were no intrasocialist bloc arguments about who was the correct Marxist-Leninist. The PRC could thus claim to represent or be working on behalf of the global proletariat without contradiction from within the ranks.

Even in this period of relatively intensive ideological-internationalist expression, however, the central element in Chinese foreign policy remained that of nationalism. The new leaders took special delight in underlining their independence from all forms of Western domination (while acquiescing at least nominally in Soviet leadership). As noted, traditional claims of sovereignty and suzerainty were asserted (again, except against the USSR). Although it was never articulated as such, a concept of national interest was very much in the minds of the new elite as they fashioned foreign policies. But there was a substantial handicap. Being extremely weak and backward, the PRC was in a position to provide the most limited material assistance in supporting its interests abroad. Only rhetoric was available in unlimited quantity.

Within Chinese rhetoric, however, were contained clues to the basic techniques employed to advance the PRC cause. PRC leaders have always kept in mind the fact that there are three sets of relationships in the international arena to be considered: state to state, people to people, and comrade to comrade. In this first period, when state-to-state relations were minimal, Beijing frequently concentrated upon an appeal to "the people," invariably defining them as "friendly" even when the state involved was "hostile." The principal targets were the emerging states of the Afro-Asian-Latin American world together with Japan and parts of Western Europe. Visits and cultural relations of various sorts were promoted, with increasing pressure thereby put upon the governments concerned to move toward formal diplomatic ties. The use of comrade-to-comrade relations involved more complexities in that it often hampered improvements in state-to-state relations with noncommunist nations. Yet in this first period, Beijing did not hesitate to assist comrades within its means (one notable example being the Vietnamese Communists), justifying this as its socialist-internationalist duty.

The Turn Toward the Third World

The second broad phase of PRC foreign policy, commencing in the late 1950s and extending into the early 1970s, can be defined as centering upon a turn toward the Third World. In the first period, as already noted, the PRC had devoted rhetorical attention to the developing nations, although the rhetoric lacked consistency. In the next phase, PRC interest in such nations by no means disappeared; on the contrary, an upswing occurred in China's Third World orientation. Concomitantly, the second period was marked by a pronounced swing away from the socialist bloc, but with no effort to seek alignment with the West. For more than a decade, the PRC seemed to be satisfied to identify itself with that great body of non-Western (and with rare exceptions, non-communist) states, most of which had come into being after World War II.[9]

The ideological-political base of this period lay in China's analysis of trends in the Soviet Union: Khrushchev and his successors, Brezhnev and Kosygin, had pursued revisionist policies, thereby destroying socialism in the world's first socialist state. The Soviet Union had become a fascist, social-imperialist nation, equal as a global menace to the United States. Thus, a socialist bloc no longer existed. Instead, the world was divided into three parts: the two superpowers, hegemonistic in nature, constituted the First World; the remaining advanced industrial states, all of them "capitalist" (Japan and the nations of Western Europe) represented an intermediate force, a Second World; and the remaining states—for the most part poor, backward, and oppressed—made up the Third World. China belonged to this Third World and would champion its causes.

Following from this analysis, the new PRC course involved three broad efforts. First, both the United States and the USSR had to be vigorously opposed via the mobilization of the world's people. Modern weapons were no match for an aroused people. Second, Japan and the nations of Western Europe had to be encouraged to exercise greater independence from the United States, giving voice to their nationalism so as to overcome U.S. hegemonistic efforts. Finally, the Third World had to advance its interests by concentrating upon unity and organization. Thus, China extolled a wide variety of Third World countries and leaders, encouraged various cultural exchanges, undertook select programs of economic assistance, and participated actively in Third World organizations.

The PRC's new course met with modest success before ultimately revealing fatal flaws. Toward the USSR, a certain ambivalence was displayed at first. It was difficult to conceal the bitterness engendered by Soviet actions, but the dispute was camouflaged for several years, with both sides avoiding open polemics as efforts were made to find solutions. After the downfall of Khrushchev, a serious attempt to reach agreement with the new Soviet leaders was undertaken and for a brief time, in 1964, relations did show improvement. But the issues were too serious and the personal affronts too rankling—thus, another failure ensued.

In some quarters, the widening Vietnam conflict was seen as making possible the mending of the breach. Actually, the threat of a U.S. attack on China did become an issue among PRC leaders, with certain voices speaking in favor of reducing tension with the USSR to meet the danger. An accommodation was also urged by Hanoi and various other Asian Communists. In particular, the Japanese Communists made a strenuous effort to bring about a Sino-Soviet rapprochement on behalf of Hanoi in 1966 and became embittered over Mao's veto.[10]

In point of fact, far from helping to bring China and the Soviet Union together, the Vietnam conflict provided yet another issue between them. Mao appeared to have accepted U.S. assurances that no widening of the war was desired by the United States. Otherwise, he would scarcely have taken the risks of plunging China into the Cultural Revolution. Further, he and his colleagues seemed determined to prove to Hanoi that without Chinese approval and support, its victory would be difficult if not impossible. Thus, various restrictions were placed on the transit of Soviet aid across China. In the end, however, it was the Soviet Union that demonstrated to the Vietnamese Communists that modern weapons are critically important, especially when combined with a successful campaign to divide the enemy at home.

Long before the North Vietnamese victory, China and the Soviet Union had moved perilously close to large-scale conflict. Certain facts regarding the 1969 Ussuri River incident are in dispute, but there can be no doubt that this episode and its aftermath had a very sobering effect upon Chinese leaders. The specter of Czechoslovakia loomed in the background, made more ominous by the Brezhnev "doctrine" that no state was free to leave socialism—and a current Soviet charge against Mao was that he and his colleagues had done precisely that. Beijing was given to understand that if war occurred, the Soviet Union would not limit the war to conventional weapons. With the debris of the Cultural Revolution scattered everywhere, Mao and those comrades who survived suddenly realized that they could neither negotiate with the Soviet Union nor fight it from a position of strength. The PRC had never been so isolated in its brief history. Major shifts in policy were mandatory, since neither "aroused people" nor powerful allies existed to come to China's assistance.

PRC relations with the United States became less tense despite the fact that tens of thousands of PLA soldiers were in North Vietnam providing aid to Hanoi's war efforts in various ways. A modus vivendi evolved, with neither side desiring an extension of the conflict. At an earlier point, in March 1961, the Kennedy administration—reversing policies of the Dulles-Eisenhower era—had made certain overtures to Beijing, offering grain shipments to ease China's serious economic plight and an exchange of journalists. These offers had been rejected with the assertion that until the Taiwan issue was settled, there could be no improvement in Sino-American relations. After the Ussuri River incident, however, Chinese leaders were brought to a realization that it was imperative to move away from isolation, and that if such a move was to be effectively consummated, it had to involve the United States.

The results of PRC policies toward Western Europe and Japan up to this point provided further illustration of this necessity. The PRC attempts to weaken NATO and cause disruptions in the Atlantic Alliance came to naught because, whatever the problems between the United States and its allies, China had virtually no leverage in the Western world. On the contrary, Beijing came to realize that although it could obtain diplomatic recognition and limited economic relations from an increasing number of West European states, unless and until the United States approved, relations with Western Europe could only be limited and participation in the United Nations impossible. When Washington chose to use its leverage on these matters, it was not without power. This was made even clearer with respect to China's relations with Japan. Sino-Japanese trade increased slowly as did cultural relations, but the Japanese government was not prepared to create a crisis with the United States over China policy. Thus, in the short run at least, a Second World policy serving China's national interests depended upon an improvement of relations with the United States.

With respect to the Third World, China's gains were significant during this period, until the Cultural Revolution. Recognition was obtained from a number of new states, especially in Africa. China extended her contacts at an early point in the Middle East, commencing with Egypt, and in all regions of the non-Western world a growing PRC presence was to be observed. To dramatize such gains, Chinese leaders including Zhou Enlai engaged in highly publicized visits. Beijing, moreover, despite its serious domestic economic problems, developed an aid program of modest but meaningful proportions toward the Third World, the most significant project being the Tan-Zam railway linking Tanzania and Zambia.[11]

From the outset, however, there were problems. The radical rhetoric dispensed by Beijing during this period proved jarring to a number of Third World leaders who felt that they had already had their revolution and now needed stability and growth. China could contribute very little to these needs, especially by comparison with the United States and the Soviet Union. Moreover, the spillover from the Sino-Soviet dispute soon produced fierce struggles within individual Third World countries, Afro-Asian-Latin American organizations, and even between contending factions within external Communist parties. Neither China nor the Soviet Union gained from these contests, although both had their partisans.

A growing number of Third World leaders wanted to avoid identification with either of the two major Communist states. In Asia, moreover, where China had always been regarded as potentially a major (and expansionist) power, there were special difficulties. Beijing's assistance to revolutionary guerrilla movements, coupled with the fierce nationalism that accompanied the Cultural Revolution, seemed to belie the principles of peaceful coexistence to which the PRC was pledged, and instead created new apprehensions. Even where an alliance was achieved with Sukarno's Indonesia, the ultimate results were devasting, with the Indonesian Left drenched in blood as a result of the abortive coup of September 1965, and China blamed by the successor government for interference in Indonesia's internal affairs.

Yet China's Third World policies of this era were most seriously damaged by the self-inflicted wounds that Chinese leadership—and more particularly Mao—imposed upon the nation. At the height of the Cultural Revolution, Chinese foreign policy had virtually ceased to exist. Chinese ambassadors had been recalled from all nations except Egypt. Antiforeign incidents perpetrated by Red Guards and others had made enemies of many countries previously regarded as friendly or neutral. By the end of 1968, the PRC had normal relations with only a handful of states. Xenophobia and ultranationalism had combined to reduce the PRC's international influence to near-zero.

Even if the Cultural Revolution had not occurred, however, and PRC policies toward the Third World had been more sophisticated, Chinese foreign policy during this period could not have served the country's national interests. First, the very concept of a Third World is a myth, albeit a useful myth on occasion. The multiple differences and divisions among that huge residue of states not fitting into the category of advanced industrial nations preclude unity of purpose or action on most issues. Beyond this, the Third World, in *whatever* form, could not satisfy either of China's primary requirements—security and development. One can understand the psychological need to identify with "the global proletariat" on some new basis after the ideological as well as political-strategic shock that accompanied the break with Moscow. But as the realities of the world were borne home at the close of the 1960s, China's near-exclusive identification with an amorphous group of new states—most of which were powerless and struggling with grave problems themselves—was recognized as hopelessly inadequate. Another major shift in foreign policy was required.

Moves Toward the Advanced Industrial World—with Reservations

The events leading to a rapprochement between the People's Republic of China and the United States are too well known to warrant detailed description here.[12] Suffice it to say that the actions taken by both parties were deliberate. No accidents were involved. The motives were sufficient on each side to enable ideological differences and recent enmity to be transcended. The Chinese need for a drastically altered foreign policy has already been set forth. On the U.S. side, the need was less urgent; however, with the U.S. position deteriorating in Vietnam, hope was kindled in the Nixon administration that the PRC could assist in achieving "peace with honor." Indeed, President Nixon had signaled even before assuming the presidency that an understanding with China would be conducive to stabilization in Asia. Implicit was the thesis that such a development would provide the United States with a more advantageous position in dealing with the USSR and at the same time insure against any restoration of the Sino-Soviet alliance.

The basic initiatives, however, were taken by Beijing, not Washington, even though the latter had made clear its receptivity to a new relationship. In assessing the results, a complex balance sheet must be drawn up. Looking briefly at the U.S. side, one can assert that from the first Kissinger-Nixon visits to China in 1971–1972, and through 1979, the U.S. strategic position vis-à-vis the two major Communist states was strengthened. Only the United States among the three nations was in a position to communicate normally with the other two, thereby occupying a "center" position. To some degree, both the Soviet Union and the PRC wooed Washington, seeking to prevent gains by the other party. The official U.S. policy was captured by the term "evenhandedness," with the goal a measured improvement in relations with both states without sacrifices of American national interests.

The policy of evenhandedness was upset largely by the Soviet invasion of Afghanistan, although there had long been voices in and out of the U.S. government favorable to a U.S.-PRC strategic alignment against the USSR, or at least so greatly committed to measures directed against the USSR, like the Jackson-Vanik amendment, as to make evenhanded treatment impossible. But generally speaking, such views were in the minority until the events of late 1979. With President Carter's shift, the minority became a majority—at least within the administration. Step by step, and continuing into the Reagan administration, a strategic alignment was proffered to the PRC.

The argument on behalf of alignment was a simple one. In a period when Soviet expansionism represented the principal global threat and when the United States could no longer bear the burden of countering that threat alone, a strategic alignment with China would increase pressures on the USSR as well as deter any possible Sino-Soviet rapprochement.

The counterarguments were also powerful: the potentially adverse long-range impact upon U.S.-USSR relations, with profound regional and global consequences; the unlikelihood of China doing more to contain the Soviet Union than it was doing in its own interests prior to any suggestion of alignment, and hence, the question of whether such an alignment would subtract from or add to U.S. burdens; connected with this recognition, the possibility of shifts in PRC foreign policy, including the unwillingness of China to play the role of a strategic ally of the United States; and finally, opposition by key U.S. partners and most Asian states, many of whom feared that a militarily strengthened PRC, as it posed a limited threat to the Soviet Union, would exercise its leverage increasingly upon neighboring Asians.

As events have unfolded, the trends have been more complex than the alternative routes signaled by either of the two positions outlined above. On the one hand, the People's Republic of China, reversing an earlier policy, rejected strategic alignment with the United States, opting instead for a policy defined as one of "nonalignment and independence." On the other hand, the Chinese economic and cultural tilt toward Japan and the West continued. In addition, U.S.-PRC negotiations over the possible transfer of military technology and U.S. sales of military equipment moved ahead, symbolized by the exchange visits of Secretary of Defense Caspar Weinberger and Minister of Defense Zhang Aiping in 1983–1984—visits supplementing those of Premier Zhao Ziyang and President Reagan. In reality, China has embarked upon a policy of "tilted nonalignment."

It should be emphasized, however, that this policy did represent a significant shift from China's previous stance. In the late 1970s, Deng Xiaoping and others frequently issued calls for a united front against Soviet hegemony—a front encompassing China and the United States, the Second World, and as much of the Third World as could be enlisted. Why was this united front policy replaced by a policy of professed nonalignment? Some observers asserted that the change was a product of unhappiness with the attitudes and policies of the new Reagan administration. Certainly, problems emerged at an early point: Reagan's expressed desire during his first presidential campaign for improved relations with Taiwan, and the subsequent elevation of the Taiwan issue by the PRC; trade issues, from textiles to high technology; the defection of the Chinese tennis star, Hu Na; and other matters. Each of these issues warrants brief additional comment because some of them are likely to be projected into future U.S.-PRC relations.

At first glance, the PRC decision in 1981 to elevate the Taiwan issue into one of central importance, and in the process to seek a change in the rules of the game, seems puzzling. To be sure, it was earlier recognized that Taiwan constituted a major obstacle to the establishment of formal diplomatic relations between the PRC and the United States. Negotiations over the wording of the Shanghai Communique on this matter were strenuous. Yet a compromise of sorts was found, and at the time of normalization more than seven years later, that formula was essentially repeated, with the key element being that the United States "acknowledged" that all of the Chinese people supported the principle of one China, with Taiwan a part of China.

At the time of normalization, however, the Deng government was fully cognizant of the fact that the United States intended to continue the sale of defensive arms to Taiwan, as President Carter had made explicitly clear. There was an agreement to disagree on this issue. Subsequently, when the U.S. Congress passed the Taiwan Relations Act, making manifest the U.S. interest in the security of Taiwan until and unless a peaceful resolution of the issue was achieved, and the president signed that act, Beijing complained but did not raise the issue to a high decibel level. Indeed, the transfer of arms continued in 1980 with minimal PRC protest. And throughout the 1970s, first Mao, then Deng and others indicated a willingness to be patient on the issue of Taiwan, waiting one hundred years if necessary. They defined Taiwan as a secondary issue, with the primary issue relating to Soviet aggression.

What transpired to cause the PRC's elevation of the Taiwan issue? Perhaps the signals from candidate Reagan of an upgrading of U.S.-Taiwan relations alarmed PRC leaders and prompted the decision to take a harder and more prominent line. When Republic of China officials were invited to the Reagan inauguration, the PRC demanded that these individuals be barred from attendance, and in order to avoid a crisis, the new U.S. administration acceded to the demand, suggesting that tough PRC policies could be effective. The hard line continued. The announcement on 17 August 1982 that the United States intended to reduce arms sales to Taiwan gradually, leading eventually "to a final resolution," was the product of lengthy, difficult negotiations. Despite certain caveats subsequently advanced by the Reagan administration, this agreement represented a substantial, though less than complete, victory for the PRC. Sometimes dubbed Shanghai II, the August communique did have a quid pro quo. Vague wording was included, stipulating that the PRC would treat as "fundamental" its aim to reach a peaceful resolution of the Taiwan issue.

Immediately after the agreement was reached, both states advanced differing interpretations of the statement. The United States indicated that it interpreted the communique as meaning that the PRC was committed to a peaceful settlement with Taiwan, and its own policies were contingent upon such a commitment. The PRC insisted that the United States was now pledged progressively to phase out arms sales to Taiwan, and that China had made no pledge regarding a peaceful settlement. U.S. arms sales to Taiwan have continued, in quantity and cost at a level Beijing deems to be a violation of the August agreement. Clearly, the dispute continues.

Apart from China's suspicions of the Reagan administration, two other factors have loomed large in the PRC decision to move the Taiwan issue to a position of greater importance. In a period of internal flux and uncertainty, with major economic and political reforms being attempted, Chinese leaders find an appeal to nationalism to be extremely useful. It is the single most potent unifying force at a time when ideological exhortations evoke limited responses. Thus, on such issues as Taiwan, Hong Kong, and the South China Sea islands—issues of "national reunification"—no compromise on the question of sovereignty is forthcoming. Chinese nationalism continues to assert itself strongly.

A third and highly important factor lies with developments in Taiwan itself. Beijing leaders cannot have missed the fact that the Taiwanization process is now accelerating. Within a decade, Taiwan will have a new generation of leaders—a mixture of children of mainland refugees and Taiwanese. Such a leadership is likely to be primarily concerned with the economic and political development of Taiwan's people, and the achievement thereby of a strong, independent state—whatever the formal rubric. Taiwan will be interested in economic and cultural intercourse with the PRC, but not formal union—unless economic and political changes on the mainland are extraordinarily successful.

In the past, the men who governed China hoped that through generous offers such as that advanced by Marshal Ye Jianying in his nine-point proposal they could deal with the aging refugees at the top of the political-military structure in Taiwan, playing upon their nostalgia for the homeland. The problem with such proposals is that they demand an abandonment of sovereignty, with Taiwan to become a province of the PRC. Guarantees of autonomy, therefore, however generous, are subject to the reassessments of future PRC leaders—and judging from the past experiences of autonomous regions of China, the prospects would not seem promising. For example, it is difficult to imagine Taiwan as a PRC province having the right to exclude the Communist party, or to make independent decisions regarding foreign policy. And under the current economic and political circumstances that prevail in the PRC, who can predict with certainty future trends on these fronts?

Thus, the Taiwan issue will probably remain unresolved in the foreseeable future and constitute a continuing problem in Sino-U.S. relations, with its importance depending upon decisions in Beijing. Neither the Reagan administration nor any successor is likely to abandon Taiwan totally. The Taiwan Relations Act has bipartisan support at present. If the PRC chooses to make Taiwan a central determinant of U.S.-PRC relations, therefore, periodic acrimony seems inevitable. PRC complaints regarding the Republican and Democratic party platforms of 1984 as they related to this issue are but one piece of evidence.

It is possible, however, that despite the rhetoric on the Taiwan issue, the precise character of Sino-American relations will be determined in greater degree by developments in the areas of trade and technology transfer. Here too, problems exist. Although interested in providing China with some military technology and defensive military equipment—and with certain agreements in principle already reached—the United States has been resistant to PRC demands for what is known as "red zone" technology—items in the highly sensitive area, in some cases not even furnished to NATO allies. It is also aware of the concerns of such nations as South Korea, fearful that if the PRC obtains advanced military technology or weapons, these might be transferred to Chinese allies such as North Korea. Agreement on nuclear energy transfer, hammered out after protracted negotiations between the PRC and the United States, has also been stalled due to Congressional sensitivities over the issue of safeguards, an issue brought to the fore in charges (denied) that China had given assistance to Pakistan's nuclear program. Finally, recent restrictions on textile imports have reopened an earlier issue, since in its new export-oriented economic program, the PRC counts heavily upon such labor-intensive products in trade with the United States and other advanced industrial nations.

Despite these difficulties, the overall trend is toward greater economic intercourse between the PRC and the United States at many levels. Trade in 1984 is likely to total between US$5 and $5.5 billion, with China enjoying a sizable surplus in the balance. That is only about one-half the current trade volume between China and Japan, but it is very much greater than the US$1.2 billion PRC-USSR trade. In all probability, a modus vivendi will be worked out with respect to military sales, although PRC leaders continue to canvas Western Europe for technology and weapons. In any case, Chinese leaders have always made it clear that large-scale military purchases are not in the offing. The United States, out of consideration for its allies and for reasons outlined earlier, will treat the matter of military-related technology and weaponry for the PRC with caution, even as it encourages a low-level strategic relationship.

In the cultural realm, the flow of Chinese specialists and students to the United States remains significant. By 1984, there were some 12,000 PRC citizens in these and related categories in the United States—approximately one-half funded by the PRC government, the other half under private auspices or with U.S. institutional assistance. The great bulk of these individuals are committed to the fields of science and technology, but a small number of social scientists and humanists are making their appearance on the U.S. scene. Not yet clear is what percentage of these individuals will seek to remain in the United States, or precisely what the PRC attitude will be toward the problem of defection. It is quite possible, however, that if the drainage is not severe and defections are handled quietly, the repercussions will be minimal. Meanwhile, for its part, the United States will seek with increasing insistence a greater measure of academic reciprocity in terms of access and other types of support for U.S. students and scholars in China, an issue not yet resolved to the satisfaction of the United States.

Another U.S. grievance of a more general nature relates to the extensive criticism of U.S. policies presented in the speeches of PRC leaders and in the Chinese media. If such criticisms represent the genuine sentiments of party and state leaders, they also reflect the effort to appear truly nonaligned. Thus, U.S. policies toward Central America, the Middle East, Africa, and other Third World areas are regularly attacked; the strategic contest in Europe is defined as a superpower battle threatening global peace, frequently with little effort to differentiate between the contestants; and the American domestic scene is often painted in exceedingly somber tones. U.S. leaders especially resent the tendency of the PRC to couple the United States with the USSR, advancing the implication that both are more or less equally responsible for the world's problems.

Notwithstanding these issues, as long as Chinese domestic policies hew to the present course, the Sino-U.S. relationship will be sufficiently important to the PRC (and to the United States) to warrant sustained cultivation. Whether the measurement is economic, cultural, or strategic, the United States is in a position to be of assistance to China's modernization. And of equal importance, it does not pose a threat to China's security. Thus, a hard-headed appraisal of China's national interests, not sentimentality, dictates the growing PRC interaction with the United States, although the basic compatibility of Chinese and Americans as individuals aids the effort.[13]

In contrast, although official PRC policy is now also directed toward the improvement of relations with the USSR, the attainment of that goal promises to be an uphill struggle. Some advances have been made. Negotiations with the Soviet Union have been reopened after a period of total noncommunication, and the PRC media have muted their attacks on Soviet domestic policies. Indeed, the charge of revisionism was dropped some time ago, signaling Beijing's willingness to readmit the Soviet Union into the socialist column. Revisionism, to be sure, had become an embarrassing issue for China in the light of sweeping PRC domestic reforms.

Accompanying the reopening of Sino-Soviet talks, increases in trade have taken place, significant in terms of percentage growth but against a very low baseline. As noted, such trade now stands at slightly over US$1 billion per annum, and under favorable conditions it should steadily grow. Cultural exchanges have recommenced, with eighty Chinese students scheduled to go to the Soviet Union in 1984, and an equal number of Soviet students scheduled to come to the PRC. Joint academic and scientific conferences have also been launched.

Firm predictions regarding the nature of future Sino-Soviet relations are hazardous, but on balance, the obstacles to mutual trust or major breakthroughs in resolving the key issues appear formidable. The ideological element of the conflict has been largely set aside, but it was never the principal issue. Ideology merely served as a means of proclaiming one's own legitimacy and the illegitimacy of the other side, in order to advance positions relating primarily to matters of security and perceived national interest. On these issues the differences remain profound, with no resolutions in sight. Deng and others have outlined the Chinese demands in three crisp demands: pull Soviet military power away from the Chinese border, including Soviet forces in Outer Mongolia; cease military assistance to Vietnam; and withdraw Soviet forces from Afghanistan. No Soviet leader is likely to accommodate the Chinese on these fronts. It is conceivable that a compromise could be struck on the first demand, with Soviet forces withdrawing a certain distance without strategic sacrifices. Even on this issue, however, complexities exist. The costs of such a withdrawal (involving the abandonment of extensive fortifications and installations in one area, and their reestablishment elsewhere) would be sizable. Moreover, the USSR, concerned about what it perceives as the emergence of a U.S.-Japanese-South Korean alliance against it in Northeast Asia (with possible Chinese involvement), is in the process of adding to, rather than drawing down, its military power in the region.

Prospects for resolving the Vietnam and Afghanistan issues to China's satisfaction are even more dim. The USSR has reason to be concerned about both situations and will not abandon causes to which it has contributed much treasure and not a few lives, and which it considers very much in its national interest. Recent Soviet statements, private as well as public, suggest an uncompromising line. Sooner or later, assert Soviet spokesmen, opponents will be forced to recognize the Heng Samrin government in Cambodia, and as that government strengthens itself, Vietnamese forces can withdraw. Similarly, they insist that the international recognition of the Babrik Kamal government in Afghanistan is inevitable, and that Soviet forces are prepared to stay twenty years if necessary to complete the "Afghanization" process currently under way. Indeed, destabilization is more likely to occur in Pakistan, assert Soviet authorities, as they put pressure upon Islamabad to end the privileged sanctuaries it affords Afghan freedom fighters.

Thus, for China, the paramount security issues that confront it in its relations with the USSR will remain acute. Soviet encirclement of China today is truly massive, much more impressive than the earlier U.S. effort at its zenith. Some forty-six to fifty-one Soviet divisions, numbering 400,000 to 500,000 troops armed with the most modern nuclear and conventional weapons, are on or near the 4,500-mile frontier. Alignments with Outer Mongolia in the North and Vietnam in the South extend the Soviet reach, as do the current control of Afghanistan and the military support of India. The growing Soviet naval presence in the western Pacific adds to this power.

Chinese leaders believe, probably correctly, that the Soviet Union will not attack China. To do so would be to risk a debilitating conflict of vast proportions. But they also recognize that the Soviet power that surrounds them inhibits or restricts Chinese foreign policies, especially with respect to Vietnam. And privately, Soviet spokesmen speak of the long-range need to block Chinese expansionism, citing the likelihood of an Indian-Indonesian-Vietnamese alliance dedicated to that end.

In sum, unless the PRC is prepared to accommodate to current Soviet policies and positions, there can be no fundamental agreement in the short term on matters of vital concern. The Soviet Union is extremely unlikely to make major concessions. In recent years, it must be noted, the critical security issues separating these two neighboring empires have grown, not diminished.[14]

Recently, however, PRC leaders, even though recognizing the Soviet Union as the principal threat, have shifted their views regarding U.S.-USSR relations. At an earlier point, Beijing encouraged the United States to develop its military strength and to challenge what it termed "the Soviet hegemonic drive." Now, in addition to criticizing both superpowers for threatening global peace, it counsels Washington to moderate its hard line and to seek some reduction in tension with Moscow. The first theme, the criticism, is amply illustrated by the following statements:

> Europe is the focus of contention between the two superpowers in their scrambling for world hegemony. . . . The Soviet-American talks on nuclear arms limitations are aimed not only at carrying on their nuclear arms

> expansion race under the cloak of peaceful disarmament, but also at restraining the other side while developing one's own strength and gaining superiority . . . the two hegemonic powers, the Soviet Union and the United States, have developed more and more nuclear weapons in the course of the talks, which have posed an increasingly serious threat to world peace. . . . The new polemics at present are but another round of their protracted contention for world hegemony.[15]

A related *Renmin Ribao* report concluded with this remark: "People can only note that a formal U.S.-Soviet discussion or a meeting of heads of state is nothing but an interlude in a protracted story marked by a long disarmament deadlock and an increasingly hot arms race."[16]

The second theme, that of urging Washington to seek reduction of tension, has been voiced mainly in private, in conversations between Deng and U.S. leaders, and at lower levels as well. Although PRC officials continue to indicate support for a strong NATO and the U.S.-Japan Mutual Defense Treaty, they suggest that in its confrontation with the USSR, the United States has been too militant and inflexible, thereby paying an excessive political price internationally.

Behind such assertions, there apparently lies a growing conviction in Beijing that China's national interest is not served by the very high level of tension presently existing between the United States and the Soviet Union, for in addition to its other risks such tension will motivate the Soviet Union to accelerate its military buildup in Northeast Asia and inhibit it from any moderation of stance on the issues most vitally affecting Chinese security.

If security and economic interests tilt China toward Japan and the West on balance, political interests present a different picture. On this front, closer ties with the West, and especially the United States, pose dangers. Liberalism and economic crimes have recently been two primary targets of Beijing officialdom, with both viewed by senior cadres as related to the turn outward. Yet the thrust toward putting economics in command and liberating major portions of the Chinese people through an extensive incentives program continues, together with the creation of free economic zones to encourage foreign investment. There is every indication that past failures of an autarkic economic system and the initial gains of the reforms, together with the broad economic imperatives now confronting China, will project these experiments into the future, with consequences as yet unknown. Meanwhile, China's present leaders, considering themselves socialists and still seeking to adhere to the Marxist-Leninist faith (modified by Mao Thought) worry about the spreading agnosticism among the rank and file. With widening access to Western ideas, the intellectual community in particular runs the risk of succumbing to heresy—and at a time when China's vast rural population is being encouraged to allow materialism full sway.

Thus, in late 1983, a short-lived campaign against "spiritual pollution" was launched—a campaign abandoned when it threatened to get out of hand and intimidate the forces upon which China's future depends. Nevertheless, the effort to reduce the appeal of "bourgeois liberalism" goes on, and the vices of liberal societies are given special attention so as to temper the enthusiasm of China's post-1949 youth for the truly revolutionary world represented by advanced industrial societies. Obviously, the type of political alignment with the United States implicit in the united front policy would jeopardize such efforts. Moreover, many contemporary PRC leaders are genuinely appalled, as Mao was, by what they regard as the absence of discipline, the excess of freedom in U.S. society. As noted earlier, the older generations of top Chinese leaders remain deeply influenced by their peasant-military origins. Their pragmatism (what will work?) is not to be confused with liberalism.

There are other reasons for the appeal of an "independent" policy. Despite all of the internationalist rhetoric that accompanied the advent of Chinese Communism, xenophobic and racist sentiments lie very deeply embedded in the Chinese past. It is also clear that the achievement of a position of greater flexibility between the United States and the Soviet Union could have strong advantages. Alignment with one of the superpowers against the other would greatly increase the costs and risks for China. At a minimum, the PRC would have to accelerate its military modernization, thereby shifting the priorities it has assigned in its drive for economic development. This, indeed, may be the fundamental reason for the policy shift.

In addition, Beijing's leaders cannot be unaware of the tactical skill with which Kim Il-sŏng, ruler of North Korea, has played Moscow off against Beijing, gaining concessions from both. It is a risky game, but also a tempting one. To improve relations with the USSR, if this is possible, might induce further concessions from Washington if U.S. leaders are anxious not to have the question of "who lost China" reopened. And if in the process of reasserting an independent, self-reliant foreign policy the PRC can identify with and, if possible, play a role in leading the Third World ("the global proletariat"), the old ideological thrust will not be totally lost.

Policies toward the Second World—Western Europe and Japan—are currently in line with these considerations. On the one hand, the PRC continues to favor a strong NATO as noted, and this requires a strengthening of the Western alliance. The PRC also gives short shrift to those whom it regards as guilty of appeasement of the Soviet Union. Hence, its attitude toward many elements of the European Left has been negative. Yet on the other hand, PRC commentators do not hesitate to underline the economic crisis encompassing the "capitalist West" and the multiple cleavages marking relations between the United States and Western Europe, as if to warn its people of Western shortcomings and the risks of alignment.[17] When the issue involves a European government being pitted against a non-Western state, even in the case of such a staunch anti-Soviet administration as that of Prime Minister Thatcher and such a dubious candidate for support as Argentina, the PRC takes its stance with the latter.

Only toward Japan does the PRC evidence minimal criticism, although the textbook crisis (over coverage of Japan's pre-1945 policies toward China in Japanese textbooks) represented a temporary departure from this policy. Beijing presently proclaims that Sino-Japanese relations have never been closer. It supports Japanese rearmament (with cautions against some bad "militarist" elements in Japan) and champions the Japanese position on the four northern islands. The Japan Socialist party is treated politely although it is regarded privately as both powerless and naive because of the quasi-pacifist, neutralist stance of its left wing. This may change if party leader Ishibashi succeeds in recasting Japan Socialist party policy. At present, however, Beijing is prepared to stand with the Liberal Democratic government, convinced that it will retain power for the indefinite future and, on balance, serve China's national interests, especially on the economic front.

To generalize, the Second World clearly remains an important consideration in PRC foreign policy. The unity and strength of Western Europe is essential if the Soviet Union is to be countered on the Western front, and this also requires a continuing U.S. commitment. Similarly, a strengthened Japan in alignment with U.S. power is a present need in the western Pacific. The current tensions in relations among the advanced industrial states, even if reflective of certain fundamental flaws of a structural nature, should not be allowed to disintegrate the key alliances through which the USSR can be thwarted. The Second World, moreover, and especially Japan, offers promise with respect to China's modernization drive. In a fashion similar to its position vis-à-vis the United States, however, the PRC has increasingly attempted to differentiate its strategic from its political position vis-à-vis the Second World, thereby deflecting the criticism so assiduously advanced by the Soviet Union that Beijing is prepared to support any "reactionary" if he or it is anti-Soviet.

There remains the topic of current PRC policies toward the Third World. Here, despite the relatively simple rhetoric employed, Chinese policies are as complex and contradictory as those of any other major state. Four predominant characteristics can be discerned. First, Beijing's central thrust is in the direction of supporting states that act "independently" of major powers, especially the superpowers. This position is most forcefully manifested with respect to Eastern Europe, where the Chinese have had closest relations with Romania and Yugoslavia for obvious reasons. Yet with respect to Poland, PRC spokesmen have been careful not to support Solidarity or the quasi-rebellion of the Polish people against their government. The movement may be anti-Soviet, but it is also anticommunist, engendering the same concerns by Beijing leaders as those raised by the Hungarian uprising more than two decades ago.

A second characteristic of present PRC Third World policy is to avoid taking a position on most issues that pit one Third World nation against another. Thus, in the Middle East, it is easy for the PRC to excoriate Israel (and the United States) and to pledge support to the PLO and the rest of the Arab world. However, with regard to the long-standing quarrel between Egypt and other Arab states, the Iran-Iraq war, and the general cleavage between so-called radical and moderate Arab states, Chinese policy is generally marked by a conspicuous silence or a neutrally phrased appeal for unity. This position is defended on the score that one must do nothing to promote Third World divisions. It is also a policy aimed at making as few enemies as possible in regions where, in any case, PRC leverage is minimal.

In Latin America, the vagueness encasing PRC policies is based on additional reasons. Because Castro—"a surrogate of Soviet hegemonism"—is no friend (although some efforts at rapprochement have commenced), it is impossible for PRC policy to support his or the Soviet activities in Central America. Thus, PRC officials generally restrict themselves to broad statements calling for respect for the independence, sovereignty, and territorial integrity of the countries of the region, and opposition to intervention "from whatever source."[18] Such statements, however, do not preclude Beijing from castigating the United States for its "mistakes in policies" toward such countries as El Salvador while denouncing the USSR for seeking to fish in troubled waters.

This brief review introduces yet another feature of PRC Third World policy. The insistence that all must direct their efforts toward Third World unity does not preclude the PRC from having special friends and enemies within this world. One quickly realizes, moreover, that such friends and enemies bear a direct relation to China's very basic national interests, especially in the security realm. Thus, the Chinese make continuous efforts to keep North Korea within their political orbit. Although privately there is no fondness for Kim Il-sŏng or his regime, Chinese leaders have gone to great lengths in exchanges of visits, economic concessions, and military assistance in their campaign to maintain a priority of position in Pyongyang. Cognizant of the fact that, despite their best efforts, they cannot match Moscow in economic and military aid, PRC leaders refuse to be outdone in rhetorical support, including acknowledgment of Kim's son, Kim Chong-il, as his successor, repeated calls for U.S. troop withdrawal from South Korea, and support for Kim Il-sŏng's reunification program. (At the same time, these overtures have not prevented China from extending its cross-contacts with South Korea, much to Pyongyang's dismay.)

In similar fashion, Beijing has been wooing the states comprising the Association of Southeast Asian Nations (ASEAN). Assistance to the Communist insurgents of this area has been drastically curtailed, with the premium upon correct state-to-state relations. Even when formal diplomatic relations are not in existence and hostility to China's policies is sometimes voiced (as in Indonesia and Singapore), neither the PRC leadership nor the Chinese media permits criticism to issue forth publicly.

On the other hand, the PRC's enemies in the Third World are treated to severe attack. Vietnam presently heads the list and it is invariably put in the same category as other "hegemonists." One commentator reported:

> It is not accidental that the Hanoi authorities regard the Soviet Union as their firmest ally because Vietnam's regional hegemonistic strategy is closely connected with Soviet global hegemonistic strategy. Vietnam needs political support and economic and military aid from the Soviet Union to conduct its aggression and expansion abroad while the Soviet Union uses Vietnam as a springboard to carry out its expansion in South Asia.[19]

At various times, past or present, the attacks upon Cuba and Israel as well as upon South Korea have been equally harsh. Some governments are ignored or dismissed because they are considered under Soviet or Vietnamese control: Afghanistan, Cambodia, and Laos. In East Asia, however, one fact cannot escape Beijing's attention. Whether other states are those it seeks to cultivate or those it opposes, they do not regard the PRC as a part of the Third World despite its lack of development. Rather, the PRC is seen as a big and neighboring state where nationalist tides run swiftly.

A final characteristic of the PRC's Third World policies is the retreat from sizable economic or military assistance. Despite some relatively small economic assistance programs advanced during a recent African trip by Premier Zhao Ziyang, there are no Tan-Zam railway projects under way or being contemplated. In part, this reflects the difficult economic problems faced by China today—but that was always the case. Of equal importance, the PRC—like other states—has discovered that when economic assistance is intended to purchase political dividends, the results are rarely satisfactory. The gains are generally short-range at best, as the Tan-Zam project itself has revealed. Chinese assistance to the Third World for the foreseeable future is likely to to be primarily in the realm of political support, reflective of its limited economic and military reach.

What are the conclusions to be drawn? In the spring of 1982, Premier Zhao Ziyang asserted: "China's foreign policy can be summed up in three sentences: strengthen unity and cooperation with the Third World countries; oppose hegemonism; and preserve world peace."[20]

Every national leader seeks to cast his nation's policies in the most favorable light, but Zhao's summarization is considerably more idealistic and less complex than the realities. For example, as indicated earlier, however satisfactory from an ideological-political standpoint, a policy placing primary emphasis on the Third World can satisfy neither the economic nor the security needs of China. Beyond this fact, such a policy is bound to harbor numerous contradictions and complexities, as the present policies of the PRC patently demonstrate. China is a backward nation in economic and military terms, but as just indicated, it is also a state that by virtue of its size and aspirations is regarded as a "major power" by its neighbors, most of whom treat it with some apprehension. Nor are the Chinese people especially drawn to other cultures and peoples, particularly those of Africa and the Arab world.

Opposition to hegemony is a laudable stance, a cause to which virtually every nation pays formal obeisance. In this connection, the PRC sometimes seems to be trying very hard to appear neutral in its attitude toward the two superpowers. Criticism is bestowed equally upon the United States and the Soviet Union as "hegemonists," with Chinese spokesmen avowing that the PRC will never pursue such a path (a pledge Hanoi is not alone in disbelieving). Yet China's basic interests are not all served by a policy of equidistance between Washington and Moscow—a fact readily acknowledged by PRC leaders. The primary security threat comes from the USSR in the eyes of Beijing, and there is no indication that this will change in the near future. Tension between these two massive neighbors—the last remaining great empires, forced to live cheek by jowl with each other—will ebb and flow, but it will not disappear in this century. Nor are China's economic interests promoted by equidistance. Whatever the benefits of Soviet assistance in the 1950s (and they were considerable), the PRC now wishes to turn to the more dynamic states leading the technological revolution—namely, Japan and the United States—to acquire advanced technology. China's developmental hopes and plans are geared to an ever-increasing economic interaction with these nations and with Western Europe. Naturally this influences cultural contacts as well.

These facts do not preclude a heightened element of universalism in Chinese foreign policy. Together with the effort to restore some normalcy to relations with the USSR, the PRC is seeking to reestablish or improve relations with various other Communist parties and states, proposing the principles of "peaceful coexistence" as the basis of a new relationship. Only a few states of the noncommunist world have been consigned to the category of pariahs by Beijing.

Whatever may be its contradictions, the present PRC foreign policy is more realistic, and hence, more in the national interest of China as defined by its leadership than at any time since 1949. The ideological quotient in this policy is strictly limited, and uniformly subordinate to other considerations. The nationalist quotient is very high and continues to mount. The traditionalist element is easily discerned, and it will remain. The recent shift from the briefly held united front policy of the late 1970s to the current position, while very important, was essentially a tactical shift. The united front policy was abandoned primarily because in the form enunciated, it was a high-cost, high-risk policy in both political and strategic terms. The present policy of tilted nonalignment is likely to endure for a much longer period because it provides flexibility and reach—with an acceptable level of costs and risks. Within the confines of this policy, adjustments will unquestionably occur on a more or less continuous basis, especially in China's relations with the United States and the USSR. But such adjustments will, in all probability, be tactical, not strategic. After considerable experimentation, a policy line has been reached that seems likely to serve PRC needs for a considerable span of time.

Notes

1. Mikoyan's trip to China has been discussed with me by both Russian and Chinese sources, although it has not been publicly revealed to my knowledge. The precise date is unclear, but it took place in early 1949, either January or February, and the meeting with Mao was at Shijiazhuang.

2. Discussions conducted in the USSR in 1979. A Soviet discussion of assistance to the Chinese Communists, written in the aftermath of the Sino-Soviet cleavage when a central target was Mao, can be found in O. B. Borisov and B. T. Koloskov, *Sino-Soviet Relations—1945–1973—A Brief History,* translated from Russian (Moscow, 1975).

3. Speeches by Mao and Zhou set the tone for this period at an early point. See the report by Mao at the 6 June 1950 meeting of the CCP Central Committee, in *Current Background,* Suppl. 1 (13 June 1950), p. 1, and the report by Zhou Enlai entitled "Fight for the Consolidation and Development of the Chinese People's Victory," delivered 30 September 1950, in *Current Background* 12, 5 October 1950, p. 2.

4. I conducted a series of interviews in the spring of 1981 with some PRC officials whose earlier careers had involved them in close interaction with the Soviet Union during the 1950–1960 period.

5. See the classic work by Donald S. Zagoria, *The Sino-Soviet Conflict—1956–1961* (Princeton, N.J.: Princeton University Press, 1962).

6. The Soviet version of the split has been given to various U.S. scholars orally, including myself, by M. S. Kapitsa who was personally involved, having gone to Beijing in the fall of 1958 with Gromyko as interpreter. Kapitsa has also written on the subject of early Soviet-PRC relations in his *Sovetsko-Kitaiskie Otnosheniia* [Soviet-Chinese relations] (Moscow: Gosudarstvennoe Izdatelstvo Politicheskoi Literatury, 1958). See also Mikhail I. Sladkovskii, *Istoriia torgovo—ekonomicheskikh otnoshenii SSSR s Kitaem, 1917–1974* [The history of trade and economic relations of the USSR with China, 1917–1974] (Moscow: Nauka, 1977).

For accounts by U.S. scholars, see A. Doak Barnett, *China and the Major Powers in East Asia* (Washington, D.C.: Brookings Institution, 1977); Harold C. Hinton, *China's Turbulent Quest,* rev. ed. (Bloomington: Indiana University Press, 1972); *Three and a Half Powers: The New Balance in Asia* (Bloomington: Indiana University Press, 1975); and A. D. Low, *The Sino-Soviet Dispute: An Analysis of the Polemics* (London: Associated University Press, 1976), among other works.

7. As examples, note the series of booklets translated into English from the *Zhongguo Jindaishi* [History of modern China], original ed. (Shanghai: Renmin Chubanshe, 1958). These booklets included *The Taiping Revolution, The Opium War, The Reform Movement of 1898, The Yi Ho Tuan Movement of 1900,* and *The Revolution of 1911.* All were compiled by members of the history departments of Fudan University and Shanghai Teachers' University.

8. See *China and the Asian-African Conference* (Documents) (Beijing: Foreign Languages Press, 1955) for key speeches and important resolutions.

9. For several interesting interpretations of this era, see Charles Neuhauser, *Third World Politics: China and the Afro-Asian People's Solidarity Organization—1957–1967* (Cambridge, Mass.: Harvard University Press, 1970); John D. Simmonds, *China's World: The Foreign Policy of A Developing State* (New York: Columbia University Press, 1970); Peter Van Ness, *Revolution and Chinese Foreign Policy: Peking's Support for Wars of National Liberation*

(Berkeley: University of California Press, 1971); and Wang Gungwu, *China and the World Since 1949* (New York: St. Martin's Press, 1977).

10. This episode is set forth in the author's *The Japanese Communist Movement—1920–1966* (Berkeley: University of California Press, 1967), pp. 266–272.

11. For details, see George T. Yu, *China's African Policy: A Study of Tanzania* (New York: Praeger, 1975), and Bruce D. Larkin, *China and Africa, 1949–1970: The Foreign Policy of the People's Republic of China* (Berkeley: University of California Press, 1971).

12. The memoirs written by Richard Nixon and Henry Kissinger are indispensable to understanding the U.S. perspective.

13. For a recent survey of selected issues in Chinese foreign policy from a PRC perspective, see Zhou Guo, ed., *China and the World* (1), *Beijing Review* Foreign Affairs Series (Beijing: *Beijing Review,* 1982).

A recent Western analysis of the PRC foreign policy process is that by Freeland Henry Carde III, *The Making of Chinese Foreign Policy: Actors and Processes* (Monterey, Calif.: Naval Postgraduate School, September 1979). See also Jonathan Pollack, *Security, Strategy and the Logic of Chinese Foreign Policy* (Berkeley: Institute of East Asian Studies, 1982), and my essay, "Foreign Policy," in *The People's Republic of China After Thirty Years: An Overview,* ed. Joyce K. Kallgren (Berkeley: Institute of East Asian Studies, Center for Chinese Studies, 1979). An interpretative essay by a prominent scholar is that of Tang Tsou, "China and the World in the Mao and Post-Mao Eras," in *The Many Faces of Communism,* ed. Morton Kaplan (New York: The Free Press, 1978).

In the Chinese language, see Chen Tiqiang, "On the Issue of U.S. Arms Sales to Taiwan from the Viewpoint of International Law," *Renmin Ribao* (5 February 1982), p. 1; Zhang Dezhen, "The Evolution and Contradictions of the Reagan Administration's Middle East Policy," ibid. (19 March 1982), p. 1; Zhang Yebai, "The Contradictions of the Reagan Administration's Foreign Policy," ibid. (31 July 1982), p. 1; and Jin Junhui, "The Foreign Policy of the Reagan Government," *Journal of International Studies,* no. 1, 1982.

14. For several recent works dealing with the Soviet role in Asia, see Allen S. Whiting, *Siberian Development and East Asia—Threat or Promise?* (Stanford, Calif.: Stanford University Press, 1981), and Donald S. Zagoria, ed., *Soviet Policy in Asia* (New Haven, Conn.: Yale University Press, 1982). See also an interesting monograph by Banning N. Garrett and Bonnie S. Glaser, *War and Peace: The Views from Moscow and Beijing* (Berkeley: Institute of International Studies, 1984). In addition, a very useful compilation entitled *Sino-Soviet Competition in Asia* is being published on a semiannual basis by the Defense Intelligence Agency, Washington, D.C.

In the Chinese language, see Shu Gang, "The Nature of the Expansionist Strategy of Soviet Hegemonism," *Guoji Wenti Yanjiu* [*Journal of International Studies*] (20 February 1982), p. 1; Xi Linsheng, "Western Technology Has Armed the Soviet Union," ibid. (9 February 1982), p. 1; and Li Huichuan, "The Crux of the Sino-Soviet Boundary Question," ibid., no. 1, 1981.

15. These quotations are taken from "New Polemics Break Out Over Soviet-American Nuclear Talks," a commentary broadcast in Mandarin for domestic consumption, Beijing, 12 April 1982, in *Foreign Broadcast Information Service (FBIS) Daily Report—China* (13 April 1982), pp. A1–2. Numerous similar statements are to be found in current PRC media reports.

16. See, for example, the article by Zhai Xiangqian in *Renmin Ribao* (15 June 1982), entitled "From Versailles to Bonn," p. 7.

17. For the remarks of Ling Qing, PRC representative to the United Nations Security Council, on 29 March 1982, see *FBIS, Daily Report—China* (30 March 1982), p. A1.

18. Geng Biao's speech is carried in ibid. (21 June 1982), pp. D1–5; the partial quotation is from p. D3.

19. Commentary by Ya Ming, "Can the DRV-USSR Alliance Be Broken Up?" Beijing radio in Mandarin, 3 April 1982, in ibid. (6 April 1982), pp. E2–3; the quoted passage is from p. E2.

20. These remarks were made during a talk with the Guinea-Bissau head of state on 19 April 1982 and were carried in the Beijing journal *Ban Yue Tan* [*Biweekly Talk*] 12

(25 June 1982), reproduced in ibid. (2 July 1982), pp. A1–4; the quotation is from p. A1. Regarding the second point, Zhao stated (quoted on p. A4):

> China lays particular emphasis on opposition to Soviet hegemonism, and at the same time she also opposes U.S. hegemonism. The foreign policy pursued by China is principled and means acting independently and keeping the initiative in her own hands. As everyone knows, the United States has consistently supported the racist regime in South Africa, and stubbornly supports Israel in the Middle East, thus being antagonistic toward the African and Arab peoples. The United States supports the reactionary forces in Latin America and opposes the local nationalist and democratic movements there. The United States refuses to withdraw its troops from South Korea and hampers the peaceful reunification of Korea. As regards China, the United States is still selling arms to Taiwan and violating our country's sovereignty. We resolutely oppose the pursuit of hegemonism by anyone in any place. We consistently support all countries endangered by hegemonism.

8
The Foreign Policy of the PRC Since 1949: A Critical Analysis

Liang-ts'ai Wei

Introduction: Components of the Foreign Policy

More than three decades have passed since the founding of the People's Republic of China on 1 October 1949. During these thirty-odd years, the PRC has witnessed some drastic changes, both in its domestic politics and in its international relations. The foreign policy of the PRC has attracted considerable attention and speculation from Western specialists, as attested to by the many books and articles on the subject.

In dealing with the PRC's foreign policy, some Western specialists are apt to emphasize ideological elements at the expense of realistic elements (such as economic development, national security, and international legitimacy) or vice versa. In reality, the PRC's foreign policy, like that of any other country, has consisted of three basic components: basic strategy, fundamental goals, and the means to achieve the goals.

Basic Strategy: United Front Doctrine

Although scholars dealing with the PRC's foreign policy have used various approaches and reached different conclusions, most of them have shared at least one common view: Mao Tse-tung played a vital, if not the sole, role in decision making about the PRC's foreign policy until his death. As for basic strategy, suffice it to say that the united front doctrine, modified and brought to maturity by Mao during the Chinese civil war in the 1930s and 1940s, became the backbone of the PRC's diplomatic strategy during the next three decades.[1]

Although the original concept of the united front doctrine can be traced back to the international Communist movement in the 1920s, it was modified by Mao to fit the situation in China. He concisely defined the united front strategy as "to make use of contradictions, win over the many, oppose the few, and crush our enemies one by one."[2] Mao further divided "contradictions" and "enemies" into two different levels: principal and secondary. By doing so, he gave the united front strategy both flexibility and maneuverability.

For four decades, beginning with his rise within the Chinese Communist party (CCP) until his death in 1976, Mao never ceased using "unite and struggle" tactics, the essence of the united front strategy, in his power struggles with his enemies in the CCP or in the CCP's life-or-death fight with the Kuomintang. After 1949 Mao also applied these same tactics in conducting the PRC's foreign relations.

Fundamental Goals

The PRC has a set of fundamental goals to be achieved through the execution of its foreign policy. They include: (1) protecting the socialist revolution at home and promoting socialism of the orthodox Marxist-Leninist-Maoist type in the international arena;[3] (2) maintaining a healthy and balanced economic development; (3) safeguarding national security; and (4) improving the country's international status. If the last three are lumped together, they can be called "the national interest." Thus, contrary to the viewpoints of some specialists, the PRC's foreign policy is characterized by a "national interest-ideology" dichotomy.[4]

Means to Achieve the Goals

In the past three decades, the PRC has used several alternate means to achieve its fundamental goals: (1) military force (such as intervention in the Korean War and the 1962 Sino-Indian border war); (2) economic aid (mainly to the Afro-Asian countries in the Third World); (3) negotiations (principally with the United States and the Soviet Union); (4) overt subversion (in some of the African countries whose governments were hostile to Peking, such as Zaire during the 1960s); and (5) covert infiltration (mostly in Afro-Asian countries whose governments were lukewarm, but not necessarily hostile, to Peking).

One needs an overall understanding of the framework of the PRC's foreign policy as outlined above to better perceive the rationale of the regime's international behavior since 1949. In this paper, the development of PRC foreign policy will be divided into three phases and analyzed accordingly.

Phase One (1949–1960)

In phase one, the PRC's foreign policy underscored two facts: first, an irreconcilable mutual distrust and hostility between the PRC and the United States continued following the Chinese civil war; and second, the PRC's warm friendship with and its dependence on the Soviet Union over the same period. The PRC's attitude toward the Soviet Union was clearly stated in Mao's famous slogan "lean to one side," proclaimed on 30 June 1949 when celebrating the twenty-eighth anniversary of the founding of the CCP:

> "You are leaning to one side." Exactly . . . all Chinese without exception must lean either to the side of imperialism or to the side of socialism.

> Sitting on the fence will not do, nor is there a third road. . . . Internationally, we belong to the side of the anti-imperialist front headed by the Soviet Union, and so we can turn only to this side for genuine and friendly help, not to the side of the imperialist front.[5]

Two-and-a-half months after the establishment of the Chinese Communist regime, Mao visited Moscow and asked Joseph Stalin for the "genuine and friendly help" he needed. A thirty-year Treaty of Friendship, Alliance, and Mutual Assistance, signed by the PRC and the Soviet Union on 14 February 1950, resulted from this visit. Both sides agreed that if either were "attacked by Japan or any state allied with it," the other would "immediately render military and other assistance by all means at its disposal." Thus, the pact apparently was directed against both Japan and the United States.[6] Moscow further provided Peking with a credit of US $300 million, an amount much less than what Mao expected. Before leaving for home, Mao forecast a roseate future for the alliance with Moscow:

> All see that the solidarity of the Great Chinese and Soviet peoples, consolidated by the Treaty, is durable, unbreakable, and steadfast. This solidarity will inevitably influence not only the well-being of the great powers China and the Soviet Union, but also the future of all humanity and will lead to the victory of justice and peace throughout the whole world.[7]

History was to prove how false and ironic his prediction was. By signing the alliance pact with Moscow, Mao thus formalized his "lean to one side" policy. During the next decade, this policy did not change, at least officially.

Prior to the 1955 Bandung Conference, Peking appeared on the world stage only infrequently, and then usually as one of Moscow's protégés. During the first six years of its existence, the PRC showed little interest in the outside world. Its main goals were domestic: to tighten control over the Chinese people, to strengthen the new regime, and, finally, to conquer Taiwan, the last stronghold of the rival ROC government. The PRC's involvement in external affairs was confined mostly to its closest neighbors, as in its large-scale participation in the Korean War and its much more limited involvement in the Vietnamese war.[8]

As the PRC consolidated its domestic position and acquired more self-confidence at home, signs began to appear that its passive attitude in foreign policy would change. Doubts about the suitability of Soviet economic policies as models for China's economic development were accompanied by incipient doubts about the congruity of Soviet and Chinese national interests in foreign policy. Peking's prestige abroad was increased significantly by its participation in both the Korean armistice negotiations at Panmunjom in 1951–1953 and the 1954 Geneva Conference that ended French colonial rule in Indochina. These events soon led to a new era in which Peking became actively involved in events in various parts of the world.

The Bandung Conference was one of the turning points in the PRC's foreign policy.[9] Unlike the conferences on Korea and Indochina, the conference at Bandung gave clear indications that the PRC's interest in more distant countries was expanding and might eventually conflict with Soviet interests.

The PRC made the most of the Bandung opportunity by sending a delegation headed by its second-highest official, Premier Chou En-lai, whose moderate and conciliatory attitude enabled him not only to eclipse India's Jawaharlal Nehru as the leader of the conference, but also to allay the apprehensions of noncommunist delegations toward the PRC's ambitions in other countries. Chou presented the PRC as a reasonable and peace-loving nation, and later reported to his colleagues in Peking that "China and many Asian and African countries had established preliminary mutual understandings as a result of direct contacts during the Asian-African Conference."[10] However, the PRC's seemingly moderate and reasonable attitude was soon to change due to both external and internal factors.

In early October 1957, the Soviets sent up "Sputnik," the first man-made satellite. Shortly afterward, Peking signed a nuclear agreement with Moscow under which the latter was to provide the technical know-how for making atomic weapons. In early November Mao led a delegation to Moscow to celebrate the fortieth anniversary of the Bolshevik Revolution. While in Moscow, Mao delivered an address before Chinese students in the Soviet Union on 18 November 1957 in which he made the famous remark, "The east wind is prevailing over the west wind. That is to say, the forces of socialism are overwhelmingly superior to the forces of imperialism."[11]

The second half of the 1950s also witnessed the intensification of relations between the PRC and the United States, due to the two Taiwan Strait crises in 1955 and 1958. Although the crisis in January 1955 was a direct reaction to the Mutual Defense Treaty signed by the United States and the ROC in early December 1954, the 1958 crisis was planned by the PRC to provide an outlet for the internal discontent and pressure produced by the failure of the Great Leap Forward. In both crises the United States committed itself to the protection of Taiwan and the Pescadores, but the Soviet Union gave the PRC only lukewarm verbal support. Peking was angered by Washington's support of the ROC; it was even more incensed by Moscow's lack of fraternal enthusiasm.[12]

Domestically, the last two years of the 1950s were not rosy for the PRC. During this period, deep-seated conflicts gradually emerged between the two factions of senior PRC officials. The internal dispute was basically between the ideologues led by Mao and the pragmatists led by Liu Shao-ch'i. These factions held different views regarding both the methods and rapidity of collectivization in agriculture, and also regarding the relative importance of ideological purity ("Red") and pragmatic competence ("expert") in economic planning, training, and development.

The ideologically motivated Second Five-Year Plan, inaugurated by Mao in 1958 under the grandiloquent slogan of a "Great Leap Forward" to surpass the Soviet Union, was a disastrous failure. Soviet criticism of Mao's economic blunders and pretensions to ideological leadership of the Communist world was matched by Chinese criticism of both the Soviet repudiation of Stalinist policies and the Soviet advocacy of "peaceful coexistence" with the West. Although Sino-Soviet disagreement had been building since the Twentieth Congress of the Communist party of the Soviet Union (CPSU) in 1956, it was not publicized in open polemics until 1960. However, by late 1959, the PRC's policy toward the Soviet Union was ready to change.

In retrospect, the Bandung Conference can be seen as an early hint of the PRC's attitude that the developing nations of Asia and Africa had a greater community of interests with the PRC, the largest and most populous of the developing nations, than with the industrially advanced Soviet Union or the United States. This attitude, however, was not fully developed until much later. Moreover, during the first five years after Bandung, the PRC continued to be more concerned with its own development than with activities elsewhere.

Phase Two (1960–1969)

At the outset of this period, the ideological polemics between Peking and Moscow intensified and relations between the two degenerated rather rapidly. They were ready to lock horns. In mid-April 1960, *Red Flag,* the CCP's main theoretical journal, printed a long article entitled "Long Live Leninism." The article severely condemned the Soviet Union for abandoning Leninist principles and for adopting a revisionist line.[13] Moscow believed that the article was written by Mao himself. It symbolized the beginning of a long and bitter ideological polemic between the two Communist giants.

On 20 June 1960 at the Third Congress of the Romanian Workers' party in Bucharest, which was attended by twelve Communist parties, Nikita S. Khrushchev openly accused the Chinese Communists of being "mad, Left-adventurist, and pseudo-revolutionary," and he warned that "only lunatics and maniacs can now come out with appeals for a new world war."[14] P'eng Chen, a CCP Politburo member and head of the Chinese delegation, took his turn at the podium the next day. He reiterated the Chinese position for the support of world revolutionary movements and called for a strong stand against imperialism.[15] Shortly after the conference, the Soviet Union recalled all its technicians and experts from China.[16]

However, as far as the PRC's Soviet policy was concerned, evidence indicated that as late as mid-1961 there was still disagreement among the top-ranking leaders in the CCP. On 30 June 1961, at a rally in celebration of the fortieth anniversary of the CCP, Liu Shao-ch'i stated that the first of the three guiding principles of the CCP's foreign policy was "to develop relations of friendship, mutual assistance and cooperation with the Soviet Union and other fraternal socialist countries."[17] Because of his sympathetic attitude toward Khrushchev, Liu later was denounced as "China's Khrushchev" in the power struggle with Mao.

Between 1961 and 1964, several events took place that were to have repercussions on both Sino-Soviet relations and the world situation. In October 1962, the long-standing Sino-Indian territorial dispute erupted into a full-fledged border war. Chinese Communist troops staged massive attacks along the McMahon Line and occupied all of the disputed territory in Kashmir. Almost concurrently, the discovery of Soviet missiles in Cuba forced President John F. Kennedy to have a showdown with Khrushchev. Khrushchev's decision to keep neutral in the Sino-Indian conflict (while both Great Britain and the United States aided India) and to withdraw the missiles from Cuba convinced Mao that Moscow was willing to sacrifice Communist brotherhood for peaceful coexistence with the imperialists.

In early 1963 the ideological arguments between the CCP and the CPSU began building up in both frequency and strength. Among the numerous letters between the two parties, two are especially enlightening. The contents of these two letters reveal that the ideological conflict between the two parties was too strong to be overcome through a limited concession. In a letter sent to the Central Committee of the CCP on 30 March 1963, the Central Committee of the CPSU defended Khrushchev's efforts toward peaceful coexistence:

> The policy of peaceful coexistence accords with the vital interests of all the peoples; it serves to strengthen the positions of socialism, to help the international influence of the socialist countries, and to increase the authority and influence of the Communists.[18]

In reply, the Central Committee of the CCP sent a long letter on 14 June 1963. The letter was full of Mao's "united front" jargon. From the CCP's point of view:

> . . . the general line [of the international Communist movement at the present stage] is one of forming a broad united front, with the socialist camp and the international proletariat as its nucleus, to oppose the imperialists and reactionaries headed by the United States; it is a line of boldly arousing the masses, expanding (developing) the revolutionary forces, winning over the middle forces and isolating the reactionary forces.[19]

The Chinese then warned:

> If the general line of the international Communist movement is one-sidedly reduced to "peaceful coexistence," "peaceful competition" and "peaceful

> transition," this is . . . to discard the historical mission of proletarian world revolution and to depart from the revolutionary teachings of Marxism-Leninism.[20]

As this ideological polemic was dragging on, the Soviet Union signed a nuclear test-ban treaty with Great Britain and the United States in Moscow on 25 July 1963. The pact intensified the PRC's fear that the Soviet Union was ready to reach an all-out compromise with the imperialists. Peking bitterly denounced the treaty as "a big fraud to fool the people of the world," through which the three nuclear powers were attempting "to consolidate their nuclear monopoly and bind the hands of all the peace-loving countries subjected to the nuclear threat."[21] Behind this bitter denunciation lay Peking's fear of Soviet-U.S. encirclement of China with nuclear weapons or even a "preemptive" attack upon China by the Soviet Union. The PRC's response was the decision to pursue a much more assertive and independent foreign policy as well as an intense drive to develop its own nuclear technology, which led to the first PRC atomic explosion on 16 October 1964.[22]

Thus, by late 1963, the PRC decided to apply Mao's united front strategy to win over Afro-Asian countries as well as to reassign Moscow's role in the scheme. Between mid-December 1963 and early February 1964, Premier Chou En-lai, accompanied by an impressive entourage numbering more than fifty, including Foreign Minister Ch'en I and ten other high-ranking officials, took a fifty-four day tour in which they visited ten African countries.[23] Visits between the PRC officials and those of nonaligned Asian countries such as Burma, Indonesia, Laos, and North Vietnam also increased.

The concept of an "intermediate zone" played an important role in the forming of Mao's united front strategy. It was first mentioned by Mao in August 1946 in an interview with the U.S. correspondent Anna Louise Strong, a Communist herself. In answer to Strong's question about the possibility that the United States might start a war against the Soviet Union, Mao said:

> The United States and the Soviet Union are separated by a vast zone which includes many capitalist, colonial, and semi-colonial countries in Europe, Asia, and Africa. Before the U.S. reactionaries have subjugated these countries, an attack on the Soviet Union is out of the question. . . . I believe it won't be long before these countries come to realize who is really oppressing them, the Soviet Union or the United States. The day will come when the U.S. reactionaries find themselves opposed by the people of the whole world.[24]

The exclusively anti-U.S. interpretation of the concept was maintained by the PRC until the Sino-Soviet split developed. The "intermediate zone" was then redefined in an important editorial in the *Jen-min Jih-*

pao or *JMJP* (*People's Daily*), official newspaper of the CCP, on 21 January 1964:

> The vast intermediate zone is composed of two parts. One part consists of the independent countries and those striving for independence in Asia, Africa, and Latin America, and may be called the first intermediate zone. The second part consists of the whole of Western Europe, Australia, Canada, and other capitalist countries, and may be called the second intermediate zone.[25]

According to this reinterpretation, countries in the second intermediate zone were said to have a dual character, exploiting and oppressing colonial peoples as they themselves were being exploited and bullied by the United States. Like the colonial states, they also wished to be free from U.S. control. This reinterpretation became the theme of a new Peking policy toward countries in the intermediate zone.

The more striking part of the 1964 interpretation, however, was the portrayal of the Soviet Union not as the head of the socialist camp and protector of intermediate zone countries, but as a sinister co-conspirator with the United States in the crime of oppressing and exploiting all countries in the two intermediate zones. As the *JMJP* expressed it:

> The Soviet leaders' hopes for U.S.-Soviet cooperation to dominate the world are but idle dreams. By undermining the unity of the socialist camp, the Soviet leaders violate the interests of the people of the Soviet Union and all other socialist countries and cater to the needs of U.S. imperialism.[26]

In other words, the intermediate zone was no longer a buffer between the Soviet Union and the United States, but an area where a united front could be formed between various socialist countries and the countries in the two intermediate zones. The struggle against both U.S. imperialism and Soviet revisionism would be led by Peking.

In 1965, a new ingredient was added to Peking's world revolution strategy. On September 3, the occasion of the "20th Anniversary of Victory in the Chinese People's War of Resistance Against Japan," the *JMJP* published an article entitled "Long Live the Victory of People's War!" written by Lin Piao, vice-chairman of the Central Committee of the CCP and minister of national defense. In the article, Lin glorified Mao's theory of and policies for people's war developed by Mao during the War of Resistance Against Japan. He emphasized particularly Mao's "thought on the establishment of rural base areas and the use of the countryside to encircle the cities and finally capture them."[27]

Then Lin stretched Mao's theory and related it to the contemporary world situation:

> It must be emphasized that Comrade Mao Tse-tung's theory of the establishment of rural revolutionary base areas and the encirclement of the

> cities from the countryside is of outstanding and universal practical importance for the present revolutionary struggles of all the oppressed nations and peoples, and particularly for the revolutionary struggles of the oppressed nations and peoples in Asia, Africa and Latin America against imperialism and its lackeys.
>
> Taking the entire globe, if North America and Western Europe can be called "the cities of the world," then Asia, Africa, and Latin America constitute "the rural areas of the world." . . . In a sense, the contemporary world revolution also presents a picture of the encirclement of cities by the rural areas. In the final analysis, the whole cause of world revolution hinges on the revolutionary struggles of the Asian, African and Latin American peoples who make up the overwhelming majority of the world's population. The socialist countries should regard it as their international duty to support the people's revolutionary struggles in Asia, Africa, and Latin America.[28]

Despite Peking's ideological and diplomatic thrust, the united front between the PRC and the selected countries in the two intermediate zones as visualized by Peking never materialized. The second half of the 1960s was not rosy for the PRC. Unprecedented internal turmoil was soon to sweep over the whole country. None of the internal events that occurred since 1949 had such a profound effect on the PRC's foreign relations as would the domestic upheaval in China from 1966 to 1969, known euphemistically as the Great Proletarian Cultural Revolution.

The chaotic Cultural Revolution affected every aspect of life in the PRC; the educational and political systems were paralyzed, economic development was interrupted, foreign policy was hindered, and relations with many countries deteriorated. Peking's foreign policy during the Cultural Revolution was affected by a wave of strong xenophobia, nationalism, and ethnocentrism reminiscent of the short-lived Boxer Rebellion in 1900. Normal and appropriate functions of the foreign affairs system were disrupted and paralyzed by juvenile Red Guards as they attempted to seize the decision-making power of the foreign ministry. The Red Guards completely paralyzed the regular operations of the ministry by criticizing Ch'en I and his vice-ministers, beating up guards, breaking open files, and ransacking documents.[29]

In December 1966, Peking began calling its ambassadors home to be "reeducated" and to answer charges levied against them by Red Guards. By late 1967, forty-five of the forty-six PRC ambassadors had returned home. Only Huang Hua, ambassador to Cairo, remained at his post. All other PRC embassies around the world were headed by charges d'affaires.[30] The Cultural Revolution and its aftermath had very negative effects on PRC relations with many Third World and other countries. Peking's relations with Afghanistan, Cambodia, Ceylon, Indonesia, Burma, Nepal, Sweden, Switzerland, Algeria, Kenya, and Tunisia deteriorated rapidly. By September 1967, Peking had been involved in incidents of varying degrees with thirty-two nations.[31]

By August 1968, the consequences of the Cultural Revolution were so devastating that even Mao and his radical followers were ready to put an end to it. On 18 August 1968, the second anniversary of the Red Guards, an editorial in the official *JMJP* said that "the Red Guards can have a sound future and carry the current great proletarian cultural revolution through to the end only by integrating themselves with the main force, the workers, peasants, and soldiers, armed with Mao Tse-tung's thought." What this opaque language meant was that the Red Guards were actually to be disbanded and sent to do manual labor on farms (the schools were still closed). Even Mao now agreed that they had gone too far. Two days later, the Soviet invasion of Czechoslovakia gave the PRC leaders a new and urgent reason to terminate the disorders of the Cultural Revolution. Like the Western powers, the PRC denounced the Soviet action, although its reasons were different.[32]

Peking's strong condemnation of the Soviet invasion reflected its fear of a similar invasion. On 2 March 1969, Chinese and Soviet forces clashed on tiny Chenpao (Damansky) Island in the Ussuri River between Khabarovsk and Vladivostok, with considerable loss of life. The incident forced the PRC to readjust its policy toward both the Soviet Union and the United States.

Phase Three (1969–1979)

The Ninth National Congress of the CCP, which was opened in conditions of strict secrecy in Peking on 1 April 1969, constituted one of the turning points in PRC history. It symbolized not only the end of the worst excesses of the Cultural Revolution but also the peak of revolutionary zealotry in PRC foreign policy. It was at this congress that Lin Piao was officially designated as Mao's "close comrade-in-arms and successor." Lin delivered a long report acclaiming the Cultural Revolution as a great success. He also reaffirmed PRC support for revolutionary struggles in Asia, Africa, and Latin America, as well as the "masses of the black people of the United States in their just struggle against the U.S. ruling clique."[33]

Despite its militant anti-U.S. rhetoric, the PRC was ready to change its U.S. policy. Admittedly this change of policy was brought about to a great extent by the acute military threat from the Soviet Union. After the clash on Chenpao Island, several more border conflicts took place; the most serious occurred in August at the Dzungarian Gate in Sinkiang.[34] Furthermore, the Russians deliberately hinted at the possibility of a preemptive nuclear strike.[35]

Considering the imminent danger posed by the Soviet Union, Mao conceded the necessity of changing the format of his united front strategy regarding both Moscow and Washington. He found a willing partner in President Richard M. Nixon. However, the PRC improved its relations with the United States rather cautiously and with pretentious reluctance.

Despite some diplomatic gestures, such as the continuation of the Warsaw talks in January 1970, the visit of the U.S. ping-pong team in April 1971, Kissinger's secret trip to Peking in July 1971, and finally President Nixon's visit to China in February 1972, the PRC's basically anti-U.S. stand remained the same.

Early in this interval of time, on 20 May 1970, Mao issued a statement entitled "People of the World, Unite and Defeat the U.S. Aggressors and All Their Running Dogs," to support Laos, North Vietnam, and Cambodia, as well as black people of the United States. Mao criticized the United States openly:

> Ever since World War II, U.S. imperialism and its followers have been continuously launching wars of aggression. . . . While massacring the people in other countries, U.S. imperialism is slaughtering the white and black people in its own country. Nixon's fascist atrocities have kindled the raging flames of the revolutionary mass movement in the United States. The Chinese people firmly support the revolutionary struggle of the American people. . . . The Chinese people firmly support the people of the three Indo-Chinese countries and of other countries of the world in their revolutionary struggles against U.S. imperialism and its lackeys. U.S. imperialism, which looks like a huge monster, is in essence a paper tiger, now in the throes of its death-bed struggle.[36]

In September 1971, the Lin Piao affair came as a shock to almost all observers in and out of China. Lin Piao reportedly planned an armed counterrevolutionary coup d'etat to assassinate Mao and to seize power. After his plan failed, Lin, his wife, and several of his closest associates boarded a plane in an attempt to flee to the Soviet Union. The plane crashed at Undur Khan in Outer Mongolia on September 13 under mysterious circumstances, and all of the passengers were killed. Lin Piao, who had been officially designated as Mao's "close comrade-in-arms and successor," was posthumously denounced as a "bourgeois careerist, conspirator, double-dealer, renegade, and traitor."[37]

After Lin Piao's purge, Chou En-lai returned to being second in rank after Mao within the CCP hierarchy. Contrary to the generally held impression that he was a moderate, Chou's stand on the PRC's foreign policy was as revolutionary as that of Mao. After the PRC entered the United Nations, Chou spoke bluntly in an interview with the British reporter Neville Maxwell in November 1971:

> On the part of using the contradiction between the United States and the Soviet Union as a whole and the intermediate zones, the major aim of Communist China is to raise the slogan of anti-imperialism and anti-superpowers with a view to forming a Peiping-centered proletarian international front by uniting the middle and small size countries of the Third World and to keep the United States and the Soviet Union as our deadly enemies.[38]

In early 1974, a new concept—Three Worlds Theory—was added to Peking's global revolutionary strategy. The Three Worlds Theory was soon to replace that of the two intermediate zones to become the essence of the PRC's world revolutionary strategy as well as its foreign policy jargon. Both Soviet and PRC sources attributed the theory to Mao himself.[39] However, it was Teng Hsiao-p'ing, the newly reinstated vice-premier, who popularized the term. In a speech delivered at the Sixth Special Session of the UN General Assembly on 9 April 1974, Teng stated:

> Judging from the changes in international relations, the world today actually consists of three parts, or three worlds, that are both interconnected with and in contradiction to one another. The United States and the Soviet Union make up the First World. The developing countries in Asia, Africa, Latin America and other regions make up the Third World. The developed countries between the two make up the Second World.
>
> The two superpowers, the United States and the Soviet Union, are vainly seeking world hegemony; each in its own way attempts to bring the developing countries of Asia, Africa and Latin America under its control and, at the same time, to bully the developed countries that are not their match in strength.
>
> The two superpowers are the biggest international exploiters and oppressors of today. They are the source of a new world war. . . . China is a socialist country, and a developing country as well. China belongs to the Third World. Consistently following Chairman Mao's teachings, the Chinese Government and people firmly support all oppressed peoples and oppressed nations in their struggle to win or defend national independence, develop the national economy and oppose colonialism, imperialism and hegemonism.[40]

Comparing the two concepts, one finds that the Three Worlds Theory adds nothing new to the old global revolutionary strategy of the two intermediate zones of a decade earlier.

In the second half of the 1970s, a series of changes took place in the power structure of the CCP. These changes were brought about by the deaths of Chou and Mao. Chou died in January 1976. Mao appointed the formerly obscure Hua Kuo-feng as premier and on the same day removed Teng Hsiao-p'ing, a protégé of Chou, from all his posts both inside and outside the party—three years after his reinstatement.[41] Mao died on 9 September 1976. With both Mao and Chou gone, the stage was set for new rounds of power struggle that saw the purge of the Gang of Four, the comeback once again of Teng, and the ouster of Hua—a process the detailed description of which is beyond the scope of this paper.

As far as PRC foreign policy was concerned, no drastic changes took place before the end of the decade. Although Peking normalized its relations with Washington in January 1979, the PRC's basic world revolution strategy remained the same as it was during the 1960s: Form a united front with the Third World countries to struggle against the two hegemonic superpowers, the United States and the Soviet Union.

Prospects for the 1980s

As the decade of the eighties moves onward, there is no indication that the PRC will change its foreign policy outlined by Mao in the mid-1960s. One explanation of this phenomenon is the fact that Teng Hsiao-p'ing still directs the foreign policy of the PRC. No Chinese Communist leader of the first generation dares to totally discard Mao's legacy lest he jeopardize his own political future. On several occasions, Teng has reaffirmed that the PRC would follow the foreign policy outlined by Mao. On 16 January 1980, Teng stated at the cadres meeting held by the Central Committee of the CCP that the first of the three major tasks for the PRC in the eighties was "to oppose hegemonism and support world peace on the international front."[42]

Less than three months later, in a conversation with Zambian President Kenneth Kaunda on April 12, Teng said: "We uphold the three worlds theory advanced by Chairman Mao. China will always remain a member of the third world; it will never pursue hegemonism, and it will always uphold proletarian internationalism and firmly oppose hegemonism."[43]

Now, several years after Teng's statement, Mao's Three Worlds Theory and united front strategy as reinterpreted and expanded by Teng still serve as guidelines for PRC foreign policy. The content of the PRC's foreign policy statements since 1980 substantiates the presumption that Peking still regards the Soviet Union and the United States, in that order, as the two major enemies in its world revolutionary strategy. Antihegemony will probably remain the central feature of the PRC's foreign policy during the rest of this decade.

Notes

1. For a detailed description of relationships between the united front doctrine and the development of the Chinese Communist party, see L. P. Van Slyke, *Enemies and Friends: The United Front in Chinese Communist History* (Stanford, Calif., 1967).

2. Mao Tse-tung, "On Policy," in *Selected Works of Mao Tse-tung,* 5 vols., hereafter cited as *Selected Works* (Peking, 1969), vol. 2, p. 289.

3. In their book *China Under Threat: The Politics of Strategy and Diplomacy* (Baltimore, 1981), Melvin Gurtov and Byong-Moo Hwang state that "the chief purpose of foreign policy in China is to protect and promote the radical socialist revolution at home" (p. 17). However, in this author's opinion, as far as ideology is concerned, PRC foreign policy tries to achieve more than this.

4. J. D. Armstrong, a U.S. specialist on PRC foreign policy, denies that national interest plays a significant role in the process of foreign policymaking. He indicates that the "national interest-ideology" dichotomy is a false one and that "it is particularly inapplicable when the ideology under consideration is Marxism-Leninism." See his *Revolutionary Diplomacy: Chinese Foreign Policy and the United Front Doctrine* (Berkeley, Los Angeles, and London, 1977), p. 4.

5. Mao Tse-tung, "On the People's Democratic Dictatorship," *Selected Works* (Peking, 1969), vol. 4, pp. 415, 417. As a matter of fact, Liu Shao-ch'i, another top-ranking leader

in the CCP, expressed the same theme a year earlier than Mao. After Tito was expelled from the Cominform, Liu wrote in 1948 that "if one is not in the imperialist camp . . . then one must be in the anti-imperialist camp. . . . To remain neutral or sitting on the fence is impossible . . . so-called neutrality . . . is nothing but deception, international or otherwise." See Liu Shao-ch'i, *Internationalism and Nationalism,* 3rd ed. (Peking, 1952), pp. 32–33.

6. O. Edmund Clubb, *China and Russia: The "Great Game"* (New York and London, 1971), p. 383; Yin Ching-yao, *Chung-kung Wai-chiao yu Tui-wai Kuan-hsi* [Communist Chinese foreign policy and foreign relations] (Taipei, 1973), p. 25; and A. Doak Barnett, *China and the Major Powers in East Asia* (Washington, D.C., 1977), pp. 25–26. For the text of the treaty, see *Sino-Soviet Treaty and Agreements* (Peking, 1951), pp. 5–8.

7. *Izvestiya,* 18 February 1950, quoted in Clubb, *China and Russia,* p. 385.

8. According to Gurtov and Hwang, the PRC's involvement in Korea was a response to the threat to its national security as well as the domestic need to mobilize the people for production. Thus, they maintain that "China's Korean War decision was influenced by and in turn affected its domestic affairs." See *China Under Threat,* p. 25.

9. The Bandung Conference of twenty-nine Asian and African nations, meeting from 18 to 24 April 1955, was organized by Indonesia, Burma, Ceylon, India, and Pakistan to oppose colonialism in Asia and Africa. One independent African country (South Africa) was not invited, as well as the Soviet Union, by far the largest Asian country.

10. Chou En-Lai, "Report on the Asian-African Conference," *China and the Asian-African Conference* (Peking, 1955), pp. 50, 52–53. This was his report to the Standing Committee of the National People's Congress on 13 May 1955.

11. Interestingly enough, the true meaning of the remark was to become controversial as relations between Moscow and Peking deteriorated. See Clubb, *China and Russia,* p. 421 and note 12 of ch. 30 (p. 546).

12. For a more complete treatment of the two Taiwan Strait crises, see Kwan Ha Yim, ed., *China & the U.S. 1955–63* (New York, 1973), chs. 1 and 5 (pp. 5–28, 83–114).

13. Irwin Isenberg, ed., *The Russian-Chinese Rift; Its Impact on World Affairs* (New York, 1966), pp. 154–155; Barnett, *China and the Major Powers in East Asia,* p. 39; Clubb, *China and Russia,* pp. 440–441. For the text of the article, see *Red Flag,* no. 8 (16 April 1960). Much has been published about the Sino-Soviet split; a convenient summary is *The Sino-Soviet Dispute: Keesing's Research Report 3* (New York, 1969).

14. Tuan Chia-feng, "Schism in International Communist Movement," *Issues and Studies* 18:1 (January 1982), p. 70; Isenberg, *The Russian-Chinese Rift,* p. 29; Clubb, *China and Russia,* p. 21. For the full text of Khrushchev's speech, see *Current Digest of the Soviet Press* (hereafter cited as *CDSP*) 12:25 (20 July 1960), pp. 3–9.

15. For the text of P'eng Chen's speech, see *CDSP* 12:26 (27 July 1960), pp. 11–12.

16. According to the PRC's own account, the Soviet Union withdrew 1,390 experts working in the PRC, tore up 343 contracts and supplementary contracts, and canceled 257 projects for scientific and technical cooperation. See *Kuan-yü Kuo-chi Kung-ch'an-chu'yi Yün-tung Tsung-lu-hsien te Lun-chan* [Polemics on the general line of the international communist movement], (Peking, 1965), pp. 82, 343.

17. The other two guiding principles were: (1) to strive for peaceful coexistence with countries of different social systems on the basis of the Five Principles and to oppose the imperialist policies of aggression and war, and (2) to support the revolutionary struggles of all oppressed peoples and nations against imperialism and colonialism. See Yin Ching-yao, "The Chinese Communists' Foreign Policy," *Collected Documents of the First Sino-American Conference on Mainland China* (Taipei, 1971), p. 556.

18. The full text of the letter was printed in *Peking Review,* no. 25 (21 June 1963), pp. 23–32.

19. *CDSP* 15:28, p. 15.

20. Ibid.

21. See the statement made by the PRC on 31 July 1963 in U.S. Foreign Broadcasting Information Service, *Daily Report,* hereafter cited as *Daily Report,* no. 148 (31 July 1963), p. BBB 1.

22. For fuller treatment of this subject, see Morton H. Halperin, ed., *Sino-Soviet Relations and Arms Control* (Cambridge, Mass., 1967); Walter C. Clements, Jr., *The Arms Race and Sino-Soviet Relations* (Stanford, Calif., 1968), chs. 1, 4, 8–10; and Alice Langley Hsieh, "The Sino-Soviet Nuclear Dialogue, 1963," in *Sino-Soviet Military Relations*, ed. Raymond L. Garthoff (New York, 1966), pp. 150–170.

23. For a concise treatment of Chou's visit, see Robert A. Scalapino, *On the Trail of Chou En-lai in Africa* (Santa Monica, Calif., 1964), and W.A.C. Adie, "Chou En-lai on Safari," *China Quarterly* 18 (April 1964), pp. 174–194. For documents, speeches, and press interviews pertaining to Chou's visit, see *Afro-Asian Solidarity Against Imperialism* (Peking, 1964).

24. See Mao Tse-tung, "Talk with the American Correspondent Anna Louise Strong," *Selected Works,* vol. 5, pp. 99–100.

25. For the full text of the *Jen-min Jih-pao* (*JMJP*) editorial, "All the World's Forces Opposing U.S. Imperialism, Unite!" see Peking, New China News Agency (NCNA) International Service in English, 0524 GMT, 21 January 1964, in *Daily Report,* no. 14 (21 January 1964), pp. BBB 5–10.

26. *Daily Report,* no. 14 (21 January 1964), p. BBB 9.

27. Lin Piao, "Long Live the Victory of People's War!" in A. Doak Barnett, *China After Mao* (Princeton, N. J., 1967), document 2, p. 206. The English translation of Lin's article was also printed in *Peking Review* 8:36 (3 September 1965), pp. 9–30.

28. Barnett, *China After Mao,* pp. 241–243.

29. For a detailed account of PRC foreign policy during the Cultural Revolution, see Melvin Gurtov, "The Foreign Ministry and Foreign Affairs During the Cultural Revolution," *China Quarterly* 40 (October-December 1969), pp. 65–102; Robert A. Scalapino, "The Cultural Revolution and Chinese Foreign Policy," *Current Scene* 6:13 (August 1968), pp. 9–10; and Daniel Tretiak, "The Chinese Cultural Revolution and Foreign Policy," *Current Scene* 8:7 (1 April 1970), pp. 1–25.

30. Daniel Tretiak, "Disappearing Act," *Far Eastern Economic Review* 59:6 (8 February 1968), p. 216.

31. Scalapino, "The Cultural Revolution and Chinese Foreign Policy," p. 83; Curtov, "The Foreign Ministry and Foreign Affairs During the Cultural Revolution," p. 85.

32. On August 23, three days after the invasion, Premier Chou En-lai, speaking in Peking at a Romanian Embassy reception on the occasion of Romania's national day, denounced the Soviet invasion of Czechoslovakia as "the most barefaced and typical specimen of Fascist power-politics played by the Soviet revisionist clique of renegades and scabs against its so-called allies." Chou declared that "the Chinese Government and people strongly condemn the Soviet revisionist leading clique and its followers for their crime of aggression—the armed occupation of Czechoslovakia—and firmly support the Czechoslovak people in their heroic struggle of resistance to Soviet military occupation." The Soviet ambassador walked out of the reception. For the full text of Chou's speech, see NCNA, International Service in English, 1515 GMT, 23 August 1968, in *Daily Report,* no. 167 (23 August 1968), pp. A 1–3.

33. For the full text of Lin Piao's report, see *Daily Report,* supplement no. 8 (29 April 1969), pp. 1–30, and Winberg Chai, *The New Politics of Communist China: Modernization Process of a Developing Nation* (Pacific Palisades, Calif., 1972), appendix 3 (pp. 209–242).

34. See *Peking Review,* 22 August 1969, pp. 4–5, cited in Barnett, *China and the Major Powers in East Asia,* p. 50.

35. *New York Times,* 18 September 1969; Lewis S. Feuer, "Has the Cold War Really Ended?" *New Leader* (18 October 1971), cited in Yao Meng-hsuan, "Communist China's World Strategy," *Proceedings of the Seventh Sino-American Conference on Mainland China* (Taipei, 1978), p. V-1-7.

36. *Peking Review,* special issue (23 May 1970), pp. 8–9.

37. See Chou En-lai's political report to the Tenth National Congress of the Chinese Communist party on 24 August 1973, cited in *Sino-American Détente and Its Policy Implications,* ed. Gene T. Hsiao (New York, 1974), appendix 1, p. 305. The full text of

Chou's report was printed in *Peking Review* 16:35 and 36 (7 September 1973), pp. 17–25.

38. See Chou En-lai's conversation with Neville Maxwell, *London Times,* 5 January 1972, cited in Yao Meng-hsuan, "The Changes in Peiping's Foreign Policy (1969–1973)," *Proceedings of the Third Sino-American Conference on Mainland China* (Taipei, 1974), p. 305.

39. A commentary entitled "Concerning the Worldwide Response to Chairman Mao's Enunciation of the Three Worlds Theory," written by a NCNA correspondent on 26 August 1977, indicated that the Three Worlds Theory was first mentioned by Mao in February 1974 during a conversation with a visiting leader of a Third World country. See Yao Meng-hsuan, "Communist China's World Strategy," *Proceedings of the Fifth Sino-American Conference on Mainland China* (Taipei, 1976), p. V-1-11. Soviet sources referred to this certain Third World leader as Zambian President Kenneth Kaunda. This view was later confirmed by Hua Kuo-feng in August 1977. See Hua Kuo-feng, "Political Report to the Eleventh National Congress of the Communist Party of China," *Peking Review,* 26 August 1977, pp. 23–57, also cited in O. Edmund Clubb, "China and the Three Worlds," *Current History* 75:439 (September 1978), p. 53. See also John F. Copper, "China's Global Strategy," *Current History* 80:467 (September 1981), p. 241, and Yin Ch'ing-yao, "Communist China's Anti-Hegemony Policy: Its Recent Development and Prospects," *Issues & Studies* 18:5 (May 1982), p. 61.

40. Teng Hsiao-p'ing's speech at the Sixth Special Session of UN General Assembly on 9 April 1974; excerpts from *Peking Review* 17:16 (19 April 1974), pp. 6–11.

41. For fuller treatment of Teng's dismissal, see Richard C. Thornton, "Teng Hsiao-p'ing and Peking's Current Political Crisis: A Structural Interpretation," *Proceedings of the Fifth Sino-American Conference on Mainland China* (Taipei, 1976), pp. 260–295, and Yao Meng-hsuan, "The Chinese Communist Internal Struggle During the Power Transition," ibid., pp. 296–319.

42. The other major tasks were: (1) to achieve the return of Taiwan to the motherland and to reunify the country, and (2) to speed up socialist construction, that is, the Four Modernizations program. See "Report on Current Situation and Tasks—Delivered by Teng Hsiao-p'ing to a Cadres Meeting under the Sponsorship of the CCPCC on January 16, 1980," *Cheng Ming,* no. 29 (March 1980), p. 11.

43. See *Peking Review,* 21 April 1980, cited in Copper, "China's Global Strategy," p. 241.

9
The Political Role of the Chinese Army: Overview and Evaluation

Ellis Joffe

In the course of the history of the People's Republic of China, the People's Liberation Army (PLA) has moved across the entire spectrum of activities associated with military intrusion into politics and then back again almost to the starting point. After more than a decade of political quiescence, the PLA became increasingly involved in politics, setting the stage for its massive and momentous intervention in the Cultural Revolution. This intervention, which brought the army to the pinnacle of China's power pyramid, was followed again by partial disengagement from politics, but the army nevertheless played a pivotal part in deciding the outcome of the succession struggle that broke out after Mao's death. In the post-Mao period the PLA has returned to the barracks, but its leadership has continued to exercise an influence in national politics. The first part of this paper will attempt to describe and explain briefly the evolution of the PLA's political role.[1]

Political Quiescence

Until the early 1960s the PLA was politically quiescent.[2] This does not mean, of course, that it was passive or apolitical, but that it did not actively intervene in the national political process to promote its institutional interests and did not involve itself in issues outside the sphere of such interests. Aside from this basic limitation, the PLA was highly active both as a civic force and as a pressure group advocating its views in policymaking councils.

In the performance of nonmilitary tasks the PLA acted as an arm of the party according to the tasks assigned to it, whether these were in land reform, emergency aid, or the Great Leap Forward. These tasks contracted or expanded in line with the direction of the party leadership, and at no time did the PLA attempt to take over positions of power on its own. This was most clearly demonstrated by its willingness to relinquish military domination of local administration in 1954, once the civil organs were ready to assume these duties.

If the military made no attempt to overstep the limits of political activity set down for it by the party, it did not hesitate to clash with the party leadership when its professional interests were involved. Such clashes began in the mid-fifties and reached a climax during the Great Leap Forward as a result of the party's efforts to reverse the trends toward military modernization and professionalism. The vehemence with which the party rejected the views of the military in the press attest convincingly to the vigor with which the military stood by these views in inner party circles. At no time, however, did the military make a move to force the adoption of its views or, as far as is known, threaten to do so.

Nowhere was the restraint of the military better demonstrated than after the dismissal of the Defense Minister P'eng Te-huai at the Lushan Plenum of the Central Committee in August 1959. Granted that conflict over military issues was not the only, and perhaps not the central, immediate reason for P'eng's downfall, there is little doubt that the buildup of tensions deriving from this conflict played a key role in the showdown. As the chief spokesman of the officer corps, P'eng had stood in the forefront of its resistance to the party's crackdown on military professionalism. Although some of his colleagues may have disapproved of his political tactics, there is no doubt that P'eng's views on military matters were widely shared in the armed forces, as evidenced by the periodic resurfacing of such views in subsequent years and their full-scale adoption in the post-Mao period. Despite this, the military made no overt move to rally to P'eng's support. Why?

The answer to this question has to be sought in the basic factors that govern the relations of the Chinese military with the civil authorities. These factors not only accounted for the political quiescence of the PLA at the time of the P'eng Te-huai affair, but also decisively affected the PLA's behavior after it intervened in politics. One central factor has been the great integrative power of modern Chinese nationalism. Fueling this nationalism is the searing memory of China's impotence and humiliation by foreign countries, especially during the warlord period, memories that doubtless inhibit China's military leaders from taking any step that even remotely smacks of "warlordism." Another factor has been the commitment of China's military leaders to the principle of civilian supremacy over the military, a commitment born out of their nationalism and buttressed by their indoctrination, training, and experience. This premise has been so deeply ingrained that the military have never violated it of their own accord, and even when they were forced by circumstances to do so, most of them obviously regarded it as an exception to their perceived role. Adding organizational strength to these factors has been the network of controls instituted by the party in the armed forces, which, despite its weakness during certain periods, has acted as a powerful check on military officers. A further check has been the innate conservatism of the professional military as well as their discipline. Finally, forged out of all these factors has been what is probably the most elusive and yet the most elemental constraint on the military: the ethic of professionalism and of nonintervention in political affairs by direct action. Given all these factors, the question that should be asked is not why the Chinese military did not intervene in the political process, but why they did.

From Involvement to Intervention

The Chinese military moved into the political arena not because the factors governing the party-PLA relationship broke down, but because of developments extraneous to this relationship. These developments are well known and need not be recapitulated in detail. They were dominated by an intraparty conflict that was triggered by the failure of the Great Leap Forward and centered on the fundamental issues relating to China's development strategy. The conflict entered a crucial phase after 1962, when party leaders opposed to Mao's concepts sought to evade the chairman's directives on the level of policy implementation. As the gap between declaratory policy and actual implementation by the party bureaucracy widened, Mao and his supporters became increasingly alienated from the party and its leaders. By the middle of the decade Mao concluded that it was necessary to shake up the party and to reinfuse it with revolutionary values in order to overcome its resistance to revolutionary policies.

To accomplish this, Mao turned to the PLA, which under Lin Piao's leadership had curbed its professionalism and revived its revolutionary qualities. Although Lin's efforts took professional interests into consideration, the revolutionary vigor of the PLA contrasted sharply with the bureaucratism and unresponsiveness of the party. Consequently, Mao began to use the PLA in order to prod the party, a process that began in 1963 with campaigns that reached a climax a year later when the entire nation was exhorted to "learn from the Army," and military officers were assigned to civilian organs.

Although the aim of these campaigns was limited to reforming the party rather than replacing it with the PLA, they marked the start of the PLA's involvement in politics. This involvement radically, if still subtly, changed the role of the PLA. For the first time it was pulled into the political arena not to carry out the policies of a united leadership, but as an ally of one group against its opponents in a leadership that was becoming increasingly divided.

The PLA thus did not intrude into politics against the wishes of the civilian leadership, but was brought into the political arena by this leadership. To be sure, Lin Piao and other senior military leaders readily responded to Mao's initiative, whether out of conviction or calculation—or a mixture of both—but there were misgivings. One who voiced them was the chief of staff, Lo Jui-ch'ing, who opposed the army's new role on the grounds that it damaged professional competence. However, his opposition, which became bound up with power relations and strategic differences, was overridden without any disruptions and he was dismissed. The way was clear for Mao to launch the Cultural Revolution with the support of the PLA.

If other army leaders viewed such use of the PLA unfavorably, they kept their views to themselves—then and, with few exceptions, later. One reason for their silence was unquestionably their discipline. Another was doubtless that during the initial stages of the Cultural Revolution the army, as distinguished from its leadership, was kept out of the struggle. When the PLA leadership intervened in the conflict, the public manifestation of this intervention was chiefly verbal. Army units remained on the sidelines, aside from providing support to the Red Guards. During this period, Lin Piao and his colleagues could reap the political benefits that accrued from backing the Maoists without subjecting the PLA to the bruising consequences of becoming entangled in the political battles that were raging throughout China. This situation, however, did not last long. As the Cultural Revolution escalated, so did the involvement of the army.

This escalation occurred due to the inability of the Maoists to purge the party organizations by using the Red Guards. Thwarted in their efforts by the unexpectedly forceful resistance of the party bureaucracy, and faced with mounting chaos as a result of these efforts, the Maoists decided that the only alternative to terminating the Cultural Revolution was to commit their remaining asset—the PLA—in support of the "revolutionary" forces. Embroiling the army in political struggles, however, was an unprecedented move that was opposed by some senior military leaders on the grounds that it would subject the PLA to dangerous strains. After these leaders were purged the PLA was ordered, in what was undoubtedly the single most important decision relating to the political role of the military, to intervene in the Cultural Revolution in order to "support the Left."

This decision, as predicted by its opponents, indeed subjected the army to intolerable strains, which became apparent from the outset of its entry into the political fray in January 1967. Confronted with contradictory directives to maintain order and to support the Left, regional military commanders generally opted for stability rather than revolution. To fill the vacuum created by the paralysis of party and administrative organs, military commanders established, in coordination with moderate leaders in Peking, "revolutionary committees," ostensibly made up of veteran cadres, representatives of revolutionary organizations, and the army, but which, in effect, the army dominated. Where such committees were not set up, the PLA ruled directly through its standing Military Control Committees.

The army's preference for order and for working with old-time cadres aroused the opposition of revolutionary activists, to which the army responded in accordance with the shifts in the balance of power among the radical and moderate wings of the Peking leadership. As the balance shifted, the behavior of the PLA alternated between repression and restraint. Eventually, proponents of the hard line against the anarchic "revolutionary" elements won out, and by the time the Cultural Revolution was terminated in April 1969, the Red Guard organizations had largely been broken up, and the power of their mentors in Peking appreciably diminished.

Since the party was still in disarray, the PLA became the supreme political and administrative authority in the provinces and, largely as a consequence of this, a central force in Peking politics. The Cultural Revolution thus completely shattered the structure of civil-military relations in China. What it did not shatter were the basic values—professionalism and the principle of civilian supremacy—that had governed civil-military relations prior to the intervention of the military in politics. The military did not set out to displace the party organization; as previously noted, political power devolved to it by default rather than by design. And it did not openly defy Peking's authority, although in the course of intervention many commanders circumvented central directives when these were confused or contradicted their desire for stability. The one commander who broke this rule, Ch'en Tsai-tao of Wuhan, was not supported by his colleagues, although he did overtly what most of them did covertly. The continued commitment of the military to these values had a decisive impact on the evolution of the PLA's political role in the aftermath of the Cultural Revolution.

Another decisive impact on this evolution derived from developments within the military. The turbulent events that brought the PLA to power also weakened it internally by creating intra-army cleavages. The main cleavage was between Lin Piao and some of his colleagues in the high command, who had become identified with the policies of the radical Left, and most regional commanders and professional military leaders, who had to bear the bitter consequences of these policies. Not only had Lin failed to protect his regional commanders from Red Guard attacks, but he dispatched main force units to support radical organizations that the regional military had suppressed—thus exacerbating intra-army rivalries. These rivalries isolated the Lin Piao group within the military establishment and undercut Lin's power base in national politics.

Disengagement from Politics

Although the Cultural Revolution catapulted China's military commanders to positions of regional rulers, the end of the upheaval did not lead to a relinquishment of these positions. On the contrary, the military continued to consolidate its political power by directing the process of party reconstruction, which got under way after the turmoil. Since the reconstituted party committees were supposed to have higher authority than the army-dominated revolutionary committees, the party leadership viewed the reconstruction process as a way of getting the military out of politics and reasserting civilian control over the army. The military, however, did not cooperate. Instead of stepping aside in favor of civilians, the military used their political posts to ensure that their representatives would be appointed to leading positions in the new party committees, either as first secretaries (21 out of 29) or as members of provincial party secretariats (62 percent). China's political system thus became military-dominated,[3] and Mao's time-honored dictum that "the Party commands the gun and the gun shall never be allowed to command the Party" was left by the wayside.

If the professional values of the military had remained intact, and if the military had been reluctant to intervene in politics in the first place, why did they refuse to withdraw from the political arena? The simplest explanation is that power, once acquired whatever the initial impetus, is not easily given up. This explanation, however, is too simple, given the readiness of the military to do just that a short time later. A more specific explanation has to take into account the hostility of most military commanders to the radical Left, and their determination to block radical representatives from gaining positions of power. As long as this possibility existed, the military were not prepared to surrender their posts and to expose China again to the threat of disorder, for it was the breakdown of order that had impelled them to intervene in politics in the first place. What they were prepared to do, as later events indicated, was to vacate their posts in favor of veteran cadres, but these cadres were prevented from returning to political activity by the Left in the immediate aftermath of the Cultural Revolution.

Another reason for the PLA's continued hold on political power was intra-army rivalry. In order to strengthen the PLA as his power base in national politics, Lin Piao sought not only to strengthen its political position, but also to replace most regional commanders (who had "accounts to settle" with him) with his supporters during the reconstruction of the party. Rival PLA groups thus had different motives for remaining in the political arena, but the result was failure to return power to the civilians.

This failure united the moderate and radical wings of the Peking leadership in a coalition against Lin Piao, who was held responsible for the domination of the military. Also working against Lin were his political ambitions and Mao's disillusionment with him as the chairman's successor-designate. Crucial to this coalition was the support or acquiescence of Lin's opponents among the regional commanders and professional military leaders at the center; with this support Mao and Chou En-lai were able to isolate Lin with relative ease. As a result of this isolation, Lin and his close colleagues acted in desperation, and Lin was apparently killed in a plane crash in Mongolia after allegedly planning to assassinate Mao.

The ignominious downfall of Lin Piao, and with him the chief of staff and other members of the general staff, had an immediate impact on the political status of the PLA. It removed a major obstacle to the reassertion of party primacy over the military. It deprived the PLA of a powerful voice at the center, and left it without an effective outlet for channeling its demands. And it discredited the military, putting it on the defensive, even though the party leadership drew a distinction between the Lin Piao group and the rest of the PLA. In these propitious circumstances the party leadership intensified its efforts to chip away at the political power of the PLA.

These efforts took several forms. First, the political profile of the PLA was lowered considerably; its prestige as a political force was diminished, and party supremacy over the military was stressed. Second, the importance of the PLA's concentration on military tasks and elevation of its professional standards was emphasized, presumably both to placate the military and to justify its withdrawal from political functions. Third and most concrete, the political power of the PLA as measured by military representation in national and regional ruling organs was reduced. Thus, in the period between the fall of Lin Piao and the death of Mao, nine of the twenty-one officers who were also first secretaries of the provincial party committees gave up their concurrent posts; PLA representatives in provincial party committees were reduced by some 16 percent, in the Central Committee by about 14 percent, and in the Politburo by some 17 percent. Military Control Committees were abolished, and eight of the eleven military region commanders were reshuffled.

The trend toward disengagement was inseparable from developments on the political scene. The fall of Lin Piao and the consequent weakening of the radical Left were used by moderate leaders to pursue policies that downplayed Maoist values, and also to rehabilitate veteran cadres who were indispensable to the implementation of these policies. To these cadres military commanders were prepared to hand over power, but their position was far from secure due to periodic radical assaults on the moderate leaders and their policies. The radicals also attacked the PLA and its veteran leaders. In this state of leadership instability and PLA antagonism toward part of the leadership, their withdrawal from politics stopped short of full-scale relinquishment of positions of power.

After Mao: Return to Professionalism

That the military remained a key force in politics in the twilight of the Maoist period was demonstrated in the succession struggle that broke out after Mao's death. The outcome of this struggle, which pitted the radical leaders against a coalition of moderates led by Hua Guofeng, was decided swiftly and without any disruptions due to the intervention of the military on the side of the moderate coalition.

Military intervention in the succession struggle had several aspects. The army carried out a coup against the radical leaders—now labeled the Gang of Four—and put them under arrest. It mounted a major propaganda effort after the coup in order to strengthen Hua's position by declaring the support of the PLA for the new leadership. And it was poised to intervene against radical resistance had the need for such action arisen. The military thus became the main prop of the Hua leadership in the transition period, gaining a central position in the post-Mao power structure.

This position began to change with the emergence of Deng Xiaoping as the dominant figure and his revitalization of the party apparatus. Much more assertive than Hua and less dependent on the military oligarchy for support, Deng has strengthened political and personal control over the armed forces. First as chief of staff of the PLA and vice-chairman of the Military Affairs Committee, and since 1980 as the committee's chairman, Deng has made many personnel changes, reduced the political power of the regional commanders, and completed the process of returning the PLA to the barracks. Under his aegis, the imbalance in the party-PLA relationship that existed during the transition period has been redressed in favor of the party.

At the same time, Deng has had to ensure the support of the military for his policies. Lacking Mao's personal charisma and political capital, Deng has had to rely to a greater degree on coalitions to maintain his political position, and the military is a central element in any coalition. And lacking Mao's personal standing among the generals, Deng cannot assume, as Mao could, that support from them will be ultimately forthcoming, whatever the differences between them over specific issues. Their support depends to a large extent upon their acceptance of party policies.

Such acceptance has formed the basis of the relations between the Deng leadership and the professional officers. Although their optimal demands for more resources and rapid updating of conventional weapons have been rejected by the leadership, the officers have accepted Deng's policy of gradual technological modernization geared to the advance of the national economy. They have also accepted the policy of basing this modernization on indigenous resources, with the understanding that there will be limited imports of military technology. The leadership, moreover, has not only held out promises for the future but, despite economic limitations, has encouraged the procurement and improvement of weapons based on existing resources. In short, both the leadership's long-term policy and current practice have done much to satisfy the technological needs of the military.

In areas not limited by economic constraints, the leadership has done very much to meet demands from the army. Maoist military doctrine has been drastically diluted. Training has been upgraded with an emphasis on operations of combined forces. Organization has been streamlined and discipline has been tightened. Educational and technical levels have been raised. Military academies and officer training have received special attention. Logistics have been improved and adapted to modern warfare.

Political work has been subordinated to the enhancement of combat capability. The dominant considerations in these far-reaching reforms have been professional. Not since the mid-fifties, and in many ways more than at that time, have professional officers carried so much weight in molding the character of the PLA.

Underlying the rapport between the Deng leadership and the professional military is a basic conceptual consensus on the fundamental policies of national development. This consensus has been a major factor behind the willingness of the professional military to disengage from the political arena and to refrain from intervening in issues that lie outside the institutional concerns of the PLA.

The same does not hold true for a different group of PLA leaders. Although these leaders share the institutional interests of the professional military, they have not confined themselves to promoting these interests. Unlike the professional officers, they have intruded into the political arena and have publicly spoken out against the national policies of the party. One contentious issue between this group of military leaders and the Deng leadership has been the evaluation of Mao's role in the history of the Chinese Revolution, an issue on which the military took a softer stand than Deng in criticizing Mao's mistakes. Related to this issue has been the discontent of this group with the consequences of what it has perceived as the drift away from Maoist values in Chinese society, as a result of the party's overemphasis on material factors and its slack ideological guidance. This group has also criticized the party's economic policies, viewed as producing greed, laxity, and corruption.

Military disaffection with party policies centered in the PLA's General Political Department and its subordinate organs and, judging by the efforts of the party leadership to counter it, was fairly widespread. It was expressed in the army paper, in speeches and meetings, and presumably in inner party circles. At no time, however, did any part of the military make any move to force the acceptance of their views by direct action of some kind.

The reaction of the party leadership to criticism from part of the military has been to crack down on the critics by means of dismissals, self-criticism meetings, and study campaigns. Although it may have made marginal policy changes in response to pressure from the military, the leadership has not been swayed from its principal policies. If anything, these policies have been consolidated and extended.

In sum, although a segment of the military elite has dissented from party policies, the party leadership has been able to overcome this dissent primarily because it has the support of the professional military, whose vital needs are being met, and who have refrained from intervening in political affairs that go beyond these needs. The ethic of professionalism, having withstood the stresses and strains of intervention and its aftermath, has under Deng's leadership again become the dominant factor conditioning the political role of the PLA.

An Evaluation

How has the evolution of the PLA's political role been viewed by specialists on Chinese military affairs? What approaches have they used in their analyses? Where have they been right and where can they be said to have gone wrong, and why? What lessons can be learned from this retrospective evaluation?

What stands out in the literature on the political role of the Chinese military is not a variety of differing views, but a consensus on the main features of this role. The reasons for this consensus are not hard to find. First, the number of analysts with a sustained interest in Chinese military affairs has been small, which naturally narrows the range of views. Second, all analysts work from the same limited published sources, which tend to propel them toward similar conclusions. Third, specialists on Chinese military affairs have not displayed any marked ideological inclinations and have not tried to fit their source material to preconceived conclusions. Fourth, writers on the military have been influenced by the dominant views of the Chinese political system prevailing at a given time, and since these views have tended to converge, so have the assessments of the military's role in the political system. Finally, the analysts have not approached their subject with a rigid conceptual framework and have not ordered their data according to distinctly different models. Had such approaches been adopted, they would have led to divergent interpretations of the same data. Since they have not, the lines between the specialists on the military have not been sharply drawn.

Nowhere was the operation of these factors more apparent than in the failure of China specialists to conceive of the possibility that the Chinese military would intervene in politics by direct action. Proceeding from the widely-held premise that China was a totalitarian system ruled by a monolithic party that dominated all other institutions of power, specialists accepted without question the Chinese maxim that the PLA was subordinate to the party and could not have an independent political role. Consequently, conflicts between the party and the PLA over a variety of issues were seen as played out within a broader framework of unity and party supremacy. The possibility of the military becoming a major force in the national political process was not even considered.

The main reason for this failure—if it can be called a failure—on the part of China specialists derived from their inability to anticipate developments that represented a sharp break with prevailing patterns. And the intervention of the PLA in politics was such a break in at least two aspects. First, the use of the army in support of one side against another in a factional struggle went completely against the grain of Chinese Communist principles and precedent. Second, the circumstances of such use were themselves unprecedented, since a leadership struggle of such magnitude and viciousness was an entirely novel phenomenon in the politics of the regime. Thus, if China specialists can be said to have gone wrong, it was in not looking beyond the confines of past examples and prevalent trends.

In that these confines could hardly have been overcome by continuing to use a China-oriented approach, could China specialists have benefited by drawing on comparative studies? This question is particularly pertinent because studies of the Chinese military have been criticized for suffering "an almost total isolation from work in related areas which are highly relevant to the field's concerns," even though "the close correspondence between the themes found in research on the PLA and the concerns raised in more general treatments of military behavior is quite striking."[4] Granted the general validity of this criticism, in this particular case a comparative approach would have been of little help, since the insights derived from such an approach were largely inapplicable to the Chinese scene.

The chief insight is that among the range of factors that account for the move of armies into politics "by far the most common and salient interventionist motive involves the defense or enhancement of the military's corporate interests."[5] Put otherwise, "officers intervene against the civilian authorities when their perceived interests are being denied or threatened by civilian policy."[6] This, however, is precisely what did not happen in China. Although, as has been seen, by the late fifties Chinese officers felt that their "perceived interests" were indeed "being denied or threatened" by the extreme reassertion of Maoist policies in the armed forces, they made no attempt to take forceful action in defense of these interests. When they did intervene, it was due to factors that lay outside the realm of their professional concerns.

Another insight derived from comparative studies is that armies intervene in politics when civilian governments fail in the performance of their duties and, consequently, lose their legitimacy.[7] The expansion of military power that results from the weakness of civilian institutions and the pressures of civilians on the military to expand the latter's role has been termed "reactive militarism."[8] Despite superficial similarities, the ascent to power of the PLA does not fit this category. Although the Chinese army moved into the political sphere due to the breakdown of civilian institutions, these institutions had been anything but weak, and their breakdown was the result of attacks launched against them by the Maoist leadership. Moreover, the initial involvement of the PLA in politics had nothing to do with the weakness of civilian institutions, for it came at a time when the regime was recovering from the crisis caused by the Great Leap Forward and was tightening its political and ideological grip over the population. In fact, it was the ability of the regime to overcome this crisis rather than its inability to cope with it that gave rise to intraparty conflict and set the stage for the intervention of the military in politics.

In short, unlike other armies, the PLA entered the political arena not to protect its corporate interests, and not due to the weakness of civilian institutions—at least not in the usual sense. Despite criticism that China specialists harbor "a lingering assumption that China somehow remains *sui generis*,"[9] it is difficult to escape the conclusion that in this particular instance China indeed was. If so, it is unlikely that any approach could have alerted specialists to the new role that the military was to assume. The circumstances that gave rise to this role simply could not have been foreseen—even by the Chinese themselves.

Once the PLA moved into politics, how did the approaches used to analyze civil-military relations until then fare in the new circumstances? The two chief approaches were the party vs. PLA approach,[10] and the field army approach.[11]

The main thesis of the first approach is that since the mid-1950s the relationship between the party and the PLA had been dominated by a conflict resulting from the growth of a professional officer corps and its espousal of views that were at variance with the basic beliefs of the politically-oriented leadership. The organizational manifestation of this relationship in the armed forces was the conflict between political commissars, who represented the party in the PLA and exercised control on its behalf, and professional commanders, who resented the excessive intrusion of political functionaries and considerations into military affairs.

When the army intervened in the Cultural Revolution, the General Political Department and the political commissars could have been expected to spearhead the implementation of policies enunciated by Mao and the radical wing of the Peking leadership. This, however, was not the case, for the political hierarchy in the PLA turned out to be an ally rather than an adversary of the professional officers. Senior political commissars were purged for attempting to limit military involvement in political activities or for protecting the PLA from radical attacks; the General Political Department operations were suspended for not toeing the radical line; and in the localities, political commissars tended to side with commanders against the onslaughts of the Red Guards.

Has it been wrong, then, to speak of a party-PLA dichotomy—as critics of this approach have maintained?[12] Their arguments may be summarized in a nutshell. First, at the top level of leadership, all senior military men are also party members. Second, there is no rigid institutional separation between the party and the PLA, because the political and military hierarchies at all levels interact closely. Third, the PLA, like the party, is not a monolithic institution, but is divided by internal cleavages that cut across institutional boundaries.

These points are valid, but they are not absolute, and they do not preclude the existence of a distinct institutional boundary between the party and the PLA: first, because the party membership of senior military leaders and the institutional interaction of the party and the army are no barrier to the growth of an organizational identification anchored in common professional interests; and second, because the existence of cleavages and coalitions that cut across institutional boundaries are no barrier to the existence of a "military view" that distinguishes the military from the civilian leadership. This distinction has been sharp when the issues at stake concerned the narrow professional interests of the army, for it was then that the military tended to coalesce around a common viewpoint—as did the civilian leaders. However, when the military became involved in issues that transcended its professional interests and had broad political relevance, the military viewpoint was overshadowed by splits and alliances that were the products of the army's political role. This was the case during the Cultural Revolution and in its aftermath, when groups in the PLA found allies in the party on certain issues *against* other groups in the PLA, which found a common cause with other groups in the party.

In short, the intensity of the party-PLA dichotomy hinges to a large extent on the level of the army's political involvement. When the military is politically quiescent and is concerned primarily with its professional interests, military leaders can be expected to present a united front to the civilians based on these concerns. However, when the army is deeply involved in politics, the party-PLA cleavage is submerged by splits and alliances that are the result of the army's political involvement and that stretch across institutional lines.

The second approach to analyzing military behavior, based on the field army thesis, postulated that the elite of the PLA were divided into five major cliques formed by long-standing associations in the field armies. The geographic regions conquered by the civil war became, after the establishment of the regime, the basis for the distribution of power among the cliques. Personnel and unit assignments were allocated in such a way as to maintain a balance of power among the field army elites.

This thesis seemed reasonable until 1967, because the main force units belonging to the field armies had been returned to their regions after the Korean War and had not been relocated after that. Furthermore, many of the field armies' leaders remained in the same locale rather than rotating from region to region.

However, the Cultural Revolution undermined the validity of the thesis. When the central leadership decided to use main force units to cope with the chaos caused by the Cultural Revolution, the selection of units was made not with the intention of maintaining a balance of power among the field armies, but with practical military considerations in mind. The main criterion for unit assignment was the state of security of the areas from which units were taken. Units in sensitive areas were left in place, and units in low threat areas were chosen for political duties regardless of their background and regardless of the fact that they had to move into areas supposedly controlled by other cliques.[13]

The conclusion was clear: The central leadership had the determination and the power to move main force units without regard for the political considerations and the personal connections that were the essential underpinning of the field army thesis. Wedded excessively to past patterns of Chinese military politics, this thesis had attached undue weight to regional military power and personal associations as determinants of

PLA behavior. As a result, it underestimated what this paper has tried to underline: the strength of central control over the military and the professionalism of Chinese officers—two sides of the same coin—which, despite enormous strains and partial breakdowns during limited periods, have remained the major marks of military behavior in China.

Notes

1. Since this paper is an overview based on my own interpretation of events, it draws on articles I have published on these events. The main articles are as follows: "The Chinese Army Under Lin Piao: Prelude to Political Intervention," in *China: Management of a Revolutionary Society,* ed. John M. H. Lindbeck (Seattle: University of Washington Press, 1971), pp. 343–374; "The Chinese Army in the Cultural Revolution: the Politics of Intervention," *Current Scene* (Hong Kong) 8:18 (7 December 1970), pp. 1–25; "The Chinese Army After the Cultural Revolution: The Effects of Intervention," *China Quarterly,* no. 55 (July–September 1973), pp. 450–477; (with Gerald Segal) "The Chinese Army and Professionalism," *Problems of Communism* (November–December 1978), pp. 1–19; and "The Army After Mao," *International Journal* 34:4 (Autumn 1979), pp. 568–584.

2. I have taken this term and some of the ideas associated with it from Timothy J. Colton, *Commissars, Commanders, and Civilian Authority: the Structure of Soviet Military Politics* (Cambridge, Mass.: Harvard University Press, 1979).

3. For a discussion of military-dominated regimes, see Samual E. Finer, "The Morphology of Military Regimes," in *Soldiers, Peasants, and Bureaucrats: Civil-Military Relations in Communist and Modernizing Societies,* ed. Roman Kolkowicz and Andrzej Korbonski (London: George Allen and Unwin, 1982), pp. 281–304.

4. Jonathan D. Pollack, "The Study of Chinese Military Politics: Toward A Framework for Analysis," in *Political-Military Systems: Comparative Perspectives,* ed. Catherine M. Kelleher (Beverly Hills, Calif.: Sage Publications, 1974), pp. 240, 261.

5. Eric A. Nordlinger, *Soldiers in Politics: Military Coups and Governments* (Englewood Cliffs, N.J.: Prentice-Hall, 1977), pp. 63–64.

6. Colton, *Commissars, Commanders, and Civilian Authority,* p. 240.

7. Nordlinger, *Soldiers in Politics,* p. 64.

8. Morris Janowitz, *The Military in the Political Development of New Nations* (Chicago: University of Chicago Press, 1964), p. 16.

9. Pollack, "Chinese Military Politics," p. 261.

10. Ellis Joffe, *Party and Army: Professionalism and Political Control in the Chinese Officer Corps, 1949–1964* (Cambridge, Mass.: Harvard University, East Asian Research Center, 1965); John Gittings, *The Role of the Chinese Army* (New York: Oxford University Press, 1967).

11. William W. Whitson (with Chen-hsia Huang), *The Chinese High Command: A History of Communist Military Politics, 1927–1971* (New York: Praeger, 1973).

12. Paul H. B. Godwin, "Professionalism and Politics in the Chinese Armed Forces: A Reconceptualization," in Dale Herspring and Ivan Volgyes, *Civil-Military Relations in Communist Systems* (Boulder, Colo.: Westview Press, 1977), pp. 219–240.

13. Harvey W. Nelson, *The Chinese Military System: An Organizational Study of the Chinese People's Liberation Army* (Boulder, Colo.: Westview Press, 1977), pp. 126–137, 153–154.

Part 4

The Economy and the Law

10
The Economy of the People's Republic of China Since 1949: A Critical Evaluation

Wou Wei

Introduction: The Power Struggle over Economic Policy

The changes in the economic policy of the Chinese Communists over more than three decades have been intimately tied to power struggles. Although the struggles have been expressed in the political arena, the most consistent factor precipitating them has been economic stress. The economy has fluctuated between bad and worse; the economic policy, between mixed public-private participation in agriculture and industry and the complete socialization and collectivization of agricultural land, industrial holdings, and the production from both.

Because the changes have been cyclic from one policy to the other, a chronological review would take more space than one that focuses on each type of policy in operation, its antecedents, and the pattern of cycling up to the prevailing economic views of today. The latter can then be analyzed and elaborated as the current views.

Historically, one policy is typified by the Great Leap Forward and the later economy associated with the Cultural Revolution; the other, by the views of the "capitalist roaders" or revisionists. Today the opposing policies are often labeled "Red" versus "expert," but the current (1980s) policy of the "experts" raises several far more complex questions than did its earlier analogs about the continuing nature of Chinese Communism.

The Great Leap Forward—First and Second Phases

From the first, successful revolution was followed by unsuccessful economic strategies. Serious unemployment and a capital fund shortage resulted from the First Five-Year Plan (1953–1957). The situation was exacerbated by pressure imposed by the Soviet Union on Chinese Communist politics and the economy, and by internal turmoil among the Peking leaders.

Seeking a way out, Mao Tse-tung fashioned an economic policy based on his Great Leap Forward. The socialization of rural land was completed in 1956, and by 1958 rural communes had begun the great collective agricultural experiment. Industry and urban enterprises, similarly socialized, emphasized the question of whether ideology and nonmaterial rewards could increase production over private incentive.

But the Great Leap Forward proved a disaster. The food and capital needed for the expansion of the Communist economy did not materialize from nonmaterial incentives. Indeed, some of the nonmaterial incentives (social, medical, and educational services) further burdened the economy. The cycle swung the other way, and some individualized or family incentive was permitted in both agriculture and urban business, although with state quotas still emphasized. This revisionist policy was interrupted by the Cultural Revolution, and the Mao-Chiang Ch'ing factions reestablished a "Red" policy that was soon headed for trouble (to be aggravated by the world recession between 1974 and 1976 and by a diplomatic and economic blockade clamped by the Soviet Union against the Chinese Communists).

It took the influence of Chou En-lai in the highly charged atmosphere of the Cultural Revolution to reinstate in an official government position Teng Hsiao-p'ing, who earlier had been deposed. Chou En-lai died in January 1976 and Mao deposed Teng again; however, after Mao's death later in 1976, Teng rose to power for the third time. To deal with the economic crisis he implemented the Ten-Year Economic Plan of the "expert" faction of the "capitalist roaders." The plan began as another ambitious "Great Leap Forward" in a second phase, at least in the sense that high-pressure methods were again employed on the population to eke out capital funds for economic reconstruction. But the operation of the plan was to become quite different through its more liberal view of the economy and of economic rewards.

If at the beginning and end of the period so far under consideration the populace was put under great pressure, the outlook each time on their future was not the same. A brief review of the policies of the Cultural Revolution and the "capitalist roaders" will highlight the differences.

The Economic Policies of the Cultural Revolution and the "Capitalist Roaders"

In fairness to the Chinese Communist regime, I will say that the economic policy framed by the Mao-Chiang groups (i.e., conservative or *against* the market economy) served its goals in the end to a certain extent. For its part, the revisionist economic policy of the "capitalist roaders" of the Liu-Teng faction, even though it allowed some market economy, did not essentially contravene the proletariat class struggle. To the extent that it was based on the principle of market economy it helped breathe some vigor into the Communist Chinese economy.

Overall, the economic policy of the revisionists was relatively moderate as viewed against the background of Chinese Communist goals. However, the economic policy of the Cultural Revolution persisted for some time. This resulted in continued impoverishment, fomenting distress and misery. With time and the demise of the Mao-Chiang Ch'ing era, the residual effects of the Cultural Revolution dissipated greatly and the economic policy of the revisionists displaced the wholly socialized economy. Although those opposed to any concession to a market economy managed to stage some sort of a comeback on a limited scale, the revisionists held on.

Doubtlessly, in the far future another cyclical power struggle will break out between these persisting factions of the Chinese Communists. It is evident that the residual force associated with the Cultural Revolution could again regain the power to attack the economic program of the "capitalist roaders." It is the essence of the proletariat class struggle that those who, with Mao, toppled Teng Hsiao-p'ing twice before could regroup shortly or immediately following Teng's demise.

However, in the immediate future the line of the "capitalist roaders" will dominate economic policy and the Four Modernizations plan. This trend is something that conservatives will find difficult to check. In short, the future economic policy of the Chinese Communists will follow a more moderate course than in the past.

The chief difference between the two economies lies more in the quantity of the economic policy, not its quality; the added provisions for some market economic functions do not basically alter the socialist system. The quality is the essence of the dictatorship of the proletariat under Marxist-Leninist Communism, with all that it implies in the absolutism of the People's Commune and the complete restriction of private ownership of property. This form of power struggle during the last thirty years of Chinese Communism bears a striking similarity to developments in the Soviet Union that led to the Kosygin policy in Russia after the year 1965,[2] as will be seen below.

The Economics of Socialist Planning and Market Mechanisms

After the October Revolution in 1917, Soviet leaders enforced a new economic system that nationalized all land and property. This move caused the deterioration of initiative in industry and agriculture due to absence of profits and lack of competition (for instance, the waste of by-products of industry and agriculture, no longer competitively utilized). As a result, a great recession was generated, forcing the Soviet Union to forge a new economic policy.

Thus the USSR started the First Five-Year Plan and its economic program in 1928. Yet this step was followed by Stalin's economic program centering on the rural collectivization system, which resulted in another massive failure. Starting again in 1965, Kosygin carried out a revisionist economic policy that liberalized the planned economic targets and the system of industrial management. Simultaneously, a revision was carried out in the policy of the "land retention of the rural areas." It was this economic strategy, hewing close to Western practice, that enabled the USSR to attain a growth in its economy, particularly through the land retention program.

The essence of Chinese Communism under the Marxist-Leninist ideology could hardly change in a much shorter period of time than taken by its counterpart in the Soviet Union. In particular, the collective national rural economy—both the focus and the fulcrum of initial efforts—did not materially improve despite years of effort; productivity of the rural villages tended to be low and food had to be imported to meet the requirements of an increasing population. By trial and error the policy slowly shifted. Today, in Communist China, Teng Hsiao-p'ing's economic policy follows the path that the Soviet Union took after 1965. Indeed, Teng's policy is more complex; the processes of importing materials, compensating trade, and establishing processing zones, among others, are factors that never cropped up in the economic formulations of the Soviet revisionists.

Insofar as form is concerned, the economic policy of the Chinese Communists is no different from that presently being implemented in the Soviet Union. However, in cultural aspects the USSR is quite different from Communist China. The essence of Communism as practiced by the Soviet Union can never be the same when applied to Communist China. China has had five thousand years of history and culture, almost all of it in association with a market economy. The tenets of Confucius have taken firm root; the innate ideology of free economy as shown by the private ownership of property and a deeply ingrained democratic system has not been successfully displaced by the Communist ideology.

The People's Commune under collective or nationalized ownership is a factor not realistically understood in the rural villages. For if the state owns everything, then its resources and its problems are beyond the rural people's calculation. The villagers have failed to perceive why, under "people's ownership" (as collectivization is proclaimed) just as under the former landlords of many of them, they could give to the economy in so much greater proportion than they can take from it. The major way their situation has changed has been in greater regulation of what they have been allowed to take despite how much or little they may have given—a consequence in part of the Peking regime's efforts to try to create an agricultural surplus as capital for the nation's industrial expansion. What this state effort created instead was a lack of incentive among the more than three-quarters of the population living in rural villages or on farms.

Teng Hsiao-p'ing's type of revisionism may therefore be said to be positive revisionism for the moment, but its limited "free" market functions do not exclude the essence of Chinese Communism. Teng apparently has recognized that the Communism of Marxism-Leninism cannot resolve the economic problems of the People's Republic of China (PRC). However, he is not fully amenable to the new market concepts and ideas. He also has a difficult political position to maintain in a collective Chinese leadership that includes many former Maoists; thus he cannot break cleanly with the past even after recognizing that the PRC has fallen into the wrong economic position.

The Contemporary Economic Design of the Teng Regime

At the Third National People's Congress of Communist China in 1980, Yao Yi-lin, vice-premier and chairman of the State Planning Commission, reported on the national economic plans for 1980 and 1981. At the same time, Wang Ping-chien, minister of finance, reported on the state budget and final account. These two reports revealed the basics of the Chinese Communist economic and financial measures, which strictly follow the Teng Hsiao-p'ing line and Chao Tzu-yang's related economic policy.

When Chao Tzu-yang was promoted to the premiership for his success in his administration of Szechuan Province, he followed Teng Hsiao-p'ing's line and adopted a new economic policy. He supplemented a planned economy with a market economy. His economic policy may be said to be based on the Yugoslavian model. He tried to apply the experience of his Szechuan success to the whole of China.

I believe this approach of delegating power to the province is just a maneuvering in economic strategy. The new policy calls for the handling of foreign trade by provinces and municipalities. Financially, it adopts the approach of "contract production." In the villages it liberates the use of "private plots" by 20 percent and, at the same time, it encourages joint enterprises of agriculture and industry.[3]

In industry, the new policy advocates that enterprises have the right to manage their own businesses and to reinvest their profits. This is, in practice, the application of features of the free economy of the West to the centralized planned economy, while preserving the pattern of socialism. In other words, it is actually the new Chinese socialist economy, not a capitalist economy. The Chinese Communist regime continues to remain in the frame of the thought of Marx, Engels, and Lenin as far as the current economic policy is concerned, but the application of this policy has been Westernized.

At the present stage, the Chinese Communists have more or less adopted the scientific management of the West in such ways as letting the banks play a role in the market economy. But this new economic system still calls for support by statutes to avoid confusion. Chao Tzu-yang hopes to use his new economic policy to save the Chinese Communist regime from its thirty-year-old crisis and to revive the economy in order to strengthen the position of the regime.

The Implementation of a New Economic Policy

I believe that implementation of this new policy will encounter three-way resistance:

1. For people of noncommunist economic societies, Chao Tzu-yang's new economic policy is just rudimentary economic knowledge, but Chinese Communist cadres will find it difficult to accept Chao's concept.
2. Even if Chinese Communist cadres can identify themselves with this new policy, the implementation will conflict with their vested interests and may therefore be resisted.
3. Despite the purge by Teng Hsiao-p'ing following Mao's death, the strength of the remnants of the Cultural Revolution faction still cannot be ignored.

Chao Tzu-yang has emphasized that there are two defects in the current economic system. First, the economic decision-making power is too centralized, depriving the leaders on the frontline of business management of their power. Second, there is no demarcation between government agencies and enterprises. To ensure its leadership in the economy, the government interferes in the enterprises with economic plans, the enactment of economic laws, and other economic measures. This interference has driven the enterprises to a passive position. In the new economy, the Chinese Communists are expected to restrain their interference by adopting price, tax, loan, and profit policies.

The New Ten-Year Economic Plan

The Chinese Communists have drafted a new Ten-Year Economic Plan for 1981–1990 to replace the old Ten-Year Economic Plan (1976–1985). The new plan combines the sixth and seventh Five-Year Plans. This new plan prescribes simpler economic targets and is to be carried out on a smaller scale. It is more balanced than the previous plan and in many ways contradicts the Cultural Revolution and Mao's Thought.

Although the Chinese Communist regime has maintained that in philosophy, party building, military doctrine, and culture, Mao's Thought still provides guidance, they also have said that some of his economic theory is no longer applicable. They have suggested that new solutions should be found. Despite this departure from the Maoist line, the regime is still reluctant to make a wholesale repudiation of Mao Tse-tung. Although portraits of Marx, Engels, Lenin, and Stalin erected at Tienanmen Square in Peking have been removed, one of Mao's portraits has remained over the entrance to the Forbidden City, indicating that he has not been entirely relegated to the past.

The case of Communist China is quite different from that of the Soviet Union, which repudiated Stalin but not Lenin or the Communist party. In China, the negation of Mao Tse-tung would be tantamount to a repudiation of the Chinese Communist party, which would shake the Communist regime to its foundation. Thus the Chinese Communist regime has to open its economic enterprises very gradually to civilians and move toward a Yugoslavian model for its economic system. The regime has to change its ownership concept, i.e., to concede that an exclusive system of all-people's ownership cannot work. In other words, "private ownership" will emerge alongside "state ownership" and "collective ownership."

Private shops have been set up in Shanghai. The regime even plans to set up wholesale markets, sales agents, and exchanges. Some consumers' cooperatives have adopted the organization of limited corporations. These developments are indications that the economic system of the PRC has undergone drastic changes that will pose a crucial test to Chinese Communism.

The Yugoslavian Pattern Under Experimentation

The Chinese Communists have recently proclaimed that people will now have free choice in their occupations. This implies a step forward in labor policy that may be interpreted, as noted above, as an adoption of the Yugoslavian model. Such a measure, however, is only one part of the economic policy of the Chinese Communist regime. Although it has not basically changed its Communist line, it adopts new measures as necessary to realize its purpose of coordinating employers and workers through the market function of the labor force. It is the Peking regime's hope to fully utilize human resources so as to upgrade working efficiency and productivity. It is adopting a two-wheel system in its economic policy. One wheel is the market system; the other is the planning system.

Generally speaking, an economy under the open market system is better for development; however, such a system is apt to lead to mass unemployment. Even if granting workers the choice of occupation seems to increase job volume, it actually works to decrease disguised unemployment and to increase real unemployment. This is contrary to the situation under the economic policy of the "Red Banner," which was most evident in the Great Leap Forward. It is notable that the Peking regime is now taking the course of the anti-Red Banner, with the result that the rate of unemployment in the PRC is likely to increase remarkably. This poses a most difficult problem for the Communist regime.

The Chinese Communists recognize the problem and are taking some preventive measures. For instance, the authorities grant loans to private sectors to help establish private enterprises and to encourage successful enterprises to grow through reinvestments. Such measures may work to a certain degree. However, the same measures promote a capitalist environment to grow and prosper. Can a tenuous balance be maintained that will not be seen as threatening the Communist regime and thus result in a renewed round of internal oppression?

A Pattern of Economic Development Under Chinese-style Socialism

The relatively liberal new economic policy can easily be predicted to have the Chinese Communists looking for a new theoretical ground on which to base this policy. To remain in power they must adopt a system that produces; however, the system must not undermine their positions.

A number of indications reflect the Peking regime's attempt to stride toward a Chinese-style socialism. For the time being, although still acting under the scope of Marxism-Leninism-Maoism, the regime is to a certain extent pragmatic in learning from foreign experiences. In the long run, the dogmas of Marxism-Leninism-Maoism face problems.

In the eyes of the Chinese Communists, there is no definite socialist approach in the pursuit of economic development. The best possible way for them to develop a socialist economy, they believe, is through constant practice and experimentation. The way toward socialism, Chinese-style, should be worked out through due coordination between the market economy and the planned economy. Such a harmonious coordination is also essential between public enterprises and private ones and between domestic capital and foreign funds, as well as in adjustments between the domestic economy and international economies.

Price Stability, Economic Growth, and Employment

Generally speaking, Communist countries cannot expect rapid economic growth if they adopt a highly centralized economic system without the free market function; under these circumstances the work ethic cannot be fully utilized. The difficulty is that when a Communist nation adopts a planned economy accommodated to the free market function, it will be confronted with severe problems of both unemployment and inflation, even though its economic development should surpass that possible under a wholly centralized economic policy. Such a dilemma is very real for Communist China.

For over three decades, Peking's economic system and policy have swung back and forth in conflicts between the Left and the Right. After such a long lingering period, the current Peking regime is now at the crossroads. The economic policy of revisionism implemented after Teng Hsiao-p'ing's return to power has been an approach for realizing the Four Modernizations. This policy, however, has caused three nonconfidence crises.

Because the Peking regime must continue to pursue a revisionist economic policy, problems of inflation and unemployment will turn from bad to worse. Statistics indicate that the inflation rate recorded a high of over 20 percent of the consumers' index in 1981. The unemployment rate was approximately 5 percent of the national population, or 10 percent of the labor force. This rate represents approximately fifty million jobless.[4] Among the jobless in the population, young urban intellectuals composed the majority. As they suffer the agony of the jobless, these young intellectuals have to struggle to cope with soaring commodity prices. The three nonconfidence crises of the Peking regime have thus been deepening day by day.

On 26 April 1982, the Peking regime promulgated its fourth draft of the revised Constitution, which contains some provisions on freedom, democracy, and private property. These rights of freedom and private property are granted under the restriction of the four unchangeables—socialism, dictatorship of the proletariat, party leadership, and Marxist-Leninist-Maoist thought. Worse, the draft Constitution vests excessive power in the Military Commission, further compromising the grant of democracy, freedom, and private property. The Constitution was drafted with a very wide range of flexibility for execution; thus, the Peking regime may enforce the Constitution according to its own perceptions of its needs. Is such a constitution designed primarily to free the people to improve the economy? Is it designed mainly to pacify the West? Or is it actually an uncertain and hard-fought compromise among the Chinese Communist leaders over the question of the necessity for revisionist measures?

Peking's policy of revisionist Communism can neither discard the burden of Communism nor release itself from the fetters of Mao's Thought; its system can take no definite shape. For example, the draft Constitution not only recognizes private ownership aside from public and collective ownership but also stipulates that People's Communes are nonpolitical. It also provides for a system of Production Cooperatives set below the People's Communes, thus scaling collective efforts down to units more readily understood by the labor force and rural villagers. But confusion is thereby introduced over the People's Communes.

Under the circumstances, People's Communes are expected to take on the status of being separate from politics and the economy, and also representing a split between reality and theory. Will the communes survive in more than nominal status? Considering that an overwhelming majority of the people—up to 80 percent of the total population—is engaged in agricultural production or activities that are almost wholly organized under the People's Communes, what will the rural people's situation be if the communes collapse of their ambiguity? For three decades the Chinese Communists have been trying to implement the system of People's Communes, and now it appears that they can no longer effectively prop up the effort. The Communists came to power using farmers and peasants as their instruments; the regime could be placed in jeopardy if it continues to lose farmers' support.[5]

An Evaluation of China's Modernization

By looking back at economic development over more than three decades in Communist China, we may come to the conclusion that the

PRC was confronted with economic recessions owing mainly to mistaken policies. It may be true in theory that a utopian ideology exists under which nonmaterial incentives can prevail over material ones, but events have shown that it is neither Soviet nor Chinese Communism.

In modernization, Communist China is caught in a dilemma: If, as in the past, it turns left again in economic policy and suppresses all free market enterprise, the economy will grow stale; but as it turns right, it skirts accusations of capitalism and will encounter grave unemployment and inflation. The current serious unemployment and inflation are not just economic problems, but also reflect social and political problems. This is an evaluation of Red China's future economic policy toward the Four Modernizations.

One of the major traits in the new Chinese Communist economic policy is reflected in the hope of stimulating production with consumption, i.e., to increase the workers' and farmers' work enthusiasm and then to promote production by increasing the production and consumption of consumer goods. This is a comparatively sensible economic policy. Apparently, the "modernization of consumer goods" has been made a precondition to carrying out the Four Modernizations. This logical economic development is an indirect application of Keynesianism.

Judging from this direction of change, one can predict that the PRC will soon follow the Yugoslavian model in economic structure. The Yugoslavian model is based on the Communist planned form of economy but allows considerable freedom in economic pursuits. In the short run, the essence of Communism will remain intact; in the long run, the system may change the nature of communism.

The economic system of Communist China is not bound like that of Eastern European nations by the Soviet-dominated Warsaw Pact and the Council for Mutual Economic Assistance (COMECON). On the contrary, Communist China is leaning toward the West in external politics and economic policy; its choices are its own for the degree to which Marxism-Leninism suits it. The Chinese Communists, after all, are Chinese. Since Mao's death they have seemed to grow less Communist and more Chinese. Pragmatism has prevailed over doctrine as necessary. What does this mean for economic policy?

The current steady readjustment in the Chinese Communist economy is caused by the following factors:

1. Since Mao's death, the regime has been relieved of the excessive baggage of Mao's Thought, Mao's quotations, and Mao deification. Therefore, it can throw off the yoke of Maoist ideology in readjusting its economic policy.
2. The economic policy since 1949 has shown that neither the leftist faction nor the rightist faction can solve the PRC's economic problems so long as the two factions merely cycle in power.

3. In the past few years, the Chinese Communist regime has come to understand as a result of its contact with the West that Western features of free economy can help make the economy prosperous.
4. The success of the Republic of China on Taiwan in pursuing a planned free economy during the past thirty-two years has helped prompt the mainland Chinese regime to reconsider its economic system.

The future course of the Chinese Communist economic system will be influenced by the following factors:

1. Soviet influence—the USSR has negated Mao's Thought and expressed its hope that Communist China will accept and travel a Moscow-led revisionist road.
2. U.S. influence—the United States has obliquely negated the Mao line and is influencing Communist China's economic system through mutual communications.
3. Rightist influence in Communist China—the rightists in the Chinese Communist regime have negated Mao's economic policy and put the economy on the track of revisionism.
4. The influence of the Chinese cultural tradition—Confucianism calls for an economic system and policy characterized by the coordination and harmonization of freedom and planning. Despite anti-Confucian campaigns this influence remains strong.

Although all four of these influences, in effect, negate Mao Tse-tung's line, they assume different meanings. Analyzing the interaction of these influences, one can ask whether in the far future the economic policy of the Chinese Communist regime will take a course closer to a Western free economy than to a socialist "planned free economy." Certainly in its economic policy the Chinese Communist regime will become more revisionistic than the Soviet Union and its associated Warsaw Pact and COMECON nations.

Notes

1. Alexander Eckstein, *China's Economic Development: The Interplay of Scarcity and Ideology* (Ann Arbor: University of Michigan Press, 1975), pp. 300–340.
2. Gertrude E. Schroeder, *The Soviet Economy on the Treadmill of Reforms—Soviet Economy in a Time of Change,* U.S. Congress Joint Economic Committee (Washington, D.C.: U.S. Government Printing Office, 1979), vol. 1, pp. 312–340.
3. Estimation made by the Advisory Office of the Ministry of Economic Affairs, Republic of China on Taiwan.
4. Estimation made by the Advisory Office of the Ministry of Economic Affairs, Republic of China on Taiwan.
5. Wou Wei, "Organizational Choice and Economic Efficiency in Communist China (1949–1969)," *Indian Journal of Economics* 55 (Allahabad, India, October 1974), p. 218.

11
Basic Trends in the Chinese Economy: An Evaluation of the Past Three Decades

Jan S. Prybyla

Introduction: Trends and Bends

A trend means a general direction, course, or tendency. It need not be a straight line. In human affairs especially, it is full of bends. The trend expresses commitment and adherence by people, particularly the more powerful ones—the leaders—to certain broad principles and goals of policy. The bends arise from disagreements about the way policy should be pursued and from the objective impossibility in some cases to express the principles and reach the goals. If alternative technologies are not available, you cannot ride to the moon on a broom, and you cannot turn 800 million Chinese peasants into selfless egalitarian beings responsive only to moral commendations—not in thirty years anyway, and perhaps not in a thousand. In Chinese socialist parlance the trend is referred to as the "basic line of socialist construction"; policy disagreements as the "struggle between the two lines"; and the objective obstacles to the line as "objective economic laws."

Trends

Principles

From the beginning of the Communist movement in China, Communist leaders and a fluctuating proportion of the people, especially parts of the intelligentsia, were committed to a general line of socialist construction (the basic trend). This line comprised two major principles of economic policy and a cluster of general economic goals. The principles concerned the replacement of China's "semifeudal," semimarket economy by a centrally planned administrative command economy modeled after the Soviet prototype of the 1930s to early 1950s,[1] and the socialization (nationalization and collectivization) of the bulk of the means of production and distribution, also on the Soviet model.

Administrative Command. The two principles of economic policy were carried out in their broadest form by 1956. After that date several attempts were made to modify the component parts of the administrative command economy and to raise or lower the level of socialization. The human cost involved in installing and then modifying the system (from right to left, and from left to right) has been high. The three elements of this cost are (1) large loss of life (land reform, Cultural Revolution), (2) loss of ability (neutralization and temporary "zombification" of rural and urban entrepreneurs and intellectuals), and (3) erosion of trust in the party and the system. The last two are especially relevant to China's future prospects; the loss of ability or intellect can be made up through formal education more easily than loss of trust.

After all the costs are accounted for and the twists and turns of policy are added, the Chinese economy today remains a centrally planned administrative command system whose Soviet origins are much in evidence. It is a Soviet-type economy at a lower level than the Soviet level of development and is marked by strong Chinese cultural infusions. As an engine of goal formulation and resource allocation it is characterized by (1) very great concentration of decision-making power in a few people at the top, with the resulting decisions mandatory (central planning or command), and (2) the key role played by physical-technical norms and accounting prices in the diffusion of information, and by about 300 centrally prepared materials-balances in the coordination of decisions—both products of a huge planning and supervisory bureaucracy (administration).

The information and coordination role of market prices and lateral buyer-seller transactions remains secondary despite the publicity it has received in recent years. This is true, I think, of both legally sanctioned and illegal or semilegal prices and transactions. Many man-hours are spent tending the family plot, working for oneself under the rural production responsibility system, and commuting to urban and rural fairs—much of this at the expense of work for the collective. Still, the mandatory state quotas are there, and they come first. The market system operates at the periphery of the command economy and under it. The two systems influence each other in many technical ways. For example, retail prices of nonstaple foods in state stores are set with some consideration of prices of similar foods on the free market and, in turn, the presence of state food stores and more or less zealous local supervisory authorities influences price levels on the free market.

The ability to sell surplus farm produce on the free market (normally at higher prices than those paid by the state) affects adversely the quality of produce delivered to the state under the mandatory quotas. The size of the market, however measured—whether by the volume of transactions, number of people involved, or man-hours spent in production and distribution for private ends—is, and probably will remain, much smaller than that of the planned economy, even if account is taken of the fact that the free market crops up in the command economy in various guises (such as the buying and selling of favors by officials, with a premium tacked onto the bribe for risk). But there is a more subtle problem involved in the unequal coexistence of command and market. It is referred to by the authorities with alarm as "spiritual pollution," meaning the spread of a market mentality. The worst interpretation is put by top officialdom on the market ethic: The voluntariness of market transactions is seen as anarchy, competition as dog-eat-dog, maximization of profits and utilities as selfishness, and the preoccupation with supply, demand, and price as rank materialism.

No doubt there is some justification for this official anxiety in an environment in which a good deal of market trafficking remains outside the slowly emerging and ill-defined law (i.e., where the traffic is forced into underground sleaziness). But there is more to it than that. Market mentality has caught on—most visibly in the large cities and suburban farm areas—in large part because of the spiritual vacuum created by the people's loss of trust in the party, the socialist ethic, and the ability of the command economy to deliver the goods. From thoughtful young people I spoke to (June 1982), faint whispers of regret could be heard that socialism and the decent life are not possible together. These people are not happy with their shattered illusions and not at ease in their newly fitted worldliness. Others wallow in it, especially around Canton and the special economic zone of Shenzhen. The problem for the future, it seems to me, is not so much whether the present unstable mix of five parts command to one part open-but-suppressed market will be reversed to purer command or relaxed to greater market, but rather how one builds a modern, materially and humanely better society on spiritual emptiness. In its heavy-handed way the party has of late mobilized children in movements of "socialist courtesy" and flag-waving cleaning-up operations, and it has resurrected the superannuated ideologues of the fifties who hanker after the allegedly ascetic ethic and probity of Yenan. This will not work, at least not in the way intended by the Dengists. The command period of the First Five-Year Plan is being built up by official propaganda (side by side with commercial posters advertising bolts, nuts, and machine tools) as a sort of paradise lost. This too will not work, at least not with those whose parents lived through that difficult time and recall it shorn of its subsequent ideological embellishments.

And so the trend in administrative command can be simply summarized. After thirty years the centrally planned administrative command economy is still in place, but it is volatile and beset by uncertainties.

Socialization of Property. Socialism, the leaders have always maintained, depends on planning and on socialization of the means of production and distribution. Planning, as we have seen, remains by and large at the helm, albeit with compromises. Socialization of property is an accomplished fact, but also with compromises. The nationalization of industry and commerce and the collectivization of agriculture were completed by 1956. The compromise was represented by "private" family plots and residual household sideline handicraft activity.

The size of family plots has fluctuated from 7 percent of the communal arable land, to zero during the Great Leap Forward and parts of the Cultural Revolution, to 15 percent now. As in other state socialist societies, the proportion of total income derived by individual peasant families from work on the plots has always been much larger than that suggested by the ratio of plots to communal arable land. In fact, the agricultural private sector was never a luxury appendage to the collective economy; it was always indispensable to the peasants' survival. In 1980 nationwide, for example, household plots and sideline activities (the private sector) provided two-fifths of the minimum income officially designated as needed for subsistence. In one-third of the production teams, private-sector income represented half of the peasants' subsistence needs.[2] There was and is, in other words, an objective need to retain the private sector in agriculture. Similarly, in urban areas the private sector furnishes many rudimentary consumer services that were badly mauled in the 1950s by the collectivization of individual handicraftsmen and peddlers.

Thus, after thirty years there are objective limits to the spread of socialization. These limits stem from the negative incentives to labor and management that accompany the socialization of assets. Public property in the means of production and distribution invariably—not just in China—causes a clean break between individual input of effort and individual reward. The concentration of inordinate amounts of power in the guardians of public property at the top of the administrative pyramid produces a highly skewed distribution of privilege and income (through "contacts") that is poorly disguised by the slogan that all property belongs to all the people. The assurance of tenured employment to workers at the bottom of the pyramid in exchange for low real wages encourages what the Chinese call "eating from the common pot" (the unbreakable iron pot) or, as we would put it, "free lunch" at public expense.

Times of economic crunch have been a result of rapid and comprehensive socialization of property. In the wake of the Great Leap Forward, from 1960 to the outbreak of the Cultural Revolution, and again after 1976, the sphere of de facto private property (nominally social property over which individual families or even individual persons are granted production and marketing rights) has invariably had to be expanded. Today the rural devolution of production responsibility to households, and in the deprived regions to individuals, represents such a compromise.[3] The ingredients of the property mix have been changed in favor of privatization, in practice if not in legal theory. The aim has been to improve incentives by expanding the individual producers' residual rights in the land they farm. Here as with the extension of markets, the real problem for the continuation of the basic line on socialization is not whether the privatization of property (including some commercial and service undertakings in the cities) will grow at the expense of social property or even whether it will be legally sanctioned at some point in land and farm capital titles granted to families. Rather the most troublesome aspect is the effect that plots and production responsibility will have on what the leaders, with growing apprehension, see as the spread of "private property mentality" (the bourgeois mentality of "petty producers"). This dimension of the problem is not readily subjected to quantification. It has enemies among the less entrepreneurial and self-reliant peasants, and there must be many of them. But seeing the multitudes of peasants single-mindedly bicycling their way to town in the morning with private produce from their land parcels dangling from their backs or waists or from the handlebars, I would be inclined to conclude that the leaders' apprehension is justified.

The Cultural Revolution has shown that it is possible to roll back the size of private plots and eliminate the Liuist (now Dengist) system of residual production responsibility at the price of an equal or greater rollback in work incentives and labor productivity. The eagerness with which the peasants seize the chance of being—if only in part—masters of the land they till in the aftermath of the Cultural Revolution suggests that it may be easier in the future (should the leaders so decide) to legislate against this particular form of property relations than to root out the idea of it (i.e., private property) from the minds of the people. In other words, it is easier to socialize land than to make that myth of the nineteenth and early twentieth centuries come true—the birth of socialist man.

Summing up, although after thirty years socialized property in the means of production and distribution is in place (100 percent in legal fiction), the socialized mind is not. What, then, about the agreed-on goals of the centrally planned administrative, socialized command economy?

Goals

In addition to the general principles of administrative command and socialization of property, China's Communist leaders and, no doubt, most of the people subscribed to a bundle of goals that the socialized command economy was to achieve and that the leaders (following Marx and Lenin) sincerely believed *only* this economy could reach at the required pace. There is not much that is original or unusual about such hopes for progress, in that the goals, if not the means, are shared at least at the rhetorical plane by all developing and developed societies.

The list is long and only a few goals can be considered: namely, growth of product; equity of distribution and security, that is, protection of the individual from physical and social risks; stability of output, employment, and prices; national economic independence (self-reliance); and scientific-technical innovation.

Growth. The overall record is respectable, given the odds. Some Asian developing countries have done much better, but others have fared worse.

Table 11.1 Growth Record: 1952 and 1981

Total and Sectors	1952	1981
National income (Net Material Product)		
National income (billion yuan)	58.9	388.0
Population at year end (millions)	574.8	996.2
National income per capita (yuan)	102	389
Index of per capita national income (1952 = 100)	100	381
Agricultural production		
Grain (soybeans and potatoes in grain equivalent included) (million metric tons)	161	325
Grain per capita (kilograms)	280	326
Availability of dehusked grain for human consumption (kilograms)	168	205
Cotton (million metric tons)	1.3	3.0
Cotton per capita (kilograms)	2.3	3.0
Industrial production		
A. Producer goods		
Coal (million metric tons)	67	620
Oil (million metric tons)	0.4	101
Electricity (billion kwh)	7.3	309
Steel (million metric tons)	1.3	35.6
Machine tools (thousand units)	14	103
Chemical fertilizer (million metric tons)	0.2	12.4
B. Consumer goods		
Cotton cloth (billion meters)	3.8	14.3
Cotton cloth per capita (meters)	6.6	1.4
Processed sugar (million metric tons)	0.5	3.2
Processed sugar per capita (kilograms)	0.9	3.0
Salt (million metric tons)	3.0	18.3
Salt per capita (kilograms)	5.0	10.0
Bicycles (million units)	0.08	17.5
Number of people per bicycle produced	7.2	5.7

Sources: State Statistical Bureau (SSB), Ten Great Years (Peking, 1980); SSB, Communique on Fulfillment of China's 1981 National Economic Plan, Beijing Review, no. 20 (17 May 1982):pp. 15-24.

The main results are summed up in Table 11.1. Four facts are significant. First, per capita national income (Chinese definition, i.e., net material product) in 1981 was still very low by any standard. Even if the figure is generously adjusted for the omission of "nonproductive" services, we come up with a per capita gross national product (Western definition) of around US $280, which puts China in the upper range of low-income countries as defined by the World Bank. (The lowest middle-income country, Egypt, has a per capita GNP of roughly US $400.)

Second, swelling population numbers have gobbled up a good part of the increase in national income. Further compression of the birthrate would greatly facilitate China's developmental take-off, on the brink of which the country now appears to be poised. The long-range, post-1949 rate of natural population increase was reduced from a little over 2 percent to 1.4 percent by 1981. Since then, the rate has been inching upward again, in part because of the side effects of the rural production responsibility system. (Under the system, the more "labor powers" you have in the household, the more you can privately produce, and the better off you are. Production team leaderships, I was told, despite disapproval by higher-ups, keep alloting land for household use according to the number of mouths in the family.)

Third, agricultural production in grain and cotton has not become fully supporting. Per capita grain output (grain continues to account by far for the greater part of the average person's diet) has risen in the last thirty years at an average annual rate of 0.5 percent. Per capita availability of husked grain for human consumption in 1981 was only about 205 kilograms (one-fifth better than thirty years earlier); of this amount, roughly ten kilograms came from imports.[4] (In the early 1960s China became a net grain importer.) Grain imports are a big drain on China's foreign exchange balance and a setback in the country's modernization effort. Per capita production of cotton (cotton is by far the most important material used in making clothes) increased over the thirty-year period 1952–1981 at an average annual rate of 1 percent. The per capita availability of cotton in 1981 was three kilograms, some of it accounted for by imports. In sum, the food situation (as represented by grains) and the clothing situation (as represented by cotton) remain precarious. Despite a huge amount of earthwork done over the years, Chinese farming is still to a dangerous extent at the whim of the elements.

Fourth, growth in output of producer goods has been more rapid than growth in output of welfare-intensive consumer goods such as cotton cloth, sugar, and salt. (Base data for 1952 for some other key consumer goods, e.g., woolen piece goods, are not available, and figures for certain other goods, e.g., edible vegetable oil, have not been reported in 1981.) The administrative command economy's tendency to expand industries for producer goods at the expense of consumer goods and food (production for production's sake), and the high investment rate involved in this, have been criticized since 1977. Both are systemic propensities that the present reformers find very difficult to bring under control. In the twenty-six years 1952–1978, heavy industry received on the average about ten times more state investment than light industry, and the rate of investment was typically over 30 percent of national income (net material product). This situation has caused all kinds of distortions, disproportions, bottlenecks, and wastages in the economy, and it has had an adverse effect on labor incentives. Under the restructuring of the economy undertaken in the last months of 1978, investment in consumer goods has been raised relative to heavy industry, but heavy industry still gets the larger share. Attempts have also been made—against spirited resistance from many quarters, especially provincial and lower-level authorities—to squeeze down the rate of investment.[5]

Equity and Security. The persistence of low income in China, due in part to the large numbers of people (32,000 more people every day) packed into a shrinking farmland area and the continued fluctuations of farm output with changing weather, make a certain amount of egalitarianism in wealth and income distribution an almost objective constraint on policy. Without a guaranteed basic grain, cooking oil, and cotton cloth ration available at subsidized prices, many people in the countryside and the cities would starve, and diseases related to nutrition deficiency would spread. For the last thirty years, except during the famine years 1960–1962 (the result in large measure of the collapse of organization during the Great Leap Forward), such an egalitarian safety net for the near-destitute has been a part of the basic trend of China's economy. Travelers in China, and not only fellow-travelers, have remarked on the attenuation of extremes of wealth and poverty so starkly visible in some other developing countries. The observation does not imply that discreet and not-so-discreet power and privilege differentials do not exist in China; they do and they are very large. But still, the burden of poverty seems to be fairly evenly spread, at least on the basis of international comparison.

The guaranteed basic ration has not always been available, especially to the "five black categories" (counterrevolutionaries, rightists, bad elements, former landlords, and former rich peasants—and the descendants of families in these categories). In 1980, for example, it was estimated that there were more than 100 million people in China whose daily food-grain consumption was below the half-kilogram guaranteed by the government.[6] Income differentials among rural households are quite significant and are on the rise (they are related to the number of people of working age in the household, but also to entrepreneurship and "contacts"). There are important income differences among production teams and among communes (the suburban ones normally well off even by comparison with urban incomes). Regional differences exist, and there also is a big gap between average rural and urban earnings.

In 1979 the highest reported total per capita earnings (social and private sector) in the countryside were 7.5 times the highest earnings of the bottom group (60 yuan a year), but the actual difference was probably much greater. That year, 10 percent of the peasants (roughly 85 million people) had total per capita annual incomes of less than 80 yuan, and 4 percent (34 million) earned less than 60 yuan. At the other end, in 2.3 percent of the production brigades (perhaps 20 million people), average per capita total income was said to have been 450 yuan.[7] The lowest income earners survive by going into debt to their production teams and through government relief. As noted before, the current comparatively laissez-faire policy stemming from the production responsibility system and private plot expansion with free marketing is

Table 11.2 Per Capita Annual Income of Urban Wage-Earning Families in 1981

Income Interval	Percentage of Wage-earning Families
720 yuan and more	6.5
600-720 yuan	11.9
420-600 yuan	42.3
300-420 yuan	31.8
240-300 yuan	5.4
Less than 240 yuan	2.1

Sources: Beijing Review, no. 48 (30 November 1981):16-17; and no. 17 (26 April 1982):15-18.

likely to widen rural income differentials. Given the basic equity-leaning trend, this development will have to be watched carefully by policymakers, for although it may spur incentives to productivity, it does not do so uniformly and carries with it short-term political dangers. There are enough Maoists around to make hay from any significant departure from the trend. The present government's agricultural tax policy (exemption of the poorest teams from the tax) takes cognizance of this danger.

Sample data from urban income distribution have been released in recent years. One such sample is given in Table 11.2. The main income (and status) gap in the cities appears to be between those employed in the more productive state sector and those working in the sweat-intensive cooperative service sector. Note the differential between the urban data and the partial data reported earlier for rural peasant families.

Another danger is attached to any further widening of the rural-urban income spread, and that is the probability of widespread migration of peasants into the cities, which would run against the basic trend (at least since 1957) of keeping more people out of the cities. The task of controlling illegal migration from country to town is a formidable one. Parts of it—those dealing with rusticated intellectual urban youths—are already in considerable disarray. A significant reversal of the trend would worsen the housing and unemployment situation in the cities, which even now assumes near-crisis proportions.[8] The economic rationalization drive currently in full swing has cooled the central planners' former ardor for the "blind" development of village industries (as was also the case for some years after the Great Leap Forward). Although there is something to be said for restraining the growth of such mini-industries, one of their by-products in the past was the provision of supplementary income for the communes, which in turn had a dampening effect on the peasants' eagerness to leave the land. How to keep them "down on the farm" once they have seen Shanghai emerges as a real problem for policymakers in the immediate future.

Insurance of the "correct categories" against physical risks (illness, death of principal breadwinner) and risks stemming from economic malfunctions (unemployment, lack of elementary education) has been a basic trend over the last thirty years. This felicitous calculus has been the subject of much publicity and eager study by Western observers in the past. Indeed, it was seen in some quarters as China's major contribution to a new, more humane model of development.[9] There is no doubt that in areas of public health and overt employment much was accomplished, but—as is usual with such things—at a price that the admirers of the achievement did not carefully compute.

The rural cooperative medical service (including barefoot doctors and public health cadres) and various social assistance measures (maternity benefits, retirement pensions, the spread of elementary education, and so on) are, on balance, constructive as supplements to income and promoters of public welfare. They were and remain rudimentary by the standards of developed and some few developing societies, but their positive impact on China's people cannot be hastily dismissed. On the other hand—and China is not alone in this regard—economic costs were involved, mainly in the area of labor productivity. This was especially true of guaranteed employment, which, although it resulted in statistically full or near-full employment, entailed much overstaffing or underemployment (suppressed unemployment) and thus contributed to low labor productivity. The near-impossibility for managers to dismiss redundant or undisciplined workers, and for others higher up to fire incompetent managers or close down money-losing firms, has exacted over the years a high price in industrial and farm efficiency.[10] In an important sense economics is the study of trade-offs. It is the one social science clearly teaching that you cannot have your cake and eat it too. There is bound to be an economic opportunity cost to what is deemed politically or socially desirable or expedient. The British economy stands as an awesome monument to this lesson.

The present danger, as I see it, is that the pendulum might swing too far in the opposite direction—toward a rule-of-thumb economic calculation based on a deficient Marxist economic art that has lots to say about capitalist crises but nothing about efficient functioning of centrally planned administrative, socialized command economies. Such a swing would be grist for the mill of frustrated radicals. It could endanger the present relative political equilibrium and fragile consensus, without which the future modernization of China would be seriously put to question.

Stability. The goal of stability has meant avoidance of significant fluctuations in output, employment, and prices, and avoidance of long-term foreign indebtedness (this last will be discussed later). Stability of employment—full overt employment—has already been touched on in the last section (Security). Statistically, full employment has been achieved in most years (1956–1957 and the immediate post-Leap period were the outstanding exceptions), but at the cost of disguised unemployment that fluctuated over time. A good case can be made for this practice in the context of China's factor proportions (too much labor relative to land and capital), so long as the productivity cost in stagnating factor is borne in mind. However, the tendency to suppress unpleasant real phenomena—which include open output and price fluctuations—is not just the product of China's skewed factor proportions. Rather it is the shared characteristic of all command economies. It amounts to consumption on the job in the form of idling at the workbench, instead of consumption after the job in the form of higher disposable income spent in stores.[11] It is one of those trade-offs mentioned earlier: in this case, the substitution of enforced on-the-job leisure for consumer goods in the shops.

A similar argument applies to overt price stability. Planner-set prices can be kept stable by definition if the planners decree it. However, the shifting underlying forces of offer and demand result in suppressed price fluctuations that show up in black markets, bribery of officials, "kleptocracy," "disguised" price increases (manipulation of weights, measures, and product quality), lines outside stores induced by shortages of particular goods, and mounting inventories of other, unsalable products. The measured vital signs show that nothing is the matter as the disease spreads through the body. A strong case can be made in China, on grounds of equity, for state control over the prices of basic necessities to keep them at or below their average cost of production—a procedure that involves huge subsidies to inefficient producers. At some point, however—and that point is fast approaching—the consumers have to be weaned away from their money illusion.[12] Otherwise a situation arises in which the state subsidizes an increasing portion of its own sources of revenue, which is no way to run the store.[13]

Abrupt and steep official price hikes are made at infrequent intervals. They are dictated by the plight of the state treasury and are made with an eye to what the traffic will bear politically. Even a slight miscalculation of the people's political tolerance leads to riots (which can be contained by the deployment of police force) and to popular alienation (which cannot be). Poland is an excellent example of the problem, and its experience should provide the newly pragmatic Chinese leadership with food for thought.

One of the command economy's self-proclaimed claims to greatness is that by ex ante planning and the abolition of market anarchy it bans forever the business cycle (periodic ups and downs in output). It is true that the causes of output fluctuations in market economies and command economies are different, but it is not true that administrative command has banished such fluctuations. Business cycles in command economies, in the bouncing output sense, are historically documented. They take two forms: (1) subsurface fluctuations in output not revealed by the official statistics and caused by defects in the planning mechanism (especially in the linkages between the planners' commands and the firms' execution of those commands—defective managerial "success indicators"); and (2) open fluctuations revealed by the statistics and induced by political instability (factionalism within the party, succession crises) or agriculture's sensitivity to natural calamities (strengthened by the inappropriateness of socialization and central command planning to the need for agricultural production). Suppressed output cycles assume the form of now more, now less defective or unusable output. For example, in China, in one particular year, out of a total steel output of 34 million tons, 20 million tons could not be used because they were qualitatively substandard or were of the wrong specifications or were not needed or could not be transported to where they were needed. The share of such useless production in the total varies from year to year as the planners crack down here and make repairs there. In addition, for built-in reasons that cannot be examined here, all command economies are subject to activity cycles: sluggishness at the early stages of the planning period and feverish production toward the end of the period. Added to open output fluctuations, these suppressed phenomena contribute to significant economic cycles in China as in other centrally planned administrative command economies.

In sum, under the heading of stability (output, employment, and price) the overt trend, by and large, in the last thirty years has been consonant with the claim. However, after suppressed fluctuations are factored into the record, China has not done any better overall than other economies in this regard.

National Economic Independence and Innovation. Because of China's size and the potential availability of all sorts of inputs needed for development, the goal of national self-sufficiency (not autarky, but self-reliance "in the main") makes more sense for it than for a country such as Hungary. On the other hand, given the relative backwardness and low income of the economy as compared with the world's developed economies, such a goal makes much less sense in terms of trying to generate the needed scientific and technological know-how and rely on the country's own capacity to generate the required amounts and qualities of capital. An important part of China's compulsion to avoid foreign economic entanglements over most of the thirty-year period is attributable to historical memories: Western capitalism before 1949 and Soviet socialism (the period of "leaning to one side") from 1950 to the Great Leap. These memories, some old, some fresh, have strengthened the not always unanimous resolve of the leaders to seek stability in the balance of external payments, i.e., to avoid excessive deficits in its foreign accounts.

Whatever the constructive results of the policy of self-reliance—and there are some, among them the resurgence of self-confidence, national dignity, and national unity as China "stood up"—they have been bought at the price of a slowdown in the economy's modernization drive and a falling-behind in China's economic standing relative to other modern and modernizing economies. As noted, the trend under this heading has been mixed: first, heavy reliance on the outside socialist world (especially during the First Five-Year Plan), followed by years of cocoonlike development, followed in turn by an unprecedented opening-up after the death of Mao. The ardor of the latest affair with capitalism has shown wide fluctuations since 1977: first a shopping spree, then, on reflection, more moderate involvement and a switch from massive purchases of up-to-date plant and equipment to acquisition of foreign knowledge aimed primarily at renovating, updating, and rationalizing the country's capital and human resources and its system of economic organization. New bad memories have been added to the older ones: The Japanese-financed steel project at Baoshan is a good example.

The enthusiasm for mutual embrace has by now considerably cooled on both sides, including the Western interest in joint oil exploration and development ventures off the China coast. The capitalists' main worries center, as one would expect, on the possibility of suffering financial losses on transactions with China (especially on commercial loans, which are now running very close to the Plimsoll line drawn by China's debt service ratio). Such apprehensions are not assuaged by the vagueness and future uncertainty of China's laws, especially those dealing with joint ventures. China's recent restraint has to do with the leaders' more accurate perception of the economy's ability to absorb foreign technology and to pay for it with exports to highly fickle and resistant foreign markets without domestic inflationary and other adverse repercussions. Among such repercussions is the already noted influence of imported market mentality on what, rightly or wrongly, the leaders believe to be the indispensable socialist ethos.

I think it is important to bear in mind that China's "reversal" of the basic self-reliance trend is (1) relative, and (2) well within the limits of the administrative command system and sanctioned by no less a doctrinal authority than Lenin. Foreign-held assets in China are subject to China's laws, and they will eventually be transferred to Chinese ownership. Using foreign capitalists to help build socialism is doctrinally orthodox and has long been practiced by most state socialist economies. Whether market-related pluralistic values will take root in China as part of the economic package, whether they will be tamed and transformed by a combination of China's millennial cultural tradition and socialist re-education, or whether they can be separated from modern technology and social organization and discarded—these are important questions that unfortunately cannot be done justice here.[14]

Bends

The bends in the trends arise from leadership disagreements on the modalities of policy trends (all of them relevant to life and limb of both leaders and people) and from objective impediments. Because of space constraints, I shall deal here mainly with the subjectively induced bends, or leadership disagreements.

Although in everyday reality the situation is more complex, a division of opinion between the party's "Right" and "Left" wings is a workable simplification that has stood up well to the test of time. The Right is a coalition of party regulars, hardened members of the structured hierarchical administrative command apparat whose philosophical positions within the Marxist-Leninist ideological universe range all the way from Stalinism to Yugoslav-type revisionism, with many points covered in between. They are now back again at the helm (with some hidden Leftists among them). During the Cultural Revolution, they were collectively branded by the Left as "capitalist-roaders"—a designation that must not be taken too seriously when their knowledge of capitalism and its pluralistic values was and is zilch (zero).

The Left, whose leaders are now serving time, was and clandestinely remains a loose radical coalition made up of diverse groups and individuals: fundamentalist interpreters of the Marxist creed; idealists and ideologues of radical persuasion (including a sprinkling of socialist utopians, populists, communards, political revivalists, and anarchists); some young people disillusioned with their career prospects in a rigidly structured society and resentful of elite privileges and privileged corruption; other young and not-so-young people who were "helicoptered" by the Cultural Revolution into universities and positions of authority by reason of their impeccable class antecedents; elements of the Liberation Army's high command who resent the effects of de-Maoization on army morale and army budgets; spiritual devotees of the late Chairman Mao (the "whatever" group); a few literary types; and some Leftist loonies. The list is longer but this will have to do for a recitation of the leadership disagreements that follows.[15]

Principles

Administrative Command. The Right emphasizes the importance of the "economic base" (Marxist jargon) to the dialectically historical progression; the tight, highly structured, centralized, hierarchical bureaucratic organization of the economy ("social relations of production") along ministerial branch lines; central physical planning by means of a growing number of material and financial balances; economic accounting (*khozraschet*); the directorial principle at the level of the firm; and the development of the labor force through professional and vocational education, capital increase (widening and deepening), and technological development (in Marxist terms, the "material productive forces"). Mass mobilization movements are seen as being handy for breaking down major obstacles in the path of economic development (including the suppression of former elites and oppositionists within the ranks of the new elite), provided such movements are organized and strictly controlled by the center. The Right stands for socialist law and order (including Stalinist-type legalism) that would give the clerks enough uninterrupted routine time to do their job of formulating commands and carrying them out "according to plan."

The Left is concerned with the Marxist "superstructure" of ideas, including individual and mass psychologies, political culture, the content of social science, "consciousness" (popular and academic ideological outlook, organized religion, the news media, the system of education, family relations), and the nature of the state (i.e., the question of in whose hands state power resides). The quintessence of the Left's position is found in Mao's essay on the *Foolish Old Man Who Removed the Mountain*—a hymn to the irresistible power of the correctly inspired collective will.[16] The Left shuns bureaucratic structures and rigid lines of command and prefers government by "cultural" mass movements held together by a shared correct ideology in which material gain plays a subordinate role to moral collective spirituality. It interprets the Marxist dialectic in its extreme antagonistic and confrontational sense and sees the process of economic development as an unending succession of "rebel dictatorial" proletarian waves (permanent revolution) that are anathema to the apparat-anchored bureaucrats.

The apogee of the Right in China was the First Five-Year Plan (1953–1957), although even this institutionally structured and disciplined period was rent by Leftist outbursts toward the end (the "little great leap" in agricultural collectivization of 1955–1956, the Hundred Flowers Campaign, and the antirightist campaign of 1957, as examples).

The Great Leap Forward (1958–1960) and the Cultural Revolution (1966–1976, especially 1966–1969) illustrate the Left's approach to the principle of economic organization. Over much of these two periods the administrative command apparatus was put to great strain, and key components of it were dismantled (e.g., the organs of central planning and the State Statistical Bureau, which supplies planners with indispensable information).

Socialization. The disagreement about this principle hinges on the pace and level of socialization, not on its desirability. The Right is sensitive to the braking influence on socialization exerted by "objective economic laws" (the "law of value" without market prices) and to the effect of the speed and level of socialization on labor incentives. It is ready to compromise, albeit not graciously, with remnant private or semiprivate property relationships and settle for lower levels of socialization for as long as necessary (i.e., for as long as modest socialization turns out the goods at little resource cost). It tends to view the pace and degree of socialization as a function of the pace and level of maturation of the material productive forces—technology being the foremost among them. The Right was opposed to rapid collectivization and the instant communization of agriculture.

The Left regards leaps in property relations—both forward in time and upward in degree—as the independent variable in the qualitative transformation of labor, land, capital, and technology (the material productive forces). When in power, it throws in the slammer those who advocate temporal and level-of-socialization restraint (e.g., the economist Sun Yefang).

The apogee of the Right for the socialization principle was the post-Leap period 1961–1964 (until the onset of the Socialist Education

Campaign), and it is occurring again in the Dengist course. The Left's perception of socialization dominated the Great Leap Forward and the larger part of the Cultural Revolution.

Goals

Growth, Equity, and Security. The disagreement over these three goals begins with the trade-off between growth and fairness. For the Right, the implied thesis is that growth, through the development of material productive forces, will at some indeterminate higher level of income enable the planners to manipulate rewards to arrive at a just and fair share for all: not just the distribution of personal income, but the provision of social insurance and public goods. Premature and too ideologically advanced exercises in egalitarianism and the free supply of public services jeopardize the development of the material preconditions for growth; they sap incentives by rewarding everybody equally for unequal contributions, impede the raising of levels of skills (labor, managerial, and technical) by lowering the professional content of education, and promote sloth rather than—as the Left claims—the "masses' enthusiasm for production." (The term "masses" is in disfavor nowadays.) For the Left, economic development rests on fairness, interpreted to mean income leveling and widespread "free supply," reinforced by nonmaterial plaudits (moral incentives). Distributive justice in this egalitarian sense (Madame Mao and her associates excepted) leads to growth—and if it does not, so much the worse for incorrect growth. Politically induced swings in the relative weights attached by leadership factions to the three goals and by the leaders' disagreement over which goal plays the motor role in development are the direct cause of the bends in the thirty-year-old trend toward growth, equity, and security.

There has also been disagreement between the Right and the Left on who is to benefit from growth, equity, and security. The Right is inclined to a united front approach to this problem. Reeducated intellectuals, for example, must not be invariably labeled "white." Many Rightists (even former Kuomintang [KMT] officials) can be used within the socialized command economy or allowed to help improve the people's material welfare by peddling small services as one-man collectives. The Left draws a sharp distinction between correct and incorrect class categories; it regards the recruitment of ideologically suspect experts in the cause of socialist construction as a spiritual time-bomb. Although both factions harbor an abiding distrust of intellectual freedom, the Right is willing to take a chance on the ability of the public security apparatus to deal with deviations. In any event, the Right does not regard book-learning, in and of itself, as a threat to socialism provided that it publishes the books.

The Right is more inclined than the Left to put up with some ideologically compromising overt unemployment, especially where this unpleasantness is forced upon it by objective circumstances (dismal productivity at the fringes). Without forsaking the goal of security of employment it is prepared to let some people seek jobs by themselves, or, put in reverse, it is not ready to have its labor bureaus waste time finding employment for everyone. The problem is sloughed off to the workings of a highly imperfect market. In the interest of productivity, and to reduce the burden of state subsidies, the Right is inclined—very reluctantly—to shut down the blatantly more inefficient enterprises. All this runs against the tenets of the Left on labor allocation and on the sanctity of the masses' collective.

Stability. This question has been dealt with earlier under the same topic heading in the section on trends. The discussion must be left at that.[17]

National Economic Independence and Innovation. By and large, the Right is more concerned than the Left with intensive growth—that is, growth through the qualitative improvement of labor, capital, and technology. To encourage such growth, the Right stands ready to open up the economy to foreign (mostly capitalist) scientific and technological imports and to send people abroad for training. It puts less trust than does the Left in the creative potential of the masses of poor and lower middle-income peasants, workers, and lineal descendants of revolutionary martyrs, and it tries to break down economically the "artificial" all-around, self-contained production units that it sees as impeding the benefits to be gained from specialization and economies of scale. Unfortunately, the Marxist economic art to which the Right adheres does not provide it with even approximate answers to questions of what constitutes an economically rational size or a skill-specialization dimension of the producing unit. Leadership disagreements between the Right and the Left do not even address the problem at such a level.

Conclusion

The basic trends in China's economy over the past thirty years have been the construction of a nearly marketless, centrally planned socialized command economy on the Soviet model (adjusted for level of development and historical-cultural legacy) and the attainment of certain broad goals in growth of product, equity of distribution, security, stability, national economic independence, and scientific-technical innovation. With various reservations, the principles of administrative command and socialization have been carried out, and the generously wide goals have been met or more closely approached. The system of economic organization and the commitment to the major goals have not changed. However, the dominant trends in pursuing the goals have been the source of much controversy. Both the commitment to a trend and the sharp divisions over the interpretation to be given to it have profoundly affected the lives of China's people.

The testimony of figures, visual evidence, and what the economists call "intuitive analysis" (gut feeling) lead me to believe that China is today poised on the edge of a developmental take-off. Whether it materializes will depend on the continuation, beyond the lifespan of the present leaders, of political equilibrium and on the ability of the socialized administrative command system to carry the weight of the lift-off and sustain future flight. There are, I think, strong indications that beyond a certain point (already reached by Eastern Europe and the USSR), the system is not the appropriate vehicle of modernization. Should this prove to be so, China will have to consider alternative systemic economic arrangements to carry it on its future course. Such arrangements would inevitably involve a considerable marketization and privatization of the economy. They are bound to meet with strong political resistance, as is clear from the experience of other state socialist countries. In view of this, one might venture to predict that much energy will be expended in the coming years on fixing-up and tinkering with the existing command engine, or in other words, on comparatively innocuous intrasystemic readjustments rather than fundamental systemic reform.

Notes

1. A more thorough treatment of the centrally planned administrative command system may be found in my *Issues in Socialist Economic Modernization* (New York: Praeger, 1980), ch. 1, and in my "Economic Problems of Communism: Mainland China—A Case Study," *Asian Survey* (Berkeley), December 1982.

2. Deng Runsheng, "Good Beginning for Reform of Rural Economic System," *Beijing Review,* no. 48 (30 November 1981), pp. 17–17.

3. A useful analysis of the rural production responsibility system is to be found in Jürgen Domes, "New Policies in the Communes: Notes on Rural Societal Structures in China, 1976–1981," *The Journal of Asian Studies* 41:2 (February 1982), pp. 253–267. A more comprehensive survey of recent reform is Martin Feldstein, "An Economist Looks at China's New Economy," *Wall Street Journal,* 8 July 1982, p. 31.

4. Per capita availability of husked grain for human consumption is arrived at as follows. Grain production (soybeans and potatoes in grain equivalent included) + net grain imports = total grain availability ÷ population at year end = total per capita grain availability − nonhuman consumption, loss in transport and storage, and loss of weight due to dehusking (together estimated at 40 percent of total grain availability per capita) = per capita availability of husked grain for human consumption.

5. "The 1981 investment in capital construction covered by the national budget was basically brought under control. But the investment not covered by the national budget exceeded the plan to a fairly large extent, and blind and duplicate construction was not eliminated." State Statistical Bureau (SSB), "Communique on Fulfilment of China's 1981 National Economic Plan," *Beijing Review,* no. 20 (17 May 1982), p. 10. See also my "China in the 1980s," *Challenge* (May-June 1980), pp. 4–20.

6. E. B. Vermeer, "Income Differentials in Rural China," *China Quarterly,* no. 89, (March 1982), pp. 18–19. Daily per capita consumption in 1980 was given as 0.60 yuan (35 U.S. cents) for the country as a whole. Total per capita consumption of the 800 million or so peasants was 0.46 yuan (27 U.S. cents). *Beijing Review,* no. 48 (30 November 1981), pp. 16–17, and no. 14 (5 April 1982), p. 27.

7. *Beijing Review,* no. 3. (19 January 1981), pp. 5–6; no. 3 (21 January 1981), pp. 6–7; no. 3 (18 May 1981), p. 20; no. 20 (19 May 1980), p. 23. Beijing, Xinhua (New China News Agency) dispatch, 30 December 1980.

8. Since the new course inaugurated in December 1978, state expenditure on residential housing has been stepped up and greater latitude and encouragement have been given to

peasants to build homes. In fact, official warnings are being issued against too much and too profligate house-building in the countryside—much of it on good agricultural land. The neglect of housing (an "unproductive" use of funds in Marxist analysis) is a state socialist systemic trait, not limited to China. Chinese figures for residential housing space in the cities must be watched with care since they appear to include hotel space, now very much the favorite type of housing construction. The impressive figures for new housing released in recent years must be adjusted for old homes that had fallen apart. During 1966–1976, according to official sources, outlays for housing construction were "almost zero" (in fact a net loss of housing space). In 1980, average housing space allocation in Peking came to 2.5 square meters per person.

9. Robert F. Dernberger, ed., *China's Development Experience in Comparative Perspective* (Cambridge, Mass.: Harvard University Press, 1980). Cf. my review of that work in *Problems of Communism* (Washington, D.C.) 31:3 (May-June 1982), pp. 38–41.

10. As a result of the production responsibility system, rural unemployment that was formerly suppressed has become openly visible. A *People's Daily* article (8 October 1981) spoke of "an immense amount of surplus labor" that has emerged in the countryside as peasants began to work more efficiently for themselves and were rewarded less from the common pot. The surplus labor in some localities was said to have been more than 30 percent of the labor force. Between 1957 and 1975 Chinese agriculture absorbed 100 million extra workers, while per capita farmland declined by about 40 percent.

11. In pre-Dengist days travelers from the West described in graphic terms the happy expressions they perceived on the faces of Chinese factory workers, a proof—they argued—of humane socialism at work. The travelers saw the employment of preschool children at various (not overly taxing) manual tasks as part of a character-building process of socialization. In their own homelands they would be the first to denounce this sort of thing as child labor. On my last visit to China (June 1982) I no longer saw toddlers putting together ball point pens. They were playing, and raucously at that, slugging away at one another for possession of the few better toys, just as they are prone to do everywhere. The late chairman's picture, I noticed, was in most classrooms conspicuous by its absence. China is no longer a special case in Western accounts. It is just another underdeveloped economy.

12. See Robert Delfs, "The High Cost of Stable Prices," *Far Eastern Economic Review* (12 March 1982), pp. 84–86; Frank Ching, "China Pays a Price to Keep Prices Low," *Wall Street Journal,* 26 December 1981, p. 15.

13. This problem is in addition to the geometric growth of the planning bureaucracy for every arithmetic increase in the work to be done. In the end, as Novozhilov pointed out for the Soviet Union, if everybody does the planning, who is going to do the producing?

14. In the meanwhile, it is reported, Chinese peasants are busy putting up shrines all over the map, at what the authorities consider to be profligate cost. The peasants argue that since the authorities are rebuilding big temples (to attract tourists and earn hard currencies), they can build little temples. Emulating the upper cadres, they hold big weddings whenever they can afford them, and despite injunctions to the contrary, bury their dead in good farmland. In the Peking metropolitan area, which includes suburban communes, an estimated forty hectares of land is lost to burial grounds each year.

15. A typology of the Right and the Left that has held up fairly well over the years may be found in my *The Political Economy of Communist China* (Scranton, Pa.: International Textbook Company, 1970), ch. 8, especially Table 8–8.

16. In 1974, when I visited Peking University, *The Foolish Old Man* was one of the three required reading texts in the curriculum of the economics department (the other two being *Das Kapital* and Stalin's *Economic Problems of Socialism in the USSR*). Since then *The Foolish Old Man* has been described by some Chinese economists as an absurdity.

17. Chu-yuan Cheng, *China's Economic Development: Growth and Structural Change* (Boulder, Colo.: Westview Press, 1982), ch. 10 ("Growth and Fluctuations in the National Economy"); Peter Wiles, "Are There Any Communist Economic Cycles?" *ACES Bulletin* 24:2 (Summer 1982), pp. 1–20.

12

Chinese Law and Justice: Trends over Three Decades

Hungdah Chiu

Introduction

Until the second half of the 1960s, Chinese Communist law was generally ignored by Western scholars in their China studies for two principal reasons. First, many scholars doubted, with some justification, whether law had any significant role to play in the People's Republic of China (PRC). Until recently, the PRC's legal system was unique even among its fellow Communist countries, with neither lawyers nor any substantive or procedural criminal and civil laws. Judges were not required to have had legal training, nor were they required or expected to cite legal provisions in rendering judgments. Second, there was a serious lack of scholars trained in *both* the Western and the Chinese legal traditions and practices. The few lawyers with this special combination of skills might have considered that the study of Chinese Communist law had no practical value or financial reward but was of academic interest only. In the mid-1960s, Harvard Law School began to undertake a systematic study of Chinese Communist law, filling a long-delayed gap in China studies. Unfortunately, even before this study of Chinese law had begun to produce any significant publications, the PRC started the Great Proletarian Cultural Revolution, which virtually suspended the operations of the PRC's legal system, legal education, and almost all scholarly writings on law. For almost a decade between 1966 and 1976, Chinese law specialists faced a frustrating lack of PRC legal materials for analysis.

After 1977, the situation underwent a fortunate reversal. Since then, barely a day has passed without the appearance of some new material relating to law in the PRC's newspapers or other publications or media. There are now voluminous materials on Chinese Communist law to be digested. The PRC government and leaders have in recent years repeatedly emphasized that China's legal system must be strengthened and perfected so as to provide an orderly environment for the national modernization program. They have also taken a series of steps, including legislative, judicial, educational, and other measures, to establish a stable legal system. In view of this development, Chinese Communist law is a subject that cannot now be ignored in China studies if one would like to get a complete picture of current Chinese society.

This paper is an attempt to analyze the trends of legal development in China in the last three decades. It begins with a survey of the stages of development of Chinese law and justice before 1977, proceeds to an analysis of the efforts of the Chinese government and leaders to build a more stable legal system since 1977, and finally assesses certain basic factors that might affect future trends in China's legal development. Several of the objectives of the conference for which this paper was prepared were to see "how we and other observers analyzed the situation in China in the past. Where have we been wrong? Where have we been right?" I shall therefore base my analysis of the past trends, to a certain extent, on Chinese writers' own assessments of the situation and, where appropriate, compare these with the views expressed in selected Western writings during the same period. However, although there are now some published Western writings on post-Mao legal development in China,[1] it seems too early to make an assessment of these writings, so I will not review them.

Stages of Development of Chinese Law and Justice Before 1977

According to a PRC article, the development of China's socialist legal system has undergone the following stages: (1) the period of the establishment of the legal system (1949–1953); (2) the period of the development of the legal system (1954–1956); (3) the period when the legal construction was subject to interference and ceased to develop (1957–1965); (4) the period when the legal system was severely undermined (1966–1976); and (5) the period of the restoration of the legal system and its further development (1977–present).[2] This division does not differ in any significant way from that used by China scholars outside the PRC such as Leng, Cohen, Lubman, and myself.[3]

1949–1953

According to a PRC article, the primary role of the PRC state with respect to law and justice during the period 1949–1953 was to demolish the old legal system and establish a new socialist legal system.[4]

Early in February 1949, before it had captured the whole mainland, the Chinese Communist party issued its Directive Regarding the Abolition of the Kuomintang's (Guomindang's) Complete Book of Six Codes and the Affirmation of the Legal Principles in the Liberated Areas.[5] This directive was later incorporated into Article 17 of the Common Program,[6] adopted in late September 1949 by the Chinese People's Political Consultative Conference (CPPCC); it served as an interim constitution until the adoption of a formal Constitution on 20 September 1954. The CPPCC was intended to serve as the provisional legislature of the country, but in fact it only exercised limited legislative functions. From 1949 to 20 September 1954, when its legislative function was taken over by the National People's Congress under the 1954 Constitution, it and the Central People's Government Council under it adopted only fifty-one laws and decrees (see Table 12.1). If one includes decrees issued by the Government Administrative Council, the total number of important laws and regulations adopted during 1949–1953 was only one hundred forty-eight.[7] Moreover, among the laws, regulations, and decrees adopted in this period there were neither criminal or criminal procedure codes nor civil or civil procedure codes. The only important criminal legislation enacted was the Act for the Punishment of Counterrevolutionaries of the PRC,[8] promulgated on 21 February 1951. This act applied retroactively to pre-1949 activities, permitted the use of analogy, and was vaguely drafted for flexible use.

In 1951, the PRC set up a three-level, two-trial (one appeal) system of people's courts: County Court, Provincial Court, and the Supreme People's Court. All people's courts were organic parts of the people's government of the corresponding level.[9] A people's procuracy was also established on a level corresponding with each people's court; the procuracy was at the same time a component of the people's government at the same level.[10] As a result, both the courts and the procuracy were, in law and in fact, under the control of administrative organs and there was no separation of power among them. At first, because of the insufficient numbers of legally trained Communist personnel, many former Nationalist legal personnel were retained to serve the people's judiciary. However, in 1952 a Judicial Reform Mass Movement was launched against such "old law" principles as "judicial independence," "no punishment without preexisting law," or "law has no class character"; the movement was intended to strengthen the Communist party's leadership over judicial work. As the result of this movement, most former Nationalist judicial personnel were dismissed from office or even condemned as counter-revolutionaries. Their positions were taken by Communist cadres who received little or no legal training at all.[11]

In fact, legal training was not essential to implementing people's law and justice, as the judiciary was frequently instructed to follow orders or policies of the government or the party in cases not covered by existing law. Also, the courts were neither required nor expected to cite the applicable provisions of law in rendering their judgments. Moreover, the dynamics of the Chinese mass movement included a disregard of law as an ordering force in society. A recent PRC article justified this approach to law and justice as follows:

> In the early years of the People's Republic, the Communist Party initiated several mass movements on a nationwide scale. Direct mass action rather than the force of law fueled these tempestuous revolutionary movements.

Table 12.1 Number of Laws and Decrees Enacted or Ratified by the Plenary Meeting of the First Session of the Chinese People's Political Consultative Conference and the Central People's Government (September 1949-15 September 1954).[1]

Types of Laws or Decrees[2]	Subdivision	Number of Enactments per Year					
		1949	1950	1951	1952	1953	1954
Constitutional Law and Organic Law for state agencies	Constitutional Law	4	0	0	0	0	0
	Highest state and adm. organs	4	1	1	2	2	1
Election		0	0	0	0	3	0
Organization of central state organs	People's courts	1[4]	1[5]	1	0	0	0
	People's procuratorates	1[6]	0	2	0	0	0
Local state and adm. organs		3	0	1	4	0	3
Appointment and removal of state organ personnel		0	1	1	0	0	0
Politics and law	Land reform	0	2	0	0	0	0
	Suppression of counterreolutionaries	0	0	1	0	0	0
	Three-anti and Five-anti	0	0	0	1	0	0
	Marriage and family	0	1	0	0	0	0
	Keeping state secrets	0	0	1	0	0	0
National defense	People's armed work	0	0	0	1	0	0
Finance		1	1	0	0	0	0
Labor		0	1	0	0	0	0
National minorities		0	0	1	2	0	0
Foreign affairs		0	0	1	0	0	0
TOTALS		14	8	10	10	5	4

1. Political-Legal Section of the Office of the Standing Committee of the National People's Congress and the Legal Office of the Legal System Committee of the Standing Committee of the National People's Congress, editors, Zhongguo renmin zhengzhi xieshang huiyi diyijie quanti huiyi, zhong yang renmin zhengfu, diyi zhi sijie quanguo renmin daibiao dahui ji qi changwu weiyuanhui zhiding hezhe pizhun de falu, faling he qita wenjian mulu (List of laws, decrees and other documents enacted or ratified by the plenary meeting of the first session of the Chinese People's Political Consultative Conference, Central People's Government, first to fourth session of the National People's Congress and its Standing Committee) (September 1949-October 1977), Beijing: Qunzhong chubanshe, 1980), pp. 3-23. Hereinafter referred to as List of Laws and Decrees between 1949 and 1977.
2. Classification made by the authors for consistency of cross-reference with Table 12.
3. Classification used in List of Laws and Decrees between 1949 and 1977, pp. 3-23.
4. Provisional Organic Act for the Supreme People's Court of the People's Republic of China, no date given in List of Laws and Decrees between 1949 and 1977, p. 11. The author believes that this law was enacted in 1949.
5. General Rules on the Organization of People's Tribunal, 20 July 1950; it was mistakenly listed under the category of "land reform" in List of Laws and Decrees between 1949 and 1977, p. 14.
6. Provisional Organic Act for the Supreme People's Procuratorate of the People's Republic of China, no date given in List of Laws and Decrees between 1949 and 1977, p. 12. The author believes that this law was enacted in 1949.

> The aim then was to break down the old, reactionary social order, and in its place establish a new, revolutionary order. Examples are the land reform movement of 1949–51 to overthrow the landlord class, the 1950 movement to suppress counter-revolutionaries and the 1952 *san fan* [three anti, i.e., anti-corruption, waste, and bureaucratism] and *wu fan* [five anti, i.e., anti-bribery, tax evasion, stealing state property, cheating in workmanship and materials, and stealing state economic intelligence] movements against the bourgeoisie. These mass movements were absolutely necessary because the reactionary forces riding on the backs of the people were still very powerful when the old society was being superseded by the new.[12]

Another PRC article, which also took a positive view of the legal development during this period, nevertheless acknowledged that the 1952 Judicial Reform Movement overreacted in denouncing the "old law" viewpoints of "judicial independence" or "inheritability" of old or bourgeois law and therefore facilitated the subsequent abnormal development in which there was no differentiation between the party and the government and between the party and the law.[13] All Chinese articles were, however, silent on the severe punishment or death sentences imposed by extralegal organs on thousands of Chinese during this period.

China scholars in the West, such as Cohen and Leng, were more willing to disclose fully the complete picture of law and justice in China during this period. Cohen wrote:

> During this period the criminal process served as a blunt instrument of terror, as the Chinese Communist Party proceeded relentlessly to crush all sources of political opposition and to rid society of apolitical but antisocial elements who plagued public order. . . . Although the Communist government created a judicial structure, much criminal punishment during these years was administered outside the regular courts . . . during the regime-sponsored "mass movements" or campaigns that swept the country, such as those instigated to carry out the land reform. To suppress revolutionary and eradicate official corruption and related illegal activities in the business community . . . ad hoc "people's tribunals," which were thinly veiled kangaroo courts, dispensed their own brand of justice.[14]

Even so, the trend in the PRC was to develop a legal system and legal education along the Soviet model; thus Soviet law books were translated into Chinese and Soviet lawyers were invited to China to help with the transplantation of the Soviet legal model.

1954–1956

On 20 September 1954, the PRC promulgated a formal Constitution[15] incorporating provisions concerning a judiciary and people's rights, which indicated a tendency to follow the Soviet model of establishing a stable legal order and a permanent judicial structure. Among the four chapters of the Constitution, Chapter IV (Articles 85 to 103) was entirely devoted to the "Fundamental Rights and Duties of Citizens." This chapter guaranteed, among other rights, equality before the law and freedom of speech, of the press, of association, of demonstration, and of religion, as well as the right to work, to leisure, to education, and to social assistance. Article 89 of the Constitution specifically provided protection against arbitrary arrest: "Freedom of the person of citizens of the People's Republic of China is inviolable. No citizen may be arrested except by decision of a people's court or with the sanction of a people's procuratorate." To implement this article, on 20 December 1954 an Arrest and Detention Act of the People's Republic of China[16] was promulgated.

The Constitution also provided in Articles 73 to 84 the basic organization and structure of the people's court and the people's procuratorate. On 28 September 1954 the PRC promulgated Organic Laws governing people's courts[17] and people's procuratorates.[18] The Constitution and Organic Laws gave the PRC judicial system a permanent structure. Under the National People's Congress (NPC) and its Standing Committee, two separate but interlocking hierarchies were established. The people's courts, headed by the Supreme People's Court, were given the sole authority to administer justice; the people's procuratorates, culminating in the Supreme People's Procuratorate, were to exercise the supervisory power over the execution of the law. Below the Supreme People's Court, local courts were divided into higher people's courts, intermediate people's courts, and basic people's courts. In 1962, it was reported that there were 30 higher courts, 200 intermediate courts, and over 2,000 or 3,000 basic courts.[19]

Both the Constitution and the Organic Laws introduced a number of democratic features to the new judicial system, including the right of legal defense and the principle of public (open) trials. For the first time, the PRC also seemed to accept in a limited form the concept of judicial independence. Article 78 of the Constitution provided: "In administering justice the people's courts are independent, subject only to the law." Article 80 of the Constitution provided that the courts should be responsible to the people's congresses at corresponding levels and should report to them. This was in clear contrast with the earlier laws that had required the subordination of the courts to the leadership of the people's government at each corresponding level.

However, people's rights and judicial independence under the new Constitution remained qualified. In the first place, both the government and the courts were under the control of the Communist party of China and both were supposed to carry out party policy. Second, the people's rights guaranteed by the Constitution were not applicable to all individuals within the country. "Reactionaries" or "class enemies" had no rights whatever under the Constitution.[20] Third, the constitutional guarantee of equality before the law did not mean that the law in the PRC would lose its class character. As a PRC scholar pointed out, such equality did not mean "when the state enacts law, it would treat individuals from different classes equally in legislation."[21]

PRC leaders such as Liu Shao-ch'i (Liu Shaoqi) and Tung Pi-wu (Dong Biwu) expressed their views in favor of establishing a stable legal system. In the political report to the Eighth CCP Congress delivered by Liu on 15 September 1956, he said:

> The period of revolutionary storm and stress is past . . . and the aim of our struggle is changed to one of safeguarding the successful development of the productive forces of society; a corresponding change in the methods of struggle will consequently have to follow and a complete legal system becomes an absolute necessity. It is necessary, in order to maintain a normal social life and to foster production, that everyone in the country should understand and be convinced that as long as he does not violate the laws, his civil rights are guaranteed and will suffer no encroachment by any organization or any individual. Should his civil rights be unlawfully encroached upon, the state will certainly intervene. All state organs must strictly observe the law, and our security departments, procurators' offices and courts must conscientiously carry out the system of division of function and mutual supervision in legal affairs.[22]

Similarly, Tung Pi-wu (Dong Biwu), then president of the Supreme People's Court, also pointed out the need for basic codes and a stable legal system:

> The problem today is that we still lack several urgently needed, fairly complete basic statutes such as a criminal code, a civil code, rules of court procedure, a labor law, a law governing the utilization of land and the like.
>
> At present . . . from the point of view of both the need and the objective possibility of building up a legal system, we should gradually complete the structure of our legal system. It would have to be regarded as a serious problem, if we allowed our legal system to remain incomplete or unduly deferred its completion.
>
> I think we also have another serious question to deal with: that is, a few of our Party members and government personnel do not attach importance to the legal system of the state, or do not observe its provisions.[23]

With respect to legal education and research between 1954 and 1956, a PRC article stated:

> Various political-legal institutes have compiled lectures and teaching materials for various subjects of law and they are basically suitable for our country's situation. At the same time, legal journals and translations of [foreign works on law] were one by one published. Generally speaking, [at that period] the development of our science of law was basically normal and achieved certain results.[24]

Despite the general trend toward establishing a stable legal system, two mass movements or campaigns were conducted during this period. The first one was launched in the spring of 1955 against counterrevolutionaries, centering on the case of a writer, Hu Feng, who was cited as an example to the whole country of a new type of counterrevolutionary. At the end of May 1955, Hu was dismissed from all his posts and later accused of having formed a "conspiratorial group with Kuomintang (Guomindang) agents." He was reported to have been tried in July 1955, but no details of the trial were ever made public. Another mass movement was launched in June 1955, again against counterrevolutionaries, aimed at certain government departments, the so-called democratic parties, and the Chinese Communist party itself, as well as at cultural, industrial, and religious circles. However, these two movements or campaigns, by comparison with those carried out in the early 1950s, were quite small in scope and in the number of people arrested, because these two were directed at specific groups.[25] Also, there appeared to have been no mass executions in connection with these two movements.

1957–1965

During 1956 and 1957, the PRC launched the movement of "letting one hundred flowers blossom and one hundred schools contend." Many jurists and scholars took this opportunity to criticize the government for the lack of basic laws and the defective administration of justice. Alarmed at the strong criticism evoked by the "blooming and contending" movement, the PRC launched an antirightist movement in the summer of 1957 to silence its critics. So far as law and justice were concerned, this meant a serious setback for the development of a stable and less arbitrary system of justice. Two years later, in 1959, another movement against "rightist opportunism" was launched within the party, further undermining the efforts to establish a stable legal system. A recent PRC article described the impact of these two movements on PRC legal development as follows:

> In 1957, it was necessary to counterattack the attack launched by an extremely small number of bourgeois rightist elements; however, this class struggle was artificially expanded. Two years later, there was improperly started the struggle against the so-called rightist opportunism within the Party, which caused unfavorable results as it undermined the democracy within the Party and people's democracy. In political-legal circles, the impact of this "left" thought was extremely obvious. The principles of democracy and [legality] provided in the Constitution were subject to criticism. The position was erroneously taken by some that the independent exercise of trial and procuratorial authority by the judicial organs was equivalent to opposing Party leadership. Moreover, the leadership over subordinate organs and the legal supervision over other state organs exercised by the procuratorial organs were accused of "invoking law to resist the Party" or "opposing Party leadership"; the principle that "all citizens are equal before the law" was considered as "disregarding the class character of law" and "talking equality with counterrevolutionaries"; the principle of "relying on facts as basis and law as criterion" [in trials] was described as "abandoning Party policy" or "favoring legal isolationism"; the emphasis

> on doing business according to law was described as a bourgeois viewpoint of "supremacy of law"; the socialist defense system and lawyer system were described as "defending bad elements and making no differentiation between us and the enemy"; and others. Thus, from idea, theory, and institution aspects, many laws and systems that were in force and had proved their usefulness were disturbed and undermined, and many comrades who defended the principles of the Constitution were declared as rightists and anti-Party elements under various false accusations that upset right and wrong. The result of such developments greatly undermined the enthusiasm of the broad political-legal cadres and encouraged the tendency of "left" rather than "right" ideas and a doctrine of abolishing the law. As a result, an adverse development emerged that despised the legal system, relying on the Party to substitute for the government and using [officials'] words to replace law. The legislative work of the state was totally suspended. . . . Our country's legal work has [since then] continued to go downward and thus opened the gate for Lin Piao (Lin Biao) and the Gang of Four to take this opportunity to usurp power and occupy government positions to engage in counterrevolutionary restoration activities.[26]

The trend toward total suspension of the legislative function can be seen from the number of laws, decrees, and other documents adopted by the NPC or its Standing Committee in each year. In 1957, 108 items were adopted, but by 1966 the number was down to seven. None were adopted between 1967 and 1974 (see Table 12.2 and Figure 12.1).

Legal education and research were also severely affected during this period, as described in a PRC article:

> In 1957 . . . in legal circles and all political-legal fronts, the error of a "left" tendency was obvious. . . . Many good comrades were declared as rightists, causing great confusion in idea and theory, and many taboos emerged in legal circles that seriously obstructed the normal development of legal research in new China.
>
> In 1959, the struggle against rightist opportunism within the Party was erroneously launched. Under the influence of left tendency thought, the Ministry of Justice was abolished, the Legal Bureau [of the State Council] was also abolished, and the phenomenon of "if there is business then handle political-legal affairs, if not engage in product work" emerged in political-legal departments. Teachers and students in political-legal institutes or schools were gradually sent down to the countryside to engage in productive labor. Different professional legal subjects in school were either abolished or combined, and professional education was replaced by political theory study. Then came a series of political movements, the doctrine of legal nihilism was spread over the whole country, and one could hardly talk of any legal research work. . . . Works concerning building the legal system, including research in law, continued to go downward.[27]

Between 1957 and 1966, when the Cultural Revolution broke out, the PRC's judiciary gradually regressed to its earlier practice, with the public security (police) organs playing a growing role at the expense of

Table 12.2 Number of Laws, Decrees, and Other Documents Adopted or Ratified by the National People's Congress (NPC) or Its Standing Committee (16 September 1954-October 1977)

Type of Laws, Decrees, and Documents Adopted	1954	1955	1956	1957	1958	1959	1960	1961	1962	1963	1964	1965	1966	1967-1974	1975	1976	1977	Total for Each Type
Constitutional and Organic Law for state agencies	6	2	1	0	0	0	0	0	0	0	0	0	0	0	1	0	0	10
NPC election, activities, and meetings	0	10	5	6	4	5	1	4	2	5	4	0	0	0	0	0	1	47
Organization of central state organs	2	3	3	1	5	3	2	2	2	4	3	3	0	0	0	0	0	33
Organization of local state organs	3	5	2	2	1	0	0	0	0	0	0	0	0	0	0	0	0	13
Delimitation of administrative area	0	2	0	2	1	1	0	0	0	0	0	0	0	0	0	0	0	6
Election, appointment, removal, punishment, and award for state personnel	9	3	2	6	4	9	1	0	3	1	0	0	0	0	2	1	0	41
National economic planning, budget and financial statement	0	4	2	1	2	2	1	0	0	2	1	0	0	0	0	0	0	15
National defense	0	10	0	1	1	0	0	0	1	1	0	2	0	0	0	0	0	16
Politics and law	3	2	7	11	6	1	2	1	0	3	3	0	1	0	1	0	0	41
Finance	1	1	3	5	8	0	0	0	0	0	0	0	0	0	0	0	0	18
Industry and commerce	0	0	0	4	0	0	0	0	0	2	0	0	0	0	0	0	0	6
Agriculture	0	2	4	2	3	0	2	0	0	0	0	0	0	0	0	0	0	13
Labor	0	0	0	8	2	0	0	0	0	0	0	0	0	0	0	0	0	10
Culture, education, and health	0	1	0	1	2	0	0	0	0	0	0	0	0	0	0	0	0	4
National minorities affairs	0	3	15	14	18	22	0	0	2	2	15	6	6	0	0	0	0	103
Overseas Chinese affairs	0	1	0	4	0	0	0	0	0	0	0	0	0	0	0	0	0	5

International affairs	3	14	17	17	15	20	31	24	14	8	11	9	0	0	0	1	0	184
Reports of work [of government][1]	3	16	18	23	7	17	20	6	30	17	21	5	0	0	4	1	2	190
Total	30	79	79	108	79	80	60	37	54	45	58	25	7	0	8	3	3	755
Total if excluding reports of work	27	63	61	85	72	63	40	31	24	28	37	20	7	0	4	2	1	565
Total if excluding international affairs and reports of work	24	49	44	68	57	43	9	7	10	20	26	11	7	0	4	1	1	381
Total if excluding national minorities affairs, international affairs, and reports of work	24	46	29	54	39	21	9	7	8	18	11	5	1	0	4	1	1	278

Source: List of Laws and Decrees between 1949 and 1977 (see Note 1, Table 12.1), pp. 27-217.

1. Items on agenda, press communiques, speeches of foreign guests, and other publication matters omitted.

Fig. 12.1. Chart on Number of Laws, Decrees and Other Documents Adopted By Chinese People's Political Consultative Conference (1949-1954) and National People's Congress or Its Standing Committee (1954-1977)

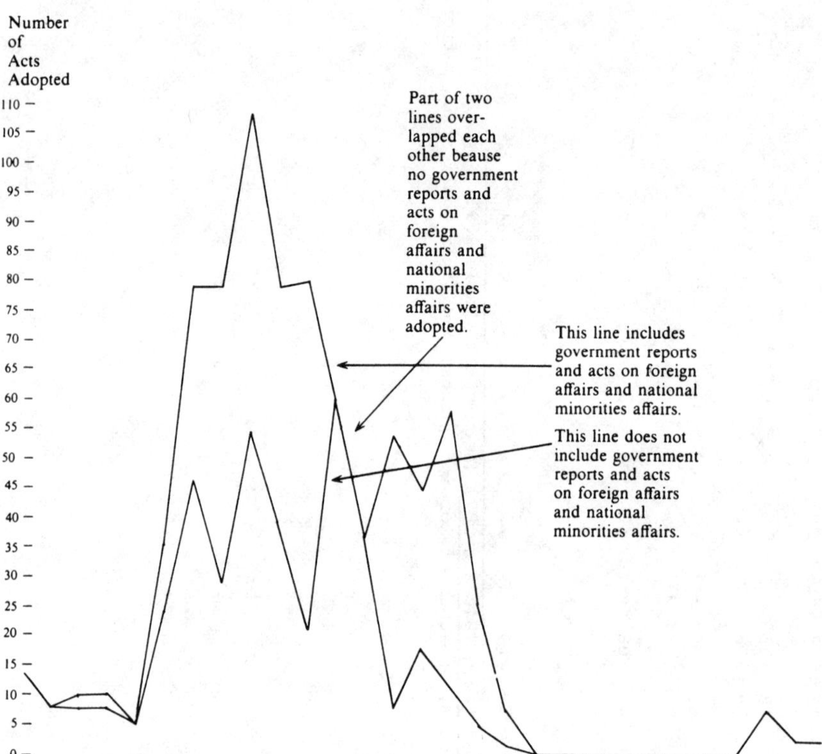

the procuracy and the courts.[28] Although some legal writings continued to appear in the PRC, those available to Western scholars did not discuss such important issues on law and justice in China as the practice of "deciding a case by the [party] secretary"[29] or how a court rendered a criminal decision in the absence of a published criminal code.[30] Thus, the comprehensive study of the Chinese criminal justice system by Leng, Cohen, and Lubman only vaguely touched on these two important questions.[31]

An important Western publication on Chinese law and justice is Bao Rue-wang's *Prisoner of Mao,*[32] which, based on his personal experience, provided many details on the actual operation of Chinese criminal justice. Unfortunately, despite his release from a Chinese prison in 1964 when France recognized the PRC, his book was not published until 1973, so that Leng, Cohen, and Lubman were unable to consult Bao's personal experience in their research on Chinese criminal justice.

1966–1976

Although law and justice were not among the major revolutionary targets at the beginning of the Cultural Revolution in 1966, they were no exception to the ensuing destruction of the "establishment." An article entitled "In Praise of 'Lawlessness'" appearing in the authoritative *Jen-min Jih-pao* (*Renmin Ribao*) [*People's Daily*] on 31 January 1967 bluntly advocated the elimination of the so-called bourgeois law:

> To destroy the bourgeois "law" and the capitalist "world" is precisely the revolutionary goal of all proletarian revolutionaries. Like the Monkey King who turns the heavenly palace upside down, we will destroy your "law," smash your "world," rebel against you, and seize your power.

A recent PRC article described the situation of law and justice during this period as follows:

> *Judicial Organs Smashed.* The socialist legal system stood in [the] way [of Lin Piao (Lin Biao) and the Gang of Four] to usurping Party and state power, so right at the start of the Great Cultural Revolution in 1966, they began dismantling the public security departments and the procuratorial organs and charged that the socialist legal system was "a shackle" and "a straight-jacket" holding back the mass movements. China's judicial organs were suspended.
>
> Abusing the power they had usurped, Lin Piao [Lin Biao] and the Gang of Four began cracking down on large numbers of revolutionary cadres and people. They let loose hoodlums and thugs to smash, grab and loot, to break into and ransack homes, illegally detain people, set up kangaroo courts, and torture innocent people to extort confessions. In places and units they controlled there was no freedom of person because socialist social order was nonexistent.
>
> *Feudal-Fascist Rule.* In those days, declared a special commentator of the journal *Chung-kuo Ch'ing-nien* [*Zhongguo Qingnian,* or *China Youth*] anyone who dared show his disapproval of Lin Piao [Lin Biao] or the Gang of Four was immediately condemned and punished for committing a heinous crime. Anything that was regarded as a slight disrespect to them constituted a "counter-revolutionary crime." One Nanking [Nanjing] worker got five years merely because he inadvertently commented in public on Lin Piao's [Lin Biao's] build. The whole thing was, of course, extremely absurd, but at least it was done with a semblance of "judicial proceedings," the special commentator added. At least, some sort of "reason" was given and it was known where the worker was imprisoned so members of his

> family could visit him occasionally. In many cases even a semblance of judicial proceedings was dispensed with. Personal property and personal freedom were willfully encroached upon and safety of people's lives was not guaranteed. In short, wherever Lin Piao [Lin Biao] and the Gang of Four held sway, socialist democracy gave way to feudal despotism married to twentieth-century fascism.[33]

The high point of the legal development during this period was in 1975 when the new Constitution[34] formally abolished the procuratorial organs and also placed people's courts under the control of the administrative organs (renamed as the revolutionary committee) at the same level.[35]

Legal education and legal research were virtually suspended beginning in 1966, as described in a PRC article:

> Under the reactionary thinking of "power is everything," Lin Piao [Lin Biao] and the Gang of Four [counter-revolutionary clique] . . . put out the slogan of thoroughly smashing the public security, procuracy and courts, and without exception, legal education and legal research were subject to thorough destruction. Basically, all political-legal institutes were abolished, legal research totally disappeared, teaching materials, books and research materials were destroyed or disappeared, some law teachers and legal researchers changed their occupations, [and] others waited to be transferred to other positions. It can be said that the 10-year period of Cultural Revolution was a 10-year holocaust for research in law.[36]

Because of the scarcity of available legal materials from the PRC during 1966–1976, there have been few Western writings on PRC law before 1977. Based on some internally circulated legal documents such as court notices, interviews with former residents of China, and other secondary sources, Randle Edwards, Tao-tai Hsia, Shao-chuan Leng, and I did put out a few articles on various aspects of China's criminal justice.[37] There are, moreover, several articles written by Western scholars based on their visits to China or interviews with Chinese officials there.[38] Those authors who had no background on China's legal system usually conveyed a favorable impression of law and justice in China.[39] There are also three more comprehensive studies on the same period. The first one is Victor Li's *Law Without Lawyers* (1977),[40] which tried to provide a theoretical basis for the legal system operating in China before 1977. The second one is Amnesty International's *Political Imprisonment in the People's Republic of China* (1978),[41] which provided a comprehensive analytical study of Chinese criminal justice up to 1978, filling a serious gap in Chinese legal teaching materials that had arisen since the publication of Leng and Cohen's books (1967–1968). The last one is Fox Butterfield's *China: Alive in the Bitter Sea* (1982),[42] which, although not entirely devoted to the study of Chinese law and justice, contains important information on the operation of the criminal justice system in China, including social control and reform through labor.

Trends of Development of Chinese Law and Justice Since 1977

In early 1978, the PRC itself began to denounce its legal system, especially the cruelty and abuses during the 1966–1976 Cultural Revolution period. At the same time, the PRC also began to end its lawlessness and attempted to build a more stable legal system. The necessity of the PRC's reversing its pre-1977 policies of antipathy to law arose from China's modernization program.

The PRC's ambitious modernization program clearly required a strengthening and perfecting of the Chinese legal system, to provide an orderly, predictable environment for economic development. Beyond that, the PRC was also confronted with a population demoralized and frightened by years of chaos and uncertainty, so it was also necessary to provide a more secure environment for the people. This was especially true in regard to gaining the confidence of the intellectuals, who had suffered most in the past decades. Without the enthusiastic participation of the intelligentsia, it would be impossible to modernize China's economy and technology. Moreover, the leaders of the PRC apparently decided that expansion of the PRC's foreign trade program and the inflow of foreign investment funds were essential to the success of the modernization program, so it became necessary to provide a legal framework for foreign trade and investment.

The trend toward establishing a more stable legal system can be discerned from following PRC efforts in the structural reorganization of legal organs, enactment of necessary legislation, restoration of a defense lawyer system, redefinition of relations between the party and the judiciary, restoration and expansion of legal education, and renewed interest in legal research.

Structural Reorganization

The 1978 Constitution[43] revived the people's procuratorates "to ensure observance of the Constitution and the law by all the departments under the State Council, the local organs of state at various levels, the personnel of organs of state and the citizens" (Article 43). It also abolished the provisions for placing courts under the control of the administrative organ at the same level.

The new Constitution adopted on 4 December 1982[44] does not have an article similar to Article 43 of the 1978 Constitution, but it has an article to ensure a more independent exercise of procuratorial power. That article, Article 131, provides: "People's procuratorates shall, in accordance with the law, exercise procuratorial power independently and are not subject to interference by administrative organs, social organizations [she-hui t'uan-t'i (shehui tuanti)],[45] or individuals." The ministry of justice was restored to take charge of the judicial administrative works, compilation of laws, and legal research.[46]

Enactment of Necessary Legislation

In 1979/1980, several major laws relating to law and justice were enacted: Arrest and Detention Act,[47] Criminal Law, Criminal Procedure Law, Organic Law for Courts, Organic Law for Procuratorate,[48] and Provisional Act on Lawyers. [49] The PRC also enacted several laws relating to foreign trade and investment.[50] In early 1982, the PRC also enacted a provisional Civil Procedure Law[51] and began the process of actively drafting a Civil Law.

Restoration of the Defense Lawyer System

Both the 1978 Constitution (Article 41, paragraph 3) and the Criminal Procedure Law (Article 26) explicitly recognize the right of an accused to defend himself, and the latter also recognizes the right to hire a lawyer to defend one's case. In 1980, the Provisional Act on Lawyers was enacted,[52] formally restoring the lawyer system. The act came into force on 1 January 1982, but before that date the PRC had already allowed certain lawyers to start practice. According to official figures in 1981, there were 6,800 lawyers, of whom 5,500 were in full-time practice. By mid-1981, 1,300 legal advisors' offices, where lawyers are supposed to conduct their practice, had been established in urban areas in all parts of the country.[53]

Redefinition of the Relationship Between the Party and the Judiciary

The present leadership of the PRC has attempted to some extent to separate the party and the government in administration. On 24 August 1980, Chiang Hua (Jiang Hua), president of the Supreme People's Court, told the Peking (Beijing) Criminal Trials Conference that the party had decided to abolish the system of party committee review (exercised through the political-legal secretary of the committee) and approval of cases.[54] The extent to which this policy will be fully implemented remains to be seen.[55] The new Constitution adopted on 4 December 1982 stipulates in Article 126 a provision for people's courts similar to that for people's procuratorates in Article 131: "The people's courts shall, in accordance with the law, exercise judicial power independently and are not subject to interference by administrative organs, social organizations [she-hui t'uan-ti (shehui tuanti)],[56] or individuals." However, the party is neither an administrative organ nor a social organization, so this provision appears not to prohibit party interference in the judiciary.

Restoration and Expansion of Legal Education

Although in 1974 the law department of Peking (Beijing) University reopened on a limited basis with about sixty students for a three-year program,[57] the students were selected on the basis of their class and political backgrounds rather than their academic competence. In 1977, the PRC restored the system of nationwide university entrance examinations for high school graduates, replacing the admission of students based primarily on political background as instituted during the Cultural Revolution period. In the same year, Peking (Beijing) University expanded its education program, including law, to four years, and began to admit new law students each year. In the fall of 1980, about 230 new law students were enrolled, bringing the total number of law students enrolled to 570.[58]

Since 1977, law departments that had existed prior to the Cultural Revolution have begun to reopen, and new law departments have been formed. Similarly, the political-legal institutes that were suspended during the Cultural Revolution have also been reopened. In September 1981, PRC First Vice-Minister of Justice Li Yün-ch'ang (Li Yunchang) said that the PRC had fifteen law departments and political-legal institutes with an enrollment of 5,500, and that more than 8,000 law students would be graduated in 1985. He also revealed that 57,000 outstanding army officers between twenty-nine and forty-five years of age were receiving judicial training and, after their graduation, would be assigned to public security departments, procuratorates, and courts at all levels.[59]

Beyond the college level in legal education, it was reported that the PRC now has two postgraduate law schools for advanced training of law graduates. There are also junior college-level (or below) cadres' schools with law divisions. Moreover, the public security (police) organs have set up their own cadres' schools, which also offer law courses.[60]

In addition to formal legal education, the PRC has launched a mass legal education campaign to familiarize the people with the substance of such laws as the Criminal Law and the Criminal Procedure Law. Also, because of the increase in juvenile criminals, the PRC has conducted campaigns in universities, colleges, and high schools on observance of laws. All college and university students since the fall semester of 1979 must complete either a special course on the legal system or a general course on politics with a strong emphasis on law. A popular weekly newspaper on law—*Chung-kuo Fa-chih Pao* (Zhongguo Fazhi Bao) [China Legal System Paper]—began publication in 1980 for promoting general legal education. Furthermore, some traditional operas and contemporary plays with the theme of law and justice are being performed on television and on the stage to attract people's interest to law.[61]

Renewed Interest in Legal Research

In 1977, the Philosophy and Social Science Division of the Chinese Academy of Sciences was separated from the academy and reorganized as the Chinese Academy of Social Sciences. An Institute of Law was established under the academy. The institute soon sponsored a ten-day conference on legal research planning, held on 21–31 March 1979. The conference set forth an outline for a seven-year legal research plan.[62] The institute also undertook translations of foreign legal works and original studies of various subjects of law.

The publication of legal journals has also been resumed. The following are four major legal journals now published in China:[63]

1. *Fa-hsüeh Yen-chiu* (*Faxue Yanjiu*) [*Studies in Law*], bimonthly starting in 1979, published by the Institute of Law of the Chinese Academy of Social Sciences;
2. *Min-chu yü Fa-chih* (*Minzhu yu Fazhi*) [*Democracy and Legal System*], monthly starting in 1979, published by the Shanghai Law Association and the East China Political-Legal Institute;
3. *Fa-hsüeh Yi Ts'ung* (*Faxue Yi Cong*) [*Law Translation Series*], bimonthly starting in 1980, published by the Institute of Law of the Chinese Academy of Sciences;
4. *Kuo-wai Fa-hsüeh* (*Guowai Faxue*) [*Foreign Law*], bimonthly starting in 1980, published by the Department of Law, Peking (Beijing) University.

Certain political-legal institutes also publish their own journals, but only for internal circulation. There are also three law journals published as restricted items, i.e., not available to the public: *Jen-min Ssu-fa* (*Renmin Sifa*) [*People's Judiciary*], published by the Supreme People's Court; *Jen-min Chien-ch'a* (*Renmin Jiancha*) [*People's Procuracy*], published by the Supreme People's Procuratorate; and *Jen-min Kung-an* (*Renmin Gongan*) [*People's Public Security*], published by the Ministry of Public Security. Moreover, increasing numbers of scholarly legal articles have been published in university academic journals on humanities or social sciences. A comprehensive law dictionary—*Fa-hsüeh Tz'u-tien* (*Faxue Cidian*)[64]—was published in 1980 and the PRC is now in the process of compiling the law section of the comprehensive Chinese encyclopedia.

In 1980 the PRC government also resumed its two important official gazettes that contain legal matters: *Ch'uan-kuo Jen-min Tai-piao Ta-hui Ch'ang-wu Wei-yüan-hui Kung-pao* (*Quanguo Renmin Daibiao Dahui Changwu Weiyuan hui Gongbao*) [*Gazette of the Standing Committee of the National People's Congress*] and *Chung-hua Jen-min Kung-ho-kuo Kuo-wu-yuan Kung-pao* (*Zhonghua Renmin Gongheguo Guowuyuan Gongbao*) [*Gazette of the State Council of the People's Republic of China*].

Since 1979, a number of scholarly conferences on various subjects of law have been held, Chinese lawyers have been sent to visit foreign legal institutes, and foreign lawyers have also been invited to China.

Four Basic Principles, Labor Camps, and Developmental Trends

Since 1977, the general trend in the PRC toward law and justice has clearly been in the direction of establishing a more stable legal system; that is why several Chinese lawyers have described the post-1977 period as the period of the restoration and further development of the legal system. However, this trend does not mean that Chinese law and justice will move closer to a Western concept of the rule of law. In this connection, the PRC itself has made it clear that its legal system is subject to the four unchangeables or four basic principles—namely, keeping to the socialist road, upholding the dictatorship of the proletariat, supporting party leadership, and upholding Marxist-Leninist-Maoist thought.[65] These principles were also incorporated in the Constitution of the PRC adopted on 4 December 1982.[66] Thus, regardless of the present leadership's pledge to establish a stable legal system, if an individual attempted to challenge one or more of the four basic principles, it would be futile for that person to rely on the PRC Constitution or statutes to guarantee him or her a fair trial.[67]

For such situations the PRC has retained some of its vaguely drafted earlier laws. The 1951 State Secret Law,[68] which includes almost everything in the PRC as "state secrets," provides under Article 13 that anyone who leaks those "secrets" to a domestic or foreign enemy is subject to punishment as a counterrevolutionary. This law was republished in 1980 to warn the public. The system of rehabilitation through labor, which authorizes the police to send a person to labor camp for up to four years without judicial review, was also retained.[69] This system has sometimes been invoked to deal with dissidents.[70] Finally, the Criminal Law still retains the principle of analogy, which may serve as the last resort for dealing with dissident elements. If the handling of a case through regular legal procedure would undermine state interests as defined by the Communist Party of China, then the regular legal procedure can be distorted to suit state interests. The trial of the Gang of Four is a vivid recent example.[71] In this connection, the PRC legal system is clearly moving in the direction of the Soviet concept of socialist legality, in that no principle, however normatively stated in a constitution or law, is permitted to conflict with the policy needs of the Communist party—although in normal situations the legal system still operates generally in a reasonable and predictable manner.[72]

The labor camps to hold criminals or political prisoners are still maintained, though the number of persons kept there seems to have been reduced. The PRC officials and legal publications have so far declined to discuss the problem of abolishing this system or of improving the miserable conditions there as revealed by several recent Western reports.[73] In 1979, the PRC republished its 1957 rules about labor reform and the *Kuang-ming Jih-pao* (*Guangming Ribao*) [*Enlightenment Daily*] even praised the success of labor reform.[74]

Overall Evaluation

In the PRC in the last thirty years, the state policy toward law and justice has been not only inconsistent but subject to several radical fluctuations. It was not until after the death of Mao and the emergence of a new leadership under Teng Hsiao-p'ing (Deng Xiaoping) in the late

1970s that the PRC government acknowledged that a stable legal system is a prerequisite for development and modernization; only then did the PRC begin to establish a stable legal system. In this connection, the question arises of whether this trend will continue. On the positive side, compared with the PRC's law program in the 1954–1956 period, present developments are more ambitious and extensive. In the 1954–1956 period, the PRC's goal was to establish a legal system based on the Soviet model, categorically rejecting any Western influence. Now, although the trend of the PRC's legal development seems clearly to be moving in the direction of the Soviet model of socialist legality, the PRC does not appear to accept the Soviet model in its totality but is also looking at the experiences of some other countries, including Western countries. This tendency is reflected in the PRC's studies or translations of some Western legal writings and laws,[75] the exchange of visits between Chinese lawyers and Western lawyers, and the sending of students to Western law schools. If this trend continues, the evolving Chinese legal system may be subject to some Western influence, especially in technical and nonpolitical aspects.

Another positive factor is that the present leadership is fully aware that during the turmoil of the Cultural Revolution, the lack of discipline among the people, workers, and peasants seriously affected production on various levels; there were also serious problems, including inefficiency, corruption, and waste, in the operation of state enterprises. To put its house in order, the PRC will find it necessary to reestablish social discipline and order and to regularize the operation of state enterprises through the mechanism of law. Moreover, the experience of the Cultural Revolution, in which the present leadership and their followers were also victims, seems to have taught the present leaders that a more stable legal system not only benefits the great majority of the Chinese people but also benefits the leaders themselves. This concern can be seen from more specific protections for personal freedoms and the explicit provisions on independence of courts and procuratorates in the 1982 Constitution,[76] prepared by the Teng (Deng) leadership, though whether these constitutional provisions will in fact be reasonably implemented remains to be seen.

On the other hand, one must realize that several negative factors may affect the trend toward a more stable legal system. The modern type of legal system, even in its Soviet style, with a separation of power among the police, procurator, and courts, was unknown to traditional China. The thirty years of Communist rule further strengthened, rather than weakened, the Chinese tradition. In order to overcome the obstacles embedded deeply in Chinese tradition, the leadership must make strenuous efforts to comply fully with the laws they promulgate and to show to the people that they are serious about implementing the laws. Most Chinese people still seem skeptical about this.[77]

Another negative factor is that Chinese society, instead of practicing the egalitarianism that some China scholars ascribed to the PRC, has been a strict class society since 1949. The higher one's position, the greater one's access to the amenities of life that cannot be purchased by money, including privileges and immunities from legal restrictions.[78] With the PRC relying on the loyalty of this privileged class to control the people, the means of implementing the principle of universal equality before the law[79] remains a challenging question for the PRC leadership.

A third negative factor is that the chronic lack of a sufficient number of trained legal personnel to run the legal system remains a serious problem. Several visiting Chinese scholars reported that in most instances only intermediate courts are staffed with persons having some formal legal training. Although China is in the process of expanding its legal education, for the forseeable future the insufficient number of legally trained personnel will continue to be a serious problem in building the legal system.[80]

The last negative factor relating to the continued progress of Chinese law is political stability in China, of which no one can be sure, based on the last thirty years' experience. In the event of a power struggle after the death of Teng Hsiao-p'ing (Deng Xiaoping), now 80, the legal system may be among the very first to be disrupted, as demonstrated by past experience. On the other hand, if Teng (Deng) and his followers continue to hold power for a considerable period of time, the outlook may be more positive. That leadership, having endorsed and publicized a fairly specific blueprint for a stable legal system as revealed in its recent enactments, has an identifiable political stake in the general implementation of the program. Therefore, under the incumbent leadership one might expect the present trend toward a stable legal system to continue.

Notes

1. The following is a selected list of major English writings on the Chinese legal system and criminal justice system (writings on trade, investment, and other technical fields not included): Jerome Alan Cohen, "Will China have a Formal Legal System?" *American Bar Association Journal* 64 (1978), pp. 1510–1515; Tao-tai Hsia and K. A. Huan, *The Re-emergence of the Procuratorial System in the People's Republic of China* (Washington, D.C.: Library of Congress, 1978); Stanley Lubman, "New Development in Law in the People's Republic of China," *Northwestern Journal of International Law & Business* 1 (1979), pp. 122–133; Jerome Alan Cohen, "Is There Law in China?" *International Trade Law Journal* 5 (1979), pp. 73–91; Tao-tai Hsia, "Legal Developments in the PRC Since the Purge of the Gang of Four," *Review of Socialist Law* 5:2 (1979), pp. 109–130; Hungdah Chiu, "Certain Problems in Recent Law Reform in the People's Republic of China," in *Comparative Law Yearbook,* vol. 3 (1979), Alphen aan den Rijn (The Netherlands: Sijthoff & Noordhoff, 1980), pp. 1–31; Victor H. Li, "Reflections on the Current Drive Toward Greater Legalization in China," *Georgia Journal of International and Comparative Law* 10 (1980), pp. 221–232; M. J. Meijer, "The New Criminal Code of the People's Republic of China," *Review of Socialist Law* 6:2 (1980), pp. 125–140; William C. Jones, "The Criminal Law of the People's Republic of China," *Review of Socialist Law* 6:4 (1980), pp. 405–423; Hungdah Chiu, "China's New Legal System," *Current History* 79:458 (September 1980), pp. 29–32, 44; Hungdah Chiu, "Structural Changes in the Organization and Operation of China's Criminal Justice System," *Review of Socialist Law* 7:1 (1981), pp.

53–72; Shao-chuan Leng, "Criminal Justice in Post-Mao China," *China Quarterly,* no. 87 (September 1981), pp. 440–469; David G. Barlow and Daniel W. Wagner, "Public Order and Internal Security," in *China, A Country Study,* Area Handbook Series (Washington, D.C.: U.S. Government Printing Office, 1981), pp. 423–455; and Hungdah Chiu, "Socialist Legalism: Reform and Continuity in Post-Mao People's Republic of China," in *Mainland China's Modernization: Its Prospects and Problems* (Berkeley: Institute of International Studies, University of California, 1981), pp. 62–92. The latter article is also in *Issues & Studies* 17:11 (November 1981), pp. 45–75, and in the University of Maryland School of Law Occasional Papers/Reprints Series in Contemporary Asian Studies, 1982, No. 1 (46).

2. Ch'en Shou-yi (Chen Shouyi), Liu Sheng-p'ing (Liu Shengping) and Chao Chen-chiang (Zhao Zhenjiang), "Thirty Years of the Building-Up of Our Legal System," *Fa-hsüeh Yen-chiu* (*Faxue Yanjiu*) [*Studies in Law*], 1979, no. 4, p. 1.

3. Jerome Alan Cohen, *The Criminal Process in the People's Republic of China, 1949–1963: An Introduction* (Cambridge, Mass.: Harvard University Press, 1968), pp. 9–18; Shao-chuan Leng, *Justice in Communist China: A Survey of the Judicial System of the Chinese People's Republic* (Dobbs Ferry, N.Y.: Oceana, 1967), pp. 27–74; Stanley Lubman, "Form and Function in the Chinese Criminal Process," *Columbia Law Review* 69:4 (April 1969), pp. 540–557; and Hungdah Chiu, "Structural Changes," *supra* note 1, pp. 54–56.

4. Ch'en Shou-yi (Chen Shouyi) et al., "Thirty Years of Legal System," *supra* note 2, p. 1.

5. Yang Ch'un-hsi (Yang Chunxi), Kan Yu-pei (Gan Yupei), Yang T'un-hsien (Yang Tunxian) and Yang Tien-sheng (Yang Diansheng), *Hsing-fa Tsung-lun* (*Xingfa Zonglun*) [General treatise on criminal law], Peking (Beijing): Peking (Beijing) University Press, 1981, p. 44.

6. Text in Yuan-li Wu, ed., *China: A Handbook* (New York: Praeger, 1973), pp. 789–798.

7. See Lan Ch'uan-pu (Lan Quanbu), *San-shih nien lai Wo-kuo Fa-kui Yang-ke Kai-k'uang* (*Sanshi nian lai Woguo Fagui Yange Gaikuang*) [Survey of the development of the laws and regulations of our country in the last thirty years], Peking (Beijing): Chun-chung Ch'u-pan-she (Qunzhong Chubanshe), 1980, pp. 3, 4.

8. Translated in Cohen, *Criminal Process, supra* note 3, pp. 299–302.

9. See Leng, *Justice in Communist China, supra* note 3, pp. 27–29.

10. See General Rules Governing the Office of the Local People's Procurators at Various Levels, promulgated on 4 September 1951. Chinese text in *Chung-yang Jen-min Cheng-fu Fa-ling Hui-pian* (*Zhongyang Renmin Zhengfu Faling Huibien*) [Collection of laws and decrees of the Central People's Government], vol. 2 (1951), Peking (Beijing): Jen-min Ch'u-pan-she (Renmin Chubanshe), 1953, pp. 86–87.

11. See Leng, *Justice in Communist China, supra* note 3, pp. 39–44.

12. "Prospect and Retrospect, China's Socialist Legal System," *Peking (Beijing) Review* 22: 2 (12 January 1979), p. 25.

13. Ch'en Shou-yi (Chen Shouyi), "A Review of New China's Research in Law During the Past Thirty Years," *Fa-hsüeh Yen-chiu* (*Faxue Yanjiu*), 1980, no. 1, p. 2.

14. Cohen, *Criminal Process, supra* note 3, pp. 9–10.

15. Text in Wu, *China, supra* note 6, pp. 799–810.

16. English translation in Cohen, *Criminal Process, supra* note 3, pp. 360–362.

17. Ibid., pp. 425–429 for English translation of essential articles of this law.

18. Ibid., pp. 379–381 for English translation of essential articles of this law.

19. See Leng, *Justice in Communist China, supra* note 3, pp. 77–78.

20. See Li Kuang-ts'an (Li Guangcan), *Wo-kuo Kung-min ti Chi-pen Ch'uan-li ho Yi-wu* (*Woguo Gongmin di Jiben Quanli he Yiwu*) [The fundamental rights and duties of the citizens of our country], Peking (Beijing): Jen-min Ch'u-pan-she (Renmin Chubanshe), 1956, pp. 7–8.

21. Ibid., p. 13.

22. *Eighth National Congress of the Communist Party of China,* vol. 1, *Documents* (Beijing: Foreign Languages Press, 1956), p. 82.

23. Ibid., vol. 2, *Speeches,* p. 87.

24. Ch'en Shou-yi (Chen Shouyi), "Review of Research in Law," *supra* note 13, p. 2.

25. Amnesty International, *Political Imprisonment in the People's Republic of China* (London: Amnesty International Publications, 1978), pp. 15–16.

26. Ch'en Shou-yi (Chen Shouyi) et al., "Thirty Years of Legal System," *supra* note 2, p. 2.

27. Ch'en Shou-yi (Chen Shouyi), "Review of Research in Law," *supra* note 13, pp. 2–3.

28. In 1957, two formerly practiced administrative sanctions, which could be imposed by the public security (police) without judicial review, became formalized. The first is the Security Administrative Punishment Act, which authorizes police to impose such minor sanctions as a fine or detention up to 15 days. For the English translation of this act, including commentaries, see Cohen, *Criminal Process, supra* note 3, pp. 200–237. The second is the Decision of the State Council of the PRC Relating to Problems of Rehabilitation through Labor, promulgated on 3 August 1957. For the English translation see Cohen, ibid., pp. 249–250. The sanction of rehabilitation through labor was designed to control vagrants, minor offenders, troublemakers who did not work properly or who refused to comply with work assignments or transfers, and people who were unemployed because they had been expelled from their places of work for breach of discipline or for being labeled rightists. There was no time limit for placing or keeping a person under rehabilitation. Thus, those intellectuals who were labeled rightists in the 1956–1957 Hundred Flowers Campaign and the antirightist campaign were detained for rehabilitation through labor for almost twenty years. The treatment of these people has been similar to the treatment of those who are subject to the criminal sanction of reform through labor. See *Political Imprisonment in the PRC, supra* note 25, pp. 82–83.

29. A recent PRC article described this system as follows: "Whether the facts of a case are clear, the evidence is convincing; the defendant should be subject to criminal sanction, and what criminal punishment should be imposed on the defendant, should be sent to the secretary in charge of political-legal affairs of the local party committee at the same level for review and approval. This is called the system of deciding a case by the secretary." The quotation is from Liao Chung-ch'ang (Liao Jungchang), "The Independence of Trial and [the System of] Deciding a Case by the Secretary," *Hsi-nan Cheng-fa Hsueh-yuan Hsueh-pao* (*Xinan Zhengfa Xueyuan Xuebao*) [*Journal of the Southwest Political-Legal Institute*], 1979, no. 1, p. 7. For a discussion of this system, see Chiu, "Structural Changes," *supra* note 1, pp. 59–61.

30. In 1962, a draft criminal law was distributed to the judicial departments throughout the country to solicit comments; it was also referred to by courts in deciding cases. See "China's Socialist Legal System," *supra* note 12, p. 26. The draft was not published and the text was not available to Chinese law specialists outside China.

31. Both Cohen and Leng did discuss the question of judicial independence but neither mentioned the system of "deciding a case by the [party] secretary." Leng, however, did report a case on direct party interference in a court's judgment. See Leng, *Justice in Communist China, supra* note 3, p. 100. Regarding the law applied by PRC courts in the absence of published written laws, Cohen did point out that, based on his interview, there were "unpublished regulations defin[ing] murder, rape, arson, and many other common crimes and set[ting] . . . the maximum and minimum penalties for each." See his *Criminal Process, supra* note 3, p. 317.

32. Bao Rue-wang and Rudolph Chelminski, *Prisoner of Mao* (New York: Coward, McCann & Geoghegan, 1973, and Penguin, 1976).

33. "China's Socialist Legal System," *supra* note 12, pp. 26–27.

34. For the English translation see Michael Lindsay, ed., *The New Constitution of Communist China: Comparative Analysis* (Taipei: Institute of International Relations, 1976), pp. 328–342.

35. For details, see Hungdah Chiu, "The Judicial System Under the New PRC Constitution," in Lindsay, *New Constitution, supra* note 34, pp. 99–103.

36. Ch'en Shou-yi (Chen Shouyi), "Review of Research in Law," *supra* note 13, p. 3.

37. R. R. Edwards, "Reflections on Criminal Justice in China, with Sentencing Documents," (document trans. R. R. Edwards and Hungdah Chiu), *Columbia Journal of Transnational Law* 16 (1977), pp. 45–103; Tao-tai Hsia, "The Tenth Party Congress and

Future Development of Law in China," in *Oil and Asian Rivals* (Washington, D.C.: U.S. Government Printing Office, 1974), pp. 390–417; Shao-chuan Leng, "The Role of Law in the People's Republic of China as Reflecting Mao Tse-tung's Influence," *Journal of Criminal Law and Criminology* 68 (1977), pp. 356–373; Hungdah Chiu, "Criminal Punishment in Mainland China: A Study of Some Yunnan Province Documents," *Journal of Criminal Law and Criminology* 68 (1977), pp. 374–398; Hungdah Chiu, "Social Disorder in Peking After the 1976 Earthquake as Revealed by a Chinese Legal Document," *Review of Socialist Law* 5 (1979), pp. 5–16.

38. As examples, Jerome Alan Cohen, "Chinese Law: At the Crossroads," *American Bar Association Journal* 59:1 (January 1973), pp. 42–44; Gerd Ruge, "An Interview with Chinese Legal Officials," *China Quarterly,* no. 61 (March 1975), pp. 118–126; Franklin P. Lamb, "An Interview with Chinese Legal Officials," *China Quarterly,* no. 66 (June 1976), pp. 323–325, and the two articles cited in note 39.

39. As examples, George W. Crocket, Jr., "Criminal Justice in China," *Judicature* 59:5 (December 1975), pp. 239–247; Derrick Bell, "Inside China: Continuity and Social Reform," *Juris Doctor* 8:4 (April 1978), pp. 23–26, 31.

40. Victor H. Li, *Law Without Lawyers: A Comparative View of Law in China and the United States* (Stanford, Calif.: Stanford Alumni Association, 1977); reviewed by R. R. Edwards, in *Journal of Asian Studies* 39:4 (August 1980), p. 803.

41. See note 25 for complete citation.

42. Fox Butterfield, *China: Alive in the Bitter Sea* (New York: Times Books, 1982), especially pp. 235–382.

43. English translation in *Peking (Beijing) Review* 21:11 (11 March 1978), pp. 5–14.

44. *Jen-min Jih-pao* (*Renmin Ribao*), 5 December 1982, pp. 1–4; English translation in *Peking* (*Beijing*) *Review* 25:52 (27 December 1982), pp. 10–29.

45. The English translation of the term appeared in the *Peking* (*Beijing*) *Review* as "public organization," which does not correspond to the Chinese original.

46. "New Ministry of Justice Interviewed," *Peking* (*Beijing*) *Review* 22:42 (19 October 1979), pp. 3–4.

47. English translation in *Foreign Broadcast Information Service* (hereinafter cited as *FBIS*), People's Republic of China (PRC), 26 February 1979, pp. E3–E5.

48. All these laws are conveniently collected in Kung-an-pu Cheng-ts'e fa-lu yen-chiu-shih (Gonganbu zhengce falu yanjiushi) [Policy and Law Research Office of the Ministry of Public Security], ed., *Kung-an Fa-kui Hui-pian* (*Gongan Faqui Huibien*), *1950–1979* [Collection of laws and regulations on public security], Peking (Beijing): Ch'un-chung Ch'u-pan-she (Qunzhong Chupanshe), 1980, pp. 87–90 (Arrest), 4–33 (Criminal), 35–65 (Criminal Procedure), 449–457 (Court), and 458–464 (Procuratorate).

49. English translation in *FBIS,* PRC, 28 August 1980, pp. L6–L9. For a summary discussion of this law, see Jerome Alan Cohen, "China's New Lawyers' Law," *American Bar Association Journal* 66 (1980), pp. 1533–1535, and Tao-tai Hsia and Charlotte Hambley, "The Lawyer's Law: An Introduction" (with translation of the complete text), *China Law Reporter* 1:4 (Fall 1981), pp. 213–221.

50. For example, "The Law on Joint Ventures with Chinese and Foreign Investments," *Peking (Beijing) Review* 22:29 (20 July 1979), pp. 3–4.

51. Chinese text published in *Chung-kuo Fa-chih Pao* (*Zhongguo Fazhi Bao*) [*China Legal System Paper*], no. 85 (12 March 1982), pp. 2–3.

52. See note 49.

53. *Country Reports on Human Rights Practices for 1981* (Washington, D.C.: U.S. Government Printing Office, 1982), p. 566.

54. *Jen-min Jih-pao* (*Renmin Ribao*) [*People's Daily*], 25 August 1980, p. 1.

55. For party officials' resistance to the abolition of this system, see Leng, "Justice in Post-Mao China," *supra* note 1, pp. 460–461.

56. See note 45.

57. See Timothy A. Gelatt and Frederick E. Snyder, "Legal Education in China: Training for a New Era," *China Law Reporter* 1:2 (Fall 1980), p. 4.

58. Ibid., pp. 44–45. For a discussion of legal education in China, see also R.S.J. Macdonald, "Legal Education in China Today," *Dalhousie Law Journal* 6 (1980), pp. 313–337.

59. "Justice Vice Minister on Training New Lawyers," *FBIS,* PRC, 22 September 1981, p. K11.

60. Information provided by Dr. Tao-tai Hsia of the Far Eastern Law Division of the Library of Congress.

61. Ibid.

62. *Chung-kuo Pai-k'e Nien-chien, 1980* (*Zhongguo Baike Nianjian, 1980*) [*China Annual Encyclopedia, 1980*], Peking (Beijing): Kuo-chi Shu-tien (Guoji Shudian), 1981, pp. 444–445.

63. Ibid., p. 447.

64. *Fa-hsüeh Ts'u-tien* (*Faxue Cidian*), Shanghai: Shanghai Ts'u-shu Ch'u-pan-she (Shanghai Cishu Chubanshe), 1980.

65. See "Quarterly Chronicle and Documentation (April-June 1979)," *China Quarterly,* no. 79 (September 1979), p. 670. One PRC writer wrote that "once our science of law deviates from the four basic principles, it would naturally lose its socialist character"; see Wang Ch'un (Wang Qun), "Upholding Four Fundamental Principles—Law Researcher's Fighting Task," *Fa-hsüeh Yen-chiu* (*Faxue Yanjiu*), 1981, no. 3, p. 1.

66. See note 44.

67. See the Wei Ching-sheng (Wei Jingsheng) and Fu Yueh-hua (Fu Yuehua) cases summarized in Chiu, "Structural Changes," *supra* note 1, pp. 62–65. For a collection of views of Wei Ching-sheng (Wei Jingsheng) and other intellectuals who demanded China practice genuine democracy, see J. D. Seymour, ed., *The Fifth Modernization: China's Human Rights Movement, 1978–1979* (Stamford, N.Y.: Human Rights Publication Group, 1980).

68. Republished in *Jen-min Jih-pao* (*Renmin Ribao*), 11 April 1980, pp. 1, 3; English translation in *FBIS,* PRC, 14 April 1980, pp. L7–L11. For two recent cases on applying the law, see Frank Ching, "Official's Punishment Gives Chinese a Message: Don't Talk to Foreigners," *Asian Wall Street Journal Weekly,* 5 April 1982, p. 10, and "U.S. Citizen is Accused of Espionage in China," *New York Times,* 2 June 1982, p. A7.

69. See "Supplementary Regulations on Rehabilitation" adopted by the Standing Committee of the National People's Congress on 29 November 1979. *Jen-min Jih-pao* (*Renmin Ribao*), 30 November 1979, p. 1.

70. For example, see the Liu Ching (Liu Qing) case reported in Michael Weisskopf, "Dissident's Memoir Provides Glimpse of the Life in China's Prisons," *Washington Post,* 15 September 1981, pp. A1, A14.

71. See Chiu, "Socialist Legalism," *supra* note 1 (in *Issues & Studies*), pp. 69–72, and Hungdah Chiu, "Certain Legal Aspects of the Recent Peking Trials of the 'Gang of Four' and Others," in *Symposium: The Trial of the "Gang of Four" and Its Implication in China,* ed. James C. Hsiung (Baltimore: University of Maryland School of Law), *Occasional Papers/Reprints Series in Contemporary Asian Studies,* 1981, No. 3 (40), pp. 27–39.

72. See Bernard Ramundo, *The Soviet Legal System, A Primer* (Chicago: American Bar Association, 1971), pp. 22–28.

73. See Fox Butterfield, "Hundreds of Thousands Toil in Chinese Labor Camps," *New York Times,* 3 January 1981, pp. 1, 4; Butterfield, *China, supra* note 42, pp. 342–369; Michael Weisskopf, "Ex-Inmate Recalls Life in China's Gulag," *Washington Post,* 12 February 1982, pp. A1, A44, and A45. See also Bao, *Prisoner of Mao, supra* note 32, and *Political Imprisonment, supra* note 25, pp. 105–131.

74. See Butterfield, "Chinese Labor Camps," *supra* note 73, p 4.

75. See, for example, Kung Hsiang-jui (Gong Xiangrui), Lo Hao-ts'ai (Luo Haocai), and Wu Hsieh-yin (Wu Xieyin), *Hsi-fang Kus-chia te Ssu-fa Chih-tu* (*Xifang Guojia de Sifa Zhidu*) [The judicial system of Western countries], Peking (Beijing): Peking (Beijing) University Press and Institute of Law of the Chinese Academy of Social Sciences, 1980; see also *Jih-pen Hsing-fa, Jih-pen Hsing-shih Su-sung-fa, Jih-pen Lu-shih Fa* (*Riben Xingfa, Riben Xingshi Susongfa, Riben Lushi Fa*) [Japanese criminal law, Japanese criminal procedure law, and Japanese lawyers' law], Peking (Beijing): Chung-kuo She-hui Ke-hsueh Ch'u-pan-she (Zhongguo Shehui Kexue Chubanshe), 1981.

76. See Articles 33–56 of the 1982 Constitution on basic rights and duties of citizens; see also Articles 126 on court independence and 131 on the procuratorate's independence *Peking (Beijing) Review* 25:52 (27 December 1982), p. 29.

77. The following comments were made by a knowledgeable observer on Chinese affairs:

> Decades of political uncertainty, characterized by numerous changes in Party line, power struggles and purges, have inculcated a sense of cynicism in young and old alike. Skepticism over the Party's true intentions and its ability to carry out its declared intentions is widespread.
>
> It won't be possible to eradicate overnight, or even in a year, the doubts and suspicions built up over decades. Only when the Party shows, through concrete actions, that there isn't any justification for such feelings, will the people be convinced of their intent. In this sense, those in power in China are still on probation, and their credibility is still being questioned.

The quotation is from Frank Ching, "China: A Major Step Toward Rule by Law," *Asian Wall Street Journal,* 11 July 1979, p. 4.

78. See Fox Butterfield, "China, for a Fortunate Few at the Top, Is Paradise of Privilege and Perquisites," *New York Times,* 2 January 1981, p. A6.

79. See Article 33 of the 1982 Constitution. *Peking (Beijing) Review,* 25:52 (27 December 1982), p. 16.

80. Information supplied by Tao-tai Hsia.

Part 5

Political and Social Developments

13
The Formation of Political Coalitions in Communist China Since 1949

John Fu-sheng Hsieh

No matter whether it is in a democratic or a nondemocratic society, people form coalitions in order to grasp governing power. No one in any large society can rule without cooperating with others. In the past twenty years, there have been quite a few studies on the formation of political coalitions.[1] However, as most of these studies treat democratic societies, relatively little has been widely known about coalitions in a nondemocratic society such as Communist China.[2]

It is obvious that there are some difficulties in studying the formation of political coalitions in the nondemocratic societies as compared with the democratic ones. First, political coalitions in a democratic society are generally based upon the free will of the participants and, according to the principle of "one man, one vote," each participant's weight can be regarded as equal to that of any other. However, in a nondemocratic society, participation often involves the use of force, and because the participants in such a case may possess different amounts of force, it is unrealistic to consider each participant's weight equal. Thus, it is much more difficult to construct a rational choice model of political coalitions for the nondemocratic societies than for the democratic ones. Even if it would be possible to set up such a formal model for nondemocratic societies, in its application one would still have a problem in assigning relative weights to the participants.

A second difficulty is that data on the formation of political coalitions in the democratic societies are relatively open to the public, but this sort of information for the nondemocratic societies is often incomplete or unavailable. The data may even be incompletely known to observers within these nondemocratic societies.

Despite these problems, the fact that such a large nondemocratic society as Communist China exists makes it necessary to find some alternative ways—perhaps less precise and definite—to study it. The purpose of this article is to explore such possibilities.

Among those studies on political coalitions, the most celebrated is that of William H. Riker elaborating the "size principle": "In social situations similar to n-person, zero-sum games with side-payments, participants create coalitions just as large as they believe will ensure winning and no larger."[3] That is to say, the participants, under the given circumstances, will try to form a minimum winning coalition—large enough to win, but no larger. In a parliamentary democracy, for instance, winning often means controlling more than a majority of seats in the lower house of parliament. Thus, according to the size principle, in situations similar to n-person, zero-sum games with side-payments, a coalition consisting of slightly more than a majority of MPs will most likely be formed.

It should be noted that the size principle refers only to zero-sum games. By zero-sum games we mean the kind of games where the total in payoffs to all participants in the game remains unchanged.[4] In political coalitions the payoffs appear in the form of governing and nongoverning. For convenience, we can assign a value 1 to governing and 0 to nongoverning. Thus, zero-sum games usually refer to the situations in which the total payoffs to all participants in the game always add up to 1 (governing plus nongoverning).

However, political situations do not always resemble zero-sum games. In quite a few situations, the total payoffs to all participants in the game may vary. For example, as a society faces a foreign threat or a serious ethnic conflict, the total payoffs may diminish from 1 to 0; or when a society asks for independence from a colonial power, the total payoffs may increase from 0 to 1. These situations are similar to a life-or-death choice for the society as a whole. It can be argued that in such situations unity may become the theme, and participants will try to form a coalition as large as possible.[5] That is, participants will form a grand coalition, much larger than necessary to win in the normal sense. Let us again take the example of a parliamentary democracy. In situations similar to a life-or-death choice for the society as a whole, it can be expected that a grand coalition consisting of, say, more than two-thirds of MPs will be set up.

It should be stressed here that whether a situation resembles a zero-sum game or a life-or-death choice for the society as a whole must be dependent upon the perceptions of the participants. If most of the participants in a game perceive the situation as a zero-sum game, it can be expected that something like a minimum winning coalition will be formed. If most participants view the situation as a life-or-death choice for the society as a whole, then a grand coalition will very likely be set up.

Obviously, there are lots of factors that may affect participants' perceptions of the situations. Suppose that there is a "threshold of crisis" above which individuals may believe that the situation is something like a life-or-death choice for the society as a whole. It is clear that participants may have different thresholds of crisis because of personalities, positions they occupy, and so on. Because this chapter is not a psychological study, I will not delve into all details regarding the individual participants' thresholds of crisis. Rather, I will concentrate upon one kind of participant, the most powerful leader in the governing position, who will be called the singular "leader in power" in the following discussions. Because he has particularly high stakes (governing power) in the game, he may be especially sensitive to any situation in which he will probably lose all the governing power he now possesses. Hence, it can be expected that he may have a lower threshold of crisis than most others in the game; that is, he may be more inclined than others to perceive the situation as a life-or-death choice for the society as a whole, and thus, to advocate the need for unity and cooperation among all participants in the game. This inclination on the part of the leader in power to advocate the need for unity will be called the Principle of Unity.[6]

There is no doubt that some other factors in the actual situation, the institutional setting, the past experience of the society, and so on may also affect in one way or another the participants' perceptions of the situation. In the case that the actual situation is really like a zero-sum game, it can be expected that a large number of participants may be induced to perceive this situation. Correspondingly, if the actual situation is similar to a life-or-death choice for the society as a whole, then many participants may be inclined to believe it to be so. Nevertheless, the relationship between the actual situation and participants' perceptions of it is not always so unambiguous. This is especially true in nondemocratic societies where information about the situation received by the participants is often distorted, in turn distorting the participants' perceptions of the situation. This event is less likely in democratic societies.

As noted, the past experience of the society may also affect participants' perceptions of the situation. For instance, if there have been experiences in undergoing disasters caused by noncooperation, or in preventing disasters by cooperation, it can be expected that a lot of participants may have a lower threshold of crisis and thus be more inclined to perceive the situation as a life-or-death choice for the society as a whole. Also, it is apparent that if the size of the game, i.e., the number of participants, is large, it will be relatively more difficult to obtain a consensus among the participants about the situation of the game.

After briefly introducing some theories of political coalitions, I will show how these theories can be applied to the case of Communist China. First, a distinction must be drawn between two types of participants: the leader in power and ordinary political actors (OPAs). The former, as defined earlier, is the most powerful leader, the one who is actually responsible for the day-to-day functioning of the government, although he may or may not occupy the formally highest position in the government. He may be a king, a president, a prime minister, the boss of the dominant single party, or whatever. The OPAs are those who are in some way directly involved in the task of selecting the leader in power. They may be members of the lower house of parliament in a parliamentary democracy, voters in a presidential election in a presidential democracy, civilian and military bureaucrats in a nondemocratic society, or some combination of these. Some OPAs in a game form a coalition with the leader in power and this coalition is referred to as the winning coalition. Other OPAs form coalitions that lose in the game.

In the case of Communist China, Mao Tse-tung was the leader in power during the period from 1949 when the Chinese Communist party (CCP) took over the reins of government until 1976 when he died. Mao derived his power primarily from his positions as chairman of the Central Committee (CC) of the CCP and chairman of the CC's Military Affairs Committee. Also, Mao was chairman of the Central People's Government Council (1949–1954) and chairman of the People's Republic of China (1954–1959). In April 1959, he resigned as the head of state, but he remained the final authority in Communist China by virtue of his positions in the CCP.

After Mao's death, Hua Kuo-feng inherited these positions in the CCP, retaining also his position of premier, which he had taken over after Chou En-lai died a few months earlier. At one time, it seemed that Hua was the leader in power; however, shortly after Teng Hsiao-p'ing, having been purged twice by Mao, was rehabilitated in the summer of 1977, Hua was overshadowed by Teng. Though Teng was only a vice-chairman of the CCP and a vice-premier, he soon became the person actually responsible for the day-to-day functioning of the government. Teng was, and still is, the de facto leader in power in Communist China. In September 1980, Hua resigned as premier and was replaced by Teng's associate Chao Tzu-yang. Teng, in a symbolic move, also resigned as vice-premier then. In June 1981, Hua was further deprived of the chairmanship of the CCP in favor of Hu Yao-pang, another Teng associate, and of the chairmanship of the CC's Military Affairs Committee, where he was succeeded by Teng himself. Hua was transferred to a vice-chairmanship of the CCP.

Now, consider the OPAs. In the case of Communist China, they may be army generals, party and state bureaucrats, and so on. However, there are some serious problems in identifying exactly who they are in such a nondemocratic society. As discussed at the beginning, since Communist China is a closed society, it is difficult for an outside observer to obtain the necessary information. Moreover, the OPAs in such a society are not in a well-defined institution like the lower house of parliament in a parliamentary democracy. This difference arises because the criterion for winning in a nondemocratic society such as Communist China is, in general, not election (at least not by popular vote), but force, and there is almost no way to specify the use of force in a well-defined institution. Besides, even if one were able to find out exactly who the OPAs are in Communist China, another disturbing problem would be raised. That is, unlike elections in which the rule of "one man, one vote" prevails, the use of force implies that someone's "vote" is weightier than those of others. Thus, each player's "vote" should be weighted before one can talk about the sizes of coalitions formed in the game. However, this kind of information is almost impossible to secure, rendering more difficult any study of the sizes of coalitions in such a society.

In order to solve or, more accurately, to bypass these problems, a two-step approach is suggested. The first step is to describe in very broad terms the power struggle in the society as a whole. One can assume that if, in the game, there are no alternative candidates for, and no or few real challenges to, the position of the leader in power, then it is likely that a grand coalition, centering upon the leader in power, exists; otherwise, the coalition will approach the minimum winning size or even slip below that size. The second step is to look into the formation of coalitions within the CC Politburo. It should be stressed that although members of the Politburo are all important participants in the game, their weights are not the same, and many other participants, probably including some of major importance, are not included in that organization. Thus, what one gets from examining coalitions in the Politburo may not reflect the real picture of political coalitions in Communist China. So Politburo coalitions will be used only as a reference to check the results from the first step above. This two-step approach is certainly not very satisfactory, but under the circumstances it seems the only possible way to study the formation of political coalitions in Communist China.

Now let me begin with the first step and carry it out. Since the mid-nineteenth century, China has sustained repeated long periods of chaos and turmoil, prompting many to try to rebuild the whole society. Indeed, the history of modern China is marked with, in Richard H. Solomon's words, "the uncompromising struggle to re-establish a unitary political structure."[7] Being one of the forces to attempt to win such a struggle, the Chinese Communist party finally succeeded in controlling all of the Chinese mainland in 1949, while its primary rival, the Kuomintang (KMT), retreated to Taiwan.

The center of political power in Communist China rests at least theoretically with the CCP, so that the leader of the CCP is generally regarded as the leader in power in the society as a whole. However, the CCP does not monopolize the whole political process. At times the army, the state bureaucracy, and even students may play important roles in the internal political process in Communist China.

During the period 1949–1958, there were few serious challenges, both in and out of the CCP, to Mao Tse-tung as the leader in power. The only notable conflict among the top leadership of the CCP during this period of time was the Kao (Kang)-Jao (Shu-shih) affair of 1954, which still remains a mystery to the outside world. However, from what little became known, it seems that it was mainly a conflict between the Kao-Jao clique and Liu Shao-ch'i, then the second most powerful man in Communist China—rather than directly aimed at Mao himself.[8] The Kao-Jao clique was charged with trying to oust Liu, resulting in the purges of Kao Kang, Jao Shu-shih, and some of their close associates. The case was handled in great secrecy—not even made public until March 1955—and without much disruption so as to reinforce the outside impression that the CCP leadership was "united and free of the internal conflicts so characteristic of the Russian leaders."[9]

In view of the fact that there were very few serious challenges to Mao as the leader in power during the period from 1949 to 1958, it seems that Mao was able to put together a grand coalition centered upon himself. However, events soon changed that, as the policies of the Three Red Banners (the general line for building socialism, the Great Leap Forward, and the People's Communes) of 1958–1960 disrupted the whole picture. These policies were promulgated mainly by Mao himself and were opposed by many of his colleagues. Thus, it is not surprising that the catastrophic results of the Three Red Banners severely eroded Mao's authority in and out of the party.

In December 1958, Mao announced his resignation as chairman of the PRC, and in April 1959 he was formally replaced in this position by Liu Shao-ch'i. However, Mao remained the leader in power through his positions as chairman of the party and chairman of the CC's Military Affairs Committee and was able, in August 1959, to purge P'eng Te-huai, minister of defense and a severe critic of the Three Red Banners policies, along with some of P'eng's associates. Yet it was apparent that Mao was no longer able to command all the resources available in the game; he was even boycotted by Liu Shao-ch'i and his men. As time went by, Mao's position was further weakened. The situation could be best summarized by Mao's own words: "At that time [referring to the winter of 1965], some departments and places in this country were controlled by the revisionists so tightly that water could not be poured in, and pins and needles could not be stuck in."[10] This observation signifies the fact that Mao's coalition was dwindling to the minimum winning size, or even losing.

The Great Proletarian Cultural Revolution, dating from late 1965, could be regarded as an attempt made by the Maoists at regaining full control of the government. After having successfully purged a number of Liu Shao-ch'i's followers in the first half of 1966, Mao was determined to recruit into the game some new elements because the Liuists remained very strong among the traditional participants, particularly the party and state bureaucrats. Thus, in mid-1966, the Red Guards were organized by the Maoists and began to attack various governmental departments controlled by the Liuists. In October 1966, Liu and Teng Hsiao-p'ing were purged; however, the remaining Liuists still resisted vigorously, so in January 1967 Mao, supported by Lin Piao, defense minister and the emerging number-two man in Communist China, ordered the formerly neutralized People's Liberation Army (PLA) to intervene. Thereafter, the PLA became the dominant force in Chinese Communist politics. Though Mao was later able to put together the PLA, the "revolutionary cadres," and the "revolutionary mass organizations" in a grand coalition, this coalition was shaky at best, for the conflicts among the three groups were intense.

In August 1970, Ch'en Po-ta, one of Mao's closest associates, disappeared. One year later, Lin Piao, Mao's heir-apparent, and a number of generals were purged for allegedly plotting a coup d'etat against Mao. This event was followed by a decline of influence of the PLA in Chinese Communist politics. The purges of Ch'en and Lin have remained a mystery to the outside world; however, what seems clear is that Mao's position as the leader in power was then very limited, and it is doubtful that Mao was able to put together a grand coalition at that time.

In early 1973, Teng Hsiao-p'ing and some others purged during the Cultural Revolution were rehabilitated. It seems to have been Premier Chou En-lai's idea and was probably reluctantly approved by Mao, for, soon after Teng's rehabilitation, Mao staged several campaigns such as the anti-Confucius campaign, apparently aimed at Chou and the rehabilitated old cadres.[11] Nonetheless, these campaigns all failed until Chou's death in January 1976. In April 1976, Teng was again purged by Mao. At this moment, it seemed that Mao was able to rebuild once more a grand coalition, but before such a coalition could really be put together, he died.

Shortly after Mao's death on 9 September 1976, the Gang of Four, including Mao's wife, Chiang Ch'ing, and some of Mao's close associates, were arrested, and Hua Kuo-feng succeeded Mao as the leader in power. Although Hua was at first able to form a grand coalition consisting of the moderate Maoists and the non-Maoists, he gradually lost the support of many of the latter. After giving in to the demand for restoring Teng Hsiao-p'ing, Hua was no longer able to put together a grand coalition and finally lost to Teng in the game. Teng replaced Hua as the actual leader in power.

Although Teng became the leader in power soon after being rehabilitated in the summer of 1977, the support for Hua did not all die down. For instance, Hua was strongly backed by Marshal Yeh Chien-ying, a powerful figure with support in the PLA. Even after Hua was deprived of both the CCP chairmanship and the chairmanship of the CC's Military Affairs Committee in June 1981, it remained doubtful whether Teng would be able to get rid of the challenges posed by the Hua-Yeh faction and thus form a grand coalition centered upon himself.

We will now proceed to the second step and examine the coalitions within the CC Politburo. In 1949 when the CCP took over the reins of government on the Chinese mainland, there were twelve members in the Politburo that was left over from the Seventh CC: Mao Tse-tung, Liu Shao-ch'i, Chou En-lai, Chu Teh, Jen Pi-shih, Ch'en Yün, Chang Wen-t'ien, K'ang Sheng, Lin Po-ch'ü, Tung Pi-wu, Kao Kang, and P'eng Chen.[12] It seems that, at that time, all these men could be regarded as Mao's loyal supporters.[13] That is to say, Mao was able to set up a grand coalition centered upon himself. Before the opening of the Eighth CCP Congress in 1956, there were some changes in the Politburo, such as the death of Jen Pi-shih in 1950, the purge of Kao Kang in 1954, and the election to the Politburo of P'eng Te-huai in 1954 and of Lin Piao and Teng Hsiao-p'ing in 1955; nevertheless, the fact that Mao was able to form a grand coalition remained unchanged. Even in the case of Kao Kang, the only notable conflict at that time involving the members of the Politburo, Kao's efforts, as mentioned earlier, seemed to be aimed at Liu Shao-ch'i rather than Mao.

At the First Plenum of the Eighth CC on 28 September 1956, a new Politburo was elected with seventeen full members and six alternate members. Except for Chang Wen-t'ien and K'ang Sheng, who were demoted to alternate status, all other members of the Politburo of the Seventh CC—Mao Tse-tung, Liu Shao-ch'i, Chou En-lai, Chu Teh, Ch'en Yün, Teng Hsiao-p'ing, Lin Piao, Lin Po-ch'ü, Tung Pi-wu, P'eng Chen, and P'eng Te-huai—were reelected as full members in the new Politburo. Several new men were added to the Politburo. Lo Jung-huan, Ch'en I, Li Fu-ch'un, Liu Po-ch'eng, Ho Lung, and Li Hsien-nien were elected as full members, and Ulanfu, Lu Ting-yi, Ch'en Po-ta, and Po I-po became alternate members. Again, Mao was able to put together a grand coalition consisting of almost all members—full and alternate—of the Politburo. In 1958, K'o Ch'ing-shih, Li Ching-chüan, and T'an Chen-lin were elected as full members of the Politburo. It seems that these three men could also be viewed as Mao's supporters at the time.

Mao's position within the Politburo was basically unchanged until after the failure of the policies of the Three Red Banners. Beginning then, Mao was gradually isolated in the Politburo. Although Mao was able in August 1959 to purge P'eng Te-huai, a severe critic of the Three Red Banners policies, along with Chang Wen-t'ien, it was clear that Mao's influence had shrunk.[14] As far as Mao was concerned, the situation became worse as time went by.

On the eve of the Cultural Revolution, among sixteen active full members of the Politburo,[15] only Lin Piao could be regarded as Mao's loyal supporter. It is only when such middle-of-the-roaders as Chou En-lai, Tung Pi-wu, Ch'en I, Li Fu-ch'un, Liu Po-ch'eng, Li Hsien-nien, and T'an Chen-lin were all included that Mao might be able to put together a minimum winning coalition against Liu Shao-ch'i, his primary rival. Even among five active alternate members, Mao was able to obtain the support of but two men, i.e., Ch'en Po-ta and K'ang Sheng.

At the Eleventh Plenum of the Eighth CC in August 1966, a new Politburo was elected, which reflected the struggle between Maoists and Liuists. In the new Politburo, there were twenty-one full members: Mao Tse-tung, Lin Piao, Chou En-lai, T'ao Chu, Ch'en Po-ta, Teng Hsiao-p'ing, K'ang Sheng, Liu Shao-ch'i, Chu Teh, Li Fu-ch'un, Ch'en Yün, Tung Pi-wu, Ch'en I, Liu Po-ch'eng, Ho Lung, Li Hsien-nien, T'an Chen-lin, Li Ching-chüan, Hsü Hsiang-ch'ien, Nieh Jung-chen, and Yeh Chien-ying.[16] There were six alternate members: Ulanfu, Po I-po, Li Hsüeh-feng, Sung Jen-ch'iung, Liu Lan-t'ao, and Hsieh Fu-chih. It seems that the Maoists had made small gains since they were able, on the one hand, to promote Ch'en Po-ta and K'ang Sheng from alternate to full status, and to elect T'ao Chu as a full member and Li Hsüeh-feng and

Hsieh Fu-chih as alternate members, and, on the other hand, to expel P'eng Chen and Lu Ting-yi from the Politburo. Among other new faces, Hsü Hsiang-ch'ien, Nieh Jung-chen, and Yeh Chien-ying could be viewed as middle-of-the-roaders, but Sung Jen-ch'iung and Liu Lan-t'ao were against Mao. Without the support of the middle-of-the-roaders, Mao was still unable to set up a winning coalition in the Politburo. Under the circumstances, Mao therefore decided to bypass the Politburo and other party and state organs, and to appeal directly to first the students and later the PLA.

Mao's tactics were very successful, for at the First Plenum of the Ninth CC on 28 April 1969 Mao was able to put together a grand coalition among the members of the new Politburo. In the new Politburo, there were twenty-one full members: Mao Tse-tung,*[17] Lin Piao,* Chou En-lai,* Ch'en Po-ta,* K'ang Sheng,* Chu Teh,* Tung Pi-wu,* Chiang Ch'ing, Chang Ch'un-ch'iao, Huang Yung-sheng, Yeh Ch'ün, Yeh Chien-ying,* Yao Wen-yüan, Liu Po-ch'eng,* Li Hsien-nien,* Hsieh Fu-chih,* Wu Fa-hsien, Li Tso-p'eng, Ch'iu Hui-tso, Hsü Shih-yu, and Ch'en Hsi-lien. There were four alternate members: Chi Teng-k'uei, Li Te-sheng, Wang Tung-hsing, and Li Hsüeh-feng.* Among the new faces, almost all were Maoists, probably except Hsü Shih-yu, who might better be categorized as a middle-of-the-roader. At that time, Mao was not only able to command those Maoists but to gain the support of most of the middle-of-the-roaders. Thus, he was able to form a grand coalition in the Politburo.

However, this grand coalition was shaky at best, for shortly afterward, Ch'en Po-ta, Li Hsüeh-feng, Lin Piao, Huang Yung-sheng, Yeh Ch'ün, Wu Fa-hsien, Li Tso-p'eng, and Ch'iu Hui-tso were purged, and the Maoists and those close to Chou did not always cooperate harmoniously. Hsieh Fu-chih died in 1972.

In 1973, the Politburo of the Tenth CC was elected. In the new Politburo, there were twenty-one full members: Mao Tse-tung,*[18] Chou En-lai,* Wang Hung-wen, K'ang Sheng,* Yeh Chien-ying,* Tung Pi-wu,* Chu Teh,* Chang Ch'un-ch'iao,* Chiang Ch'ing,* Yao Wen-yüan,* Liu Po-ch'eng,* Li Hsien-nien,* Ch'en Hsi-lien,* Hsü Shih-yu,* Chi Teng-k'uei,* Wang Tung-hsing,* Hua Kuo-feng, Wu Teh, Ch'en Yung-kuei, Wei Kuo-ch'ing, and Li Te-sheng;* the four alternate members were Su Cheng-hua, Saifudin, Ni Chih-fu, and Wu Kuei-hsien. Among the new faces, almost all except Wei Kuo-ch'ing, Su Cheng-hua, and Saifudin were Maoists. Teng Hsiao-p'ing was elected a full member of the Politburo in 1974. In the Politburo of the Tenth CC, though the Maoists were able to set up a minimum winning coalition by themselves, it was only after gaining the support of some others that they could form a grand coalition. As discussed previously, the relationship between the Maoists and those close to Chou was not very good.

In 1975, Tung Pi-wu and K'ang Sheng died; in January 1976, Chou En-lai died. In April, Teng Hsiao-p'ing was purged. In July, Chu Teh died. It seemed that finally Mao was again able to put together a grand coalition. However, he himself passed away in September 1976.

After Mao's death, the Gang of Four (Chiang Ch'ing, Wang Hung-wen, Chang Ch'un-ch'iao, and Yao Wen-yüan) were arrested. As mentioned earlier, Hua Kuo-feng then became the leader in power. Following the arrest of the Gang of Four, there were only twelve full members plus four alternate members left in the Politburo. Hua, as the leader of the remaining Maoists, was able to form a grand coalition in the Politburo with the help of some non-Maoists such as Yeh Chien-ying and Li Hsien-nien. However, soon after the rehabilitation of Teng Hsiao-p'ing and the opening of the Eleventh CCP Congress in the summer of 1977, Hua was no longer able to command a grand coalition and eventually lost to Teng.

In the Politburo of the Eleventh CC, elected on 19 August 1977, there were twenty-three full members: Hua Kuo-feng,*[19] Yeh Chien-ying,* Teng Hsiao-p'ing,* Li Hsien-nien,* Wang Tung hsing,* Wei Kuo-ch'ing,* Ulanfu, Fang Yi, Liu Po-ch'eng,* Hsü Shih-yu,* Chi Teng-k'uei,* Su Cheng-hua,* Li Te-sheng,* Wu Teh,* Yü Ch'iu-li, Chang T'ing-fa, Ch'en Yung-kuei,* Ch'en Hsi-lien,* Keng Piao, Nieh Jung-chen, Ni Chih-fu,* Hsü Hsiang-ch'ien, and P'eng Ch'ung. There were three alternate members: Ch'en Mu-hua, Chao Tzu-yang, and Saifudin.* Wu Kuei-hsien, who had been close to the Gang of Four, was not included in the Politburo this time. Among the new faces, no one could be viewed as Hua Kuo-feng's man. It was a victory for Teng Hsiao-p'ing. Among twenty-three full members of the Politburo, Hua was able to control only about eight: Hua, Wang Tung-hsing, Chi Teng-k'uei, Li Te-sheng, Wu Teh, Ch'en Yung-kuei, Ch'en Hsi-lien, and Ni Chih-fu. Even with the help of Yeh Chien-ying and Li Hsien-nien, it was difficult for Hua to set up a winning coalition. It is, thus, not surprising that Teng finally replaced Hua as the leader in power.

In 1978, four more of Teng's supporters—Ch'en Yün, Teng Ying-ch'ao, Wang Chen, and Hu Yao-pang—were elected as full members of the Politburo. This further strengthened the position of Teng Hsiao-p'ing and his followers. In 1979, Su Cheng-hua died, and later, Chao Tzu-yang was promoted from alternate to full membership in the Politburo, and P'eng Chen was also elected as full member. In February 1980, Wang Tung-hsing, Chi Teng-k'uei, Wu Teh, and Ch'en Hsi-lien, who were all Hua's close associates, were expelled from the Politburo. Thus, it seemed that Teng was eventually able to form a grand coalition against the Hua-Yeh faction.

After completing the discussions using the two-step approach, it is surprising that the results one gets from the second step are generally quite consistent with those obtained from the first step, with probably only one exception, i.e., the size of Teng's coalition at present. According to results from the second step, Teng should have been able to form a grand coalition, but according to the first step, he would be unable to do so. What is the problem here? The problem, I think, rests with the strength of the Maoists represented by the Hua-Yeh faction. In view of the fact that Teng was not free of the challenges posed by the Hua-Yeh faction, and the Hua-Yeh faction still had, or has, some influence in places including the PLA, it is quite possible that we may in the second step have underestimated the strength of the Hua-Yeh faction. Thus, it seems that a more appropriate assessment may be that Teng has been able to command a large winning coalition in the whole game, but not large enough to be called a grand coalition.

Now, the remaining question is: What are the factors affecting the formation of political coalitions in Communist China? According to the Principle of Unity, the leader in power is inclined to have a lower threshold of crisis and thus is more likely to perceive the situation around him as a life-or-death choice for the society as a whole. So it is likely that he will try to form a coalition as large as possible. In such a nondemocratic society as Communist China, the leader in power is usually able to control the mass media, the armed forces, and the recruitment process so that he can try several major moves: (a) intensive propaganda to convince others to perceive the situation in the same way he does; (b) depoliticization, imprisonment, and execution to remove from the game those participants who disagree with him; and (c) penetration into the recruitment process to enlist into the game only those who agree with him. This final kind of maneuver is a constant factor in Chinese Communist politics. Nonetheless, these repressive methods alone cannot guarantee the formation and maintenance of a grand coalition, especially in a large society like Communist China.

Other factors as mentioned earlier, such as past experience and the actual situation, may also affect the formation of political coalitions in Communist China. If there have been disasters in the past because of noncooperation, or benefits because of cooperation, it can be expected that many participants may lower their thresholds of crisis. In case the actual situation is really like a life-or-death choice for the society as a whole, then a lot of participants may be induced to perceive the situation as such and to try to form a coalition as large as possible; otherwise, people may view the situation as a zero-sum game. The disunity and turmoil in China since the mid-nineteenth century, the experience of cooperation among the CCP members and supporters in the pre-1949 military struggle, the Korean War of 1950–1953, the U.S. containment policy in the 1950s and 1960s, the Soviet threat since the 1960s, the continued confrontation with the Nationalists on Taiwan, and the turmoil remembered during the Cultural Revolution all may, at one time or another, bring some participants to perceive the situation as a life-or-death choice for the society as a whole. As these factors become less significant, more and more people may consider the situation a zero-sum game.

To summarize, the repressive methods used by the leader in power and his followers, the fear of the recurrence of the great turmoil prior to 1949, the experience of cooperation among the CCP members and supporters in the earlier period, the Korean War, the U.S. containment policy, and the confrontation with the KMT all may have contributed to the formation of a grand coalition in Communist China in the period of 1949–1958. Since the late 1950s, most of these factors, such as the fear of recurrence of the turmoil prior to 1949, the past experience of cooperation, and the Korean War, have become less relevant. Even repressive methods could not be monopolized by the leader in power. Thus, it has not been surprising to see the breakdown of the grand coalition. As for the formation of a grand coalition in the late 1960s, it resulted mainly from the use of force by the leader in power, plus, to a lesser extent, some concern about the past experience, the Soviet threat, the U.S. containment, and the confrontation with Taiwan. Because it was, for the most part, a result of the use of force, such a grand coalition, as might be expected, was not stable. Later, Hua was able to form a grand coalition immediately following the arrest of the Gang of Four primarily because, apart from the use of force, fear existed about recurrence of the turmoil of the Cultural Revolution. As this fear attenuated, the formation of a grand coalition became more difficult, in that more and more people started to think of the situation as a zero-sum game.

Notes

1. Among studies on the formation of political coalitions, the classic one is William H. Riker's *The Theory of Political Coalitions* (New Haven, Conn.: Yale University Press, 1962). Other important works include Sven Groennings, E. W. Kelley, and Michael Leiserson, eds., *The Study of Coalition Behavior: Theoretical Perspectives and Cases from Four Continents* (New York: Holt, Rinehart and Winston, 1970); Abram De Swaan, *Coalition Theories and Cabinet Formations* (San Francisco: Jossey-Bass, 1973); and Lawrence C. Dodd, *Coalitions in Parliamentary Government* (Princeton, N.J.: Princeton University Press, 1976). Nonetheless, it should be noted here that all the above works deal mainly with a particular kind of coalition, i.e., the minimum winning coalition, or some of its variants. As for the formation of grand coalitions, see Fuh-sheng Hsieh, "The Formation of Grand Coalitions in Politics," Ph.D. dissertation, University of Rochester, 1981. (The terms "minimum winning coalition" and "grand coalition" will be defined later.)

2. The theories of political coalitions cited here are concerned with the kinds of coalitions being formed in the political games on the assumption that the goal of the participants in such games is to gain the governing power. In these games, people—individuals or groups of individuals such as factions and parties—form coalitions in order to win, i.e., to govern. Andrew J. Nathan touches on some of these points in his "A Factionalism Model for CCP Politics," *China Quarterly,* no. 53 (January/March 1973), pp. 34–66. However, his model is less formal, and he does not elaborate on these points. It seems that he cares more about whether Communist China has factional politics than about how the factions coalesce to obtain the governing power.

3. Riker, *Political Coalitions,* p. 47.

4. A more accurate term for the kind of games where the payoffs to all participants in the game always add up to a constant should be constant-sum games. Only when the constant is 0 does the game become zero-sum. However, since all constant-sum games can be transformed into zero-sum games simply by subtracting an appropriate constant, in order to be consistent with Riker's statement, zero-sum instead of constant-sum will be used to refer to the situations where the total payoff to all participants in the game remains a constant.

5. It can be proved by using the notion of the core that in a situation similar to a life-or-death choice for the society as a whole, participants will try to form a coalition as large as possible. See Hsieh, "Formation of Grand Coalitions," pp. 21–23.

6. For a discussion of the threshold of crisis and the Principle of Unity, see ibid., pp. 35–36.

7. Richard H. Solomon, "Mao's Effort to Reintegrate the Chinese Polity: Problems of Authority and Conflict in the Chinese Social Process," in *Chinese Communist Politics in Action,* ed. A. Doak Barnett (Seattle: University of Washington Press, 1969), p. 272.

8. Tu Feng, "Can the Kao Kang Issue Be Solved?," *Cheng Ming,* 1 November 1980, pp. 18–19. Cf. Harold C. Hinton, *An Introduction to Chinese Politics* (New York: Praeger, 1973), pp. 30–32.

9. Lucian W. Pye, *China: An Introduction,* 2nd ed. (Boston: Little, Brown, 1978), p. 230.

10. Mao Tse-tung, "Speech at Receiving the Albania Military Delegation in Peking" in *Important CCP Documents of the Great Proletarian Cultural Revolution* (Taipei: Institute for the Study of Chinese Communist Problems, 1973), p. 209.

11. The Maoists attacked Confucius' words "to elect the able men living in seclusion," implying Chou's move to rehabilitate old cadres, including Teng.

12. The members of the CC Politburo (1949–1977) listed here are cited from Parris H. Chang, *Power and Policy in China,* 2nd ed. (University Park, Pa.: Pennsylvania State University Press, 1978), appendix B. As for the latest developments since 1978, the data are gathered from the news reports.

13. In view of his special background, Chang Wen-t'ien's role was dubious; however, there seems no strong evidence to indicate that he was then against Mao.

14. Both P'eng Te-huai and Chang Wen-t'ien retained their positions in the Politburo, though they were no longer very active.

15. Lin Po-ch'ü, Lo Jung-huan, and K'o Ch'ing-shih died earlier.

16. Chu Teh is not included on P. Chang's list. However, several other sources suggest that Chu should be put in. See, for example, Jürgen Domes, *The Internal Politics of China 1949–1972* (New York: Praeger, 1973), p. 161.

17. Those members with asterisks following their names were members of the old Politburo. Hsieh Fu-chih was promoted from alternate to full membership.

18. Those members with asterisks following their names were members of the old Politburo. Chi Teng-k'uei, Wang Tung-hsing, and Li Te-sheng were promoted from alternate to full status.

19. Those members with asterisks following their names were members of the old Politburo. Su Cheng-hua and Ni Chih-fu were promoted from alternate to full status.

14
The Politics of Life Chances in the People's Republic of China

Martin King Whyte

How has the structure of stratification and of mobility opportunities affected people's lives in China since 1949? The focus in investigating this question will be as much or more on popular perceptions of life chances as on the objective facts of stratification and mobility, for two primary reasons. First, data concerning most aspects of stratification in contemporary China do not exist. Second, political inclinations and popular moods do not reflect the objective facts of stratification directly, but are influenced by the subjective perceptions of life chances that the population holds.[1] Yet even gaining a clear idea about popular perceptions in China is no easy matter. Popular perceptions there, as in any other society, are diverse rather than uniform, and judgments about subjective views cannot help also being subjective and tentative. The following pages contain many "seat of the pants" generalizations on these matters that are based upon several stints of refugee interviewing in Hong Kong, a wide reading of personal accounts of life in the PRC, accounts in the Chinese press, Chinese short stories, and the Western secondary literature. Although some of the judgments rendered here will require qualification and modification, a preliminary effort of this type still seems worthwhile.[2]

The basic assumption underlying the analysis that follows is that public perceptions about life chances can be of considerable importance politically. Support for governments everywhere depends in part on the degree to which subjects feel that their aspirations for security and mobility are being satisfactorily met, and the recent events in Poland demonstrate what can happen when such feelings are eroded or negated.

In Chinese history, at least part of the evaluation of dynastic cycles and the changing "mandate of heaven" was seen in terms of altered perceptions of life chances. New and vigorous dynasties established order, revived the economy, recruited able men into official service, and created conditions for prosperity and social mobility. Over time, rising corruption, declining tax bases, less public-spirited officials, and other problems were seen as contributing to rising economic problems, heightened threat of famine and banditry, and a general decay of confidence in the government—trends that made conditions ripe for efforts to overthrow the dynasty.

The government established after 1949 is not a traditional imperial house, and it does not ordinarily allow direct voicing of public dissatisfaction with life chances. Nevertheless, I will argue here that public perceptions still influence behavior in important ways and create conditions that the government must be concerned about. So perceptions of life chances remain politically important even if they cannot be directly expressed or form the basis of protest groups.

It must be clear at the outset that the perceptions of life chances discussed here form a concept much broader than, say, a desire for "material incentives" that some see lodged in "human nature." Probably the post-Mao leadership has placed more faith in the beneficial power of bonuses and piece rates than is justified. This and earlier problems with such material incentives (as well as the experience of other countries) make it clear that long-term prospects may be more important than immediate rewards, that rewards are compared with expectations and with those rewards received by peers, and that incentives other than direct material ones are important.

What sorts of perceptions are conducive to positive feelings toward the political system in which one lives? First, a perception of economic security and predictability would seem to be important—a feeling that starvation and penury can be avoided, that diligent efforts will be rewarded, that gains will not be unexpectedly wiped out, and that life can be planned with some degree of certainty so that marriages can be entered into, children given birth to, new housing can be built, and so forth.

Second, it helps if there are perceptions that legitimate opportunities for upward mobility exist in some abundance, whether through education, trading, diligent labor, or other devices, and that one can pursue such opportunities with some degree of confidence rather than hold an overriding fear of failure and downward mobility. The use of the term "legitimate" refers to a perception that those who get ahead, for the most part, have followed culturally approved means and thus deserve the success and advantages that they have achieved.[3] The political elites, as perhaps the most advantaged group, should particularly be seen as meriting their positions and as making some contribution to providing economic opportunity and mobility opportunities for society as a whole. In other words, inequality is not necessarily resented, but inequity—the perception that the inequality existing does not coincide with what is "just"—inevitably is resented.

Given these considerations, it also helps if the public sees instances of economic insecurity, poverty, and downward mobility as not due to government action or neglect, elite callousness, or some other "systemic" source, but rather to external or uncontrollable factors—fate, weather, foreign imperialism, or whatever. It also helps if those who do perceive the government as arbitrary, unjust, and the source of much of the insecurity and downward mobility that exists are kept politically isolated so that they are not able to get such views widely communicated and accepted. This is not necessarily an exhaustive list of the aspects of perceptions of life chances that can be politically important, but it should suffice for the consideration of trends over time in contemporary China.[4]

If one accepts this list of considerations, then the erosion of public support for the Nationalist regime that preceded the Communist regime in China fits readily within this framework. On the one hand, many new kinds of opportunities for social mobility arose in the twentieth century. But on the other hand, many of these new routes lacked the legitimacy of the official examination route dismantled in the closing days of the Qing. Military prowess, compradoreship, commercial manipulations, and other paths were not seen entirely in positive terms. Efforts were made to regularize a new school system and civil service procedures, but much social mobility was still seen as taking place through other means. In an extreme example, one study of social mobility in the Republican period illustrates an illegitimate path—a family who murdered a group of seven traveling ox merchants and then became wealthy by trading the goods they had thus acquired.[5] A further complication was that some of the elites in these years were foreigners, and their privileges and the extraterritorial powers that buttressed them were widely resented.

Widespread perceptions of venality and corruption within the political elite and a sense that the government was not taking effective measures to improve "the people's livelihood" (one of the three people's principles of Sun Yat-sen) further undermined the government's legitimacy. In the closing years galloping inflation, banditry, and civil war made life quite unpredictable and led to feelings that life chances were quite inequitable. Some of the blame for economic insecurity could be diverted to other sources—the Japanese, the CCP, local warlords, and so forth—but by the post–World War II period enough blame was left over for the feelings of government ineptitude and corruption to prepare the way for the passing of the "mandate of heaven" to the CCP. Also important was the fact that, in spite of police repression used by the Nationalists, disenchantment could still be readily, if cautiously, communicated to others, and complaints and protests were not effectively prohibited.

The "Golden Years" in the 1950s

In terms of developments and popular perceptions from 1949 through the latter part of the 1950s, one has to acknowledge dramatic changes for the better that did much to contribute to public support for China's new rulers. Political unity and stability were achieved to a much greater extent than at any time since the fall of the Qing. In the countryside, land reform led to perceptions of some improvement for the majority of peasants and severe losses for the landlord elite, but the latter were politically muzzled (when not physically eliminated). And in spite of recurring efforts to keep peasants from streaming into the cities, large numbers of them managed to get established in urban places anyway in these years and take advantage of the new opportunities opening up. The army also provided an increasingly important mobility channel for rural youths, leading to high status jobs in the countryside or city after demobilization. The government managed with some success to convince the remainder of the peasants who were still in the villages that collectivization would provide the structural basis for greater economic security and gradual improvement, and the expansion of rural schools and other facilities provided evidence for rural parents that their children's lives would be better than their own had been.

In urban areas the rampaging inflation was brought under effective control within a relatively short time, and the new government showed itself capable of taking firm measures to deal with other problems in the distribution system. The power of "gang bosses" in urban unskilled labor recruitment was broken, secret societies and criminal syndicates were smashed or driven underground, foreign property was for the most part confiscated, and the remaining privileges of foreigners in China were ended.[6] A standardized system of wage ranks and fringe benefits was developed that seemed to promise relatively humane and predictable working conditions, secure employment, and chances for future wage increases and promotions.

The combination of the flight of much of the Nationalist apparatus and sympathizers, the swelling of the bureaucracy of the new government, and the launching of ambitious economic development projects all led to high demand for many different kinds of personnel. Crash training programs and recruitment drives were launched to fill the newly created slots, and many besides the veterans of the Revolution were swept upward into better and more secure jobs. In the early 1950s career ladders were not seen as rigidly fixed, and personnel were shifted from one agency or bureaucratic system to another in a way that would be unusual in later years. A general sense existed that those who worked diligently and made real contributions could count on promotions to higher status jobs in the future. Schooling was expanded even more rapidly in the cities than in the countryside, and for a period in the fifties there were actually more university places available than there were applicants coming out of China's secondary schools.[7]

The early years of the CCP in urban areas were thus seen as a "golden age" for upward social mobility. Of course, downward mobility was occurring as well. But at least for a portion of the formerly advantaged groups who were cooperative and acceptable politically, the descent was considerably "gentler" than it was for rural landlords. Capitalists who cooperated were allowed to receive interest payments on the (undervalued) official evaluation of their former capital and were in many cases given salaried positions in their former firms as well. Other relatively well-paid individuals who passed muster were given specially set "retained wage" levels, often above the new standard wage scales, when the shift to socialist property relations and employment occurred. And in this period the offspring of former "exploiting classes" were not heavily stigmatized. The pressing need for skilled personnel meant that such youths could continue up through the school system and take advantage of new career opportunities, with only ritualistic criticisms of the class standpoint of their families demanded of these youths for them to qualify.[8]

Of course there were still others in these years whose downward mobility was anything but gentle. In a series of campaigns up through 1957, large numbers of people were made targets, stigmatized, arrested, and even executed. This widespread coercion clearly had an unsettling effect on many segments of the population, and the population rapidly became aware that politics was a tricky minefield in the new society. Statements questioning new policies or leadership became a quick route to downward mobility. Even the rewards of loyalty and activism were not entirely predictable, in that changes in line or a falling out of favor of one's superior and patron could leave an activist isolated and vulnerable. But several perceptions in the 1950s seem to have helped to keep these political uncertainties from offsetting enthusiasm about new opportunities. First, much of the population was told, and wanted to believe, that most targets of coercion were enemies of the new society rather than helpless victims, and even when repression hit close to home they could assume that it was due to the mistakes and overzealousness that could not be avoided in a revolutionary situation. Second, even within these initial years there were signs that the scope of coercion was becoming more limited and life more predictable. In particular, the launching of the First Five-Year Plan seemed to indicate a shift from political activism to technical expertise in the criteria for upward mobility, and the announced deemphasis on class struggle and class labels at the Eighth CCP Congress in 1956 reinforced this impression. The new government was clearly a harsh and demanding one, but its demands seemed to be becoming more predictable.

Other factors besides widespread official coercion were sources of public concern in the 1950s. For one thing, the new government set out to erect a new status structure and establish an aura of legitimacy around that structure, and at least substantial segments of the population found it hard to accept all the new rules of the game. Several controversial ideas were involved: that long-time party members, military veterans, and members of formerly oppressed classes should receive some preference in access to new opportunities, that political loyalty or being "Red" should carry greater weight in many cases than expertise, that contact with Western influences tainted one and made one in need of thought reform whereas contact with Soviet influences made one especially worthy, and so forth. These official preferences to some extent ran counter to centuries-old Chinese respect for book-learning, and to a newer respect for Western learning; an intensive propaganda effort had to be waged to persuade the population to accept the new rules of the game. That this effort was not fully successful is shown by the fact that in the 1957 Hundred Flowers Campaign complaints about "Reds" and Soviet-oriented individuals lording it over "experts" and Westernized Chinese were a primary focus.

One other issue during these years concerned the privileges enjoyed by the new elites. Were China's new leaders seen as careerist privilege-grabbers? Or were they seen instead as selfless public servants or as legitimate recipients of earned rewards? On this point the evidence is mixed; I would argue that the perceptions correspondingly differed. On the one hand, it became apparent to any discerning citizen that China's new elites enjoyed a variety of benefits and privileges. Even before a regular salary system was implemented in the mid-fifties, leading personnel enjoyed special dining rooms, servants, access to limousines, and other privileges that set them apart from their subordinates. To some extent a status competition was visible, with new leading cadres using rank and seniority within the party and honor from the Revolution to acquire preferential access to housing and other scarce resources. The consolidation of the wage system in 1956, with the highest leaders earning about twenty-five times as much as the lowest state personnel, made income disparities public for all to contemplate.

On the other hand, a number of considerations led many Chinese to see their new leaders in positive terms and feel that they were different from their predecessors. First, equity and not equality was the standard of judgment, and this involved considering whether the privileges of leaders were earned and deserved. On this score there was considerable support for elite privileges. Individuals who had risked their lives and lived under arduous conditions during the Revolution were generally seen as entitled to special consideration after 1949. (As early as 1929 Mao had gone on record against "excessive" egalitarianism.) In addition, the new government seemed very concerned that leading personnel not abuse their privileges. The Three-Anti Campaign of 1951/1952 and subsequent publicity given to cases of cadre corruption convinced much of the population that the government was concerned about keeping cadre privileges under control. And official corruption was seen as sharply diminished.

Another factor in creating a positive impression was the relative invisibility of the lives of the top elite and the successful public relations effort that surrounded their contacts with the public. Not until the Cultural Revolution was the "bourgeois" behavior of leaders in private laid open to public view. In the 1950s the public saw pictures of top leaders visiting farms and factories and taking part in manual labor stints along with the ordinary population. Junior personnel working in state organs in Peking at the time described being favorably impressed by the way Zhou Enlai, Chen Yi, Mao, and other leaders mixed informally with their subordinates during dances and swimming outings during these years. So there was a fairly widespread impression during this period that China's new leaders were living more spartan and accessible lives than their predecessors and were not using their posts for personal profit.[9]

In general, then, and in spite of a number of concerns and discordant notes, the fifties were mostly an optimistic period in which a reservoir of good feelings on the part of the population toward the government was built up. Declared enemies of the new order were dealt with harshly, but for the most part the government succeeded in convincing the population that the numbers involved were not overly large and that this coercion was both necessary and popular. And in spite of continuing political uncertainties, the population perceived this as an era of expanding opportunities in which life chances were less dependent upon fate and personal connections and more determined by following the new rules of the game. In this new atmosphere many individuals felt they could put their disrupted lives in order. Individuals married, looked for better housing, began families or added children, and made plans for future careers and purchases.

The Great Leap Forward and Its Aftermath

In many respects the years after 1957 can be seen as ones in which both the opportunities available and the public perceptions of life chances began to become less favorable—not constantly year by year, but still gradually and perceptibly. The difficulties produced by the Great Leap Forward were obvious to all, although reactions to them differed. In the cities reduced rations, shortened working hours, experiments with laboratory-produced food substitutes, new unemployment caused by the closing of some enterprises, and plain ever-present hunger were felt by all. In the countryside conditions were of course worse, with starvation conditions and heightened mortality common in a number of locales. Hopes for continued material improvement had clearly been dashed, but interpretations of what had happened differed.

In the cities it appears that acceptance of official explanations of the collapse was fairly general, even if not universal. The government tried to argue that the problems were "nonsystemic" in large part, being a product of disastrous weather, the abrupt withdrawal of Soviet aid and advisers in 1960, and irrational demands made by poorly trained local cadres. Continuing pride in the new factories, reservoirs, and public buildings constructed during the Great Leap Forward as well as a perception that urbanites, high and low, were sharing in the severe belt-tightening promoted a sense of shared crisis rather than an inclination to blame Mao and the government.[10] And many urbanites were not aware of the full extent of suffering in the countryside and did not become aware of the details of Peng Dehuai's critique of the Great Leap until later.

In the countryside, not only were conditions worse but reactions were often more negative. Communications to and among the peasants were not as strictly controlled as in the cities, and so anger and blame directed toward the government could spread more readily in China's villages. The result was the severe morale and leadership crisis that the subsequent rural socialist education campaign was designed to combat.

Even when the economy began to revive from 1962 onward, the situation had changed in comparison with the earlier years. To begin with, the urban migration restriction system was finally effective after 1958, making it very difficult for peasants to come to the cities and take advantage of opportunities there. The old city walls may have been dismantled, but a much more impermeable set of administrative walls around urban places had been erected instead. So apart from a few exceptions provided by army recruitment and university admissions, peasant youths and their families could not realistically look beyond their local communities to satisfy their ambitions. Within the countryside contradictory forces affected mobility chances. On the one hand, the beginnings of the drive for rural industry and the building up of the local educational and health care system provided new opportunities apart from agricultural labor. On the other hand, the "Four Cleanups" campaign was in many places very brutal, with the actions taken against local cadres and peasants who engaged in off-farm activities severe enough to make other mobility channels appear much less inviting than formerly.

A second important difference concerned demography and educational enrollments. The cutbacks in the economy and in university enrollments occasioned by the collapse of the Great Leap Forward meant that ever-larger cohorts of urban youths finishing middle school found the competition for opportunities getting more severe. As of 1965 the percentage of general upper middle school graduates who could be accepted in the university each year had declined to 45 percent, and it was perceived as decreasing year by year. For those not selected for the university, the chances of placement in a state job were also less favorable than in the 1950s, and the phenomenon of "social youths"—urban school graduates with no jobs—grew in seriousness. The authorities attacked this problem by trying to induce "social youths" to volunteer for rural resettlement, although without all of the coercive devices used to this end after 1968. The sense of diminishing career opportunities was heightened in many cases by comparisons urban youths could make with their own older siblings. Not uncommonly an upper middle school graduate with no job assignment would have an older sibling who had completed only primary or lower middle school three to four years earlier but who now had a secure job and good career prospects.

The competitive atmosphere was made more unpredictable by the rapidly shifting political winds of these years. The populace was told in 1961 that apolitical experts were worthy but learned the next year that they should "never forget the class struggle." A stiffening of the class line and an emphasis on army models in 1964 was followed in 1965 by a new relaxation of the class line in regard to admission to the Communist Youth League. In this situation two perceptions were fairly widely shared—that political criteria were becoming generally more salient in affecting life chances, but that the rules of the game might change suddenly, so that a strategy of school performance devised to meet one set of rules might mean losing out in the competition when the rules changed.[11] The result was a growing level of competitiveness and anxiety in urban schools, marked by a keenly felt uncertainty about how students could distinguish themselves from their classmates.[12]

For urban adults, things looked somewhat different during this period. For the most part they had secure jobs and a range of fringe benefits, and they continued to feel grateful for the security they enjoyed. But with urban wages largely frozen throughout this period (except for a minor adjustment in 1963) people found their earlier hopes of moving up through the ranks as they gained experience and increased their qualifications disappearing. Instead they remained stuck for the most part at the same salary levels they had held before the Great Leap Forward. Supporting a family of growing children became an increasing concern with such frozen wages, although the added family income resulting from the large-scale mobilization of women into the work force during the Great Leap helped to compensate somewhat for the freeze. The frequent shifting around of personnel that had characterized the early 1950s was perceived by this time as having given way to employment stability, with most individuals contemplating remaining in the same work and work unit for the duration of their careers. So urban adults came increasingly to see their life chances not as fairly wide open, but as highly restricted and subject to the whims of the leaders in their work units as such units came to have more and more power over their members.[13]

Not surprisingly, in this environment the value of traditional tactics of cultivating favor and establishing connections with superior patrons in the work unit became evident to all concerned. The dangers of running afoul of such superiors in the political campaigns that followed 1957 also became clear, as colleagues were demoted, transferred, or simply publicly stigmatized. So for many urban adults the issue of the day became not how to prepare oneself to take advantage of future mobility opportunities, but how to build a secure nest with benevolent patrons that would enable one at least to maintain one's position.[14] Many adults in urban areas "dug in" and tried to stay out of trouble while hoping that the economic revival would eventually allow the wage freeze to be lifted and promotion opportunities to be opened up once again.

The Cultural Revolution Decade

The Cultural Revolution and ensuing campaigns again changed the opportunity structure and public perceptions. Initially the Cultural Revolution seemed to promise a shake-up of the social and political system that would reopen clogged channels to upward mobility. Large numbers of elites who had become "revisionists" and "capitalist roaders" were to be attacked and purged, and those who "established merit" in this struggle would, as in previous campaigns, expect to earn honors and promotions. People whose careers had been sidetracked or who had been downwardly mobile could hope to regain lost status if they could successfully blame the capitalist roaders for their troubles and procure a "reversal of verdicts." Youths who had been stigmatized because of their "impure" class origins could hope to prove their mettle in the Cultural Revolution and earn a better fate.[15] I do not wish to suggest that most Red Guards were simply cynical careerists, but it does seem clear that the rigidities of the status structure in previous years and the spreading insecurities about the future, especially among the young, helped to provide an important emotional basis for the Red Guard response to the new campaign.

There were a number of immediate effects of the Cultural Revolution. The campaign exposed in much more lurid detail than any previous rectification campaign the range of privileges and luxuries enjoyed by China's elite and subjected these phenomena to scathing criticism. The various confidential files raided by the Red Guards also revealed details of abuses of power and elite vindictiveness. The rhetoric of the campaign reinforced this new information by espousing a new perception of elite privileges not as earned and legitimate rewards but as signs of creeping revisionism and the incipient formation of what later came to be called the new bureaucratic stratum. The anti-elitist enthusiasm that was spawned led to many novel phenomena in this period: raiding homes and destroying "four old" possessions, eliminating separate dining halls based upon bureaucratic rank, demanding that servants be dismissed, having doctors empty bedpans and nurses experiment with surgery, moving bureaucrats out of spacious apartments and into cramped hovels, and so forth. All of these efforts had the immediate political purpose of undermining elite authority and mobilizing mass enthusiasm for the campaign, but they appear to have had a longer-lasting influence as well. The eyes of the public were opened by the many revelations about the behavior and character of authority figures at all levels, and a suspiciousness about elite motivations was inculcated that would carry over to later years.

The consequences of the Cultural Revolution for mobility opportunities turned out to be less favorable than originally expected. To be sure, there was substantial upward (as well as downward) mobility in this period, with a flood of new party members, the ascent of workers and soldiers into local power in revolutionary committees, and even the catapulting (or "helicoptering") of some Cultural Revolution stalwarts into national prominence. But for some this mobility was a mixed blessing. For one thing, political mobility was often not accompanied by economic mobility, when in the spirit of the times people were expected to accept more important and difficult jobs with no change in pay. For another, by the early 1970s many of the purged old cadres were being rehabilitated, which meant that new cadres had to share power with their former targets in a situation far different from the "lean troops and simple administration" that was constantly espoused. The sense of competition and animosity within organizations was fed by the various political campaigns that followed the Cultural Revolution in rapid succession—"the cleaning of class ranks," "one-hit and three-anti," and so forth. As a result, the predominant perception among employed urbanites during the early 1970s was not one of lots of new channels opened for upward mobility, but of spreading political victimization in which avoiding downward mobility became an overriding concern.[16] Given these hazards and the general decline of institutionalized procedures, the effort to cultivate patronage and protection from the uncertainties of future campaigns became even more highly accentuated.

By the mid-seventies not only was the danger of political stigmatization more widely felt, but the prospects for economic improvement looked highly uncertain. The wage freeze remained in effect, except for minor adjustments at the lowest ranks in 1971/1972. So most urbanites continued to receive the same wage they had received for a decade or more. The elimination of bonuses and incentive payments of other kinds actually reduced wages in some cases.[17] The combination of the wage freeze and continuing shifts in work assignments produced a widespread sense of inequity within work organizations, with individuals doing the same work as others—or producing more—ending up earning less because they started work a few years later.[18] The stored-up gripes about such inequities helped to make the eventual overall wage adjustments in 1977 and 1979/1980 extraordinarily contentious and arduous.

General material conditions in the cities were also not perceived as improving. True, articles such as radios and bicycles were being manufactured in larger numbers and were more readily available than before. But urban housing had been neglected for many years, and citizens now found themselves with less room than in the 1950s and faced with great difficulty in getting assigned to better housing.[19]

Food products were also not consistently well supplied. Grain was for the most part available in sufficient quantities, but meat, fresh vegetables, fruit, and other desirable food items were often not—pork began to be rationed in the seventies even in Peking, where it had been sold without ration coupons before. The Cultural Revolution campaign against private enterprise, free markets, and even urban collective enterprises meant that urbanites had to rely more exclusively than in the past on state enterprises and shops, and the inadequate quantity and variety of goods there and the poor service offered gave rise to increasing consumer frustrations. Urbanites who had to get up early to stand in line in the hope of being able to buy rarely seen fresh chickens or eggs quite generally perceived that the food situation had been better before the Cultural Revolution or even in the mid-fifties.

The combination of frozen wages, inadequate housing, an uncertain food supply, and other constraints of urban life led many urban parents to reduce their fertility aspirations even before the government began to make small families mandatory. And just as within work units the importance of personal ties and patronage was seen as on the increase, so in the urban distribution system, with bureaucratic allocation and widespread shortages, it became clear that using connections and "going by the back door" were crucial in meeting one's needs. To a considerable extent this became a game that all urbanites played insofar as they were able, using relatives and friends who had contacts with shop personnel, doctors, truck drivers, staffs of housing offices, and other people with special access to scarce resources. Again urbanites perceived that such use of special connections was more widespread than in the fifties or sixties, although it is difficult to be sure how accurate this perception was. But accurate or not, the effects of this perception were clear—people increasingly felt that bureaucratic authorities were not simply honest public servants, and that the higher your position was, the more likely and able you were to use your power and contacts to benefit your own family and friends.

If for urban adults the situation in the early seventies was one of continuing to try to hold onto one's niche in an increasingly insecure environment, for urban youths the situation became even more bleak. Most of the Red Guards found their life chances harmed rather than helped by the Cultural Revolution, as they were mobilized to settle down in the countryside. The majority of their younger brothers and sisters then had to follow in their footsteps—17 million urban, educated youths were settled in the countryside in the decade after 1968. For these younger siblings uncertainty about the future was even greater than it had been in the past. With the Cultural Revolution reforms in place, one could no longer go directly from middle school to the university, and from kindergarten onward one repeatedly was subjected to messages designed to prepare one for eventual rustication. With grades and examinations deemphasized and promotion in grade made automatic, and with no direct connection any longer between school performance and future prospects, much of the motivation for studying and behaving was lost.

Political activism and enthusiasm for manual labor were honored, but even these qualities did not provide much guarantee against rustication. Young people came to feel that their lives were quite unpredictable, and parents found it difficult either to advise their offspring on how to plan their lives or to persuade them of the virtues of behaving themselves and working hard.[20] Those with powerful parents and personal connections were perceived as most likely to be assigned to urban jobs or the army, thus escaping rural exile. The Cultural Revolution strictures on private and collective enterprise and the coercive nature of the rustication drive after 1968 did not provide even the low-status urban employment alternatives that had been available to "social youths" before the Cultural Revolution.

Some of the rusticated youths did content themselves with rural life and made a niche for themselves there, but most kept their options open by not marrying and kept hoping to be able to get back to the city—either through approved channels, such as by university selection or reassignment to an urban job or, failing that, by fleeing illegally back to the cities they had come from.[21] Some of these sent-down youths were so eager to get back to the city that they were willing to accept assignment to urban jobs of low prestige just to escape their rural exile. So for urban youths in the early seventies the name of the game was how to avoid downward mobility (into the countryside) and, if not successful in this, how to find ways to climb back onto any available rung in the urban hierarchy.

In urban China the aftermath of the Cultural Revolution saw a continued erosion of the popular view about life chances and of confidence in the elites and the distribution system. In rural China the trends were more diverse and complex, so that capsule generalizations are difficult. The economic revival of the early sixties and the initiation of China's "green revolution" began new trends in many rural locales that increased opportunities within the countryside. Agricultural experiment stations, barefoot doctors, propaganda teams, rural industry, and other innovations increased the options available to rural youths. Rural schools were expanded to produce a rising number of lower middle school graduates capable of filling many of the new posts. And some communes, particularly in suburban areas, experienced a fairly steady increase in production and incomes, fostering satisfaction among their membership. The urban migration restrictions remained in effect, but peasants saw some important loopholes appearing even in this realm. Peasants continued to provide the bulk of manpower for the PLA, and the role of the military in revolutionary committees in urban areas meant that not a few peasant recruits found themselves assigned to urban places and had hopes of staying there later on, rather than being demobilized back to the village.

The recruitment of "worker, peasant, soldier" students for the post-Cultural Revolution universities also seemed to promise better chances for rural youths to attain the lofty goal of a college education. It is true that the modest university enrollments of the period, combined with competition from sent-down youths and others, meant that the objective chances for a rural youth to get into college remained very slim indeed. But still this change in enrollment policy was generally received positively in the countryside.[22]

In the early seventies, then, a certain amount of optimism about improved life chances spread in at least significant portions of rural China. By the mid-seventies, however, much of this optimism had dissipated in all but the most successful rural locales. The high cost of new agricultural inputs and social overhead expenditures and the negative consequences of higher level commands in controlling crops planted, income distribution, and other matters meant that peasant incomes in many locales stagnated or declined, even in cases where agricultural yields were increasing. A new campaign after 1975 to shift to brigade-level accounting helped poorer teams, but penalized the teams that had been most successful in improving their incomes in the past. And the slim prospects for escaping from the village seemed to be closing up. The phasing of the PLA out of civilian leadership organs was accompanied by new directives specifying that veterans should be demobilized back to their native villages and not remain in the cities, a change that led to new protests by veterans.[23]

Peasants also seem to have become increasingly aware that most university slots were being monopolized by sent-down youths, high cadre children, or at best the children of ranking rural cadres, with little room left for ordinary peasant youths. The increasing stress on the final stage of academic screening by the universities by the mid-seventies also helped to make prospects for rural youths more difficult.

Changes in the rustication program also affected rural opinions. Peasants and rural youths who in some cases felt resentment at being saddled with sent-down youths nonetheless gained some awareness of urban life and culture through such contacts, and then saw most of these sent-down youths able to gain reassignment back to the cities, although their hosts remained confined to rural life. In general, then, the changes in both prospects and perceptions in these years were not as sharp in the countryside as in the city, but still they eventually took the same direction—of increasing pessimism and skepticism.

Life Chances After Mao

By the time of Mao's death in 1976 one could argue that much of the good will that had been built up after 1949 as a result of improved life chances and a more equitable society had been dissipated. Broad sectors of the population felt that chances of improving their lot had declined, and chances for getting in trouble had increased. It was also common to see the status hierarchy as increasingly competitive and unpredictable. And just as the government had taken much of the credit for the improvements after 1949, by the mid-seventies it received a significant part of the blame for the deterioration in life chances that had occurred subsequently. No longer were "external factors" convincing explanations for disappointed expectations. Not only was the government not seen as living up to its commitment to provide better lives for the population, but high ranking cadres were seen by many as using their power for personal and family advantage. In this atmosphere poor academic performance, low productivity, surly service attitudes, rising crime, and other unhealthy phenomena were visible, as well as occasional outbreaks of open protest—even before the death of Mao.

Even though Mao's successors did not face the danger of large-scale, organized opposition, still they sensed that they faced a general crisis. Many of the changes they have introduced since 1977 can be seen as efforts to restore the sort of public confidence in life chances that had existed earlier. Yet there is in these efforts something of the dilemma faced by the king's horses and men in trying to reconstruct Humpty Dumpty. Chinese society has changed in many ways, and it is not possible to return to the sort of situation that prevailed thirty years ago.

The reforms adopted are familiar matters and will only be touched upon briefly here: a return to the highly competitive educational system of the pre-Cultural Revolution years; new general wage increases and the restoration of bonuses, piece rates, and other incentive devices; a relaxation of restrictions on private and collective enterprises; the use of examinations to place people in jobs and determine promotions (and demotions); the phasing out of the program of sending urban youths to the countryside; efforts to institutionalize legal codes and other procedures to make life more predictable; increased procurement prices and new rural reforms to foster peasant incentives; a large-scale housing construction drive; and other efforts to improve the living standards of much of the population.

These and other related reforms are designed to provide (or restore) a clear set of opportunity ladders to structure the lives of the populace and to convince individuals that if they study hard, work productively, increase their qualifications, and in other ways become more valuable contributors to society they can expect improving income and career prospects, more access to perquisites, and better lives for their families. (The reverse is also being forcefully communicated—those who do not apply themselves and who cause problems will not benefit and may be downwardly mobile—the "iron rice bowl" guarantees will no longer protect them.) The government is also attempting to persuade the population that it is concerned to check bureaucratic privilege and abuses of power, and that problems in these realms are cases of idiosyncratic "bad apples" rather than systemic to Chinese socialism. (Hence the vigor with which the notion of a "new bureaucratic stratum" is argued against, even as bureaucratic abuses are being exposed.)

A number of problems disrupt these aims. One of the most serious problems is simply demographic. In spite of the vigorous birth control campaign, for some years to come there will continue to be too many young people finishing their schooling for the economy to absorb easily. The previous tactic of sending excess urban youths to the countryside is being phased out, but this fact has made it increasingly difficult to arrange job placements to satisfy such youths. Most of the new jobs are in urban collective and even private sector enterprises, often oriented to providing services, and these tend to be looked down on as low-prestige jobs with limited career prospects. With the threat of forced rural reassignment no longer hanging over their heads, many youths would prefer to wait for a more secure job in the state sector or to try repeatedly to pass the university entrance exams. But the chances of success in the latter are even much slimmer than they were in earlier years (see Table 14.1).

Most urban youths are being oriented to compete academically and try to gain university admission, but clearly the vast majority of them

Table 14.1 Changing Prospects for College Admission in China

	Year			
	1953-1956	1965	1976	1979
New enrollments/ Upper middle school graduates	115%	45.6%	4.2%	3.8%

Sources: For 1953-1956, Robert Taylor, Education and University Enrollment Policies in China, 1949-1971, Contemporary China Centre Paper no. 6 (Canberra: Australian National University, 1973); for other years, Stanley Rosen, "Obstacles to Educational Reform in China," Modern China 8:1 (January 1982).

will fail and will be disappointed. Most will end up taking one of the available urban jobs, often after a long wait for assignment, but here too they are likely to feel frustrated. Various tactics are being adopted to cope with these problems, such as converting some general middle schools to technical or vocational schools fostering more limited aspirations and encouraging parents to retire early so that a son or daughter can be given a job in their unit, but still the mismatch between numbers and aspirations on the one hand and opportunities on the other is not something that can be readily solved.

In the countryside the situation in regard to youths is again somewhat distinctive. The urgent sense of crisis surrounding urban unemployment has generally kept the barriers to migration to the city closed as tight or tighter than before.[24] Furthermore, in the post-Mao consolidations significant numbers of secondary schools have been closed, disproportionately in rural areas, so that the numbers of students enrolled in middle schools has actually decreased.[25] This factor, combined with the restoration of the college entrance exams, appears to have made the prospects for rural youths getting into the university even bleaker than before. One other traditional route to mobility for peasant youths appears to be narrowing as well—that provided by the PLA. Apparently in the early 1980s a shift was made toward recruiting more urban youths and fewer rural youths into the PLA.[26]

All of these changes are occurring in the midst of organizational reforms in the countryside that foster the family as an economic unit and encourage contributions to the family economy rather than ascent of the career ladders provided by the state or the commune as the main route to a better life. Whether this new (or actually very ancient) route to improvement is successful enough to compensate for other avenues that are being closed off is a major question.

One other element of the post-1976 changes has been an official attempt to change the way the population views the status structure. This effort has involved trying to develop support for a shift in the rules of the game toward a technocratic meritocracy. Intellectuals, people with bad class backgrounds, individuals with foreign ties, and a variety of other formerly suspect groups are now welcomed back into the fold, and a mania for examinations, degrees, credentials, and academic skills has suffused the contemporary status competition. As in previous shifts in other directions, this one has proved difficult to carry out. There are significant and powerful groups that fear they will lose out under the new rules—beneficiaries of the Cultural Revolution, old party members and military officers, and simply the poorly educated. There are signs of some discontent with some of the privileges being granted to technocrats and intellectuals, and popular resentment may have contributed to the modification of some of the most extreme meritocratic devices such as the use of tracking into "slow" and "fast" classes within individual schools. Signs also exist of resentment against the range of privileges accorded to foreigners.

In a curious fashion the resentment of those losing out under the new rules does not appear to be fully balanced by the gratitude of those who are gaining. Some of those who have been rehabilitated and promoted are of course heartened, but at the same time many appear to feel that it was the least that was due them, and that such measures still do not compensate for the disrupted lives and disappointed expectations that have been their lot in previous periods, nor for the way in which many of their children have had their educations cut short and their aspirations thwarted. So in general the public mood appears to be something other than a feeling of satisfaction that a new set of rules of which all can approve is being implemented.

On the brighter side of things, there have clearly been important improvements in both rural and urban incomes and in the supply of food, housing, and consumer goods since 1976. These changes are a vital part of the government's effort to restore confidence, and they are meeting with considerable success. Yet even here there are dark clouds around the edges. Inflation has reappeared on the scene, reawakening bad memories of the erosion of living standards before 1949 and reinforcing skepticism of government claims of economic improvement. Considerable doubt exists about whether the Four Modernizations program will deal successfully enough with China's many economic problems to provide for the long-awaited steady improvement in living standards. In this atmosphere of skepticism and uncertainty individuals continue to scrutinize market supplies and price rumors and make use of their back-door connections even as they enjoy their new television sets and contemplate eventual purchase of goods still more precious, such as washing machines.

In its effort to restore morale and public confidence the government has adopted a strategy that is both bold and risky—of loosening some of the restrictions on information flow in Chinese society. The goals of such a loosening appear quite laudable—a desire to publicize problems, stimulate criticism from the public, encourage new ideas and innovation, and so forth. But given the past track record, the results of this effort have not always been to restore a sense that the government is working in the interests of the public. Revelations about abuses of power during the Gang of Four period rival the exposés provided by the Red Guards a decade earlier and reinforce the idea that China's bureaucrats tend to be power-hungry and corrupt.

The modest liberalization in the mass media and the arts, the wider contact with people and information from outside of China, and simply the somewhat safer atmosphere for communicating with others all provide new bases for sharing critical ideas about China's leaders and institutions. Individuals can now more readily realize that not only have they suffered and accumulated grievances, but that large numbers of other people share their anger and discontent. As the leadership strives to convince the population that the main problems are in the past and that equitable rules and procedures are now taking hold, the widespread knowledge that many children of the elite are studying abroad or have been assigned to cushy jobs, and that elite families continue to live in a fairly luxurious style leads these claims to be received skeptically.[27]

In a number of ways life has improved and become more predictable for most since the death of Mao, and people are able to plan their lives and formulate career objectives as they were not able to in the previous decade or so. But still many remain skeptical and frustrated. They see the chances for general economic improvement and personal advancement as less favorable than before the Cultural Revolution. Many see the chances for their children to use their talents to the maximum as much less certain than before, and as a result they worry about how their offspring will be able to attract a desirable spouse and establish a family and a career. In the countryside the cities appear closed off as much as or more than before, with life chances depending to a predominant extent on the efforts of family and kin rather than on the avenues of mobility provided by the state. Gratitude that society has been made orderly again is tinged with suspicion that the people at the top continue to benefit disproportionately, and with doubt that China's bureaucratic and economic problems can ever be fundamentally solved. The greater ability that people have to express their views and communicate their cynicism to others makes it difficult to restore the sort of general public support that existed in earlier periods.

The government can still argue that the lives and material prospects of most Chinese are more secure than was the case before 1949, but given the generally deteriorating trends since the optimism of the fifties, the time-honored tactic of "recalling the bitterness" (of pre-1949 days) and "thinking of present sweetness" now tends to fall flat. Long-embellished tales of starvation, selling children, and eating the bark off trees may still stimulate some anger and tears. But for most of the population today there are more salient comparisons to make—with the situation a decade or two earlier, with one's own past aspirations, or with the experiences of older siblings and friends. In these terms the present situation is bittersweet at best—improved in many ways by comparison with the Cultural Revolution decade, but still far from satisfactory.

These popular sentiments are of political importance even if they are unlikely to provide the basis for an organized challenge to the Chinese political system. Perceptions of life chances can affect student motivation, labor productivity, political commitment, and social order. They can influence whether young people are inclined to volunteer for campaigns, attend a Christian church, or rob a purse; whether peasants are eager to join the army, engage in illicit peddling, or simply to diligently tend their crops. If open conflict should reemerge at the top of China's political system in the future, the existence of popular discontent would provide a basis for mobilizing support into a potent political weapon. For all of these reasons the public's view of their life chances cannot lightly be ignored. The strategies that produced the wave of optimism and commitment in the fifties cannot be repeated, and the degree of public support that existed then cannot readily be restored. The reasons for this "fall from grace" can to some extent be attributed to government actions—the mismanagement of the economy, political witch hunts, and so forth. But the causes are more complex and involve things like the unanticipated consequences of demographic trends set in motion by the earlier optimism, along with other factors that are not so easy to deal with and control. In the future the preoccupation of China's leaders is not likely to remain focused on how to restore the spirit of earlier years. Rather, concern with how to manage the economy, the opportunity structure, and public opinion so that public resentments can be kept within bounds and some level of public support or acquiescence can be maintained is likely to remain a constant preoccupation of China's bureaucratic elite.

Notes

1. The term "life chances" is used to refer to a global sense of the chances for an individual to achieve various kinds of security and mobility in society.

2. The writing of this paper took place while the author was enjoying a faculty fellowship at the Center for Asian and Pacific Studies at the University of Hawaii, and I would like to thank the director of that center, Stephen Uhalley, for making this opportunity possible.

3. Perceptions of what channels are legitimate will of course vary from one culture to another. Generally, in Chinese culture use of kinship connections and patron-client relationships have been seen as more legitimate than they are in modern Western societies, although since 1949 efforts to "change the rules" have made the use of such channels more controversial.

4. The reader will note that these ideas have been stated in universal terms, implying that the same considerations apply in all societies and that one could contemplate them as hypotheses to "test" in the case of contemporary China. However, since they were not derived from some general theory but from thinking about ways to interpret trends in China, no claim is made that this paper is testing universal propositions. It is also important to note that I do not mean to imply that perceptions of life chances are the only things

or even the most important things that affect how subjects feel about their government, although I do assume that they are among the most important things. For an example of how a similar framework has been used to explain trends in things as varied as crime frequency, divorce rates, and faith in the government in the United States, see Richard Easterlin, *Birth and Fortune* (New York: Basic Books, 1980).

5. See Yung-teh Chow, *Social Mobility in China* (New York: Atherton, 1966), pp. 58–59.

6. By exception, Soviet advisers did have a privileged position during the 1950s, but this was a position granted by the Chinese government in return for services rendered, rather than demanded by the foreigners on the basis of extraterritorial rights. (Extraterritoriality was renounced by the allied powers in 1943, but considerable privileges and even gunboat protection remained up to 1949.) And there were some efforts to make the position of Soviet advisers appear different from that of earlier privileged foreigners—e.g., by forbidding them to ride in rickshaws.

7. See Robert Taylor, *Education and University Enrollment Policies in China, 1949–1971,* Contemporary China Centre Paper no. 6 (Canberra: Australian National University, 1973).

8. This generalization assumes that the parents were cooperative and acceptable. If the parents became a target in a campaign or were arrested, then even a less ritualized denunciation of the parents might not salvage the opportunities for the offspring. Still, social mobility data show that into the 1960s children from capitalist and other "bad class" families continued to do better in terms of years of schooling and wage level on the job than children from "good class" worker or poor peasant families. See Martin King Whyte and William L. Parish, *Urban Life in Contemporary China* (Chicago: University of Chicago Press, 1984).

9. On the cadre rectification campaigns of the earliest years, see Frederick C. Teiwes, *Elite Discipline in China: Coercive and Persuasive Approaches, 1950–1953,* Contemporary China Centre Paper no. 12 (Canberra: Australian National University, 1978). It should be noted that Chiang Kai-shek managed to preserve a relatively spartan personal image, but that many of those surrounding him were seen as profiting greedily.

10. Of course, not all urbanites did, in fact, suffer equally, and in the early 1960s there were minor campaigns to require those in a position to escape from the belt-tightening (e.g., people in foreign affairs or overseas Chinese work who could attend banquets or get access to "care" packages) to confess their errors.

11. The analysis presented here differs somewhat from that presented in Michel Oksenberg's seminal article, "Getting Ahead and Along in Communist China: The Ladder of Success on the Eve of the Cultural Revolution," in *Party Leadership and Revolutionary Power in China,* ed. John W. Lewis (Cambridge, U.K.: Cambridge University Press, 1970). Oksenberg argues, as do I, that there were two primary routes to career success in post-1949 China, the political or "Red" route, and the academic/professional or "expert" route. However, he departs from the analysis here in arguing that by the early 1960s there was increasing predictability in the system permitting more conscious planning of careers. In the sense of familiarity with campaigns and political rituals this may have been so, but this factor is in my view counterbalanced by the sheer effect of numbers in relation to opportunities, which made career planning for young people more problematic.

12. On the school atmosphere in these years, see Susan Shirk, *Competitive Comrades: Career Incentives and Student Strategies in China* (Berkeley: University of California Press, 1982); Jonathan Unger, *Education under Mao* (New York: Columbia University Press, 1982); and Stanley Rosen, "Obstacles to Educational Reform in China," *Modern China* 8:1 (January 1982). It should be noted that in low quality and people-run middle schools the perception of life chances was often so pessimistic that instead of competitive anxiety the atmosphere was one of fatalism and low motivation. In other words, the highly competitive atmosphere was most characteristic of high quality, keypoint middle schools.

13. The growth of unit power was due to a number of factors, but particularly to the socialist transformation and the decline in market distribution of housing, medical care, and other resources, which meant that employees had to increasingly go through their work units to get their needs met. See Whyte and Parish, *Urban Life in Contemporary*

China. The shift toward a strategy of striving for security rather than advancement was previously noted in Oksenberg, "Getting Ahead and Along in Communist China."

14. Not all urbanites followed this strategy, of course. For instance, some employees in state factories quit their jobs and took work in urban collective enterprises, lured by the fact that the wage freeze did not apply to such enterprises. In most cases the gamble turned out poorly, because during the Cultural Revolution new regulations were adopted that prevented collective firm pay from exceeding that in comparable state enterprises.

15. On the differentiated response to the Cultural Revolution, see Ezra Vogel, *Canton under Communism* (Cambridge, Mass.: Harvard University Press, 1969), ch. 8; Anita Chan, Stanley Rosen, and Jonathan Unger, "Students and Class Warfare: The Social Roots of the Red Guard Conflict in Guangzhou," *China Quarterly*, no. 83 (September 1980); and Gordon Bennett, "Political Labels and Popular Tension," *Current Scene* (26 February 1969).

16. Data collected from a sample of urban adults shows the proportion of people in trouble with the authorities to have spread significantly beyond the mythical 5 percent figure of "bad guys" quoted in campaigns during the 1970s, with groups like intellectuals particularly vulnerable. See Whyte and Parish, *Urban Life in Contemporary China*, ch. 9.

17. During the Cultural Revolution many kinds of incentive payments (e.g., royalties for writers, innovator prizes) were simply abolished, but in factories the funds previously used to pay bonuses were generally converted into egalitarian wage supplements after 1966. Efforts to phase these supplements out subsequently led to much complaint and industrial unrest. See Michel Korzec and Martin King Whyte, "Reading Notes: The Chinese Wage System," *China Quarterly*, no. 86 (June 1981).

18. The variety of inequities perceived in industrial enterprises is discussed in Andrew G. Walder, "Work and Authority in Chinese Industry," unpublished Ph.D. dissertation, University of Michigan, 1981.

19. A survey in 1978 found housing space per capita in China's 192 largest cities 20 percent less than it had been in 1952—a decline from 4.5 sq. meters to 3.6 sq. meters. See Zhou Jin, "Housing China's 900 Million People," *Beijing Review*, no. 48 (1979), p. 18.

20. In this atmosphere of uncertainty some urban youths turned to fortune-tellers and other mystical means to try to gain help in planning their lives. Some youths without powerful connections were able to devise strategies that they felt provided them with at least somewhat improved chances of landing an urban job—for instance, by developing athletic or musical skills, or even by mastering a foreign language. For a personal account of basketball prowess as a route to such salvation, see Liang Heng and Judith Shapiro, *Son of the Revolution* (New York: Knopf, 1983).

21. Starting in about 1973 an effort to transfer rusticated urban youths back to urban jobs began, and since 1976 the pace of this reassignment effort has accelerated.

22. In special rural locales the chances were not so objectively slim. The national model Dazhai brigade, with only some 80-plus families, was reported to have four or five of its youths enrolled in college during the early 1970s.

23. The exact details of this shift are not clear to me, but travelers to China reported seeing wall posters on this issue in the mid-seventies. On the problems of demobilization in an earlier period, see Gordon White, "The Politics of Demobilized Soldiers from Liberation to Cultural Revolution," *China Quarterly*, no. 82 (June 1980).

24. In earlier times major industrial expansions in particular locales often led to recruitment of new workers from the countryside, but it is not clear whether this is so common now. In one instance observed, the development of a new port in Shandong, not a single neighboring peasant benefited from the new jobs, which all went to urbanites moved in from other parts of the province. Norma Diamond, personal communication.

25. See the details in Suzanne Pepper, *China's Universities: Post-Mao Enrollment Policies and Their Impact on the Structure of Secondary Education* (Ann Arbor: University of Michigan Center for Chinese Studies, 1983).

26. Some documents argue that the PLA was forced to make this shift because peasant youths were no longer so willing to serve in the army after the rural change to contracting

to the household. See *Foreign Broadcast Information Service* (*FBIS*), 9 December 1981, p. W–2.

27. It appears that there was some popular support for Hua Guofeng, and regret at his demotion, based largely on the fact that he was perceived as less inclined to take advantage of elite power and privileges than other top leaders.

15

Agricultural Strategies and Rural Social Changes in Communist China Since 1949: A Macrosociological Assessment

Hsin-huang Michael Hsiao

This paper examines the nature and changes of Communist China's agricultural strategies and their respective impact on the agricultural-rural sector since 1949. By analyzing the origin and changes of the agricultural strategies adopted by the Communist regime, it can be assessed that the prevailing character of Communist China's strategy on agriculture has been to make "squeezing," the exploitation of agriculture for the benefit of industrial growth, an instrument for overall economic growth. The rural social structure has been induced to change in the direction the squeezing strategy required.

Under the squeeze, agriculture as a socioeconomic sector has not been developed and modernized and, as a result, the rural population has been exploited vis-à-vis the policy of urban-industrial development in the past thirty years of growth experience.

It is important to point out that the Communist regime had indeed turned its back on the countryside after it seized power in 1949. The "revolution" based on the countryside did not bring about a just, fair, and equal development and well-being for the Chinese peasants as had been promised by the Communists.

Introduction: Agricultural Strategies in the Third World

Having reviewed a dozen or so early models of development, Reynolds admits that existing models all regard industry as the focal point of

---

This paper has previously been published in the Academia Sinica's *Bulletin of the Institute of Ethnology*, no. 53 (June 1983), pp. 155–177, Taipei, Taiwan.

economic development in the Third World, with agriculture playing the role of a "resource reservoir" (Reynolds, 1975:1). Much attention, in fact, has been paid to the "contributions" of agriculture as a sector to overall economic development in the initial stage of Third World development. It is also often argued that the extent of agriculture's "contribution" to overall growth can largely be determined by government strategy in the Third World. The success or failure to put agriculture to work for national economic growth can be critical to a Third World government's development achievement. The path of government intervention is often referred to as the "developmental squeeze on agriculture." Boulding and Singh (1962:31) maintain that a "squeeze on agriculture seems to be a feature of all developing societies, whether socialist or capitalist." Owen (1966) further delineates two aspects of what he terms "the double developmental squeeze on agriculture."

On the one hand, the production squeeze requisitions increments of farm production. On the other, the expenditure squeeze requisitions residual farm income for essentially nonfarm uses. The classical discussion in agricultural economics of the "functions" agriculture is assigned to play overwhelmingly stresses the two squeezes. Viewed from this perspective, a government strategy for agriculture is mainly designated to squeeze agricultural growth and transfer it to the nonagricultural sector. The difference between an effective and an ineffective agricultural strategy lies in the way in which the squeeze has been applied and in the relative efficiency with which the process has operated in each case (Owen, 1966: 44). The whole question of how much the agricultural sector and its related population actually gain and benefit from the overall growth remains largely unanswered in most literature on the economics of agriculture development.

However, it also has been argued that a successful squeeze on agriculture ought to be accompanied by an effective development program for the agricultural sector itself (Reynolds, 1975). Without it, the squeezing strategy would be detrimental to long-term economic development. This ambivalent view about agricultural development, unfortunately, has not yet been fully appreciated by the elites and planners in the Third World in the post-World War II context. As a result, Third World agriculture is squeezed in one way or another, but without having been "developed" simultaneously. The very existence of slow growth and general underdevelopment in agriculture throughout much of the Third World can be largely attributed to either "ignorance" or "oversqueeze" of agriculture by government strategy.

Johnston and Kilby (1975:133–139) have spelled out three general objectives for an agricultural strategy usually taken by any Third World government:

1. To increase the output of the agricultural sector so that overall economic growth and structural transformation will be promoted.

Full advantage is taken of positive interaction between agriculture and other sectors. This policy encompasses what has often been referred to as agriculture's "contributions" to development. It is evident that this objective aims at the developmental squeeze on agriculture.

2. To achieve broadly based improvement of the well-being of the rural population. Included are the improvement of income opportunities, health services, and other public services.
3. To induce changes in attitudes, behavior, and institutions that have a favorable impact on the process of social development in rural communities.

However, there exist many potential conflicts and contradictions in implementing the above three objectives. The most serious of these lies in avoidance of a clash between the first and second. To achieve a net flow of resources from agriculture required in the first objective can constitute a dilemma for the second objective, i.e., to improve the welfare of the rural-agricultural sector (Lipton, 1977). As for the third objective, there are doubts as to its validity, given the conflict between the first two objectives. In the Third World today, most efforts are primarily devoted to realizing the first objective; the importance of the second objective has been neglected. The third objective, consequently, is thus employed to serve the materialization of the first objective. In other words, changes induced in attitudes, behavior, and institutions in the rural sector are also "instrumental" for the successful implementation of policies aimed at squeezing agriculture.

In order to realize the squeezing objective, several policies and means have been popular in the Third World. Low prices for agricultural products are a major policy tactic for keeping wages low in the industrial sector. Higher agricultural input price is another way to absorb rural cash income to stimulate domestic industrial growth. Other policies such as taxation on land, water, irrigation facilities, etc., are usually, in fact, unfavorable to the agricultural sector. Some attitudinal, behavioral, and institutional changes are also expected, though in various forms, in order to generate more efficient outflow of agricultural growth. Programs such as induced acceptance of biotechnological innovation, i.e., the "green revolution," and rural local institutional changes, either radical or conservative, all have the same ends. Even land reform policy, redistributive and collectivized alike to some extent, also has been employed as the means to achieve the first objective in the name of the third objective. All the above squeezing policies are found in most Third World countries, despite their different political ideological inclinations (Hsiao, 1981).

In most available sociological studies of Third World agriculture under development, attention has been paid to the so-called capitalist states. This paper intends to take Communist China as a socialist case in point, with two major issues to be raised and analyzed.

The first issue tackles the extent to which the agricultural strategies in Communist China since 1949 can be assessed as typical or atypical cases in terms of the squeeze on the agricultural sector. The continuities and changes in the agricultural strategies will be analyzed in brief in order to grasp the basic character of Communist China's strategy in agriculture for the past thirty years.

The second issue concerns the extent to which the rural Chinese social structure and rural life have been altered and transformed as expected and as planned by the Communist state in the course of implementing its specific agricultural strategies. Special attention will be focused on the ways the rural sector has persisted and/or has changed, as well as the manner in which the rural society responded to governmental agricultural strategies.

The sources on which the following discussions are based are mainly secondary data drawn from available documents and related published research findings.

Changes in Agricultural Strategies in Communist China Since 1949

Though the important features of Communist China's recent economic strategy consist of its "shift in priority" to agriculture and its adjustments in the rural commune system, agricultural strategies in Communist China have undergone several fluctuations in the past thirty years. And it would be misleading to think that Communist China opted for "agriculture first" as its official developmental strategy simply because it was blinded by the fact that its power had been rooted in the countryside since the 1920s.

There is little doubt that the Communists under Mao, before seizing power, i.e., from 1927 to 1949, had indeed taken the agricultural-rural sector as the backbone for advancing revolutionary strategy (Lai and Hsiao, 1981:79–81). But in 1949 Mao became apprehensive about entering the cities. He explicitly required his party to search for a new developmental strategy to meet the new problem—city and industry. In other words, the urban-industrial sector since then has occupied the Communists' attention in dealing with domestic socioeconomic problems. Mao had made the points quite clear:

> From 1927 to the present the center of gravity of our work has been in the village in order to surround the cities and then take the cities. The period for this method of work has now ended. The period of "from the city to the village" and of the city leading the villages has now begun. The center of gravity of the Party's work has shifted from the villages to the city . . . We must do our utmost to learn how to administer and build the cities . . . If we do not pay attention to these problems . . . we shall be unable to maintain our political power, we shall be unable to stand on our feet, we shall fail. (Mao, 1965:363–364)

Interestingly, this also reveals Mao's anxiety about reentering the cities. As Gurley puts it:

> Mao had come full circle: he had in the 1920s turned his back on the cities and found revolutionary fires in the countryside; the fires had eventually spread across the lands of China until Mao stood again facing the cities and once again fearful of them. The cities were destined to haunt Mao in the coming years as they had puzzled and frustrated him in the past. (Gurley, 1975:121)

Facing a new and strange situation, the Communists started the task of economic rehabilitation with a gradualism in transforming Chinese society and economy. During the period from 1949 to 1952, the overall economic strategy was the establishment of an economic law and order with a vision of a socialist framework. For the agricultural and rural sector, a redistributive land reform was initiated first, and was then followed by a gradual socialization of farms. Mutual aid teams and "low level" agricultural produce cooperatives were set up step by step. By 1952, 39.9 percent of the peasant households were members of the mutual aid teams, but only 0.1 percent had joined in the "lower level" cooperatives and none were in "high level" cooperatives (Prybyla, 1970:151). It shows that a central planning apparatus was in the process of being established in the countryside, a socialist way of institutional change for the agricultural sector. An agrarian social and economic order was gradually organized. This order laid the groundwork for the transformation of the rural economy into a Soviet-type command economy destined to be further squeezed in the succeeding period.

Greatly influenced by Soviet leanings, the First Five-Year Plan (1953–1957) was initiated in 1953. In this Soviet-like model of economic strategy, priority was given to heavy industry, with agriculture in the service of industry. The development of agriculture was to be directed to ensuring adequate supplies of grain and industrial raw materials, and to increasing the agricultural surplus with which to finance industrialization. A clear picture of a developmental squeeze on agriculture for the sake of the industrial sector was provided for in the plan. Over 50 percent of the state investment funds was given to the capital goods industries, and only 7.8 percent was devoted to agriculture. Simultaneous with this vigorous squeeze, an agricultural collectivization campaign was launched in 1957; "high level" or "advanced" agricultural producers' cooperatives were established, and 97 percent of peasant households were members of these cooperatives. The collectivization was designed to have great impact on farm labor mobilization and agricultural growth. But the drastic institutional change without supporting growth policy for agriculture could only lead to a squeeze without development in the agricultural sector.

It was not long before critical obstacles emerged. The most crucial of these was the lack of sufficient growth in the agricultural sector. At that time, 80 percent of Chinese light industry (and 50 percent of all industry) depended on agriculture for its raw materials. Agricultural output was lagging behind expectations and needs, due to the squeezing strategy without supporting policies and the effects of devastating floods. Population growth continued unchecked, and this made the problem of sustaining a per capita growth increasingly difficult. In addition, the special backwardness of agriculture in some areas created extra burdens on a strained transportation system to move food from grain-surplus to grain-deficient regions. In short, the policy of "agriculture serving industry" soon came up against the barriers of China's physical environment: the rapid growth of population, the shortage of transportation facilities, and natural disasters. Industrialization could not advance without an upsurge in agricultural output and could not succeed at the expense of the agricultural sector alone. The "imbalanced growth" strategy as planned for in the First Five-Year Plan suffered a serious setback that forced the Communists to alter their overall economic strategy.

The Second Five-Year Plan (1958–1962) was swept aside in 1958 by the establishment of communes and by the Great Leap Forward. The Great Leap Forward was Mao's hasty answer to the above-mentioned agricultural crisis.

During the Leap the Communists abandoned the Soviet model and adopted a new development strategy, the Maoist model, designed both to accelerate growth and to promote Mao's revolutionary political and social values. "Politics" was placed "in command." The aim was to "walk on two legs"—to speed growth in both agriculture and industry. The general line of "going all out, aiming high and achieving greater, quicker, better, and more economic results in building socialism" was the character of the Leap. A distorted "balanced growth" strategy was adhered to without a careful study and adjustment of the previous "imbalanced growth" strategy. For example, instead of relying on capital investment and modern technology as the primary determinants of economic advance and full employment, the Leap pursued the opposite principle of relying extensively on the maximum utilization of labor to create "capital." An outstanding illustration was the mobilization of the rural population to maximize water resources. Before the Leap, most of the investment in this area was devoted to large undertakings for flood control financed and planned by Peking. The new departure encouraged local authorities and agricultural cooperatives to organize the labor force and use their own resources for smaller projects of water storage and irrigation (Barnett, 1974:124).

Rather than take a progressive agricultural strategy with a priority given to agricultural "development," the state transferred responsibility to the peasants with extra burdens in confronting agricultural crisis. Radical institutional change to establish rural communes was another agrarian strategy in the Great Leap that had a seriously adverse impact on peasants' economic motivation and incentives. The result of the Great Leap approach to the agricultural problem combined with three consecutive years of bad weather (1958–1961) was a sharp decline in production and a severe nationwide shortage of food. Agriculture and its rural population once again suffered from the ignorant government strategy from the top.

The failure of the Great Leap did force the regime to take a new economic strategy between 1961 and 1965. The "New Economic Policy" advocated a reversal of the accepted sectoral priorities (i.e., heavy industry, light industry, agriculture), which had been the faithfully adhered to development strategy during the First Plan period and implicit in the Great Leap in spite of the furor about agriculture.

Chou En-lai's statement in December 1964 is clear on this point:

> The plan for national economic development should be arranged in the order of priority of agriculture, light industry, and heavy industry. The scale of industrial development should correspond to the volume of marketable grain and the industrial raw materials made available by agriculture. (*Peking Review,* 1 January 1965, p. 10)

Guided by the "agriculture first" strategy, agriculture was conceived as the foundation of economic construction. The priority within the industrial sector was also placed on the development of light industry and handicrafts, which serve agriculture. And the agricultural sector shared 21.3 percent of the total state investment in 1962, the highest percentage devoted to agriculture since 1949.

Within the agricultural strategy, several modifications were also introduced. Not only were private plots reestablished and free markets reopened, but modern industrial inputs into agriculture—including chemical fertilizers—were steadily increased. In order to increase the total agricultural output, the policy of "san zi yi bao" (Three Self and One Assignment) allegedly was promoted from 1960 through 1962. The policy consisted of: (a) giving up commune land to individual households, (b) setting up free markets, (c) giving more responsibility to enterprises in the handling of their own profits and losses, and (d) the assignment of production quotas to households. Moreover, the communes were sharply reduced in size; communal small-scale industry was discouraged, and the production team (20–30 households) became typically the planning and accounting unit within the commune. Even the households became much more autonomous economically, and peasants engaged in "side-line" production such as the raising of pigs and the planting of vegetables. Peasants enriched themselves, rather than "serving the people" as required before.

Material incentives were reintroduced into the agricultural sector as well as into industry. The squeezing strategy on agriculture was indeed loosened a little during the period. However, affected by the increased military budget and a new campaign on "learning from Tachai in agriculture," requiring local self-reliance, the investment for agriculture dropped to 14.6 percent in 1965.

Through late 1968, the agriculture-rural sector was left more or less alone by the Cultural Revolution (1966–1969). But during the late Cultural Revolution period, a crackdown began in the countryside. Material incentives and private plots were denounced. Production teams, which under the readjustment policy had assumed the principle responsibility for basic production planning and income distribution, were superseded by production brigades. This move was aimed toward the formation of "great production brigades" and eventually communes. This was the "Tachai Work Point System" under which commune members' performance was to be measured not only by the amount of work done, but by the degree of the workers' revolutionary spirit. Moral and political incentives were introduced into the agricultural sector again. But the impact was not great. All in all, the agricultural sector was not seriously affected by the Cultural Revolution.

Judged by the further decline of agriculture's share to an average 11 percent in state investment during the period from 1966 to 1975, the Cultural Revolution and its aftermath did have a negative impact on the regime's strategy toward agriculture. Though since the New Economic Policy period the developmental priority had not been officially changed, greater emphasis given to industry, especially heavy industry, was gradually evident. This was also demonstrated in the governmental reorganization in 1975 (Ch'en, 1982:4). Also, the investment in agriculture for that year again dropped, to only 9.8 percent. Agriculture in overall economic development strategy, in fact, had not received as important a role as claimed by the regime during the ten-year period. No effort was made by the regime to challenge the basic strategy of squeezing agriculture under a somewhat "imbalanced growth" ideology.

After a short-lived increase in state investment in agriculture during the period from 1976 to 1978 (12.1 percent average), it then dropped again to 11.6 percent in 1979 due to serious financial deficits.

At the Fourth Session of the Eleventh CCP Central Committee in September of the same year, decisions were adopted on "Some Questions Concerning the Acceleration of Agricultural Development" in which criticisms were made of the previous twenty years of agricultural strategy.

> The sluggish expansion of agriculture in the past 20 years or so was due to the following reasons: the absence of a stable social and political environment after the completion of socialist transformation; *the adoption of some policies and measures which were unfavorable to arousing the peasants' enthusiasm for production; inadequate and ineffective state aid;* neglect of technical innovation and agricultural research and education; and inefficient implementation of the principle of all-round development of farming, forestry, animal husbandry, sideline occupations and fishery. (*Peking Review*, no. 4, 28 January 1980)

In spite of the above self-criticism and the launching of the Four Modernizations, no actual strategic change was made immediately; a cutback in state investment in agriculture was even apparent for the year. A year later, in September 1980, when the CCP Central Committee issued Document No. 75, entitled "Some Questions Concerning the Strengthening and Improvement of the System of Production Responsibility in Agriculture," a strategic shift in agriculture was observed. Under the system of "fixing output quotas based on individual households," the individual peasant household was given more freedom and incentives, and the existence of "high level" and "pure" collectivization and even the commune system was therefore questioned. The rural institutional change and the reoccurrence of material incentives for peasants, in fact, resembled the New Economic Policy in the early sixties. By February 1982, over 90 percent of the production teams practiced the production responsibility system, and the agricultural output did increase in areas where the new system was enacted. And this institutional change can be considered as a temporary strategic adjustment of halting the continued squeeze on agriculture. However, still no clear strategic alteration has been evident as to the priority given to agriculture in the overall economic development strategy (Baum, 1980).

Given the fact that the highest priority has been placed on the rapid expansion of the light industrial sector in the 1979 economic readjustment for the Four Modernizations campaign, the agricultural sector will be expected to play a supporting role to the industrial-urban sector. Agriculture is to be squeezed on its surplus production and income, with the excess being transferred to the newly induced industrial sector. In other words, in the foreseeable future, agriculture will continue to be extracted and squeezed for the modernization of the PRC.

In conclusion, the history of agricultural strategies in the PRC since 1949 has indeed revealed an apparent squeezing character for the whole period. Dernberger (1980:450) maintains that the PRC's economic strategy and practices have been designed to exploit agriculture and have succeeded in doing so. Tang and Huang (1980:374) make a similar assertion by saying that "the role of agriculture is to support priority (selective) industrialization with (extracted) savings articulated by real resource transfers in the form of food (the principal wage good), labor, raw materials, and exportable farm products." After analyzing the direction and quantity of intersectoral resource flows in Communist China, Lardy also concludes by saying that:

> My own view is that the farm sector was a large net contributor of financial resources to the rest of the economy in the 1950s and that this continued even after the mid-1960s. That is, the burden of increased costs of farm production was to a large degree borne by the peasantry in the form of stagnant and reduced consumption and was not fully borne by the state in the form of reduced outflows (or increased inflows) of resources from the farm sector. (Lardy, 1980:412)

Lardy also asserts that, in money terms, the urban-rural income ratio appears to have been the same in 1957 as in 1979 (Lardy, 1978:179).

Table 15.1 International Comparison of Rural-Urban Inequality

	Ratio of Average Urban Income to Average Rural Income	
	Per Capita	Per Household
China, 1979	2.2	1.7
Bangladesh, 1966/1967	n.a.	1.5
India, 1975/1976	1.9	1.8
Sri Lanka, 1969/1970	n.a.	1.7
Indonesia, 1976	n.a.	2.1
Malaysia (Pen.), 1970	2.2	2.1
Philippines, 1971	n.a.	2.3
Thailand, 1975/1976	2.2	n.a.
Brazil, 1976	2.3	n.a.

Source: World Bank, 1981. China: Socialist Economic Development.

Actually, for some of the intervening period (prior to the large increase in agricultural procurement prices in 1979) the income inequality has even been substantially greater. Nationwide, on the average, data suggest that in money terms urban per capita income is currently about 2.2 times rural income. According to a World Bank report, due to the fact that the "cost of living" has risen faster in rural areas than in urban areas, the gap appears to have widened considerably: urban per capita incomes are estimated to have increased in 1957–1979 at an annual average real rate of 2.9 percent, but rural incomes at only 1.6 percent. The results of recent household surveys in Sichuan and nationwide indicate that the urban-rural ratio of per capita meat consumption is 2.4, and that the urban-rural ratio of per capita consumer durables ownership is 4.6 for bicycles, 3.8 for sewing machines, 4.3 for radios, and over 4 for watches and clocks. It is also estimated that the urban-rural per capita grain consumption ratio is 1.6 (World Bank, 1981:56–57).

Evidence also indicates that in rural areas, per capita consumption of foodgrains declined 5.9 percent between 1957 and 1978, edible vegetable oils 43.2 percent, and cotton cloth 5.7 percent. On the other hand, per capita urban consumption of these items was either unchanged or rose significantly (Lardy, 1980:426). Under the squeeze, the rural living standards were actually depressed and exploited in order to preserve or increase urban living standards.

Even by comparison with other Asian developing countries, the urban-rural income inequality in Communist China in 1979 was not very different and certainly not very progressively better, despite the ideological promise made by the Communists (see Table 15.1).

In the twenties, Mao had turned his back on the cities and clung to the countryside for revolutionary force. It seems that for the past thirty years, since 1949, the Communist regime has been marching in exactly the opposite direction in the course of its economic development strategies.

Rural Social Change in Communist China

Under the squeezing agricultural strategies, Chinese rural society was also expected to change. This socialist "economic" strategy of squeezing agriculture in the PRC has, in fact, demanded changes in rural social structures. In addition, a series of social and political campaigns was launched in order to transform the rural society, where the majority of the Chinese population resides. These planned social changes were conceived as necessary for the implementation of Communist China's squeezing strategy on agriculture.

Two types of planned rural change occur in the squeezing agricultural strategies as adopted by the Communist regime. The first one, at a macro level, relates to the changes in rural local organizations, i.e., the establishment of the various levels of new collectivization institutions (the rural commune system).

One objective is to set up a collectivized commune for rural China. A second, at a micro level, concerns the required change in peasants' everyday life, social interactions, and a certain world view and outlook. The image of a "socialist peasant" is expected to be realized for collectivized peasantry.

These planned changes were initiated vigorously in the countryside during the past thirty years by means of power-coercive strategies (Chin and Benne, 1969). This section will explore the extent to which the two planned changes have been achieved. Special attention will be paid to the dynamism with which the traditional Chinese rural social structure has persisted or even resisted the governmental agrarian strategies.

Continuity and Change at the Macro Level

The commune system of Communist China consists of four organizational parts: commune, brigade, team, and household. As described earlier, the macro change was intended to reorganize the traditional rural institutions and social structures, replacing them with a total socialist sociopolitical apparatus. This system was established in the Great Leap Forward but was reduced to a skeleton during the period of the New Economic Policy. It since developed greatly, however, until 1980, when the system of "fixing output quotas based on individual households" was adopted (Crook, 1975:366–410; Dernberger, 1980:445–501).

Skinner first made his assertion in 1966 as to the proper unit for cooperative production under the Communist collectivization movement. He argued that the traditional standard marketing community would be an optimal unit for the rural commune. The Communist decision to make communes larger than basic marketing systems with the objective of circumscribing and diminishing the pernicious particularism of traditional social relations had, in fact, confronted serious functional resistances in the countryside. Skinner pointed out that the Chinese Communist efforts to build up organizational strength and to develop solidarity would face the difficulties arising from mutually antagonistic loyalties already existing in the component natural social groups. And as a result, the commune system was forced to be subdivided to compromise with the traditional marketing structure. For example, in Guangdong, the scale of rural communes was halved; the 803 communes of September 1958 had increased in number to approximately 1,600 by April 1963 (Skinner, 1966:382–399).

Stavis, in a comparative study of rural local institutions, found that the functions of the "production team" in the rural reorganization scheme were actually fulfilled not by the three levels of ownership but rather by a variety of cooperative organizations in the traditional rural communities, including labor exchange groups and irrigation management associations, as well as the marketing communities (Stavis, 1976:381–396).

Ahn also discussed the problems of rural structural change faced by the Communists in the process of establishing rural People's Communes in the period of 1958 to 1974. Similar to the finding in Skinner's study, Ahn discovered that during the whole period, the rural commune systems had experienced changes, continuities, and problems and that their size and ownership had been scaled down. He disclosed that:

> We find a surprising durability of the traditional social units which correspond, though with different names, to the market town, the village, and the neighborhood. Accompanying the reduction of scale has been the evolution of three-level ownership allowing for the free market and private plots. These changes represent a compromise between revolution and development necessary for intensive farming based on human labor and self-sufficient production. (Ahn, 1975:656)

On balance, Ahn argued that the rural commune system has resulted from the constant dialogue between the Communist revolutionary goals and development imperatives. The organizational and attitudinal changes involved in the rural commune system were perceived to be contributory to equality as well as to productivity. In a sense, the establishment of the rural commune reorganization was, in fact, designed to be instrumental for the simultaneous resolution of scarcity and ideology as Eckstein (1976) has observed. And the end result is the extraction and squeeze on agricultural productivity.

The squeezing strategy on agriculture generated great pressure on the production management and especially on the brigade and team leaders to keep after the household to work for compliance with the production schedule and quantity. In order to cope with this squeezed production pressure under Communist China's centralized economy, in which production demand has been determined administratively, the existence of a "second economy" has been observed in rural China. Burns has delineated a wide range of informal, extra and illegal strategies that were created by the team and brigade cadres and the peasants to enhance collective/private income. The case of rural Guangdong, under study from 1962 to 1974, revealed the following informal local strategies: altering the size of production units, speculation, fraudulent loan applications, corruption, theft, withholding goods or services, false reporting, and violence or demonstrations (Burns, 1981:629–644). The continued existence of the "second economy" is an evidence of the reaction and resistance of the rural locality and particularly the peasants to the rigid and ever-squeezing agricultural strategies.

With the temporary strategic accommodation to adopt the system of "fixing output quotas based on individual households," the peasants might obtain some temporary relief from the squeeze. And the organization pressure faced by the team and brigade leader could also be minimized. But this must not be misconceived as a basic strategic change in squeezing agriculture. Judged from the past historical course, a new wave of squeeze on the agricultural and rural sector is to be expected by means of further control through collectivization and command forces.

Persistence and Change at the Micro Level

In Communist ideology, family commitment and loyalty should be minimized with a stronger commitment to the state and the collective, and individuals should all be socialist in their outlook and have a larger collectivity orientation.

According to Parish and Whyte (1978), the rural family as a corporate economic unit within the commune system has remained a basis of rural life. Many old functions (e.g., support of the elderly, early child care, the arrangement of consumption and domestic work, animal raising, and the provision of housing) are still kept. The organization of daily farm labor and later socialization of the youth are replaced by the production teams and other collective bodies in the countryside. Also, the decline of nepotism, lineage conflict, and ceremonial life are apparent in the collectivized rural sector. Moreover, major changes in the structure of rural life took place in the fifties when the collectivization movement was most actively implemented. In the sixties and seventies, changes in health care, education, and female leadership have been observed, but no successful actions to further the collectivization of rural economic activities were made. A great persistence of the Chinese family system is still in action even under the commune system.

As for change in individuals, the said conflicts between old and new values, selfishness, and socialist consciousness are not as evident in the degree to which peasants accepted or resisted social change advocated by the Communist policy. What matters is the extent to which the structural change actually makes new ways of cooperative behavior rewarding to the peasants. Communes and collectivization of rural economic life have placed restrictions on peasants in pursuing economic opportunities, but in recent years, peasants have been allowed to ignore the orthodox ideals of communism as long as they can work diligently for increasing production within the existing sociopolitical framework.

Parish and Whyte then conclude that:

> In the future gradual evolution of commune life the peasants are best seen not as ardent Confucianists or as modernizing men or as new socialist men, but as flexible, family-oriented individuals striving to deal with the unique set of problems and opportunities existing in their local village environment in order to maximize the security and satisfaction that this environment can provide. (Parish and Whyte, 1978:337)

It can be said that under the squeezing agricultural strategy accompanied by collectivization, the Chinese peasants have been and will continue to be more and more situation-oriented in order to get by through many expected and even unexpected policy changes in years to come.

Concluding Remarks

From the foregoing analyses of the nature and changes of Communist China's agricultural strategy and its impact on the agricultural-rural sector, it can be assessed that the Communists have taken to squeezing agriculture as an instrument for economic growth and development. The rural social structure has also been induced to change in the direction that the squeezing strategy required.

Under the squeeze, agriculture as a socioeconomic sector has not been developed and modernized, and the rural population has been exploited vis-à-vis the policy of urban-industrial development in the past thirty years of growth experience. The Communist regime, with an urban-industrial bias since 1949, has turned its back on the countryside in which it had seized power before 1949. The "revolution" in 1949 did not bring about just, fair and equal development and welfare for the Chinese peasants as had been promised by the Communists.

From a humanist perspective, Communist China's agricultural squeezing strategy manifests the "myth of revolution" adhered to in Chinese Communist ideology for development and change (cf. Berger, 1976). Moreover, the PRC once again demonstrates another case of the sad experience of Third World agriculture in the post-war era suffering under the worldwide urban bias for development (cf. Lipton, 1977).

References

Ahn, Byung-joon. 1975. "The Political Economy of the People's Commune in China: Changes and Continuities." *Journal of Asian Studies* (May), pp. 631–658.

Baum, Richard, ed. 1980. *China's Four Modernizations.* Boulder, Colo.: Westview Press.

Barnett, A. Doak. 1974. *Uncertain Passage: China's Transition to the Post-Mao Era.* Washington, D.C.: Brookings Institute.

Berger, Peter. 1976. *Pyramids of Sacrifice: Political Ethics and Social Change.* Garden City, N.Y.: Anchor Books.

Boulding, Kenneth, and P. Singh. 1962. "The Role of the Price Structure in Economic Development." *American Economic Review Proceedings* 52 (May), pp. 28–45.

Burns, John P. 1981. "Rural Guangdong's 'Second Economy': 1962–1974." *China Quarterly* (December), pp. 629–644.

Ch'en, Ting-chung. 1982. "Mainland China's Current Agricultural Policy: A Review of the "Diversified Economy" and "Fixing Output Quotas Based on Individual Households." Papers presented at the Eleventh Sino-American Conference on Mainland China held in Taipei, June 7–13.

Chin, Robert, and Kenneth Benne. 1969. "General Strategies for Effective Changes in Human Systems." In *The Planning of Change,* ed. W. G. Gennis et al. New York: Holt, Rinehart and Winston.

Crook, Frederick. 1975. "The Commune System in the People's Republic of China, 1963–74." In *China: A Reassessment of the Economy,* Joint Economic Committee, 94th U.S. Congress. Washington, D.C.: U.S. Government Printing Office, pp. 366–410.

Dernberger, Robert F. 1980. "Micro-Economic Analysis of the Farm in the PRC." Conference on Agricultural Development in China, Japan, and Korea. Taipei: Institute of Economics, Academia Sinica, pp. 444–497.

Eckstein, Alexander. 1976. China's Economic Development: The Interplay of Scarcity and Ideology. Ann Arbor: University of Michigan Press.

Gurley, John. 1975. "The Foundation of Mao's Economic Strategy: 1927–1949." *Monthly Review* (July-August), pp. 50–132.

Hsiao, Hsin-huang Michael. 1976. "A Model Outside the Models: Communist China's Developmental Experiences." M.A. thesis, State University of New York at Buffalo.

______. 1981. "Government Agricultural Strategies in Taiwan and South Korea: A Macrosociological Assessment." Taipei: Institute of Ethnology, Academia Sinica.

______. 1982. "Changes in Communist China's Economic Development Strategies, 1949–1975: A Chronological Examination." *Journal of Sociology* (Taipei), no. 15, pp. 82–116.

Johnston, Bruce, and Peter Kilby. 1975. *Agricultural and Structural Transformation: Economic Strategies in Late-Developing Countries.* New York: Oxford University Press.

Lai, Tse-han, and Hsin-huang Michael Hsiao. 1981. "Rural vs. Urban Strategies in Modern China: 1911–1949." *Thought and Word* (Taipei) 18:6, pp. 75–84.

Lardy, Nicholas. 1978. *Economic Growth and Distribution in China.* New York: Cambridge University Press.

______. 1980. "Intersectoral Resource Flows in Chinese Economic Development." Conference on Agricultural Development in China, Japan and Korea. Taipei: Institute of Economics, Academia Sinica, pp. 405–431.

Lipton, Michael. 1977. *Why Poor People Stay Poor: Urban Bias in World Development.* Cambridge, Mass.: Harvard University Press.

Mao Tse-tung. 1965. *Selected Works of Mao Tse-tung.* Vol. 4. Peking: Foreign Language Press.

Maxwell, Neville, ed. 1979. *China's Road to Development.* Elmsford, N.Y.: Pergamon Press.

Owen, W. F. 1966. "The Double Developmental Squeeze on Agriculture." *American Economic Review* (March), pp. 43–70.

Parish, William L. 1975. "Socialism and the Chinese Peasant Family." *Journal of Asian Studies* (May), pp. 613–630.

Parish, William L., and Martin K. Whyte. 1978. *Village and Family in Contemporary China.* Chicago: University of Chicago Press.

Perkines, Dwight H. 1975. "Constraints Influencing China's Agricultural Performance." In *China: A Reassessment of the Economy,* Joint Economic Committee, 94th U.S. Congress. Washington, D.C.: U.S. Government Printing Office, pp. 350–365.

Prybyla, Jan S. 1970. *The Political Economy of Communist China.* Scranton, Pa.: International Textbook Company.

______. 1982. "Economic Problems of Communism: Mainland China—A Case Study." Paper presented at the Eleventh Sino-American Conference on Mainland China held in Taipei, June 7–13.

Reynolds, L. G. 1975. *Agriculture in Development Theory.* New Haven, Conn.: Yale University Press.

Schran, Peter. 1980. "Agriculture in the Four Modernizations." Conference on Agricultural Development in China, Japan, and Korea. Taipei: Institute of Economics, Academia Sinica, pp. 503–539.

Skinner, William G. 1966. *Marketing and Social Structure in Rural China.* Ann Arbor, Mich.: Association for Asian Studies, Reprint Series No. 1.

Stavis, Benedict. 1976. "China's Rural Local Institutions in Comparative Perspective." *Asian Survey* 16:4 (April 1976), pp. 381–396.

Tang, Anthony M., and Cliff J. Huang. 1980. "Changes in Input-Output Relations in the Agriculture of the Chinese Mainland, 1952–1979." Conference on Agricultural Development in China, Japan, and Korea. Taipei: Institute of Economics, Academia Sinica, pp. 371–400.

Walder, Andrew. 1982. "Chinese Communist Society: The State of the Field." Paper presented at the Eleventh Sino-American Conference on Mainland China held in Taipei, June 7–13.

World Bank. 1981. *China: Socialist Economic Development.* Washington, D.C.: The World Bank.

Part 6

Intellectuals, Dissidence, and the Cultural Scene

16
Intellectual Dissent in the People's Republic of China

Merle Goldman

The Cultural Revolution and its aftermath of 1966–1976 and the movement for human rights that burst forth in 1978–1979 were not aberrations in the People's Republic of China. Both repression and dissidence have been inherent in the relationship between the Chinese Communist party and the intellectuals since even before the establishment of the People's Republic of China in 1949. They reflect the effort of the party to subordinate intellectuals to its shifting political line and the effort of a small number of intellectuals to uphold individual and intellectual values. The ability of intellectuals periodically to express their own views stems from the party's need for their services in its drive to build a modernized society. Thus, while the party presses the intellectuals to conform, it cannot press to the point of producing an atmosphere that might permanently stifle the intellectuals' initiative and creativity.

Therefore, the CCP has carried out a contradictory policy toward the intellectuals. On the one hand, it has indoctrinated them in Marxism-Leninism, which has been imposed more comprehensively and intensively than Confucianism had been on the traditional literati. On the other hand, it has tried to stimulate the intellectuals to be productive in their professions. This contradictory approach has resulted in a policy toward intellectuals that has oscillated between periods of repression and periods of relative relaxation in which the intellectuals have been granted some responsibilities and privileges in order to win their cooperation in carrying out modernization. These shifts are in part determined by economic and political factors and sometimes by international events. Particularly in periods of economic crises as in 1956 after the collectivization, in the early sixties after the Great Leap Forward, and in the late seventies after Mao's death, the party eased its pressure somewhat in order to gain the intellectuals' help in solving its problems.

The shifts in policy toward the intellectuals also have had a dynamic of their own. The party has pushed toward orthodoxy until the intellectuals appeared reluctant to produce; then it has relaxed until its political control appeared threatened. In the intervals of relative relaxation, the party fostered, or at least permitted, intellectual debates, Western influence, and criticism of the bureaucracy in order to root out abuses of the system. The party initiated and established the framework within which, at least in the beginning, intellectuals were to express themselves. But, although the party limited the scope and laid down the terms in which the criticism was to be expressed, it could not fully control the response. Some intellectuals demanded individual self-expression not only in their own work but on broader political issues as well. Similarly, criticism of the bureaucracy went beyond criticism of individual officials to criticism of the system itself. The party would then crack down with varying degrees of intensity.

The Dissident Intellectuals

Even during the dogmatic imposition of Mao's thought on intellectual and artistic activity, a minority of the educated elite never completely abandoned their professional and artistic values. The very nature of their work propelled them into confrontation with the party's encompassing political control imposed by less knowledgeable officials. Within this minority, a tiny group of intellectuals demanded not only professional autonomy, but the right to comment on past and present political events. As the most outspoken segment of China's intellectuals, they led the way in exposing intellectual repression, bureaucratic privilege, arbitrary rule, and irrational practices.

Most of them were Marxists-Leninists, influenced by late nineteenth- and early twentieth-century Western thought and engaged in the creative arts, history, literature, and philosophy. Within this general stance, there was wide variation. Some stressed traditional aspects of Marxism; others stressed radical aspects of Maoism. Some emphasized Western-style professionalism; others emphasized intellectual pluralism. Most desired industrialization, but some criticized its accompanying human costs; others criticized its skilled and managerial elite. What they shared was a disagreement at certain times with the way the party or Mao or both were carrying out Marxism-Leninism in practice. They pointed out the contradiction between the ideals of Marxism-Leninism-Maoism and the realities of political life. Most sought change not by destroying the prevailing political order, but through the prevailing political order. Their protest was not to overthrow the political leadership but to win concessions from it. Though perhaps more courageous and sensitive than their colleagues, they were not untainted heroes or selfless idealists. A few may have been, but most of them were motivated by personal and power ambitions as well as by ideals.

There was only a sprinkling of scientists within this group. Because their work was more abstruse and theoretical, the scientists enjoyed more relative autonomy than the nonscientific intellectuals. The political leadership admitted less understanding of their discipline. Moreover, because their discipline is crucial to industrial, military, and technological modernization, they received greater material rewards and were more isolated from political campaigns. Though they were inevitably affected by campaigns, they felt the impact later and less severely. Similarly, in periods of relative relaxation, they felt the effect earlier and more generously. The very nature of their work gave them a greater stake in the system and more to lose by protest than the nonscientific intellectuals.

The May Fourth Mode of Protest

Intellectual dissidents in the People's Republic of China have been heirs to the May Fourth movement of the early decades of the twentieth century, which sought to create a new Western culture as a solution to China's social, political, and economic plight. Though the precise remedy was new, the method of cultural regeneration as a key to survival was traditional. The May Fourth writers of the twenties and thirties in particular regarded their writings as tools with which to fight social and political ills and shape political consciousness. In the chaotic political situation of those decades, and under the influence of Western liberalism, they conceived of their activities as free and independent of political control. Even those May Fourth intellectuals committed to the Communist movement believed in intellectual autonomy.

At various times the party has had to contend with this May Fourth spirit. In the mid-thirties, when it directed left-wing writers to write about the united front, China's pre-eminent modern writer, Lu Xun, protested against the party's dictate over creative activity. In Yan'an in the early forties, when the party and Mao sought to impose political criteria over intellectual and creative activity, a group of left-wing writers protested and continued their role as critics of political abuses as they had done under the Guomindang. As the party increasingly came to dominate all aspects of intellectual activity by the mid-fifties, a close follower of Lu Xun, the writer Hu Feng, in a letter to the Central Committee in 1955, protested against the stifling of intellectual life and pleaded for individual and intellectual autonomy. Party officials denounced these dissident intellectuals and in the forties and fifties launched ideological remolding campaigns to compel intellectuals to accept party authority. Hu Feng was imprisoned and the Hu Feng campaign of 1955 became a massive movement that moved beyond the intellectuals to the nation as a whole.

However, the May Fourth spirit was to revive shortly afterwards in the Hundred Flowers Campaign of late 1956 and the first half of 1957. But, unlike the previous protests, it did not arise spontaneously. To prevent Polish- and Hungarian-style uprisings, which Mao regarded as movements of repressed discontent, he encouraged intellectuals to criticize the bureaucratism of party officials. He also granted intellectuals a relative degree of intellectual freedom in the expectation that they would help the regime with its economic problems. In the belief that the intellectuals had been sufficiently indoctrinated, he expected them to stay within the limits he set. Though the response was cautious at first, by the spring of 1957 the Hundred Flowers Campaign had become a large-scale movement in the large cities, particularly in the universities. Intellectuals and students expressed themselves not only in the established journals and newspapers, but also in wall posters, unauthorized pamphlets, and large-scale meetings and demonstrations. Though they had been isolated from the West by China's alliance with the Soviet Union, they continued to express May Fourth values. They criticized the domination of Soviet-style scholarship and sought a return to a Western orientation. They demanded a separation of intellectual and creative activity from political direction and the right to express themselves in a style and with a content of their own choosing.

Even intellectuals such as the writer Lao She, who had tried to conform to every dictate of the party line, pointed out how difficult it was to function under the control of the revolutionary regime they had helped bring to power. "A writer who is always scared stiff of overstepping set principles or doing damage to the revolution is certain to find himself bound hand and foot and incapable of writing boldly."[1] The demand for nonpoliticized intellectual activity was not only a protest against party direction of one's work, it was also an effort to allow literature to fulfill the function it had in traditional times and in the May Fourth era: to criticize and speak out on political issues.

The most controversial literary works were not by the old left-wing writers, but by two young writers, Wang Meng and Liu Binyan, published in *People's Literature* in 1956. They had been brought up in the Communist system and had a strong commitment to its principles. They were not only influenced by the May Fourth spirit, but also by the intellectual thaw that occurred in the Soviet Union in the wake of Stalin's death. Using the prototype of Soviet stories in which characters who lived up to Communist ideals came into conflict with bureaucrats who did not, they depicted courageous, resourceful, idealistic young men and women who were frustrated in their efforts to improve the well-being of the people by apathetic, inefficient, cautious bureaucrats.

Some intellectuals went beyond criticizing the abuses and arrogance of the party bureaucrats, as Mao had urged, to criticize the party's domination itself as the root of China's problems. The editor-in-chief of the intellectuals' newspaper *Guangming Ribao,* Chu Anping, charged that " 'The world belongs to the Party.' I think a party leading a nation is not the same as a party owning a nation."[2] These charges and growing student demonstrations against one-party rule and demands that Hu Feng, who had been imprisoned, be tried in open court in accordance with legal procedures, went beyond the limits Mao had set. With Mao's disillusionment with the intellectuals and students and with increasing pressure from the bureaucracy, the Hundred Flowers Campaign ended abruptly in early June 1957. A campaign against critics of the party who were labeled rightists was launched. It is estimated that from 400,000 to 700,000 intellectuals were dismissed from their jobs and forced to undergo varying degrees of labor reform. The circles of May Fourth writers and Western-educated social scientists, which had continued to function as distinct communities with shared values after 1949, were smashed by the antirightist campaign of 1957–1959.

The Confucian Mode of Protest

The form and method of intellectual protest were influenced not only by contemporary pressures and precedents but also by long-term historical forces. In the early sixties the party once again relaxed its political grip on the intellectuals in order to gain their cooperation in repairing the damage to the economy caused by the Great Leap Forward and the withdrawal of Soviet experts. Since the antirightist campaign crushed the expression of open dissent, the intellectuals resorted to a form of dissent more in the Confucian mode than the more Westernized May Fourth mode. Like their literati predecessors, they camouflaged their dissenting political views in indirect, figurative analogies and allusions used in discussions of history, literature, philosophy, art, and the theater. Some, like the editor Deng Tuo, the historian Wu Han, and the playwright Liao Mosha, used a quintessential Chinese genre of dissent, the zawen—short, subtle satirical essays seemingly on innocuous subjects but actually discussing political issues. This political device was used by the great Confucian thinkers Han Yu and Ouyang Xiu and by Lu Xun.

Intellectuals in the People's Republic of China were under even more pressure to mask their dissent because they were more tightly controlled than the Confucian literati ever were. It was not only the use of secret police and prison camps, but party control of all aspects of an individual's life from education to economic livelihood. Intellectuals who wished to protest or who did not wish to serve the state could no longer withdraw to their libraries or to a mountaintop. They had to participate actively in the tasks the party set for them. Thus, the only way for them to express dissent was subtly in their work.

Tradition resonates even more strongly in the strategies the intellectuals used to carry out their dissent. Although some aspects of Confucianism generated conformity and orthodoxy, other aspects generated criticism and protest. Confucianism encouraged discussion and criticism of its practices in order to renew itself. Semiofficial dissent was inherent in the Confucian system. Confucian literati were obliged to admonish the government and ruler when they failed to live up to Confucian humanistic ideals and fair treatment of the peasantry. Since the literati had no legal or institutional protections, they risked punishment and even death to act as the "conscience" of society. Although some literati became martyrs, most criticized only when they had patrons and protection within the top leadership. Moreover, they could get a hearing only when they had allies in positions of power. Most often this occurred during periods of factional conflict when literati were used in the political struggle. In the process of articulating their patrons' position, some literati inserted views and values that differed not only from the prevailing orthodoxy, but also from those of their political patrons.

A similar process occurred in the People's Republic of China in the early sixties, when a small number of well-known intellectuals in the Beijing Party Committee and Party Propaganda Department protested against the suppression of intellectuals and exploitation of the peasants in the Great Leap Forward. Even some of the concerns of these modern-day critics resembled their literati predecessors. Despite their Marxist proletarian orientation, they were more like their predecessors in their concern for the peasants' well-being. Deng Tuo and his colleagues pointed out in their zawen that the peasants had been victimized by Mao's untested economic and social experiments. They argued that Mao's methods of mass campaigns and ideological mobilization were no longer applicable to a modernizing society and advocated more conventional economic practices. These views overlapped with those of the bureaucratic leaders in the early sixties, who could not express them openly without threatening the leadership consensus necessary to rule. Under the high-level patronage of Peng Zhen, Politburo member and secretary of the Beijing Party Committee, and Zhou Yang, vice-chairman of the Party Propaganda Department and cultural czar, a group of May Fourth-educated intellectuals expressed these views in the national and Beijing media clothed in philosophical discussion, historical discourse, literary criticism, and the Beijing Opera.

However, a number of these intellectuals went beyond espousing their patrons' positions to try to influence policies in ways their patrons had not sanctioned. They not only expressed the interests of the educated elite in their demand for a degree of intellectual autonomy, they also asked for scholarly input into political decision making. Intellectuals associated with Deng Tuo in the Beijing Party Committee praised Song, Ming, and Qing scholars, poets, artists, and advisers who spoke out against harsh rulers and extolled rulers who sought advice from diverse sources. Deng Tuo coined the phrase "welcome miscellaneous scholars," by whom he meant nonconforming intellectuals who not only served their governments in a professional capacity but also in a political capacity. He asserted that "It would be a great loss to us if we now failed to acknowledge the general significance of the wide range of knowledge of 'miscellaneous scholars' for all kinds of leadership as well as for scientific research."[3]

The bureaucratic leaders in the early sixties desired more intellectual ferment and a loosening of ideological restraints on intellectuals in order to help solve the problems brought on by the Great Leap Forward. But they were as unwilling as Mao to give up political control over scholarship and allow intellectuals a voice in policymaking or in public criticism of their political decisions. Some dissenting intellectuals were silenced by their own patrons in the 1964 rectification when their views diverged too far from the views of the bureaucracy.

Their patrons were also under pressure from the Maoist political faction that was galvanized into action by the intellectuals' criticism of Mao's policies. Under the political patronage of Mao and his wife Jiang Qing, a group of younger, more radical intellectuals rebutted the arguments of Mao's critics. They came from the Philosophy and Social Sciences Department of the Chinese Academy of Sciences and the Shanghai Party Committee's Propaganda Department. They also were skilled in intellectual debate but differed from the older intellectuals in that they had a more Marxist-oriented education and were lower in the intellectual hierarchy. Thus their opposition was generational as well as ideological. The arguments, rhetoric, and symbols used by the radical intellectuals in rebutting the older intellectuals in 1963–1964 provided the ideological foundation for the Cultural Revolution. Using similarly indirect methods, they expressed the views of their mentor that socialist transformation of the economy did not transform bourgeois ideology. Therefore, it was necessary to wage ideological class struggle against bourgeois ideas and values that prevailed in the intellectual establishment and the party bureaucracy. As the older intellectuals expressed the consensus of the educational elite, the younger intellectuals expressed another consensus—genuine socioeconomic grievances of a segment of the educated youth against the lack of mobility in the hierarchy and the inequalities between the older, better-trained intellectuals and the younger, less well-trained ones.

When Mao, with the support of the army under Lin Biao, moved the surrogate struggle from the defined limits of an intellectual debate into the open as a political struggle in the Cultural Revolution, the radical intellectuals became the core of the activists. Their prominent role in rebutting the established intellectuals in the early sixties gave them the opportunity to move from the periphery to the center of power in the Cultural Revolution. However, when Mao compromised his revolutionary vision because of outside pressure and an unwillingness to accept its inherent anarchy, the radicals refused to forsake Mao's original call to overthrow authority and establish a new order. As they moved in a more radical direction than Mao in ideology and in practice in 1967–1968, most of them were purged and imprisoned as were the older intellectuals they had attacked. The intellectuals who participated in politics, whether Westernized or radical, party or nonparty, suffered fatal consequences in the Cultural Revolution. Even some intellectuals who had not taken an active role in politics were purged or killed or forced to commit suicide just because they were intellectuals. Virtually a whole generation of intellectuals was decimated. The institutions they helped to establish—universities, research institutes, journals, libraries, and theater companies—were also decimated. The destruction of China's cultural life was so widespread that it would take generations to repair.

Post-Mao Policy Toward Intellectuals and the Intellectuals' Response

The emerging pattern of the party's policy toward the intellectuals and the intellectuals' response in the post-Mao era in some respects resembles that of the Soviet Union in the post-Stalin era. The indiscriminate terror and massive coercion of the antirightist and Cultural Revolution campaigns have given way, as they did in the Soviet Union, to a mixture of cajolery, manipulation, and intimidation. As in the past, a small number of intellectuals continue to express criticism through official channels, but, more like the Soviet Union, some also express criticism through unofficial channels. Still, as in the past, neither official nor unofficial dissent is possible without some degree of official sanction.

As in the Maoist era, the post-Mao leadership has sought to win the intellectuals' cooperation in repairing the devastation of the previous campaign and to use the intellectuals in factional rivalries by allowing them to speak out and criticize in the fashion of the Hundred Flowers Campaign and the early 1960s. This time Deng Xiaoping has used them against Maoist holdovers in the Politburo. In 1978–1979, a spontaneous, grass-roots response burst forth that resembled similar protests in the Soviet Union but that also was not unique in the People's Republic of China. There have been a number of earlier precedents: the large-scale demonstrations and unofficial pamphlets on university campuses in May 1957; the Shengwulian manifesto by suppressed Red Guards in 1967 (upholding the utopian revolutionary vision from which Mao had retreated); the Li Yiche poster in 1974 written by a group of young students in the midst of the anti-Confucian campaign (denouncing the cult of the personality and echoing some of the socialist democratic principles espoused in the Hundred Flowers Campaign); and the Tiananmen demonstration of workers, students, and intellectuals of 5 April 1976 against Mao's radical policies and in support of Zhou Enlai's and Deng Xiaoping's more pragmatic policies. However, these protests were singular events and were suppressed very quickly.

What was different in 1978–1979 was that the protest was nationwide. In contrast to earlier protests that took place primarily in urban areas and university centers, this unofficial protest took place in the countryside as well as in the cities. Moreover, it lasted much longer. Its heyday was from the fall of 1978 to the spring of 1979. This seething underground protest was allowed to explode aboveground for a period of time because open condemnation of Mao had not yet become official and because Deng used it in his battle with the remnant Maoists. Equally important, it expressed the wide and deep revulsion of officials as well as nonofficials against Mao's use of terror and chaos as an instrument of rule.

The 1978–1979 protest movement had many of the same trappings as the Soviet underground movement in the post-Stalin era. It circulated hand-to-hand stories, poems, petitions, magazines, and documents. It put up wall posters and made contact with foreign journalists in order to publicize its cause. Like its Soviet counterparts, it attacked the supreme former leader and demanded laws that protected human rights. Although the demands for greater cultural and political freedoms were similar to those of the Hundred Flowers Campaign, the protesters of 1978–1979 called for regularized institutions and legal procedures to guarantee these freedoms and to prevent the lawlessness and chaos they had experienced in the antirightist and Cultural Revolution campaigns. The emphasis was not so much on moral appeals to the leaders for moderation and self-restraint, as in the Hundred Flowers Campaign, but on laws to protect civil liberties and prevent arbitrary treatment.

Within this general framework, the 1978–1979 protest was a heterogeneous movement more in the mold of the Soviet underground movement than in the more ideologically orthodox semiofficial form of Chinese dissent. It was produced by the Cultural Revolution and led to a wide range of views on how to prevent a reoccurrence of the Cultural Revolution. Some wanted traditional Marxism cleansed of Maoism. Others wanted Western-style democracy combined with a socialist economy. Some stressed cultural pluralism; others stressed economic pragmatism. However, unlike in the Soviet Union, there were few religious or ethnic dissenters and, with the exception of individuals like the human rights activist Wei Jingwei, few rejected the prevailing political system outright. Most expressed a different opinion or alternative view within a Marxist-Leninist context, perhaps because they knew no other context. Similar to the semiofficial Chinese dissenters, they were like a loyal opposition, addressing their messages to the political elite and trying to influence public opinion in order to change or negate certain policies.

As in the Soviet underground, the roots of the dissent were in the dissenters' own personal experiences or those of close relatives who suffered persecution and injustice. But the Chinese dissenters differed from the Soviet dissenters in that they did not include eminent intellectuals with the prestige of a Sakharov or a Solzhenitsyn. They were led by unknown younger workers and students who, but for the Cultural Revolution, would have been intellectuals. Many were children of middle- and upper-level cadres and intellectuals who were deprived of a university education and sent to work in factories and the countryside. Some had known one another as Red Guards; others met at their place of work. They were without much expectation of higher education and were working in jobs incommensurate with their aspirations. David S. G. Goodman has called them "the underprivileged privileged," an apt phrase to describe the potentially most revolutionary group in any system.[4] However, after the Maoist segment was purged from the Politburo and these youths were demanding more democracy as a prerequisite for modernization—and a few were denouncing the Chinese invasion of Vietnam—the protest movement was quickly and harshly suppressed. Some of its leaders were imprisoned; Wei Jingwei was sentenced to fifteen years.

Although the "underprivileged privileged" have been forced underground once again, it is likely that if a crisis occurs they will burst forth as they have in the past, either through official sanction or spontaneously, if only momentarily. Yet despite the publicity given such unofficial protests, they are marginal movements. Though they may have many sympathizers, the number of *active* participants even in the 1978–1979 movement was no more than several thousand youths who could easily be suppressed.

The more traditional semiofficial dissent continued and was more difficult to repress. This form of dissent was published in the most prestigious national newspapers and journals such as *Renmin Ribao, Guangming Ribao,* and *Renmin Wenxue,* and its exponents were some of China's most eminent writers. In the immediate post-Mao era, literature, as in traditional times and in the Soviet Union, was the principal means for expressing dissent. It began with stories, plays, and poems on the officially approved topic of persecution by the Gang of Four during the Cultural Revolution. These works came to be called the "literature of the wounded," after a story written by a Fudan University student, Lu Xinhua, about a young woman who suffers because of her blind faith in the regime. But by the fall of 1979, this genre had become outmoded as the mood of the nation turned more to the present and future than to the past. It was replaced by a more controversial genre, "exposure" literature, in which the injustices, social ills, corruption, and official privileges were blamed no longer only on the Cultural Revolution activists and the Gang of Four, but also on those presently in power and those in power before the Cultural Revolution. In the tradition of Lu Xun and the May Fourth writers, this literature exposed the abuses in society in order that they might be corrected.

An example of this genre in the theater was *If I Were Real,* written by three members of the Cultural Revolution generation and patterned on Gogol's *Inspector General.* The play depicts a young man who deceives officials in Shanghai by pretending to be the son of a high military officer in Beijing. Because of his supposed good connections, the young man is granted all kinds of privileges, from theater tickets to having a friend released from prison. When he is finally caught, he protests that he has done nothing wrong. He explains: "If I were really the son of some high party official, then whatever I would have done would be considered legal."[5] Thus the play went beyond criticism of the Gang of Four to criticize the prevailing system, which promoted such abuses due to the extraordinary power of its officials. Though the leadership itself called for criticism of bureaucratism, the play was banned shortly after it opened.

Some of the most daring exponents of the "exposure" genre have been the writers who burst forth in the Hundred Flowers Campaign and were purged in the antirightist campaign. Closer to the May Fourth era than the younger writers, they have also been more willing to take risks than the older May Fourth writers who were so active before 1949.

Such older writers as Ai Qing, Ding Ling, and Cao Yu, victims of campaigns since the early 1940s, were too old and too broken to seek anything more than peace and security. These Hundred Flowers writers had been silenced for virtually twenty years, not by the Gang of Four, but by the very people in power when they were rehabilitated in the late seventies. They sought to expose the system that allowed the Cultural Revolution to happen. The army writer, Bai Hua, in the Confucian and May Fourth tradition, called on his fellow writers at the Fourth Writers and Artists Congress in 1979 to fulfill their "sacred duty" of courageously criticizing the abuses of officialdom.[6] In his scenario *Bitter Love,* he depicts an artist who returns home from abroad out of a feeling of patriotism. But he is persecuted in the Cultural Revolution and finally dies a hunted criminal. In one scene, his daughter questions him: "You love your motherland, but does your motherland love you?" This line and the scenario were interpreted as expressing disillusionment not only with the Cultural Revolution but with China's political system.

Another former rightist who has been active in the post-Mao period is Wang Meng, author of the controversial story "New Man in the Organization Department," published in 1956. However, his dissent has taken a different form than in the Hundred Flowers Campaign. He dissents artistically rather than ideologically. He writes less of political issues and more of the emotions and relationships of everyday life and experiments with a variety of styles. As Leo Lee has pointed out, with the few exceptions of Lu Xun and some experimental poets working in their own styles, even before the party prescribed socialist realism the nineteenth-century Western realist style with a social message had dominated Chinese writers, ever since the twenties and thirties.[7] Wang Meng, more than any other established writer, has attempted to break the bounds of the realistic narrative and experiment with intricate language and stream of consciousness to evoke memories, inner feelings, and random associations. To be artistically apolitical in a society in which politics permeates every aspect of life is a rejection of political interference in one's creative work. However, in the post-Mao era, the party has encouraged greater leeway in style than in content, as if this concession might placate the writers.

Artistic dissent is safer than ideological dissent. Nevertheless, Wang Meng explained at the 1979 Fourth Writers and Artists Congress that his less politically oriented approach was based on his belief that concern with political issues in literature stultifies the writer's ability to express human emotions and create artistic works. It could be that Wang Meng's more artistic, seemingly safer approach might lead others to experiment with new techniques and will stimulate a new outburst of creativity. Moreover, it is an indirect challenge to the party's politicization of culture. Yet, can a writer who experiments artistically but continues to express the party's view of society and human relationships be truly creative?

Another former rightist, Liu Binyan, presented just the opposite view at the Fourth Writers and Artists Congress. He upheld the May Fourth tradition that literature should continue to expose the ills of society. He also harked back to the early sixties' literary presentation of the peasant as caught between revolutionary ideals and harsh realities. Describing his own experience of being sent down to the countryside in the antirightist campaign, he charged that writers had falsified the life of the peasant by not depicting its difficulties and bitterness and ignoring the indifference of the officials to peasant suffering. In the manner of his Confucian predecessors, he exhorted his fellow writers to assume their "responsibility" by telling the truth. He denounced those who would "break the mirror" rather than correct the ugliness it reflected.[8]

Liu's mirror in the post-Mao era, as in the Hundred Flowers Campaign, has reflected the ugliness of the new class of officials spawned by the Communist system. But whereas in the Hundred Flowers Campaign he presented enthusiastic, idealistic youth who struggled against cynical, opportunistic officials, his most controversial work of the post-Mao era, "Between Men and Monsters," published in 1979, focuses on corrupt bureaucrats. In the form of an investigative report—"reportage literature"—he has described a female official who uses her connections (guangxi) and a widespread system of corruption to embezzle huge sums of public money to build her own financial empire in which party officials are obedient to her rather than to the party. Hers is a powerful political and economic organization, unrestrained by any laws, institutions, or moral code. His description recalls Lu Xun's condemnation of traditional society as "man-eating." Liu wrote: "Party cadres were gradually transformed into parasites who devour the people's flesh and blood."[9] Moreover, unlike the "wounded literature," the phenomenon Liu describes is not just the aberration of the Cultural Revolution but is inherent in the system: "The Communist Party regulated everything, but would not regulate the Communist Party."[10] As opposed to Liu's earlier works and as opposed to the renewed party policy in the late seventies that literature should present socialist realistic heroes, no idealistic hero came forth to rectify the system. The future as well as the present in Liu's work was bleak.

"Between Men and Monsters" supposedly was in line with Deng Xiaoping's efforts to reform the bureaucracy. However, by the early eighties, as the aftereffects of the Cultural Revolution subsided and as the Deng Xiaoping leadership consolidated its power, the party no longer wanted such critical works. The "crisis of the socialist spirit," which the party initially attributed to the Cultural Revolution, intensified with Deng's reforms rather than diminished as the party had anticipated.

Fitfully in 1980 and repeatedly by 1981 the party charged that literary works were exaggerating the gloom, weariness, and cynicism within the population and were spreading a feeling of utter hopelessness. As in the Maoist era, literary works were singled out as examples to be criticized and held responsible for the ills of society. Specifically, *If I Were Real* and particularly *Bitter Love* were blamed for inducing disillusionment with the system. As always, political factionalism was involved. The initial attack on *Bitter Love* was by the army newspaper *Liberation Army Daily* in April 1981, and it was not until August 1981 that the party newspapers fully joined the attack. But in the intervening months, as the epithets against these works, such as "bourgeois liberalism," grew louder and more frequent, it became evident that the party leadership also was increasingly concerned with the continuing disrespect for authority and growing Western influence.

Although this concern subsided somewhat in 1982 and early 1983, it surfaced again in a campaign launched in the fall of 1983 against "spiritual pollution," which party leaders attributed to increased contact with the West. The leaders were particularly concerned with Western ideas that evoked questioning of the party and its policies. Thus, they attacked Sartre's existentialism, Kafka's antiauthoritarianism, and even some views associated with Marx, such as his theory of alienation. They also attacked a number of Chinese ideologists such as the cultural czar Zhou Yang, writers such as the outspoken Wang Ruowang, and journalists such as *Renmin Ribao* editor Wang Roushui for criticizing bureaucratism, injustice, corruption, and social ills in present-day China. They charged that instead of solving the problems of Chinese society, the discussion of these issues had caused confusion and weakened unity. As opposed to the 1981 campaign against Bai Hua, this campaign was not restricted to literary circles; it was carried out on a nationwide scale in all the media and in factories and youth groups, signifying the support of the top leadership. Like the 1981 campaign, this campaign was involved with factional conflict. The old guard party leaders such as Peng Zhen and Chen Yun pushed the campaign, fearing dilution of party control, whereas the younger leaders such as Hu Yaobang and Zhao Ziyang sought to limit it, fearing its negative effect on the reforms. When the campaign got out of hand and was used against the economic reforms, Deng Xiaoping swung his support to the younger leaders and the campaign was gradually brought to an end in early 1984. Thus the post-Mao leadership, although its approach is more moderate and more selective, has resorted to the old Maoist methods of campaign and suppression against the Western pluralistic ideas and their exponents because the Chinese leaders fear erosion of the ideological unity on which the one-party state is based.

The campaigns of the early eighties were much more restrained than those of the Maoist era. They lacked the ideological fervor and mass mobilization of earlier campaigns. Whereas in the past the targets and their associates, as well as their works, were condemned, this time only the individual's works were criticized. The writers continued to write and be published. One of the authors of *If I Were Real,* Sha Yexin, produced another play, Bai Hua was awarded a prize for his poetry, and Zhou Yang and Wang Roushui continued to publish. Moreover, whereas in the past all of one's colleagues turned against the individual under attack, this time few of Bai Hua's colleagues participated. A number of Zhou Yang's old enemies criticized him, but others of his colleagues held back, though few wrote articles in his defense. Furthermore, not all the media criticism was consistent. Whereas the *Liberation Army Daily* repudiated *Bitter Love* repeatedly and harshly, other journals such as *Wenyi Bao* and the media of some of the provincial journals avoided sweeping repudiation. Similar inconsistencies occurred in the spiritual pollution campaign. Yet the effect of even limited campaigns put pressure on writers, editors, journalists, and even nonliterary intellectuals to conform and be less daring.

The party's semicampaign against Bai Hua and its interrupted campaign against spiritual pollution did not signify a lessening of its will to prevent any challenge to its authority, but it did signify a concern that the kind of wide-ranging, intensive campaigns of the past might incapacitate the intellectuals needed for modernization. Even though writers and ideologists may be expendable in industrialization and scientific development, the way in which the party treats them may affect the response of the scientists and technicians. The latter may be less willing to participate actively in modernization if they fear that they will be treated like the writers. Thus, even though the party once again repressed dissent when it threatened political stability and party power, it did not resort to the kind of disruptive, arbitrary campaign of the past for fear of paralyzing all intellectuals. Instead it used the more restrained, selective method used in the Soviet Union of choosing a few intellectuals as examples to keep the whole intellectual community under control. If the limits of the permissible are still wider than at any time since the Hundred Flowers Campaign, the attack on Bai Hua and on spiritual pollution narrowed the limits from what was allowed in the late seventies. Specific bureaucratic defects may be criticized, but not the political system itself, which must be depicted as leading the nation toward a glorious socialist future.

The Future of Intellectual Dissent

Intellectual dissent in the People's Republic of China is not the product of a particular moment in history or the result of the personal qualities of individual dissidents. It is a structural phenomenon inherent in Confucian tradition and the Communist commitment to modernization. The need for intermittant relaxations with their accompanying expressions of criticism has kept alive the tradition of semiofficial dissent. The party cannot simply crush the intellectual dissidents without alienating the educated elite needed for modernization.

The intellectual critics have no real power or mass base. Even the great majority of the educated elite are products of a tradition and current political system that primarily fears anarchy and accepts the monopoly of political power. Nevertheless, in the limited, fragmented intervals of relative relaxation, the intellectual dissenters have expressed the criticisms, frustrations, and aspirations of the intellectual and professional elite as a whole. At the same time they have continued to examine public issues and influence public opinion as they have throughout Chinese history.

Although the party regards any criticism of the party as a challenge to its political power, it would be incorrect to judge a group's influence by the party's reaction to it. However, the fact that the party deploys enormous resources to discredit a small group of dissenters demonstrates that the dissenters have important social roots. Moreover, the fact that despite increasingly devastating campaigns against them, the dissenters reemerge periodically, reflects a resilient, vital movement beneath the surface of conformity and coercion.

Because there are no laws or institutions to protect dissident intellectuals and no rules that define permissable criticism, the intellectuals, as in the past, will be allowed to speak out only at the party's discretion. Nevertheless, history seldom repeats itself. Mao, with his charismatic leadership and particular animus against the intellectuals, is gone. The party's cyclical policy toward intellectuals will continue, but the shifts may be more moderate. It is unlikely that nationwide campaigns against intellectuals as a group will be carried out with the ideological fervor and intensity of the past because they are so disruptive to economic modernization. The party still has the power to isolate, discredit, and coerce a self-criticism from any intellectual it wishes, for its own political purposes, as it did with Bai Hua in 1981 and Zhou Yang in 1983. But this is a more selective instrument of control than the massive, arbitrary, and sometimes terrorizing campaigns of the past. Moreover, since Mao's death, China has been more open to the West for a longer period than in any previous relaxation. There has been an influx of Western learning and scholars and an efflux of Chinese intellectuals to the West. The skepticism engendered by radical shifts of policy, together with the expression of semiofficial and unofficial dissent with the policies of past decades, makes it unlikely that the party will be able to impose the kind of monolithic ideological control that existed in the early years of the regime.

Although they do not represent the mainstream and have evolved in a different framework than in the West, a small number of intellectuals continue to express political dissent, loyal opposition, nonconformity, and even individuality in the People's Republic of China. As long as the party's goal remains modernization, the dissenters are likely to increase in numbers and become more outspoken because the party cannot completely repress them without jeopardizing modernization. Yet to give the dissenters too much leeway would jeopardize party control. Although the degree of arbitrariness and terror may lessen, as long as the Communist party rules China, it will be locked in an inextricable and troubled relationship with China's intellectuals.

Notes

1. Hualing Nieh, *Literature of the Hundred Flowers* (New York: Columbia University Press, 1981) vol. 1, p. 47.

2. Roderick MacFarquhar, *The Hundred Flowers* (Atlantic Books), p. 51.

3. Deng Tuo, "Is Wisdom Reliable?" *Yanshan Yehua* (Hong Kong), vol. 4, pp. 17–19.

4. David S. G. Goodman, *Beijing Street Voices: The Poetry and Politics of China's Democracy Movement* (London: Marion Boyars, 1981).

5. *Chishi Niandai* [*The Seventies*], published monthly in Hong Kong, no. 1 (1980), p. 9. See also *China News Analysis,* no. 1205 (24 April 1981).

6. Howard Goldblatt, ed., *Chinese Literature for the 1980s* (Armonk, New York: M. E. Sharpe, Inc.), pp. 56–67.

7. Leo Ou-fan Lee, "Technique as Dissidence: A Perspective of Contemporary Chinese Fiction," paper given at the Conference on Contemporary Chinese Literature, St. John's University, New York, 28–31 May 1982.

8. Goldblatt, *Chinese Literature for the 1980s,* p. 107.

9. Liu Binyan, *Baogao Wenxue Xuan* (Beijing: Chubanshe, 1981), p. 162. "Between Men and Monsters" first appeared in *Renmin Wenxue,* no. 8, p. 197, translated in *People or Monsters,* ed. Perry Link (Bloomington: Indiana University Press, 1984).

10. Link, p. 43.

17
Chinese Communist Party Policy Toward Intellectuals Since 1949: A Critical Analysis

Byung-joon Ahn

No other issue better illustrates the basic dilemma for a Communist party in simultaneously building socialism and promoting modernization than its policy toward intellectuals. The evidence is clearly discernible in the policy that the Chinese Communist party (CCP) has pursued toward intellectuals since 1949. In general, when the party stresses revolution or building socialism, its policy tends to make intellectuals the targets for ideological remolding. But when the party stresses modernization, its policy tends to elicit their support by allowing greater freedom for their activities. Since the death of Mao, the CCP has taken the latter approach—the middle of the road between dogmatic control and unlimited liberalization.

The "intellectuals" are those who deal with ideas and knowledge and who—more specifically—are engaged in science and technology, education, and art and literature. The "policy" toward them is comprised of the basic stand and the concrete course of action that the party takes with regard to these people. It is a central theme of this essay that the CCP's policy toward intellectuals alternated between two lines until Mao's death: what Mao consistently advocated and what his opponents preferred. Since his death, however, the policy has ceased to be dichotomized and has tended to diversify into more complex directions that are quite difficult to identify, even though the party's basic policy line has reverted to the one adopted at the Eighth CCP Congress in 1956.

Within these broad observations, we can try to account for changes in the CCP's policy toward intellectuals and examine the influence of change upon the party's different sources of legitimacy. While Mao was alive, the primary base for party legitimacy was the commitment to transform Chinese society into a socialist utopia according to the dictates of Marxist-Leninist ideology as Mao had defined it. After Mao passed away, however, his successors have regarded the accomplishment of modernization as the primary goal of the party; hence, the bases for legitimacy have multiplied as the exigencies and results of the modernization program have posed major constraints for party policy. It is in this changed context that the role of Chinese intellectuals is being redefined; the new leadership is trying to build a new ruling coalition and a new consensus best suited to the task. But one thing still remains constant: the party continues to determine for the intellectuals the limits of their acceptable activities.

The Party and Intellectuals: An Overview

Tensions are inevitable between the party and intellectuals because of their divergent expectations of each other's roles. Basically, the party wants to control and utilize the intellectuals in order to advance its legitimacy and to solve imminent problems. However, the intellectuals want to be free from party control and seek their own professional, academic, and artistic goals. The party is a highly organized entity, whereas the intellectuals are not necessarily attached to a single organization even in the Communist system. It is rare, therefore, that these two maintain a harmonious or synchronized relationship.

The precise state of the party-intellectual relationship is predicated upon the context within which it was established. During the Maoist era, the party's policy was designed to change the values shared by the old intellectuals who had been active before 1949 and to educate (socialize) in the Communist ideology those who had begun their intellectual activities since 1949. The scientists, professors, writers, and most other intellectuals sought to accommodate themselves to this party policy. Intervening in this interaction were the elite politics within which Mao often waged intense power struggles with his opponents.

The relationship between the party and intellectuals in the Maoist era was characterized by swings or cycles back and forth between two models. For lack of better terms, we call the first one Maoist and the second one non-Maoist. As shown in Table 17.1, there were significant differences in the party's policy toward intellectuals under these two models, although differences were largely a matter of degree rather than kind.

The contrast between the Maoist and the non-Maoist models derives from different perceptions of the party's task, the status of intellectuals, and the means of control. The Maoists regarded class struggle as the party's main task in the "socialist period," during which the party had to concentrate its efforts on transforming the "productive relations" and the superstructure into socialist ones to ensure that China would never change back to the old capitalist society. Under this notion, the intellectuals became part of the superstructure, a bourgeois element who had to be struggled against. In fact, Mao consistently called for the political education of intellectuals as a precondition for undertaking socialist transformation, and to achieve this central goal, he repeatedly

Table 17.1 Two Models of Party Policy

	Maoist	Non-Maoist
General trends		
Party line	Class struggle	Modernization
Status of intellectuals	Superstructure	Productive forces
Means of control	Ideological campaign and coercion	Professional autonomy and persuasion
Science and Technology		
Party line	Applied research	Basic research
Status of intellectuals	Popularization	Professionalization
Means of control	Politicization	Professional autonomy
Education		
Party line	Work-study equality	Quality of study
Status of intellectuals	None: "open schools"	Selection by examination
Means of control	Worker control	Professorial autonomy
Art and literature		
Party line	Revolutionary	Free choice
Status of intellectuals	Conformity	Diversity
Means of control	Party control	Partial autonomy

called upon the party to undertake ideological campaigns or "thought reform." In theory, these campaigns were to be conducted in the form of criticism and self-criticism, but in practice, physical or at least psychological coercion was invariably used as a means to control the ideologically undesirable. Two prototypes of these campaigns were the antirightist campaign along with the Great Leap Forward in 1958–1959 and the Cultural Revolution and its aftermath in 1966–1976.

The non-Maoists presented a different model. According to their views, after China had completed agricultural collectivization and industrial nationalization, class struggle was basically over. Hence, the party's main task was to accomplish modernization by rapidly developing the "productive forces" so that China could overcome her economic backwardness as soon as possible. In this view, the intellectuals became part of the productive forces; the party had to seek their support and participation in the modernization process. To secure such participation, the party could not help but grant them a degree of professional autonomy. If they had to be controlled, persuasion rather than coercion was suggested. As for the party's stand on class struggle, Liu Shaoqi elaborated the view already summarized above in his report to the Eighth CCP Congress in 1956 and Hu Yaobang reaffirmed it in his report on party history to the Sixth Plenum in June 1981. For the intellectuals, the Hundred Flowers Campaign in May 1957 and its revival in 1978–1979 approximated this model.

From these general models the more refined policies applied to scientists, educators, and artists can be delineated. For science and technology, for example, the Maoists favored a utilitarian model. By emphasizing the importance of applied research, they sought to maximize the results of science and technology to meet China's immediate needs; they placed greater emphasis on mobilizing existing knowledge and technology than on producing more—and on developing appropriate technology for the masses. Mao often called for "popularization" of science and technology in such a way that the peasants and workers could learn from the scientists and vice versa. In implementing this policy, the Maoists called on party committees or workers to assume leadership over scientists and technicians. Under this arrangement the scientists and technicians had to carry out physical labor under party or worker supervision; as a result, science was highly politicized.

The non-Maoists' ideal of science was a professional model whereby basic research, specialization, and autonomy were stressed. They appreciated the importance of basic and pure research for scientific discoveries and technical inventions, and they favored specialization in research so that the scientists in each field could occupy themselves with pursuing their own interests and satisfying their theoretical curiosity. To permit the scientists to do their work without being influenced by extraneous forces, the non-Maoists wanted the party to allow a maximum degree of autonomy in the governance of scientific activities.

In many ways, the party's education policy paralleled its science policy. The Maoists selected policy instruments designed to enhance equality in education for all. Both in his 6 May 1966 letter to Lin Biao and his 27 July 1968 comment on the Shanghai Machine Tool Company, for example, Mao asked professors, teachers, and students to combine work and study at all levels. This idea was also reflected in the admission policy for universities. The "open school" system enabled workers, peasants, and soldiers to enter universities without taking examinations. In fact, the Maoists let the outsiders control the educators by encouraging the workers and peasants to assume leadership over the professors and teachers.

By contrast, the non-Maoists favored policy instruments designed to enhance quality education. They stressed full-time and regular studies and supported the "two tracks" of academic and vocational schools. To maintain academic standards and excellence, they defended the selection of students by examinations. And to protect some degree of academic freedom in pedagogics, they emphasized respect for the authority of professors and teachers. The professors were supposed to govern their universities.

The CCP's policy toward artists and writers was more controversial than that in any other area. The Maoists consistently espoused revolutionary art and literature. Mao laid down this theme in his *Talk at the Yenan Forum on Art and Literature* in 1942. Art and literature were to be subordinated to the revolutionary tasks prescribed by the party. Artists and writers had to select their topics so as to portray the contemporary lives of workers, peasants, and soldiers. In the name of socialist realism, the artists and writers were asked to portray or describe heroic or, at least, positive aspects of life instead of darker or negative aspects; in effect, they were called upon to conform with the party's instructions. The party thus not only supervised but directly interfered in artistic and literary activities.

The non-Maoists advocated humanistic art and literature. Even though they also supported party control, they were more disposed toward giving artists and writers a certain degree of free choice so that the latter could depict human nature without too much inhibition. Overall, the non-Maoists called for more diversity in the selection of topics and forms so that the artists could portray not only socialist themes but others, including traditional ones. In effect, this policy was more conducive to permitting professional autonomy among the artistic and literary associations.

These two models contended with each other until 1976. Since then, the non-Maoist or a similar model has been sought by the CCP even though the details of the party's policy and the way in which the policy has been effected are different from those of the non-Maoist model before 1976. Significantly, there has been no swing back to the Maoist model. As of 1982 it appears that the party is trying to reach consensus in response to the demands emanating from the intellectual circle. As we shall see, the CCP's current policy approaches a middle ground between the two preexisting policies in their simplified form as described above.

It should be clear that the non-Maoist model is the one the majority of intellectuals support. When some members of the intellectual community speak for variants of these models, it usually means that they have some powerful backers at the top level of the party hierarchy. When party policy in the past shifted from one model to the other, it indicated a power struggle and the related viability of a given policy.

Party Policy in the Maoist Era, 1949–1976

During the Maoist era (1949–1976), Mao and his supporters tried to have the CCP adopt their preferred policy. But this effort was often resisted or even sabotaged by those party leaders and intellectuals who seriously disagreed with the Maoist policy. When Mao set out to impose his ideas on the party and they became party policy, they had to undergo a process of "reality testing" in practice, interacting with China's own reality. In the course of this interaction, Mao often encountered setbacks, causing such stiff resistance within the party that he frequently found it impossible to continue to press his original ideas. In such cases he either retreated temporarily from his position or let other associates take command of party policy, but whenever he judged that policy unacceptable, he came back and sought to change it by engaging in campaign after campaign.

Table 17.2 Cycles of Party Policy, 1949-1976

Policy Development	Period
1. Three- and Five-Anti Campaigns	1949-1953
2. First Five-Year Plan with thaw in relations with intellectuals	1953-1954
3. Anti-Hu Feng campaign	1954-1956
4. Hundred Flowers Campaign	1956-1957
5. Antirightist campaign and Great Leap Forward	1957-1960
6. Adjustment and Notes from the Three-Family Village	1960-1962
7. Rectification in science, education, and cultural circles	1962-1966
8. Cultural Revolution	1966-1971
9. Anti-Lin Biao campaign and modernization	1971-1973
10. Anti-Lin Biao, anti-Confucius, and anti-Water Margin campaigns	1973-1976

From such processes a number of cycles affecting the CCP's policy toward intellectuals occurred after 1949. As shown in Table 17.2 we can discern at least ten such cycles.

Within the party's policy toward intellectuals, the policy for natural scientists was the least controversial, and that for artists and writers the most controversial. During the formative years of the People's Republic in 1949–1953, the CCP applied a double-edged policy: inducing many intellectuals to cooperate with the cause of communism, and reeducating those who refused to do so. In the name of "new democracy," Mao actually welcomed collaborating intellectuals as partners in building the new republic, keeping in mind that there were not many educated people. But in the wake of land reform at home and the Korean War abroad, he switched to the policy of restricting the activities of intellectuals through the Three- and Five-Anti Campaigns that were followed by the "suppression of counterrevolutionaries" campaign in 1950–1953.

While the CCP was making preparations in 1953–1954 for the First Five-Year Plan in China's economy, it sought to emulate the Soviet example of highly professionalized scientific, educational, and literary institutions. Such efforts brought about a thaw in the party's campaigns directed at the intellectual community, but this thaw turned out to be short-lived. It was followed in 1954–1956 by the campaign criticizing Yü Pingho and Hu Feng. Yü was accused of having defended "art for art's sake" in his critique of the *Dream of the Red Chamber;* the critique also represented an indirect attack on Hu Shih because Yü had studied under Hu Shih. Hu Feng was said to have demanded literature portraying human life without the constraint of party policy, arguing that if socialist realism means Marxism, then literature must in effect be destroyed.[1] The anti-Hu Feng campaign branded this view as a "bourgeois poison," creating a chilling atmosphere for the intellectuals.

The atmosphere began to change again as the party slowly eased its control in 1956–1957 by initiating a new slogan: Let One Hundred Flowers Bloom and Let One Hundred Schools Contend. In a report to the National People's Congress in January 1956, Zhou Enlai signaled this new policy when he said that the majority of 3,840,000 intellectuals were either favorably disposed or neutral toward socialism.[2] Lu Dingyi, director of the Party Propaganda Department, revealed the gist of a speech Mao made in May 1956 encouraging comradely criticisms for mistakes existing "among the people." In the aftermath of the Hungarian uprising, Mao further elaborated on this idea in his secret speech of February 1957, in which he called upon nonparty intellectuals to voice their criticisms of the party. Despite the objections of most party leaders to this novel idea, Mao went ahead with the Hundred Flowers Campaign, expecting it to be as "gentle as a breeze or mild rain." When the blooming and contending started in May that year, scientists, professors, students, and writers all complained about the lack of professional autonomy under the "party kingdom" (dang tianxia); eventually they came to challenge the very legitimacy of the Communist party.

Confronted with this storm of dissent, Mao, in an abrupt turnabout, began in June 1957 the antirightist campaign, accusing the dissenting intellectuals of being "ghosts and monsters." When the revised version of his speech of February 1957 was made public, Mao laid down six criteria for criticism; in doing so, he banned any criticism harmful to socialist transformation and the party. Seriously concerned with the possibility of regression in China's revolution, Mao launched another mass movement, the Great Leap Forward. At the peak of this movement in 1958, he directed Chen Boda to start a new party journal, *Red Flag,* to smash what he called the fear of and respect for intellectuals. Amidst calls for "walking on two legs," applied to industry, agriculture, and, in general, mental and physical labor, Mao decreed that nonprofessionals must rule professionals because the masses have been wiser than the intellectuals throughout history![3] In the heat of such mass mobilization zeal, scientists, professors, and writers were sent down to the countryside to till the soil along with the peasants in the newly emerging People's Communes.

Once the Great Leap Forward was recognized as a colossal failure, the party was forced in 1960–1962 to make drastic adjustments and allow some degree of liberalization toward the intellectuals. It was during this period that a considerable number of intellectuals derided the Great Leap Forward as being "a blowing of trumpets and an indulgence in empty talk." Those intellectuals who worked in Beijing under Peng Zhen used the guises of ancient allegories or satires to systematically review the theoretical assumptions underlying the Great Leap Forward and refute them. Wu Han's play, *Hai Rui Dismissed from Office,* was a famous example that ridiculed Mao's firing of Peng Dehuai. The newspaper column *Notes from the Three-Family Village* by Wu Han, Deng Tuo, and Liao Mosha was another example in which these talented writers questioned every premise of the Great Leap Forward as having substituted illusion for reality through wishful thinking. In this translucently masked manner the intellectuals expressed their yearning for a measure of freedom and autonomy for their crafts.

At this time, Zhou Yang must have spoken for these people when he said, "The most serious crime in the world is the rape of the spirit! Literature should observe the spirit of the time, not the orders of an individual. . . . We must not harm people spiritually and throw them into a spiritual prison."[4] Indeed, under the leadership of Lu Dingyi and Zhou Yang, the party revised its policy toward the intellectuals to restore professionalism, quality, and humanism to science, education, and art. Zhou Yang and Jiang Nanxiang, vice-minister of education, formulated a set of regulations governing the natural sciences—the "Fourteen Articles" of February 1962, which were designed to restore orderly conduct in scientific research and a system of ranks and titles based on merit and seniority. In June of that year they drafted a document on education—the "Sixty Articles on Universities," which emphasized regular teaching and research, specialized education, and the authority of teaching staffs over party committees. In April 1962, Zhou Yang produced the "Eight Articles on Literature and Arts," which called for some freedom in choosing artistic forms and themes and warned that politics must not replace art.

About the relationship between politics and art in particular, Chen Yi was most outspoken at the Canton conference on drama in March 1962, where he asked, "If everywhere there are invisible nets, how can I survive?" and answered, "Yes, the netless net is a big net. It kills people! . . . It is this that I must fight against today." On the role of politics, Chen Yi had this to say: "What price is your goodness in politics? Can you sell it to me and can I weigh it for you?"[5] This liberal trend was approved by Liu Shaoqi and Deng Xiaoping, who were in charge of the adjustment policies; actually these top leaders actively invited the contributions of scientists, academics, and writers in order to help the party weather the acute crisis wrought by the Great Leap Forward.

Such liberalization could not last for long unchallenged by Mao. In September 1962, at the Tenth Plenum, he reiterated the thesis that class struggles invariably find their expression within the party in the form of class enemies who seek to create public opinion first before actually overthrowing political power. The years 1962–1966 were a long period during which Mao continued to attempt silencing the challenging voices of the Chinese intellectuals by warning the party never to forget class struggle. During these years a series of debates and conflicts were generated by Mao's demands for rectification in the intellectual community and the Party Propaganda Department's efforts to accommodate to his demands while still trying to preserve most of the adjustment policies of 1960–1962.

In February 1964 Mao's antiintellectual attitude flared up again and he demanded a far-reaching reform in the schooling, teaching, and examination system. This attitude was reflected in his statement that a student would become a bookworm or revisionist if he read too many books. Mao wanted to shorten school years, combine work and study in teaching, and do away with competitive examinations. It was already well known that his wife, Jiang Qing, was working toward reform of art and literature. Together with such supporters as Zhang Chunqiao and Yao Wenyuan, Jiang Qing initiated the movement to reform Peking opera in Shanghai, thus challenging the propaganda authorities in Beijing in 1963–1964. When Lu Dingyi and Zhou Yang tried to moderate her efforts, Mao intervened by endorsing Jiang Qing's activities in June 1964, when he directed the party to carry out a rectification movement in the All China Federation of Literary and Art Circles, arguing that literary associations had already become revisionist like the Hungarian Petofi Club.[6]

Once this directive of Mao was made known, such unknown young Turks as Zi Benyu came out to question the philosophical views of Yang Xianzhen, the middle character thesis of Shao Chuanlin, and the human nature view of Feng Ding. In this way the Maoists raised political questions, but Peng Zhen and Zhou Yang responded with philosophical and artistic discussions. Finally the Maoists directly questioned the political nature of Wu Han's play on Hai Rui in September 1965, and Peng Zhen and Zhou Yang responded again with academic debates, claiming that everybody including Mao was equal before the truth. At last, in May 1966, Mao himself disavowed the February 1962 outline that Peng Zhen had prepared for cultural reforms and authorized the summary of the Forum that the People's Liberation Army prepared, thereby launching the Cultural Revolution to purge those party members and intellectuals who had been sabotaging his cultural policies.

During the Cultural Revolution the Maoist model of science, education, and art was tried again in the form of "newly born things." For example, scientists were sent down again to farms and factories, and research institutes were decentralized under the supervision of peasants and workers. All universities were asked to combine labor and study; their school period was reduced from five to three years; the "open school" concept enabled only those who had at least two years of practical experience and the recommendation of their work units to enter the university; and the so-called Workers Propaganda Teams administered these institutions of higher education. In the field of art and literature, only those eight model operas that Jiang Qing had helped reform were allowed to be performed in slightly different forms for the Chinese people; all other works were banned as "poisonous weeds." Indeed, China at this time became a great school for Chairman Mao's Thought.

As these ideological fervors adversely affected China's economic development and national security, Zhou Enlai attempted to modify some of the radical aspects in 1971–1973. In 1972, for example, he asked

Dr. Zhou Peiyuan, then vice-president of Beijing University and vice-chairman of the Chinese Science and Technological Association, to draft a document on revitalizing basic and pure research at universities and research institutes. At Beijing and Qinghua, regular instruction was resumed and some form of examinations and interviews became required for the applicants to these universities after they had been recommended by their work units. Most important of all, Zhou Enlai brought back Deng Xiaoping to take charge of facilitating these policy reviews.[7]

Seeing these measures as a trend that would reverse the verdicts of the Cultural Revolution, the Jiang Qing faction came out in defense of the "newly born things" by directing oblique attacks at Zhou and Deng under the guise of the campaign against Lin Biao and Confucius. Despite these attacks, Zhou issued his call for the completion of China's modernization in agriculture, industry, national defense, and science and technology by the end of the century, in his report to the National People's Congress in January 1975. As soon as he was restored to the post of vice-premier, Deng took charge of the State Council on Zhou's behalf. Deng directed Hu Yaobang to draft a comprehensive policy outline for the Academy of Sciences in 1975. In Deng's view the academy was neither "one of cabbage nor of beans but one concerned with sciences."[8] Deploring the phenomena that professors and students did not study, or if they did they did so in secret as if it were a crime, Deng asked Zhou Rongxin, minister of education, to restore academic studies and the authority of professors at universities. He also complained about the model operas as being devoid of interesting stories.

It was against this background that in September 1975 the *People's Daily* opened the veiled campaign criticizing Mao's favorite ancient novel, *Water Margin,* by advancing the new argument that one of the heroes, Song Jiang, betrayed the cause of the rebels by capitulating to the emperor. These insinuations and renewed attacks on Zhou and Deng continued even after Zhou died in January 1976 and Deng disappeared from public view; eventually they precipitated a violent reaction from Zhou and Deng's supporters in the open riot at Tienanmen on 5 April 1976. On this occasion there was a spontaneous expression of poems, one of which read: "We spill over blood in the memory of the hero . . . Gone for good is Qin Shi Huang's feudal society."[9] The ailing Mao blamed Deng for this incident and dismissed him again, appointing Hua Guofeng as premier. Only after Mao died on 9 September 1976 was the Jiang Qing faction purged as the Gang of Four.

In summary, the party's policy in 1949–1976 was characterized by a constant swing back and forth between the policy the Maoists favored and the one the intellectuals and their supporters preferred. Mao defined these interactions in terms of what he called the struggle between the Two Lines: i.e., between the socialist and the capitalist lines. Because Mao himself acted as the final arbiter of conflicts and the final legitimizer of policy, his cult and thought set heavy constraints on the range of party policy. Only when he retreated from active policymaking or when

Table 17.3 Contrasts Between the Maoist Era and the Post-Mao Era

	Maoist Era	Post-Mao Era
1. The party's task	Revolution and modernization	Four Modernizations
2. Policy debate	What to do between the Two Lines	How to achieve modernization: several lines about allocation of resources
3. Party policy	Shifts between two models	No abrupt shift but a middle ground

his policies failed could the party shift to a more liberal policy as manifested in the form of adjustments and consolidation. But during the last years of Mao's life there were some indications that party policy tended to be less coherent, as the elite became involved in factional struggles in anticipation of Mao's death.

Party Policy in the Post-Mao Era, 1976–1982

In the post-Mao era, the party's policy has shown on the whole the thrust of the non-Maoist model, although the detailed application of the model may be different. The new leadership has committed itself against resorting to another campaign like the Cultural Revolution, for many reasons. This may mean that Chinese Communism also has entered a postmobilization stage in which the party is making peace with society.

The CCP's resumption of the non-Maoist model is vindicated by several developments. First, the party not only purged the Gang of Four but immediately launched a campaign criticizing them. Second, the party reversed most of the old verdicts and rehabilitated those cadres including Liu Shaoqi and virtually all the intellectuals who had been persecuted by Mao and his close supporters ever since 1956. Third, the party adopted a formal decision on its history by declaring that Mao had made mistakes since 1956. Fourth—and most importantly—the party leadership is making every effort not to repeat the past excesses and to make the Four Modernizations program succeed. These efforts are comparable to those it made after the Great Leap Forward, during the adjustment period in 1960–1962. In fact, those who were in command of those adjustments, including Deng and Zhou Yang, are again in charge of the current reforms.

Thus, the party posture both toward intellectuals and domestic affairs in general in the post-Mao era shows important differences from the shifting posture in the Maoist era. In turn, these differences have a direct bearing on party policy as shown in Table 17.3.

In the Maoist era, the party was constantly reminded to simultaneously carry out both revolution and modernization. But in the post-Mao era it is seeking mainly to achieve the Four Modernizations while paying lip service to revolution. The policy debates in the Maoist era usually centered on what to do between the Two Lines as Mao defined them, but the debates in the post-Mao era are no longer so simple. Instead they are concerned with the complex problems of how to achieve modernization while developing in several directions the allocation of scarce resources. Political conflicts have also ceased to be between Mao and his opponents but now are waged among the elite themselves and their constituencies, i.e., bureaucracies, groups, and factions. In the Maoist era, the party's policy toward the intellectuals shifted from one to another pattern, but in the post-Mao era it is staying in a middle ground between total party control and complete autonomy. The intellectuals themselves are being co-opted into the party's decision-making arena and are playing increasingly important roles.

As in the Maoist era, however, the party's policy has been a function of power struggle. When Hua Guofeng was directing the campaign against the Gang of Four, the party initially took up the restoration of research institutes and universities by rehabilitating scientists and professors to their original posts. After Deng assumed real power at the Third Plenum in December 1978, he supported the thrust for blooming and contending among students and young writers until a new appraisal of the Tienanmen incident was made. However, when some of the unofficial press used its new freedoms to attack Deng's leadership, he began to crack down on the blooming and contending. Especially in literary circles, the party has reasserted its prerogative in setting the range of acceptable limits since January 1980. What really distinguishes the current policy from that in the Maoist era, therefore, is that the intellectuals are now asked to serve the cause of the Four Modernizations rather than to serve workers, peasants, and soldiers as Mao used to require.

At the outset of the National Science Conference that was convened in March 1978, Deng stressed that intellectuals and scientists should be respected as part of the nation's productive forces. According to his views, the overwhelming majority of intellectuals were of the proletariat; the only difference between them and the workers was in their different roles in the social division of labor.[10] Under Fang Yi's leadership, the CCP reorganized the Chinese Academy of Sciences in such a way that each institute could carry out its professional research work more autonomously, with less interference from the party committee. After Lu Jiaxi, a prominent chemist, became president of the academy in 1980, the academy instituted the Scientific Council to be its decision-making body and the National Science Awards Committee to make recommendations on awarding ranks, titles, and citations.

More important than these changes was the separate establishment of the Chinese Academy of Social Sciences in August 1977 under the leadership of Hu Qiaomu, an economist. Hu told the State Council in July 1978 that the basic political task of the party henceforth was to understand the "objective economic laws" of development.[11] This new academy has resumed research and publications on economics, philosophy, history, and sociology. Even political science is being revived at universities and institutes. Another noteworthy fact is that with the party's approval there have been a growing number of contacts and exchanges between Chinese and foreign scholars in all specialized fields. A conspicuous example was the joint participation of a group of historians from Beijing and another group from Taipei on the same panel (for the first time since 1949) on the 1911 revolution, at the Association for Asian Studies meeting held in Chicago in April 1982.

The March 1978 National Science Conference was followed in April 1978 by the National Educational Conference. Here, too, the message was similar. The new education minister, Liu Xigao, spoke out decisively for the resumption of quality education when he emphasized the importance of regular studies, rigorous examinations, and professorial authority. With this new policy such remnants of the Cultural Revolution as work-study programs, "open schools," and the Workers Propaganda Teams disappeared. Essentially, the school system went back to the pre-1966 system of "double tracks"—one academic and the other vocational. A striking example of elite education is the resurrection of "priority schools" (Zhongdian xuexiao) to which only the most gifted students are directly recruited after passing competitive examinations.

Unlike the policy toward scientists and educators, the party's policy toward artists and writers has become one of the most delicate issues in post-Mao politics, for it is more political in nature. The official line is the blooming of One Hundred Flowers as provided by Article 14 of the 1978 state Constitution. But its actual application has been subject to the political winds blowing at the top level of the party bureaucracy. While the initial criticisms of the Gang of Four were being urged by Hua Guofeng, the party allowed those who had been victimized during the Cultural Revolution to air their grievances, thereby providing the atmosphere for the rise in 1977–1978 of a genre called "scar literature" or "literature of the wounded." Under this category, for example, Liu Xinwu published a story called "Class Teacher" ("Ban zhuren") in July 1977 in *People's Literature* (*Renmin Wenxue*) portraying a young girl who had been a leftist heroine during the Cultural Revolution but later turned into a juvenile delinquent. In Shanghai's *Wenhui Bao* on 11 August 1978, another young writer named Lu Xinhua published "Scar" ("Shanghen"), a story of another young girl who volunteered to leave Shanghai to settle in the countryside and thereby make a clean break with her widowed mother who had been suspected of having betrayed the party. Only after the Gang of Four fell did the girl learn that her mother's crime had been framed up by the Gang of Four, but when she hurried back to Shanghai her mother was dead. While these writings were being published, most of the writers who had been labeled rightists since 1957 were rehabilitated. In November 1978, the Tienanmen incident was officially declared to have been correct.

It was at the Third Plenum in December 1978 that Deng called upon the intellectuals to "emancipate their minds" and to break into previously forbidden zones so that they all could make positive contributions to the party's new task. Responding to this was an unprecedented explosion of publications including the unofficial press and wall posters. In the diversity of opinions expressed, some welcomed the "scar literature," others were opposed to it, and still others wanted to go beyond it to complete democracy. What made these lively debates possible was the new emphasis that the party placed on "seeking truth from facts." As a result, all sorts of ideas and news were recorded on Xidan Wall or Democracy Wall in Beijing. Many young writers published their works in a growing number of unofficial journals. A most famous example of such a journal was *Exploration* (*Tansuo*); an editor of this journal, Wei Jingsheng, courageously advocated a "Fifth Modernization," i.e., democracy. Wei was arrested in March and brought to trial in October, attesting to the changing political balance within the CCP in 1979. In June, for example, an obscure writer named Li Jian published an article, "Praise and Shame," in *Hebei Literature and Art* to argue that any writer who fails to praise Chairman Mao is shameful. Many critics refuted this stand and dubbed its supporters the "whatever" faction.[12]

The Fourth Congress of Literary and Art Workers in November 1979 provided a forum for discussing these views. Zhou Yang apparently took charge of literary policy again and Huang Zhen, minister of culture, assumed administration. Discouraging both "extreme dogmatism" and "bourgeois liberalism," Zhou at this congress tried to offer a middle ground. Just as Mao Zedong Thought was not a panacea for the economy, as Hu Qiaomu pointed out, neither could it offer a ready-made solution to all problems in art and literature, according to Zhou Yang. He also commented favorably on China's long cultural traditions. Responding to this straightforwardness, several contemporary writers expressed their candid views at this congress. Bai Hua, for example, pointed out the potential danger that intellectuals might again be suppressed when they revealed their innermost thoughts; he nevertheless defended making "breakthroughs" in literature. Liu Binyan was most forthright when he said, "When literature mirrors what is undesirable in life, the mirror itself is not to blame; instead, disagreeable things in real life should be spotted and wiped out. An ugly person cannot be turned into a beauty simply by smashing the mirror."[13] But Liu Xinwu cautioned the writers to be on guard against the extreme Left. It was in this relatively blooming mood that Bai Hua had written his filmscript *Unrequited Love* (*Ku Lian*) in April 1979 and published it in the journal *October* (*Shiyue*) in September 1979, shortly before this congress was held. But the filmscript became a target for criticism in April 1981, as noted below.

After this congress was over, the party slowly began to limit the area of blooming. Apparently the party judged this move necessary to uphold domestic stability as a first priority. The first sign was the closing of Democracy Wall in December 1979. More to the point was a secret speech that Deng made at a Central Work Conference; in it, he laid down four fundamental principles (also known as the "Four Adherences") that all writers must abide by: (1) the socialist road of development, (2) the dictatorship of the proletariat, (3) the CCP's leadership, and (4) Marxism-Leninism-Mao Zedong Thought. In another speech he made on the current situation on 16 January 1980, he deplored those youth who had been infatuated by "bourgeois liberalism" and asked artists and writers to uphold the four principles. On the question of literature and politics, he maintained that literature does not necessarily serve politics, but neither can it be completely divorced from politics. His message seems to be that only when art and literature serve the party's imminent task for the Four Modernizations are they acceptable. At a conference on playwrighting in January-February 1980, Hu Yaobang, then secretary-general of the party's Central Committee, delivered the keynote speech in which he echoed Deng's view on literature and politics and called upon the playwrights to uphold the superiority of socialism and the role of the party in carrying out the Four Modernizations.[14]

What worried the party most was the social impact (shehui xiaoguo) of art and literature. For example, immediately after the January-February conference in 1980, the filmscript *If I Were Real* (*Jiaru wo shi zhende*) received criticisms. The filmscript was a satire depicting the corruption of party officials, and it contained a passage with the message that if one were really a son of a high official, he would be able to do whatever he liked with impunity. Deng, who was busy trying to put together a viable coalition of collective leadership by emphasizing unity and stability, may have feared the negative impact of such muckraking literature on his fragile coalition.

In September 1980, Zhao Ziyang replaced Hua Guofeng as China's premier. The press carried a number of exhortations that literature should serve the people, if not politics, and openly declared that Marxism and humanism were incompatible.[15] At the Central Work Conference in December 1980, Hu Yaobang referred to the need for a "socialist spiritual civilization," perhaps to compensate for the lack of ideological ferver among cadres and intellectuals.

In the spring of 1981, the CCP signaled a change in its policy toward writers when it banned the filmscript by Bai Hua, a People's Liberation Army (PLA) writer. First, the *Liberation Army Daily* published a critique that began by pointing out that Bai Hua's *Unrequited Love* had violated the four principles; then the *People's Daily* reprinted this article.[16] The reprinting may have been an indication that the PLA still contained leftist elements. The filmscript itself was a sad story of an overseas Chinese painter who returned to China out of patriotism, only to be persecuted as a counterrevolutionary during the Cultural Revolution. At one point, his daughter raised a poignant question: "You have loved this country so much . . . but does this motherland love you?" Obviously, this embarrassing question touched upon the very system in which her father was persecuted.

In criticizing Bai Hua, the party took some pains not to turn the criticism into a political campaign. In a speech made in July 1981, Deng distinguished between criticism and "wielding sticks"; he approved of the former but disapproved of the latter.[17] In a speech made in September 1981 on the centennial of Lu Xun's birth, Hu Yaobang, who became the chairman of the party at the Sixth Plenum, also made a distinction between a writer and his work, saying that the former would not be persecuted but the latter would be subject to criticism. Indeed, a mild critique of Bai Hua's work was published in the October issue of *Literary Gazette* (*Wenyi Bao*) by two editors. Then Bai Hua published his self-criticism, apologizing for not having drawn a clear line between the Gang of Four and the socialist motherland, and expressing his gratitude to the party for its guidance.[18] Thus, the party was reaffirmed as the final arbiter of cultural policy. In December 1981 this criticism was declared to have ended, suggesting the advent of a compromise between the party and the cultural community.

In trying not to repeat the excesses perpetrated during the Maoist era, the party under Deng and Hu is seeking to steer a middle ground by allowing some degree of flexibility for intellectual endeavors, so long as they do not challenge the party. Even within this perimeter, there remain serious disagreements as to the precise scope and pace of reforms. Hence, party policy seems to result from complex processes necessary for building a winning coalition and consensus within the party and the intellectual circle. It should be noted here that the 1982 draft Constitution, unlike the 1978 state Constitution, does not have a provision on the One Hundred Flowers. Its Article 20 merely says that the state promotes the planned socialist development of science, education, culture, and art.[19]

Conclusion: Legitimacy and Intellectuals

It is important to note that the major constraint on intellectual policy now is not Mao's Thought as such but the party's legitimacy. Before 1976, the party sought to remold the intellectuals with Mao's Thought, but since then, it has tried to co-opt their participation in the modernization process. What this means is that the party expects the intellectuals to help enhance its legitimacy, and that as long as they do so they can enjoy some freedom. But the intellectuals seek by nature unlimited ideas, truth, and creativity; they can hardly trust the party and vice versa. In the final analysis, the party always exercises a monopoly on truth.

Despite the restrictions of the post-Mao era, the Chinese intellectuals have gained substantial influence in determining their own fate. It should be noted that more than 90 percent of the existing 22 million intellectuals have been born since 1949. Their leaders have been actively co-opted into the decision-making processes of the party and the state. Their linkage with foreign counterparts is bound to have some impact on party policy, and as men of learning, their roles and power are likely to clash sometimes with those of party, state, and army cadres. Thus, the CCP is concerned with their social impact along with their contributions to economic development and national unity.

Since the Third Plenum in 1978, the CCP has staked its legitimacy on three separate but interrelated tasks: democratization, economic development, and national unity and security. The first of these has already been diluted, if not abandoned completely, except in the effort to achieve some semblance of socialist legalism. The second task is identical with the Four Modernizations program, which is being readjusted—but by no means smoothly. The third task is expressed in what the party calls "the liberation of Taiwan" and China's struggle against Soviet hegemony. The evidence suggests that the CCP is deliberately trying to harness the forces of nationalism and patriotism.

The most important challenge that the CCP is currently facing is how to enhance its legitimacy by means other than the Communist ideology that is being eroded in China. In this task, the intellectuals have the capacity either to undercut or promote the party's legitimacy. Traditionally, China's rulers had always tried to cultivate better rapport with men of letters (wen ren) than with men of arms (wu ren), for these literati have had enormous influence in shaping public opinion. In post-Mao China, too, there seems to have emerged something like public opinion, and the intellectuals seem to have some influence in it. Therefore, in order to maximize its own legitimacy, the party is involved in delicate processes of reciprocal dialogues and compromises with the intellectuals, although how these interactions may change remains to be seen.

Notes

1. Adrian Hsia, *The Chinese Cultural Revolution* (London: Orbach and Chambers, 1972), pp. 83–87.
2. Ibid., p. 78.
3. Byung-joon Ahn, *Chinese Politics and the Cultural Revolution: Dynamics of Policy Processes* (Seattle and London: University of Washington Press, 1976), p. 27.
4. Ibid., p. 59.
5. Ibid., p. 61.
6. Ibid., p. 173.
7. Byung-joon Ahn, "Science and Higher Education in Flux," *Contemporary China* 1:6 (March 1977), pp. 21–26.
8. Byung-joon Ahn, *Chinese Politics and the Cultural Revolution,* p. 253.
9. Ibid., p. 259.
10. *Renmin Ribao* (22 March 1978).
11. Ibid. (6 October 1978).
12. *Guangming Ribao* (20 July 1979).
13. *Beijing Review,* no. 52 (28 December 1979), p. 13.
14. "Hu Yao-pang's Speech to the Forum on Script Writing," *Issues and Studies* 17:12 (December 1981), pp. 67–106.

15. *Renmin Ribao* (15 August 1980).
16. Ibid. (20 April 1981).
17. *New China News Agency* (30 August 1981).
18. *Renmin Ribao* (24 December 1981).
19. *Beijing Review*, no. 19 (10 May 1982), p. 33.

Part 7

Methodology

18
Social Science and the Methodology of Contemporary Chinese Studies: A Critical Evaluation

Yung Wei

The field of China studies has entered a critical stage of self-evaluation, self-criticism, and soul searching. Never before have there been so many books, journal articles, and conference papers that deal with the problems of reliability and validity of scholarly work and press reports.[1] A prevailing disillusionment over the performance of the Communist regime in China has led to rising dissatisfaction over the inability of China specialists to provide reliable and timely analysis of the situation. The first serious challenge to the analytical skill of China scholars occurred during the Great Proletarian Cultural Revolution. This unprecedented movement came as a major shock to those who had long argued for the gradual evolution of Communist China into a more normal political system willing and able to interact with the West on a more cooperative and rational basis. Nevertheless, the cruelty and irrationality demonstrated by both the leaders and the followers of the Cultural Revolution did not deter the more "sympathetic" Western observers from rationalizing such bizarre behavior as a purifying and rejuvenating process for the increasingly bureaucratized Communist political system. Even the almost total absence of any legal remedy for the prosecuted during the Cultural Revolution was defended as a kind of "revolutionary justice" in a society dedicated to the eradication of "class enemies."

The setbacks of the Four Modernizations plan, however, presented a quite different set of problems for the pro-Peking scholars. Because the Chinese Communists used the old-fashioned Western criteria of "modernization" that are not so much different from the "self-strengthening" movement of the late Ch'ing Period, success or failure of this movement must be measured by rather concrete materialistic indicators. No longer can the continuation of rampant poverty and poor sanitary conditions, or the lack of administrative efficiency be defended by the mere need for revolutionary spirit. With the gradual opening up of China to Western visitors in recent years, the "discovery" of the actual living conditions of the Chinese people led two U.S. reporters to write books that have gained considerable attention from both academics on China and the general public in many countries.[2]

Why have so many China scholars, particularly those in the United States, failed not only in predicting developments in Communist China but also in perceiving the reality of Chinese society under Communist rule? Does this failure reflect an innocent lack of intellectual sensitivity to detect the real conditions, or is it due to the normative and willful orientation of the China scholars themselves? Should China studies remain an area study devoted to detailed description and analysis of specific problems in a well-defined geographical region or historical period, or should these endeavors go beyond this and become part of the social sciences related to the larger question of understanding human behavior at the global level? Should China studies be limited to the examination of Chinese society under Communist rule or include all societies in which the Chinese people predominate and the Chinese culture prevails? What types of approaches and research methods have been used by scholars in the China field and how successful have these approaches and methods been with regard to their particular subject matter? What are the requirements a competent China scholar should fulfill in order to do a good job in the field? Finally, what are some potentially rewarding areas of research in which future studies should be conducted?

Obviously it is impossible for any single scholar to address himself to all the above-mentioned questions. This paper is not intended to cover all the problems raised in those questions or even to conduct an exhaustive review of literature in the China field. Instead, the main thrust of this paper is to present a critical review of the methodological problems facing contemporary China scholars from a social science perspective. In the course of the discussion, the nature and scope of China studies, the intellectual connection between China studies and social science, the contribution of various approaches and research methods to the analysis of the Chinese society under Communist rule, and the intellectual tools that China scholars should possess in order to do a competent job in the field will be examined one after another. Finally, in the closing section some recommendations will be presented on both directions and methods of investigation, along with suggestions for further cooperation among China scholars in the Republic of China, Japan, the United States, and European and other countries.

China Studies: What Has Gone Wrong?

If we accept the criticism that China studies have fallen short of their goal in accurately analyzing and predicting events in Communist China, then a failure to determine the nature and scope of the field has been one of the major contributing factors. We may differentiate three major types of research interests in the China field: the sinological tradition, problem and policy analysis, and disciplinary studies. There has been a rough chronological sequence of development, with the sinological approach predominating in the pre-1950 period, problem and policy analysis during the 1950s and early 1960s, and the disciplinary approach in the post-1960s period.[3]

The sinological school does not need much clarification. Generally speaking, it refers to scholars influenced by China studies in Europe that focus on the historical, cultural, and linguistic aspects of Chinese society. Their interest lies in discovering the unique features of the various facets of traditional China. Not much effort has been made in producing or testing general hypotheses concerning the subject matter.

Problem and policy analysis is a type of research that treats Communist China as an issue in the foreign policy of a specific nation. Scholars of this group use a combination of research methods, ranging from sheer speculative reporting to documentary analysis to some limited employment of social science methods.

Disciplinary studies refers to the mode of investigation that relies on the theories and methods of a particular discipline or a combination of several disciplines within the social sciences. Researchers in these studies differ from sinologists in terms of their more professed interest in discovering the regularities rather than the uniqueness of certain things about events in Chinese society. The discipline-oriented scholars also differ from scholars of problem analysis in the sense that the former's concerns go beyond the immediate utility of the research results, whereas the latter are primarily interested in producing data for problem-solving and policy analysis.[4]

Since the disciplinary or social science-oriented scholars basically are not preoccupied with the immediate utility of the knowledge produced by their research, accuracy in predicting specific events or developments in the Chinese setting is a desirable and indispensable quality of their research. They are more interested in discovering the probabilistic relationships among different variables concerning a broad range of problems or phenomena. To these scholars, the building of heuristic, interpretive, and organizing models and theories is more important than becoming a successful fortune-teller in the China field.

Having made the above distinctions, one can turn to the prevailing complaint on the "failures" of China studies. Essentially, there could be two major types of problems afflicting China scholars. The first is that of orientation, the second that of inadequate research procedures. The first is a matter of preconception; the second, methodology. One may divide scholars affected by the first type of failure into two subgroups: those whose bias and prejudices derive from their social background and the milieu in which they find themselves, and the others whose problems lie in a deliberate manipulation of data to suit their ideological or personal purposes. Given the complexity and intensity of the China issues, there is no shortage of individual scholars in the China field who have basically already made up their minds. For these scholars, sophisticated research procedures are simply a better packaging process for the delivery of goods already selected.

The development of the China field in the United States was so closely related to the emergence of the Communist regime in China that policy debates within the U.S. government tended to carry over into academic research. The witchhunt procedures in the investigation for Communist-sympathizers within the U.S. government and its advisory personnel during the McCarthy era in the 1950s caused a backlash among an extremely influential group of China scholars and their students who to this day have remained dedicated to the rectification of the wrongdoings of McCarthyism. It was only natural for these scholars to feel positively toward Peking and less positively or even negatively toward the Republic of China on Taiwan. For many of these scholars who have become very successful in their profession but still feel "persecuted," their writing and research have become instruments for fighting back. With this group of China scholars in the United States, all the sophisticated reasoning processes and complicated methodology are merely instruments with which they try to influence policymakers and "educate" the general public.

A large part of the "failure" to produce a reliable account of conditions in Communist China can be traced back to preconceived biases among certain China specialists in almost all countries. Two cases must be differentiated. When a scholar deliberatively distorts reality, it is a failure in academic integrity. When, however, one unconsciously or innocently analyzes the problems in the China field with a particular tilt, it is then a matter of *Wissenssoziologie,* or sociology of knowledge.[5] That a scholar's mental process is influenced by his social position, cultural background, and belief system is not unique to China scholars. It ought to be pointed out, however, that because the post-1949 development of the China field has been so much related to an unhappy chapter of U.S. domestic and foreign policy in the era of McCarthyism, a "group think" phenomenon has appeared to develop in analysis in the China field—a phenomenon that still has an impact on scholarship in China studies.

Social Science and China Studies: The Need for Mutual Fertilization

Having recognized the problems of orientation and preconception, we may now turn to the more basic problem of China studies, i.e., that of research methodology. But first a fundamental question must be asked: why should we study China? Do we study China only because its mainland is now occupied by a gigantic Communist regime that is a major concern for foreign policymakers of many nations? Do we study China because of the "unique" cultural heritage of the Chinese people? Still more fundamentally, what is the meaning of "China"? Does it mean only Communist China or both Communist China and Taiwan? Or does it refer to a more abstract concept of the "Chinese communities" in various parts of the world? Trying to answer these questions will make us aware of the different perspectives through which one can observe "China" phenomena.

In my opinion, the key to success in China studies lies in the adoption of a broader definition of the term "China" and the application of a more rigorous social science methodology. China studies should not be limited to the analysis of the structure, processes, and behavior of the Chinese Communist system, nor should it be focused only on the examination of the Chinese society under Communist rule. Instead, we should broaden the scope and elevate the level of analytic focus from that of area studies to that of a study of the Chinese people under different social and political systems.[6] Examination should be made of the responses and readjustment of the Chinese people not only to different political regimes but to social, cultural, and economic changes at different stages. By adopting this approach, we shall be able to move from a preoccupation with "issues" or "problems" to an orientation focusing on "phenomena" or "social facts"[7]—a move that, in my opinion, will bring China studies into the mainstream of social science research.

Whether China studies should be area studies or a part of the interdisciplinary studies of the social sciences has been a topic of persistent debate among academicians. Lucian W. Pye, Robert C. Tucker, and Alex Inkeles all have argued strongly that it is the contemporary social science approach rather than area studies that has provided most of the promising conceptual tools for the study of Communist societies.[8] Only by adopting a social science approach can we move from an "idiographic" description of area studies to a "nomothetic" analysis in comparative research.[9] The larger proportion of social scientists is basically nomothetic, whereas the larger proportion of area specialists is idiographic.[10] This differentiation between the two groups, however, is not an absolute one. Many area specialists also try to generalize in their own geographic areas. Likewise, social scientists develop substantive knowledge of a specific geographic region for which they possess more comprehensive sources and more detailed data.

The need for mutual fertilization between the social sciences and China studies is evident in several important aspects. From the perspective of China studies, given the complex and ever-changing nature of the various Chinese societies such as Communist China, Taiwan, Singapore, and Hong Kong, it is no longer possible to rely upon a simple historical, cultural, or descriptive political analysis to unravel the meaning of various events and developments. More than ten years ago, this author pointed out the potential contribution that the social sciences, particularly the behaviorally oriented social sciences, could make to the studies of problems in the Chinese settings. Suggestions were made on the employment of social science theories and models such as structural-functional theory, system theory, decision-making theory, social mobilization, developmental theories, elite theories, and political communication to the examination of problems in China studies. Recommendations were also made on the utilization of the research tools of the social and behavioral sciences to investigate various problems in the China field. It was argued that research techniques such as survey methods, content analysis, statistical analysis and inference, information retrieval, computer analysis, and simulation all could be used to tackle the problems in China studies, although some modifications might be necessary to overcome the limitation on data collection and the generally lower quality of the data sources.[11]

Encouragement of a merging of China studies and social science research also can be defended by the need for extending the social sciences as a branch of human knowledge that hitherto has relied heavily on theoretical tools developed in the West and on data sources collected primarily in Western society. As G. William Skinner pointed out, "those disciplines which, like sociology, economics, and political science, developed not only *in* the Western world but as studies *of* Western institutions—those disciplines remain essentially rooted in particular societies, economies, and polities found in the Western world and its outputs."[12] Skinner lamented in a 1964 article that none of the empirical studies completed in the period between 1958 and 1963 dealt with a non-Western community.[13] If the social and behavioral scientists have any intention at all to make their particular field of human knowledge a universal science based upon global human experience, then it is absolutely necessary to include the Chinese societies in the arenas of rigorous empirical research.

On a more practical level and in more concrete terms, one of the major reasons for our interest in Communist China lies in the fact that it occupies the Chinese mainland, which is the seat of a society having a continuous social and political structure for more than 4,000 years. Thus, to study China in this context represents an effort to keep track of social and political developments in one of the oldest continuous civilizations of the world.

A second such reason for studying China is to be found in the enormous dimension of this political system in terms of the size of its territory and of the population under its domination. Indeed, it rules one-fourth of the people on earth and is the biggest country in Asia, with a central location in the eastern part of that continent.

A third reason for an interest in Communist China among social and political scientists is that it is the largest Communist nation in the world, not excepting the Soviet Union. The success or failure of this Communist regime will have a decisive impact on the Communist movements in various parts of the world. The recent Sino-Soviet split with all its consequent effects on Communist parties and governments throughout the world has further intensified concern for the role played by Communist China in the unity or division of the Communist camp.

A final reason that has motivated social and political scientists to study Communist China is that this Communist regime stands not only for a totalitarian political system of tremendous dimension but also for a distinct model of sociopolitical development that differs from both the Western democratic model and the Soviet Communist model. An understanding of this regime would shed much light on the nature of totalitarian rule and the process of sociopolitical development of the emerging nations in Asia, Africa, and Latin America.

Social Sciences and China Studies: A Preliminary Review of Approaches and Research Results

If one is not satisfied with the current state of affairs in China studies or the accuracy of reporting on China, the sources of the shortcomings are not so likely to be found in the quantity or quality of research as in the orientation and preconceptions of individual scholars or groups of scholars. As for the research itself, for the past three decades Chinese studies unquestionably has been one of the most active and productive fields of scholarly pursuit. This was particularly true in the 1960s and 1970s. Between 1958 and 1970, more than US $25 million were given by various private foundations to support research in the China field. For example, the Ford Foundation poured large amounts of funding into various China and Asian programs in the United States and other countries in order to recruit competent scholars, improve language training, expand course offerings, compile indexes and bibliographies, and establish research centers in various Chinese settings. These efforts by private foundations, coupled with equally well-financed efforts by the U.S. government, have led to the mushrooming of academic programs on China and a phenomenal increase in the number of specialists in China studies. For instance, during the decade 1960–1969, some 1,700 students in U.S. colleges received B.A. degrees in China studies; at the university level, some 1,000 received M.A. degrees and 412 the Ph.D. degree.[14]

The vitality and dynamism of China studies during that period was also manifested in the voluminous publications and the increasing attention given to the investigation of problems of contemporary China. The Social Science Research Council (SSRC), for instance, pumped a considerable amount of funds into research on carefully chosen topics submitted by young scholars and doctoral candidates. Almost invariably the methods employed in research projects supported by the SSRC were far more social science-oriented than oriented toward area studies or sinological inquiries. The fruits produced by social science-oriented research on China have been documented by a great number of bibliographical studies that stand as monuments celebrating the achievements in this field.[15]

In such a short paper it is impossible to thoroughly review the contributions made by various scholars in the China field. It is possible, however, to identify some fields that, in my opinion, have made progress toward more rigorous social science-oriented research in the China field. Tables 18.1 and 18.2 represent a rudimentary and impressionistic examination of the relationship between social sciences and China studies. Although the device is extremely crude and may be highly subjective, it does show that political science, sociology, and psychology have had the highest associations with different fields within China studies. Data in Table 18.1 also demonstrate that among the subfields of China studies, "political culture and socialization" and "population and social relations" are the two more oriented to an interdisciplinary approach. These findings are quite close to the observations made by Maurice Freedman in 1969.[16]

Table 18.2 shows that quantitative research techniques are used in the study of "political culture and socialization," "population and social relations," "elite recruitment," and "economic development" more frequently than in "political participation" and "external relations." The data also show that simple statistical analysis, contingency analysis, and computer data processing are already being used rather widely in certain fields of China studies.

Judging by the information summarized in the two tables, political culture and socialization is without question one of the most sophisticated fields in China studies, so far as both an interdisciplinary approach and research methods are concerned. The number of books and articles published on the subject testify to the vigor and resourcefulness of this research.[17] Two impetuses behind these efforts are the emergence of a "behavioral" approach to China studies and the development of political science subfields in "political culture" and "political socialization." The development of an empirically or behaviorally oriented school of China studies is closely related to the emergence of a "behavioral" approach in political science. To put it in grossly simplified terms, the behaviorally oriented political scientists have forged ahead by advocating an empirical political science based upon quantitative analysis with an interdisciplinary emphasis; that is, they increasingly use the theories and methods of other behavioral and social sciences such as anthropology, sociology, psychology, and economics in the analysis of political phenomena. In brief, they have called for a cross-fertilization of theories and methods between political science and other social sciences.

Given this background, it is no wonder that the majority of scholars who are pushing for an empirical-behavioral approach in China studies are political scientists. From the writings of Lucian W. Pye, Chalmers Johnson, Richard W. Wilson, and Yung Wei, several basic positions of empirically oriented China scholarship can be derived. First, it is maintained that in conducting research in the China field, scholars must try to adopt or develop certain analytical frameworks to use as a guide for data collection and hypothesis testing. Second, any propositions or statements that are not supported by empirical data should be regarded as untested hypotheses, not as conclusions. Third, in order to have a broader theoretical as well as methodological approach, scholars should adopt an interdisciplinary orientation, borrowing for application those

Table 18.1 Social Science and China Studies: The Degree of Mutual Fertilization (Rating: 3>2>1)

Social Science Discipline	Subfield in China Studies: Population and Social Relations	Political Culture and Socialization	Political Participation	Elite Recruitment	Economic Development	External Relations	Total
Sociology	3	3	1	1	1		9
Political science	1	3	3	3	1	1	12
Psychology	1	3	1	1	1	1	8
Anthropology	1	1					2
Economics	1		1		3	2	7
Total	7	10	6	5	6	4	38

Table 18.2 Research Methods in China Studies: The Extent of Utilization (Rating: 3>2>1)

Research Method	Subfield in China Studies						Total
	Population and Social Relations	Political Culture and Socialization	Political Participation	Elite Recruitment	Economic Development	External Relations	
Simple statistical analysis	3	2	2	3	3	1	14
Contingency and correlational analysis	2	2	1	3	2		10
Computer data processing	2	2		2	3		9
Content analysis	1	2					3
Survey research	1	2		1			4
Total	9	10	3	9	8	1	40

theories (especially middle-range theories[18]) and methodologies that are available in political science, sociology, psychology, anthropology, and economics. Finally, efforts should be made to refine the hypothesis-testing process by collecting and developing quantitative data rather than relying on qualitative descriptions.[19]

It should not be a surprise that in searching for a focus of interdisciplinary, quantitative research, China specialists turned to one of the most explored subfields in empirical political science, i.e., the study of political culture and political socialization. According to Lucian W. Pye, "political culture is the set of attitudes, beliefs, and sentiments which give order and meaning to a political process and which provide the underlying assumptions and rules that govern behavior in the political system."[20] Generally speaking, four basic approaches to the study of Chinese political culture can be identified: the psychohistorical approach, the psychocultural approach, the sociopsychological approach, and the communication approach. Scholars applying a psychohistorical approach try to combine psychoanalytical methods with historical analysis. In Robert Jay Lifton's words, this approach is "a combination of psychoanalytic sensitivity and historical imagination."[21] Lifton's interest in the Chinese culture derived from his study of "brainwashing" techniques of the Chinese Communists. During 1954 and 1955, he interviewed forty "victims" of the "brainwashing" process; among them, twenty-five were Westerners and fifteen were Chinese.[22] Being a psychiatrist, Lifton used primarily the method of clinical interview, emphasizing techniques of "free association." Through these interviews, he discovered that the basic techniques used by the Chinese Communists in "brainwashing" included coercion, exhortation, therapy, and realization. By depriving an individual of opportunities to satisfy basic physical needs and comfort, by isolating him from the outside world, by exposing him to a specially arranged environment, and by creating intense mental stress, the Chinese Communists were able to produce confession, self-criticism, and open repentance from individuals who ordinarily would not have been perceived as capable of such self-deprecating responses.

Another leading effort to understand Chinese political culture has been made through the psychocultural approach. In the words of Lucian W. Pye, psychocultural analysis is simply "a psychologically oriented study of political culture." The actual content of this type of study, however, goes far beyond this description. It involves not only the examination of the personality structure of members of a society and of a political system, but also the relationships among personal identity, political authority, nation-building, and political modernization. Pye first tried this method on Burma and then developed, along with other political scientists such as Sidney Verba, Myron Weiner, and Robert E. Ward, a general framework for studying political culture and political development. In regard to the study of Chinese political culture, Pye's major contribution is his thesis on the problem of "authority crisis" in the modernization of Chinese society.[23]

Although Pye advanced the thesis of an "authority crisis" in Chinese political culture, he did not proceed to collect empirical data to test his hypothesis. This job was left for his student, Richard H. Solomon.[24] Central to Solomon's theme of Chinese political culture is the relationship between child-rearing practices and the development of a model Chinese political personality and political culture. Solomon "discovered" that the golden age of the life experience of the Chinese people is their preteen childhood. During this period, the parents assume a very permissive and protective attitude toward the child, especially in regard to satisfying the child's desire for food, hence the development of an "oral character" among the Chinese. Yet once the child reaches his teens, this tolerant attitude on the part of his parents is suddenly changed into strict discipline, threat of isolation, severe physical punishment, endless indoctrination with the orthodox Confucianist teaching on filial piety, and subjection to shaming techniques.[25]

A third approach is the sociopsychological approach, by which I mean the analysis of Chinese political culture by examining the process of how the values, norms, and attitudes have been transmitted from one generation to another through social learning, i.e., the process of political socialization. Among the scholars who have studied political socialization in the Chinese setting are Richard W. Wilson, Sheldon Appleton, Song-hsi Yüan, and Yung Wei.[26]

During the school year 1965/1966, Richard W. Wilson collected data on political socialization by observing and interviewing children in three elementary schools in the Taipei area on the island of Taiwan. He used four procedures to collect his data: (1) actual classroom and school observation; (2) questionnaire-based interviews with children (using open-ended questions, a pictorial political symbol questionnaire, and projective questionnaires based on pictures of authority situations); (3) face-to-face interviews with children, educational authorities, and parents; and (4) intensive examination of educational materials, primarily textbooks.[27]

One of Wilson's major conclusions is that the emphasis on the importance of "face," involving the "shaming" techniques used by both parents and teachers, has a lasting effect on a child's political behavior. By denying love and shaming the child publicly, the parents and teachers of Taiwan are able to generate a deeply internalized identification with the group as well as with the leader of the group. Wilson found an intense, uncritical loyalty toward the authority figure, yet there were also feelings of insecurity, doubt, fear, inner rage, hostility, and cynicism. These hidden hostilities could usually be released against sanctioned outside groups, which in the case of Taiwanese children are the Chinese Communists.[28]

In addition to the psychohistorical, psychocultural, and sociopsychological approaches, another approach applied to the study of political culture is communications research. In this regard, studies conducted by Fredrick T. C. Yu, Richard H. Solomon, Alan P. L. Liu, and Arnold B. Urken[29] have uncovered some important findings on the interplay of political ideology, the mass media, and elite-mass relations in Communist China. Although it may be questioned whether studies of this kind are really relevant to the study of Chinese political culture, it should be recognized that, given the emphasis by Mao Tse-tung on the importance of "mass line" and the extent of the efforts made by the Chinese Communists in this respect, political communication is definitely an important link between political culture on the one hand and the behavior of the mainland Chinese people on the other.

Besides the four approaches already discussed, one may add still another, i.e., the ideological approach to Chinese political culture. By "ideological approach" I refer to studies of the relationships among Chinese culture traits, Communist ideology, and the political practices of the Chinese Communists. Studies done by Franz Schumann, Chalmers Johnson, Benjamin I. Schwartz, James Chieh Hsiung, and John Bryan Starr[30] have definitely shed much light on our understanding of the behavior of the Chinese Communists in relation to Marxism-Leninism and the thought of Mao Tse-tung. As in communications research, one may question the utility of examining the political culture of China from an ideological point of view. But unless the Chinese background of the Communist leaders can be completely dissociated from their application of Communist ideology to the solution of concrete problems in China, one cannot examine the interaction between culture and ideology in the Chinese setting.

Other than political culture and socialization, another very fruitful field of research in China is elite studies. Studies of political elites have been closely related to the investigation of revolutionary movements. In the China field, a great many studies have been made of the important political leaders of Communist China. The number of such studies increased in the years after the Great Proletarian Cultural Revolution. Various models have been developed to describe and analyze relationships among Chinese Communist leaders.[31] For example, the "Red versus expert" model attempts to picture the struggle between the Maoists and the non-Maoists in the Cultural Revolution as a conflict between those who stressed revolutionary experience and ideological purity and those who stressed practical and technical knowledge for solving concrete problems. A second model—the "palace coup"—treats the conflicts of the Cultural Revolution as an internal power struggle, focusing on political intrigues among a handful of the more powerful members of the elite and observing the spread of these intrigues to the lower echelons of the political and bureaucratic structures and the general populace in China.

A third model may be called the "regional versus central government" model. Here, conflicts between elite groups are viewed as a continuous process of readjustment of relationships between the political elite whose power base is in or near the capital and the elite whose power rests in the provinces. Scholars applying this model have pointed out that even before the Cultural Revolution, regionalism was a subject of frequent attacks by Mao and other Communist leaders. The purge of Kao Kang and Jao Shu-shih is a good case in point.

A fourth model rests on group conflict theory, viewing the Cultural Revolution as a struggle for domination among the party, the bureaucracy, and the military elites, each claiming to be the true disciples of Mao Tse-tung. The emergence of Lin Piao as vice-chairman of the party has been interpreted as a victory for the military elite in the struggle. We may call this model the "military-party-bureaucratic struggle" model.[32]

A fifth model was developed by Jürgen Domes, who tries to analyze intraparty conflicts in Communist China by examining the decision-making process. He discovers two distinct types of groups in the intraparty conflicts. The first is the opinion groups that exist in the short and middle term, having been initially formed on the basis of conflict between individuals within clearly defined limits. The second is factions that exist on a longer-term basis—the groups who are struggling for alternative programs and demanding exclusive access to leadership. By carefully examining the process of leadership formation at different stages in the development of Chinese Communist politics, Domes concludes that the course of domestic politics does not substantiate the assumption that the key to an understanding of political change in Communist China is through concepts and actions of a single charismatic leader.[33]

Another fertile field of social science research in the China field is to be found in the study of local communities. Skinner, Vogel, Ahn, Parish, and Whyte have done major works in this field.[34] By carefully examining fragmented official documents and statistics, interviewing emigrants, and occasionally visiting rural China under Communist rule, scholars of rural sociology have been able to put out an amazing quantity of serious work on the living conditions in local communities in China. Of these studies, the work by Parish and Whyte deserves special attention both in its findings and methodology. Parish and Whyte discovered that it is incorrect to interpret the willingness of the peasants to change in the 1960s and 1970s primarily in terms of outdated class labels. Instead they found that only when and where the rural social structure is supportive of particular changes is ideological persuasion likely to be effective. Parish and Whyte also discovered that the modernization perspective, in its broader conception of indirect structural sources of change, is superior to the Chinese Marxist perspective. The methodological notes made by Parish and Whyte in regard to the handling of refugee interviewing are informative as well as reflective. By pointing out the bias and selectivity of the interviewing process, they have demonstrated the painful limitation confronted by scholars doing research on closed or semiclosed systems. Yet despite all the restrictions put on them, scholars of rural and urban sociology have emerged as a group receiving one of the most abundant harvests in the China field.

From the foregoing review on political culture, elite studies, and rural sociology, one should be able to get a general idea of the types and extent of application of social science theories and methods to China studies. The list could be extended to other fields in China studies, for instance, study of the economy of Communist China, an enterprise almost monopolized by Western scholars, especially ones from the United States. Although their assessment of the Communist Chinese economy is somewhat tilted to the more optimistic side, it is far more accurate than the official figures of the U.S. government.[35]

Deductive modeling is another promising field that has witnessed creative contributions by younger scholars. Using game theory and coalition theory, models of elite behavior with a rather high explanatory power can be built.[36] If the Chinese Communists continue to increase the supply of more reliable official data on various aspects of the society on the Chinese mainland,[37] more can be done in the areas of deductive modeling as well as inductive testing of hypotheses.

Conclusions and Suggestions

From the foregoing review of the methodology of contemporary China studies, one may draw several conclusions. First, there has been a clear tendency among China specialists to move from the historical-cultural approach to more empirically oriented studies, and from pure area studies to social science-oriented research. Second, extensive efforts have been made to generate testable hypotheses by building both deductive models and inductive research designs. Third, a gradual merging of the theories and methods of various branches of the social sciences has occurred in China studies, making mutual fertilization a reality, not just a slogan. Reports on the results of serious social science-oriented research have started to appear with increasing frequency in various disciplinary journals, thus enriching and broadening the content of specific subfields within the social sciences.

Through the process of reviewing the literature for this paper, one thing has become very clear. The orientation and "group thinking" of certain China scholars, more than the lack of methodological sophistication, has prevented the emergence of a true picture of Communist China. Whether the cause is innocent or is due to the deliberate manipulation of data in the reporting process (either from pressure by a subculture of a scholarly community or a perceived need to follow the "official line," both in the West and in Communist China) I leave to my colleagues.

In the future, the key to more dynamic China studies is more interdisciplinary approaches using the theories and methodology of the social sciences. We may compare the Chinese Communist political system with other political systems along several mutually complementary spectra over time and space. For instance, we may place Communist China on the familiar traditional-transitional-modern spectrum and see how it differs from other political systems in terms of the relationship between the social and economic conditions of a society and its political style and development. Comparison along this line will help us gain much insight into the appeal of the Chinese version of communism for countries in Asia, Africa, and Latin America.

We may also compare Communist China with other nations of the world along the line of a competitive-semicompetitive-authoritarian model. Using this classification of political systems, we may compare the Chinese Communist political system with other political systems in terms of the degree of "openness" and "competitiveness" in processes affecting interest articulation, interest aggregation, elite recruitment, rule making, and other functions. However, a word of warning must be expressed: we must be careful not to let our ideological preferences lead us to quick, subjective conclusions as to the nature of the Chinese Communist political system and thus lose sight of the real purpose of the comparison.

A third type of comparison can be made between Communist China and other Communist nations, against an orthodox-revisionist spectrum. By doing this, we may see how differences in commitment to the original Marxist-Leninist dogma have affected the behavior of the Communist nations. We may also see how the historical, geographical, and cultural elements of a society can lead to different interpretations and application of the Communist political model to fit local conditions.

Finally, we may, and should, compare the Chinese Communist political system with other Chinese social and political systems in Taiwan, Singapore, and Hong Kong. What we need is detached and dispassionate comparison based upon empirical data and with some kind of theoretical framework. Given the common cultural and historical roots of the four Chinese systems, each could serve as a control group for the others. In such studies we may examine the effect of different social and political systems on the lives of Chinese people living in different geographical areas.

Han Yü, an outstanding scholar of the T'ang dynasty, once said "Wen ch'iung erh hou kung" (Scholarship gets better when one becomes poorer). The problems of China studies in the recent past may have been derived from the abundance of funding, the high relevance to policymaking, and easy access to media exposure. Consequently, one of the most important ingredients of fine scholarship, i.e., the self-imposed solitude and detachment from worldly motive, was diluted and in some cases lost. From this perspective a limited academic recession may do us some good. When funds for research become limited, the fever for quick fame lowered, and the limelight dimmed to a reading level, we shall all become more reflective and better able to move China studies onto a higher plane.

Notes

1. For examples, see Ramon H. Myers and Thomas A. Metzger, "Sinological Shadows: The State of Modern China Studies in the United States," *Washington Quarterly* (Spring 1980), pp. 87–114; Chalmers Johnson, "What's Wrong with Chinese Political Studies?"

paper presented to the Eleventh Sino-American Conference on Mainland China, Taipei, Taiwan, Republic of China, 7–13 June 1982; and Harry Harding, "From China, with Disdain: New Trends in the Study of China," also a paper presented to the Eleventh Sino-American Conference on Mainland China.

2. See Fox Butterfield, *China, Alive in the Bitter Sea* (New York: Times Books, 1982) and Richard Bernstein, *From the Center of the Earth* (Boston: Little, Brown, 1982). See also Simon Leys, *Chinese Shadows* (New York: Viking, 1977); Edward Luttwak, "Seeing China Plain," *Commentary* (December 1976), pp. 27–33; and Susan Shirk, "Human Rights: What About China?" *Foreign Policy* 29 (Winter, 1977–1978), pp. 109–127.

3. For a discussion on the changing orientation of China studies, see Yung Wei, "The Behavioral Sciences and China Studies: Some Thoughts on Theories, Methods, and Data Sources," paper presented to the Second Sino-American Conference on Mainland China, San Francisco, California, 14–16 June 1972, later included in Yung Wei, *Science, Elite, and Modernization* (Taipei: Hsueh-Sheng Shu Chu, 1980), pp. 37–55; Eugene Wu, "Studies on Mainland China in the United States," in *Collected Documents of the Conference on Mainland China* (Taipei: Institute of International Relations, 1971), pp. 29–46; and Kenneth Scott Latourette, "Far Eastern Studies in the United States: Retrospect and Prospect," *Far Eastern Quarterly* 15 (1955), pp. 3–11.

4. For a review of the different approaches to China studies and the role of social science, see Chalmers Johnson, "The Role of Social Sciences in China Scholarship," *World Politics* 17 (January 1965), pp. 256–271; Yung Wei, "The Chinese Communist Political System: An Introduction," in *Communist China: A System-Functional Reader,* ed. Yung Wei (Columbus, Ohio: Charles E. Merrill, 1971), pp. 1–13; and Richard W. Wilson, "China Studies in Crisis," *World Politics* 33 (January 1971), pp. 296–317.

5. Marx, Scheler, Mannheim, Durkheim, and Sorokin all have addressed the problem of interaction between the mental process of a scholar and his social as well as cultural milieu. For a thorough discussion, see Robert K. Merton, *The Sociology of Science, Theoretical and Empirical Investigation* (Chicago and London: University of Chicago Press, 1972), pp. 7–40.

6. For the need to broaden the scope of China studies, see Maurice Freedman, "Why China?" presidential address to the American Anthropological Association, 1969.

7. See Emile Durkheim, *The Rules of Sociological Methods,* trans. Sarah A. Solovey and John H. Mueller, ed. George E. G. Catlin (New York: Free Press, 1950), pp. 1–13.

8. See Lucian W. Pye, "Comparative Politics and Communist Studies," paper delivered at Conference on Communist Studies, American Political Science Association, New York, September 1966); Robert C. Tucker, "On the Comparative Study of Communism," *World Politics* 19 (January 1967), pp. 242–257; and Alex Inkeles, "Models in the Analysis of Soviet Society," *Survey* 60 (July 1966), pp. 3–17.

9. Frederio J. Fleron, Jr., ed., *Communist Studies and the Social Sciences* (Chicago: Rand McNally, 1969), pp. 1–33.

10. Ibid., p. 6.

11. Yung Wei, "The Behavioral Sciences and China Studies," pp. 48–54.

12. See G. William Skinner, "What the Study of China Can Do for Social Science," *Journal of Asian Studies* 23 (August 1964), pp. 518–529.

13. Ibid., p. 518.

14. Leonard D. Gordon, with Frank J. Shulman, ed., *Doctoral Dissertations on China: A Bibliography of Studies in Western Languages, 1945–1970* (Seattle: University of Washington Press, 1972).

15. For instance, see William Skinner, ed., *Modern Chinese Society: An Analytical Bibliography* (Stanford, Calif.: Stanford University Press, 1973).

16. Freedman, "Why China?" pp. 7–8.

17. Notable examples include: Lucian W. Pye, *The Spirit of Chinese Politics: A Psychocultural Study of the Authority Crisis in Political Development* (Cambridge, Mass.: M.I.T. Press, 1968); Richard W. Wilson, *Learning to Be Chinese: The Political Socialization of Children in Taiwan* (Cambridge, Mass.: M.I.T. Press, 1970); R. W. Wilson, *The Moral State, A Study of the Political Socialization of Chinese and American Children* (New York: Free Press, 1974); R. W. Wilson, "The Learning of Political Symbols in Chinese Culture,"

Journal of Asian and African Studies 3 (July–October 1968), pp. 246–254; Robert Jay Lifton, *Thought Reform and the Psychology of Totalism: A Study of Brainwashing in China* (New York: W. W. Norton, 1963); R. J. Lifton, *Revolutionary Immortality: Mao Tse-tung and the Chinese Cultural Revolution* (New York: Vintage Books, 1968); Richard H. Solomon, *Mao's Revolution and the Chinese Political Culture* (Berkeley: University of California Press, 1972); Sheldon Appleton, "The Political Socialization of College Students on Taiwan," *Asian Survey* 10 (October 1970), pp. 910–923; S. Appleton, "Regime Support Among Taiwan High School Students," *Asian Survey* 13 (August 1973), pp. 750–760; and Charles Price Ridley, Paul H. B. Godwin, and Dennis J. Doolin, *The Making of a Model Citizen in Communist China* (Stanford, Calif.: The Hoover Institute Press, 1971). For a critical review of studies on China political culture, see Yung Wei, "A Methodological Critique of Current Studies on China Political Culture," *Journal of Politics* 38 (February 1976), pp. 114–140.

18. For a discussion on the "theories of the middle range" see Robert K. Merton, *Social Theory and Social Structure* (New York: Free Press of Glencoe, 1957), pp. 5–10.

19. Wilson, "China Studies in Crisis," and Yung Wei, "Behavioral Sciences and China Studies."

20. Lucian W. Pye, "Political Culture," in *The International Encyclopedia of the Social Sciences* (New York: Macmillan and Free Press, 1968), vol. 12, pp. 218–225.

21. Robert Jay Lifton, "On Psychohistory," *Partisan Review* (Spring 1970), pp. 11–32.

22. Lifton, *Thought Reform and Psychology of Totalism.*

23. For the idea of "authority crisis," see Pye, *The Spirit of Chinese Politics;* see also Pye, *China, An Introduction* (Boston: Little, Brown, 1972), pp. 349–351.

24. Solomon, *Mao's Revolution and the Chinese Political Culture,* p. *xvii.*

25. Ibid., pp. 39–46.

26. See note 17 for the works of Wilson and Appleton in the area. As for the study done by Song-hsi Yuan and Yung Wei, see Yuan, "Children and Politics [in Taiwan]," *Annals of the Chinese Association of Political Science* 1 (September 1971), pp. 67–113, and Yung Wei, "The Political Socialization of College Students in Taiwan" (unpublished research report).

27. Wilson, *Learning to Be Chinese,* pp. 16–17.

28. Ibid., pp. 99–120.

29. See Frederick T. C. Yu, "Communication and Politics in Communist China," in *Communications and Political Development,* ed. Lucian W. Pye (Princeton, N.J.: Princeton University Press, 1963), pp. 259–297; Richard H. Solomon, "Communication Patterns and the Chinese Revolution," *China Quarterly* 32 (October-December 1967), pp. 101–110; Alan P. L. Liu, *Communication and National Integration in Communist China* (Berkeley: University of California Press, 1971); and Arnold P. Urken, "The Logic of Maoist Political Communication," paper presented at the 1973 Annual Meeting of the American Political Science Association, Jung Hotel, New Orleans, Louisiana, 4–8 September 1973.

30. See Franz Schurmann, *Ideology and Organization in Communist China* (Berkeley: University of California Press, 1966); Chalmers Johnson, ed., *Ideology and Politics in Contemporary China* (Seattle and London: University of Washington Press, 1973); Benjamin Schwartz, *Chinese Communism and the Rise of Mao* (Cambridge, Mass.: Harvard University Press, 1958); James Chieh Hsiung, *Ideology and Practice, the Evolution of Chinese Communism* (New York: Praeger, 1970); and John Bryan Starr, *Ideology and Culture, An Introduction to the Dialectic of Contemporary Chinese Politics* (New York: Harper & Row, 1973).

31. For notable examples, see Robert A. Scalapino, ed., *Elites in the People's Republic of China* (Seattle: University of Washington Press, 1973); James R. Townsend, "Intra-Party Conflicts in China: Disintegration in an Established One-Party System," in *Authoritarian Politics in Modern Society: The Dynamics of Established One-Party Systems,* ed. Samuel P. Huntington and Clement H. Moore (New York: Basic Books, 1970); John M. Lindbeck, ed., *China: Management of a Revolutionary Society* (Seattle: University of Washington Press, 1971); and Ying-mao Kau, "The Urban Bureaucratic Elite in Communist China: A Case Study of Wuhan, 1949–1965," in *Chinese Communist Politics in Action,* ed. A. Doak Barnett (Seattle: University of Washington Press, 1969).

32. See Lucian W. Pye, *The Dynamics of Chinese Politics* (Cambridge, Mass.: Oelgeschlager, Gunn & Hain, 1981); A. Doak Barnett, *Cadres, Bureaucracy, and Power in Communist China* (New York: Columbia University Press, 1967); Michel Oksenberg, "The Political Group, Political Participation and Communication," in *The Cultural Revolution: 1967 in Review,* Michigan Papers in Chinese Studies, no. 2 (Ann Arbor, Mich.: Center for Chinese Studies, 1968); and John W. Lewis, "Leader, Commissar, and Bureaucrat: The Chinese Political System in the Last Days of the Revolution," in *China in Crisis,* ed. Ping-ti Ho and Tang Tsou (Chicago: University of Chicago Press, 1968), vol. 1, book 2, 449–481.

33. Jürgen Domes, *China After the Cultural Revolution, Politics Between Two Party Congresses* (Berkeley and Los Angeles: University of California Press, 1975).

34. G. William Skinner, "Marketing and Social Structure in Rural China" (in three parts), *Journal of Asian Studies* 24 (November 1964, February and May 1965), pp. 3–43, 195–228, 363–399; Ezra Vogel, *Canton Under Communism: Programs and Politics in a Provincial Capital, 1948–1968* (Cambridge, Mass.: Harvard University Press, 1969); Byung-joon Ahn, "The Political Economy of the People's Commune in China: Changes and Continuities," *Journal of Asian Studies* 34 (May 1975), pp. 631–658; William C. Parish and Martin King Whyte, *Villages and Family in Contemporary China* (Chicago and London: University of Chicago Press, 1978); Martin King Whyte, "Inequality and Stratification in China," *China Quarterly* 64 (December 1975), pp. 684–711. For a review of sociological research on Communist China, see Andrew G. Walder, "Chinese Communist Society: The State of the Field," paper delivered to the Eleventh Sino-American Conference on Mainland China, 7–13 June 1982.

35. Kang Chao, "The China-Watchers Tested," *China Quarterly* 84 (March 1980), pp. 97–104.

36. For example, see William Pany-Yu Ting, "Conditional Behavior Among the Chinese Military Elite: A Nonrecursive, Simultaneous Equations, and Multiplicative Causal Model," *American Political Science Review* 73 (1979), pp. 428–493.

37. For a discussion on this, see W. Klatt, "Chinese Statistics Updated," *China Quarterly* 84 (December 1980), pp. 737–748.

19
The Methodology of Contemporary Chinese Studies: Political Studies and the PRC

David S. G. Goodman

Any paper pretentious enough to address itself to a consideration of the methodology of contemporary Chinese studies is subject to a number of pitfalls. Not the least of its problems is the varied and diffuse nature of its source material and the lack of precision or uniformity in the meaning and use of terms such as methodology, model, and theory.[1] It may all too easily become simply an attempt to catalogue the various visions of the People's Republic of China that have emerged in the academic press, or an attack on past scholarship, or an attempt to reconcile mutually exclusive belief systems. Here, the focus is on the work that has been published—largely in the English language—related to the study of domestic politics in the PRC. The intention is not to present any new theory for the study of politics in the PRC but to review the literature in order to provide comment on the future development of that field of academic investigation.

Particularly since the mid-1960s there has been a considerable growth in the literature on politics in the PRC. At first sight that development seems impressive not only on quantitative grounds but also because of the wider range of topics chosen for investigation and the greater variety of approaches employed. Before the Cultural Revolution, PRC politics were described almost solely in terms of a totalitarian model, or variations on that theme, with attention focused on national leadership and policies and their immediate political and ideological environments. The unsurprising conventional wisdom, which resulted largely from the lack of countervailing evidence, held inter alia that the leadership was (and had remained) cohesive and united around the generation of revolutionary leaders; and that, in large measure, PRC politics not only revolved around but was determined by Mao Zedong and Mao's Thought. As a result, what literature there was reflected those concerns, focusing on Mao, and the ideology and organization of the new Communist party state.[2]

Though variants on an explicit totalitarian approach have not been totally abandoned,[3] other perspectives have since made their presence felt. Thus, for example, one can now find explanations of politics and political phenomena in the PRC that range from the more obvious (in terms of a reaction to the totalitarian model) attempts to highlight what is seen as pluralistic tendencies in the political process[4] to the more controversial (but inherently more stimulating and interesting) applications of psychoanalytical[5] and psychodynamic[6] techniques. Above all, the study of politics in the PRC has been dominated methodologically by considerations of policy cycles[7] and factionalism.[8] Moreover, the literature on the policy cycles is generally regarded as highly developed by comparison with studies of other systems, and of a wider significance both spatially and in terms of discipline.[9]

Similarly, though the earlier concerns with biography, ideology, and organization have been far from forgotten during the period since the mid-1960s,[10] the range of topics chosen for investigation has expanded considerably. Thus, there is now greater emphasis on politics as process, and as an activity not confined to the more traditionally defined "center." For example, there have been studies of the central decision-making process through its formal communications network;[11] of the intermediate[12] and basic[13] levels of the politico-administrative hierarchy, as well as of economic enterprises;[14] of social categoric (though not necessarily political) groups;[15] and of specific local areas.[16] Though it would be incorrect to argue that since the mid-1960s the major focus of attention in the literature as a whole has shifted from considerations of policy to those of power, a less one-sided emphasis in the study of politics in the PRC has certainly emerged.[17]

The emergence of a larger and more varied literature on politics in the PRC undoubtedly owes much to the Cultural Revolution. It is not just that the way the Cultural Revolution evolved brought politics more out into the open (particularly in contrast to the early 1960s) and released new sources of information, however biased and suspect, nor is it just that the Cultural Revolution appeared to challenge almost every conventional wisdom about the nature of politics in the PRC. The Cultural Revolution drew attention first to the politics, but later to other aspects of the PRC in a spectacular way. More people were drawn to Chinese studies and there was a need—or at least a market—for more secondary literature among both the general public and the academic community.

It is probably the case that many of the developments in the study of PRC politics would have occurred regardless. After all, in relative terms the study of PRC politics was still a new area for academic investigation before the mid-1960s. Much of the academic literature was concerned with outlining the basic contours of politics in the PRC,[18] and in quantitative terms there were relatively few opportunities for those with an academic interest in the PRC. For example, from a British perspective, the *China Quarterly* started only in 1960, and as far as can be ascertained there was no one specializing in PRC politics employed in that context in a department of politics or government within a British university. There was clearly room for further development, both intellectually and organizationally, and the work of (for example) Barnett and Schurmann indicates that at least the former was already under way before 1966. Nonetheless, the Cultural Revolution was clearly an extremely useful catalyst to the study of politics in the PRC.

The impact of the Cultural Revolution on the study of politics in the PRC highlights methodological problems that have remained despite the advances since the mid-1960s, and to a certain extent these problems make that progress seem less impressive. As has already been mentioned, it is no exaggeration to claim that the onset of the Cultural Revolution destroyed almost every conventional wisdom about politics in the PRC. Academic observers of politics in the PRC were for the most part caught flat-footed.[19] The response was in many ways an overreaction: a near panic that led to radically new arguments and theories, some of which were readily discounted by their authors within a short space of time.[20] That pattern, if less spectacularly, has repeated itself since. Events in the PRC, and very often the accompanying propaganda, not only take students of politics by surprise[21] but also determine the perspectives adopted until the next "crisis" or change in direction.

It is of course "right and proper" that the study of politics in the PRC should be concerned with, and take account of, contemporary developments within the PRC. Not least, they may provide new sources of information either directly in themselves or indirectly through the release of previously unknown and untapped sources of information as, for example, the unofficial publications of the Cultural Revolution or the more recent official releases of the last four years. However, it is surely problematic that the perspectives on politics in the PRC should be so dependent on contemporary developments in that country. For them to be so is tantamount to an invitation to be faulted for sins of either commission or omission. Of course, this is not a general criticism of all the literature, nor of all contemporary commentary. Nonetheless, it remains remarkable how many students of PRC politics persist with linear explanations;[22] they did not learn the lessons of the Cultural Revolution and were surprised if not disappointed by the change from the pre- to the post-Mao era.[23]

In short, the study of PRC politics does not have a good record of either prediction or explanation. Prediction in the social sciences is a notoriously hazardous (and some might argue, dubious) activity. It would be all too easy to isolate and criticize the predictive failures. Few if any commentators predicted or *could* have predicted the Cultural Revolution, the events of September 1971, or the rapid developments during the autumn of 1976. Indeed, had they done so, it must remain doubtful that they would have been taken seriously. The fact that Wu De was eventually removed from the leadership can hardly be regarded as a success for those professional "China watchers" who had been predicting his imminent "purge" for the best part of four years.

More serious is the relative poverty of explanation—that is, not "a story" but social science explanation, and not the description of the "truth" but the search for testable hypotheses. Thus, for example, there are remarkably few accounts or interpretations of any aspect of politics in the PRC that could encompass future change.[24] It is perhaps significant that much of the more memorable canon of explanation was written before the Cultural Revolution or is concerned with Chinese Communist politics from a wider and often historical perspective.[25] Of course, there are different levels of explanation, and the search for testable hypotheses cannot but be a cumulative or perhaps additive process. Nonetheless, there would appear to be a tendency in the more recent literature on politics in the PRC to be more concerned immediately with specifics—be they personalities, policies, or periods—than with the longer-term explanation. In his somewhat tongue-in-cheek debate with Winckler about the relevance of policy oscillations, Nathan argued that political phenomena and periods in the PRC should be analyzed more as unique historical events.[26] The implication appears to be that this is not the case at present. However, if anything, the opposite scenario seems more likely. One consequence of the concern with the contemporary, stimulated by the Cultural Revolution, is a near-obsession with data collection as an end in itself. Since the mid-sixties the literature on politics in the PRC has expanded greatly, but it has expanded in terms of description rather than in terms of explanation. The real achievement of that period has been the attention to detail.[27]

One explanation for that development is that the expansion in the number of approaches brought to bear on the study of politics in the PRC is more severely limited than at first appears to be the case. The impact of the Cultural Revolution on the study of politics in the PRC stimulated, to some extent, the search for perspectives that would provide alternatives to the "united elite/Mao in command/ideological determination" model(s). On the other hand, the result has been far from the ideal of methodological pluralism. Though, as already indicated, different and unusual methodologies have been employed, the range of approaches is much more limited than in the study of politics of many other specific areas. For example, even the briefest comparison of political studies of the PRC with the variety of approaches to the study of Soviet politics available over a decade ago suggests the relative breadth of the latter.[28] However, the argument here is essentially qualitative, not quantitative. Whereas a number of perspectives to the study of politics in the PRC have been utilized, the literature has been overwhelmingly dominated by three conceptual frameworks. Considerations of socialism, factions, and policy cycles have formed the "golden triangle" for the study of politics in the PRC.

Moreover, wider focus to the study of politics in the PRC has not really broken the pre-Cultural Revolution mold in two important respects.

The first is that the ability to describe in detail has reinforced the hermetic study of the PRC. Discussions of socialism, factions, and policy cycles may have become more detailed, sophisticated, complex, and even interrelated, but on the whole they have tended to remain PRC-specific.[29] It is thus hardly surprising (and perhaps less surprising now than before the mid-sixties) that, as several writers have indicated, normal academic judgment often appears to become suspended when focused on the PRC.[30]

The second sense in which there has been less methodological change in the study of politics in the PRC than might appear at first sight is in the continuation of an essentially totalitarian perspective. That perspective is far from invariably explicit. However, it does underlie much of the literature, no doubt at least partially because of the emphasis on description and detail. "Totalitarian" in this context does not imply rigid adherence to the Friedrich and Brzezinski (five- or) "six-point syndrome," with its pejorative "cold war" overtones. Rather, as Brown indicates with respect to the USSR, it refers to the exclusive concentration (and outreach) of power within a political system and to its organizational consequences—an important and potent analytical concept.[31] Few accounts of politics in the PRC have abandoned such an implicit totalitarian perspective on either the system as a whole or on the choices of particular topics for investigation.

Moreover, considerations of socialism, factions, and policy cycles have not really contradicted but to a certain extent have supplemented or have been predicated upon a totalitarian model. Strangely enough—given the undoubted intention from some quarters to counter the totalitarian model—the various socialist perspectives on the PRC have tended to reinforce the totalitarian model, not least since they come closest to its earliest formulations. Those that have approved of the PRC's variety of socialism have highlighted the power of mobilization of its leadership and ideology, the regime's goals as defined by that ideology, and the absence of political intermediation. To take but one example of the genre, there are more than distinct echoes of, inter alia, Kornhauser's "Mass Society" explanation for the totalitarian polity in the description of Mao's "revolution from above":

> He set out to break down the gulf between the elite group and the masses, to spread a new outlook at the centers of decision-making, to motivate decisions differently, and to substitute for the "invisible hand" of the price mechanism the visible bond of Mao Tse-tung's thought; Mao preaches a socialist morality, a collective selfless attitude, and a concern for world revolution, as against an individualistic, competitive morality.[32]

It is frequently difficult to escape the conclusion that pro-PRC perspectives have identified socialism, as opposed to totalitarianism, in that country only in moral terms and, moreover, that the morality in question is more a product of the writers' environment than of political reality in the PRC. Those socialist perspectives that have disapproved of the PRC's variety of socialism are even more easily identifiable as at least quasi-totalitarian explanations (and on occasion the totalitarian epithet is even explicit) in that there is not even an appreciation of "correct" ideology. There is emphasis on the power and nature of the ruling elite, class, or strata, depending on political persuasion, and there is criticism, for example, of the "cult of personality," the extent of centralized state power, and of "purges."[33]

Factional accounts, through emphasizing elite-level conflict and coalition formation, have sometimes—but by no means always—purported to be presenting an alternative (frequently pluralism) to the totalitarian model.[34] However, it is clearly misleading, if not mistaken, to regard elite-level conflict as an indication of pluralism. Indeed, in the light of the available evidence it seems more reasonable but not necessarily advisable to regard conflict confined to elite-level factions, whether programmatic or not, as a hallmark of totalitarian systems. The observation of conflict in any political system—or for that matter, consensus—ought not to surprise the student of politics. That to some extent it has done so is more a function of the pre-Cultural Revolution conventional wisdom rather than political reality in the PRC. Nor for that matter is the description of elite-level factions and conflict mutually exclusive to a totalitarian perspective, not least since it has been argued that in the Chinese context it is the factions that create the conflict rather than the reverse.[35] On the contrary, the fact that the majority of factional analyses focus on what has remained a relatively cohesive elite in its self-image and to those outside emphasizes the shared perception on the concentration and exercise of power.[36]

Interpretations of politics in the PRC that employ a perspective based wholly or partly on policy cycles similarly do not contradict but are, to a certain extent, predicated on a totalitarian model. Nathan identifies three general explanations for the appearance of policy cycles: the interaction between ideology and environment; the inherent dynamic of Mao Zedong Thought; and elite-level conflict between two major power blocs.[37] Though all three stress the uneven nature of development, it is the existence of a totalitarian polity with its characteristic concentration of power and the ability and will to mobilize that provides the infrastructure through which the patterns emerge.

It would, of course, be easy to overstate the extent to which the vestigial totalitarian vision permeates the literature on politics in the PRC. As indicated, there have been bold attempts to break with that past. Communist or "Red" China may have become the "People's Republic," but its disproportionate influence remains, not least because the study of politics in the PRC has been relatively short of meta-theories. It may be that the totalitarian perspective, particularly in its later formulations, is so abstract and generalized that its influence is relatively inescapable. Or it may be that the totalitarian approach is entirely appropriate, if not necessarily the *most* appropriate approach, for the study of politics in the PRC, in terms of the perceived political reality and the academic interests of its interpreters. However, there can be little doubt that the totalitarian perspective does not present or allow a fully rounded picture of politics as both an activity in the PRC and as the subject that academics within that field more generally choose to investigate. As several writers pointed out when the study of politics in the USSR was at a similar point in its development, the totalitarian perspective restricts the area of investigation, prevents nonrelated but equally valid questions from being asked, and to a certain extent becomes a self-fulfilling prophecy.[38]

There have been advances in the study of politics in the PRC, but there remain limitations. Neither should be overstated. The problems of studying politics in the PRC are clearly not to be minimized and are largely obvious. In the first place, there are the more practical problems. Lack of both data and access hamper the student of any Communist state. However, from 1961 to 1978 the study of politics in the PRC was hindered further by the relative dearth of even official sources of information. Moreover, in addition to political and physical barriers there are probably greater linguistic and cultural barriers, which not only hamper investigation vicariously but would also frustrate analysis were access to be permitted directly to the PRC, at least for the majority of non-Chinese academics. In the second place, there is the more pedagogic problem that "politics" is not clearly defined. That problem is one of wider relevance than simply a discussion of the PRC. However, it is particularly pertinent here not least because there are those who argue that the PRC's form of rule is not primarily political.[39] Finally, there is the problem that for most of the period of the PRC's existence the very notion of that state has been a political football. For all these reasons, it would not be surprising if the uncommitted academic, in terms of either political persuasion or interest in the PRC, were to question the extent of objectivity attainable—even in terms of Weberian "objective possibility." In England, at least, those problems have led some academics to question whether the study of politics in the PRC is feasible, possible, or even desirable, and there are still departments of politics or government that remain divided over the issue.

None of these problems—blind prejudice apart—is inherently insurmountable. However, the response to the problems has been more in organizational than intellectual terms and undoubtedly helps to explain the development and shortcomings of the study of politics in the PRC, as previously outlined. On the whole, the study of politics in the PRC has emerged from the study of Chinese culture and civilization rather than from the social sciences or, more generally, the humanities. There is a consequent if often subconscious tendency to equate the study of politics in the PRC more generally with the study of the PRC—a tendency that is reinforced by the PRC's own *Weltanschauung*. The result, at least from a European perspective, is that those who choose to study politics in the PRC are often frustrated in their desire to bridge the gap between sinology and political studies, whatever their academic location. They are frequently considered to be "a race apart" and at least a little eccentric by their colleagues in either field. Paradoxically, whereas sinologists often regard them as dilettantes for their concentration on the ephemeral, the more general students of politics frequently see them as specialists in exotic and unfathomable territory.

Despite—or perhaps more accurately, because of—the encouragement of area studies, that isolation has led to a kind of academic introversion. It is thus hardly surprising that the study of politics in the PRC has developed more in terms of an obsession with the contemporary and an emphasis on description and detail. Moreover, the hermetic nature of the study of PRC politics has also undoubtedly contributed to the maintenance of the vestigial totalitarian vision. The simple idea that underlies much of the earlier comment on the development of the literature since the mid-1960s is that there is an apparent reluctance, though there is a need, to venture far from the parental home. One obvious strategy, then, for the development of the study of politics in the PRC is that it should have more confidence in itself as a field of academic investigation and that it should move intellectually more toward the social sciences. To be sure, as already suggested, that process has already started in the United States, and in some respects the impact of the Cultural Revolution has resulted in a diversionary interlude. However, the process is far from complete, particularly in Britain and to a lesser extent, the rest of Europe.

That strategy does not imply that the study of politics in the PRC should forsake its origins. Nor does it imply that the social sciences contain a universal panacea to all the problems that confront the study of politics in the PRC. Rather it is a recognition that the cross-fertilization of ideas between, on the one hand, the study of politics in the PRC, and on the other, analyses of other political systems and the social sciences generally, can be of assistance to the former as well as being essential to the development of a wider political analysis.

Thus, one obvious tactic is that consideration of the more general literature can provide balance and a wider perspective to an otherwise hermetically-sealed universe. For example, much of the literature on politics in the PRC has been concerned with the existence and identification of elite-level factions, as though they were a peculiar characteristic of that political system. However, the experience of other political systems would appear to indicate the universality of factions rather than their particularity. As Eisenstadt and Roniger, among others, have recently suggested, a central question in the analysis of factionalism within a specific system is not whether there are factions, but the extent to which their existence is either the major determinant or simply a supplementary characteristic of that system.[40] With one notable exception, that concern would appear to have remained relatively unaddressed in the literature on the PRC.[41]

A second and equally obvious tactic is that there may be concepts, theories, and approaches derived from the study of other political systems and other disciplines that can be either directly applied or adapted to the interpretation of politics in the PRC. At the more theoretical level an excellent example is to be found in Hiniker's application of the theory of cognitive dissonance to explain the evolution of the Cultural Revolution.[42] On the more conceptual level, the notion of the "political middlemen," originally pioneered by anthropologists investigating the political roles of African headmen,[43] has proved useful in two contexts. In a direct application, it has helped explain the Chinese Communist party's strategy for integration immediately after 1949 in those areas where its presence previously had been negligible.[44] In an adaptation, it has been employed to emphasize the pivotal position and dual role of the provincial first party secretary for any explanation of the relationship between center and province.[45]

Of course, concepts, theories, and approaches derived from the study of a single political system, set of systems, or discipline are rarely found to be completely transferable. However, experimentation is not a luxury if there is to be explanation. That the results may prove a relative failure or unconvincing in terms of their applicability[46] is at least an aid to the development of future perspectives. Thus, it is easy to recognize the reluctance of academics to apply pluralist or "group" approaches to the study of politics in the PRC—outside the context of the Cultural Revolution. On the other hand, as Ferdinand indicates, that does not deny the validity (nor justify the absence) of the attempt. The "group" approach and its successor in terms of perspectives on Communist states, the corporatist model, may not be totally adequate models on their own of the PRC's political system as a whole. However, they remain useful explanatory devices for specific aspects of the political system, particularly as middle-range theory, and useful as indicators of both possibly important relationships, as within the decision-making process, and potential hypotheses for further examination.[47]

A final, and perhaps the most obvious, tactic is that of direct comparison. Comparison between the PRC and other political systems, either in whole or in part, may be evaluative of performance, and indeed such comparison can be both valuable and interesting.[48] However, that is not normally its major concern. Comparison is useful not only because it identifies the common characteristics of the systems or political phenomena under investigation, but also because it crucially highlights the differences. To some considerable extent, this tactic has already been used to good effect in the study of politics in the PRC.[49] Here the problem of exhortation is of a different order. Though comparison is used, it is frequently between the PRC and some other Communist state, usually the USSR. Without denying that such comparison is inherently valid, it seems reasonable to suggest that comparison is also possible with other regimes, particularly in the Third World. Though the opportunities for comparison at the meta-level are obviously limited, some of the PRC's major characteristics provide ample grounds for further investigation; examples are its overwhelmingly peasant population, its single-party control, and the maintenance of that ruling elite that first came to power in 1949 through a protracted process of external and civil war.

Appeals to extend academic horizons notwithstanding, the first stage in the strategy proposed here is to recognize that there is a crisis of identity. So far, it has been possible to refer to the study of politics in the PRC. However, as already indicated, there is the problem that neither as a subject of study nor as an analytical approach is "politics" clearly defined. The problem is not insurmountable, but there is a need for awareness of it if the study of politics in the PRC is to develop as a field of academic investigation (however much of a subdiscipline of a subdiscipline it may be considered). In terms of the subject of study, definitions vary. For example, there is the "black box" interpretation of politics with the emphasis on policy outputs; the attention to politics as an activity or process, frequently related to decision making; the focus on political institutions; and even the tendency to regard everything that occurs in the PRC as politics—a tendency influenced by the totalitarian perspective that emphasizes the absorption of society by the state. In general, a broader rather than a narrower definition is clearly more desirable if only because academic fashions change.

However, a latitudinarian attitude to what constitutes studies of politics in the PRC does not entail that any individual study should leave politics undefined. On the contrary, there is a clear need for both a precise definition of, and focus to, politics particularly if there is to be explanation and not just description. The problem that is highlighted here is not one (despite superficial appearances to the contrary) that refers back directly to the discussion of a decade ago about the relative academic merits of area studies as opposed to the social sciences.[50] Rather, it is a problem that results from the tension between history and the social sciences. Historical method and historical perspective are central to the social sciences, and both history and the social sciences are engaged in explanation. However, their kinds of explanation are of a radically different intent and to some extent incompatible. To put it crudely, history is more concerned with understanding finite events, whereas the social sciences focus on continuing processes. The search for testable hypotheses and the notion of contingent history can at most only be (and in practice are rarely employed as) tactics of historical analysis. On the other hand, the social sciences accept that they have a more contingent universe to observe, and from which to generalize. Moreover, the search for testable hypotheses is an essential part of social science strategy.

Of course, the study of politics in the PRC can incorporate both kinds of explanations. Indeed, both history and the social sciences are necessary for this study's development. However, it is clearly important to recognize that there is a difference, if not so much in method then in intent, not least because of the evolution of the study of politics in the PRC. Thus, it would be misleading to imagine—as is sometimes the case—that all studies of politics in the PRC are political science. They are not, and though the achievement of that result would be equally as undesirable, there is much to be said for a more determined move in that direction.

Notes

1. An interesting discussion of methodological and terminological problems may be found in F. Fleron, "Soviet Area Studies and the Social Sciences: Some Methodological Problems in Communist Studies," *Soviet Studies* 19:3, pp. 313–339.

2. Three seminal works that were all written before the Cultural Revolution and that together reflect the major academic preoccupations of that period are: A. Doak Barnett, *Cadres, Bureaucracy and Political Power in Communist China* (New York: Columbia University Press, 1967); S. R. Schram, *The Political Thought of Mao Tse-tung* (New York: Praeger, 1963); and H. F. Schurmann, *Ideology and Organization in Communist China* (Berkeley: University of California Press, 1966).

3. For example, see R. C. Thornton, *China: The Struggle for Power* (Bloomington and London: Indiana University Press, 1973).

4. For example, see P. Chang, *Power and Policy in China* (University Park, Pa., and London: Pennsylvania State University Press, 1975) and A. P. Liu, *Political Culture and Group Conflict in Communist China* (Oxford: Clio Books, 1976).

5. L. Pye, *Mao Tse-tung: The Man in the Leader* (New York: Basic Books, 1976).

6. P. J. Hiniker, *Revolutionary Ideology and Chinese Reality* (London: Sage, 1977).

7. A stimulating debate about the analytical significance of "policy cycles" (and a review of the literature) may be found in *China Quarterly*, no. 68 (1976): A. J. Nathan, "Policy Oscillations in the People's Republic of China: A Critique" and E. A. Winckler, "Policy Oscillations in the People's Republic of China: A Reply."

8. Since the Cultural Revolution, much of the literature has been devoted to factions and factionalism. A useful review of the literature may be found in L. Pye, *The Dynamics of Chinese Politics* (Cambridge, Mass.: Oelgeschlager, Gunn and Hain, 1981), itself a masterful and entertaining examination of the phenomenon.

9. See, for example, R. L. Petrick, "Policy Cycles and Policy Learning in the People's Republic of China," in *Comparative Political Studies* 14:1, p. 101.

10. An excellent example of a post-Cultural Revolution work that skillfully blends a concern for all three is L. Dittmer, *Liu Shao-ch'i and the Chinese Cultural Revolution* (Berkeley: University of California Press, 1974).

11. K. Lieberthal, *Central Documents and Politburo Politics in China*. Michigan Papers in Chinese Studies no. 33, 1978.

12. As examples, see D. Solinger, *Regional Government and Political Integration in Southwest China* (Berkeley: University of California Press, 1977) and L. T. White III, "Leadership in Shanghai, 1955–69," in *Elites in the People's Republic of China*, ed. R. Scalapino (Seattle: University of Washington Press, 1972).

13. For example, see G. Bennett, *Huadong: The Story of a Chinese People's Commune* (Boulder, Colo.: Westview Press, 1978).

14. For example, see W. Brugger, *Democracy and Organization in the Chinese Industrial Enterprise* (Cambridge, U.K.: Cambridge University Press, 1976).

15. For example, see M. Goldman, *China's Intellectuals: Advise and Dissent* (Cambridge, Mass.: Harvard University Press, 1981) and G. White, *Party and Professionals: The Party and the Role of Teachers in Contemporary China* (New York: Sharpe, 1981).

16. Two of the many studies of particular localities that are significant because they mark new departures in the evolution of the literature are E. Vogel, *Canton Under Communism* (New York: Harper & Row, 1971) and L. T. White III, *Careers in Shanghai* (Berkeley: University of California Press, 1978).

17. Two studies that expertly blend an analysis of power constellations and a discussion of policy implications are M. J. Blecher and G. White, *Micropolitics in Contemporary China* (London: Macmillan, 1980) and Tsou, Blecher, and Meisner, "Policy Change at the National Summit and Institutional Transformation at the Local Level: The Case of Tachai and Hsiyang in the Post-Mao Era," in *Selected Papers from the Center for Far Eastern Studies,* no. 4 (1981), ed. Tang Tsou, University of Chicago.

18. A good example is J. W. Lewis, *Leadership in Communist China* (New York: Cornell University Press, 1963), which now appears somewhat stilted and dated.

19. Surprise is clearly reflected in the pages of the *China Quarterly* from no. 27 (September 1966) on for a number of issues. Thus, for example, Joffe at that time described the Cultural Revolution as not so much the "titanic struggle" described by the *New York Times* of 26 June 1966, but rather as a "titanic riddle"; see "China in mid-1966: 'Cultural Revolution' or Struggle for Power?" in *China Quarterly,* no. 27, p. 123.

20. A good example is Schram's reaction to Mao's attack on the party; see "The Party in Chinese Communist Ideology," in *China Quarterly,* no. 38, especially p. 23.

21. And by all accounts, very often the Chinese themselves; for example, see Pye, *The Dynamics of Chinese Politics,* p. 40.

22. This point is made forcefully by Winckler, when with not a little justice (and hindsight) he indicates the relative success of cyclical explanations; see Winckler, "Oscillations, A Reply," p. 741.

23. There is clearly no shortage of examples here. Perhaps a classic example is the comparison to be made between the two volumes edited by Brugger: *China: The Impact of the Cultural Revolution* (London: Croom-Helm, 1978) and *China Since the "Gang of Four"* (London: Croom-Helm, 1980).

24. On the macro-level, there is Pye's *The Dynamics of Chinese Politics* (1981); there is also Skinner and Winckler's "Compliance Succession in Rural Communist China: A Cyclical Theory," in *A Sociological Reader on Complex Organizations,* 3rd ed., ed. A. Etzioni (New York: Holt, Rinehart and Winston, 1980), p. 401. On the micro-level, there is Domes's explanation of the evolution of intra-elite conflict and its consequences, in *Politische Soziologie der Volksrepublik China* (Wiesbaden: Akademische Verlagsgesellschaft, 1980), p. 187 ff.

25. As examples, see Schurmann, *Ideology and Organization;* B. Schwartz, *Chinese Communism and the Rise of Mao* (London: Cambridge University Press, 1958); C. Johnson, *Peasant Nationalism and Communist Power* (Stanford, Calif.: Stanford University Press, 1962); K. Wittfogel, *Oriental Despotism* (New Haven, Conn.: Yale University Press, 1957); and F. Wakeman, *History and Will* (Berkeley: University of California Press, 1973).

26. Nathan, "Oscillations, A Critique," pp. 730–731.

27. Two excellent examples of detailed analysis are R. MacFarquhar, *The Origins of the Cultural Revolution,* vol. 1 (London: Oxford University Press, 1974) and Byung-joon Ahn, *Chinese Politics and the Cultural Revolution* (Seattle: University of Washington Press, 1976).

28. See, for example, F. Fleron, ed., *Communist Studies and the Social Sciences* (Chicago: Rand McNally, 1969).

29. One account of politics in the PRC that does combine discussion of socialism, factions, and policy cycles—although it is perhaps too sophisticated and unnecessarily complicated—and that is quite definitely PRC-specific is B. Brugger, *Contemporary China* (London: Croom-Helm, 1977).

30. A recent and provocative example is L. T. Sigal, "On the 'Two Roads' and Following Our Own Path: The Myth of the 'Capitalist Road'," in *Australian Journal of Chinese Affairs,* no. 7 (1982), p. 55.

31. A. Brown, "Pluralism, Power and the Soviet Political System: A Comparative Perspective," in *The State in Socialist Society,* ed. N. Harding (London: Macmillan, 1983).

32. E. L. Wheelwright and B. McFarlane, *The Chinese Road to Socialism* (Harmondsworth, Middlesex, U.K.: Penguin, 1973), p. 126.

33. Two examples are N. Harris, *The Mandate of Heaven: Marx and Mao in Modern China* (London: Quartet, 1978), which considers the PRC to be "state capitalist" and L.

Maitan, *Party, Army and Masses in China* (London: New Left Books, 1976), which takes a more "orthodox" Trotskyist position.

34. One account that does purport to present a pluralist alternative is W. Ting, "Coalitional Behavior among the Chinese Military Elite: A Nonrecursive, Simultaneous Equations, and Multiplicative Causal Model," in *American Political Science Review* 73:2 (1979), p. 478. Another account that most definitely does not so purport is contained in J. Domes, *The Internal Politics of China* (London: Hurst, 1973).

35. Pye, *The Dynamics of Chinese Politics,* especially ch. 7.

36. The exceptions that prove the rule are those that consider the wider factionalism extending beyond the elite during the height of the Cultural Revolution. For example, see H. Y. Lee, *The Politics of the Chinese Cultural Revolution* (Berkeley: University of California Press, 1978).

37. Nathan, "Oscillations, A Critique," pp. 724–727.

38. For example, see H. G. Skilling, "Soviet and Communist Politics: A Comparative Approach," *Journal of Politics* 22 (1960) and R. C. Tucker, "Towards a Comparative Politics of Movement Regimes," *American Political Science Review* 55 (1961).

39. Expressed most forcefully in B. Crick, *In Defence of Politics* (Harmondsworth, Middlesex, U.K.: Penguin, 1964), p. 34.

40. S. Eisenstadt and L. Roniger, "Clientelism in Communist Systems: A Comparative Perspective," *Studies in Comparative Communism* 14:2 and 3 (1981), p. 233.

41. The exception is Pye, in *The Dynamics of Chinese Politics.*

42. Hiniker, *Revolutionary Ideology.*

43. Barnes, Mitchell, and Gluckman, "The Village Headman in British Central Africa," *Africa* 19 (1949), p. 89.

44. Solinger, *Regional Government and Political Integration.*

45. D. Goodman, "The Shanghai Connection," in *Shanghai: Revolution and Development in an Asian Metropolis,* ed. C. Howe (London: Cambridge University Press, 1981), p. 127.

46. A good example is the totally unconvincing attempt to provide a cleavage analysis of the PRC leadership during the 1970s, to be found in D. Goodman, "Changes in Leadership Personnel after September 1976," in *Chinese Politics after Mao,* ed. J. Domes (Cardiff: University College Cardiff Press, 1979).

47. P. Ferdinand, "The 'Group Politics' Approach to the Political Process in the People's Republic of China," in *Groups and Politics in the People's Republic of China,* ed. D. Goodman (Cardiff: University College Cardiff Press, 1983).

48. For example, see N. Eberstadt, "Has China Failed?" in *New York Review of Books* 26:5 (1979), p. 33; no. 6, p. 41; and no. 7, p. 39.

49. For example, see T. Bernstein, "Leadership and Mass Mobilization in the Soviet and Chinese Collectivization Campaigns of 1929–30 and 1955–56: A Comparison," in *China Quarterly,* no. 31 (1967); and R. Donaldson and D. Waller, *Stasis and Change in Revolutionary Elites: A Comparative Analysis of the 1956 Party Central Committee in China and the USSR* (Beverley Hills, Calif.: Sage Publications, 1970).

50. Or at least only to the extent that area studies are "dominated by historians," to quote Chalmers Johnson from "Political Science and East Asian Area Studies," in *Political Science and Area Studies—Rivals or Partners?,* ed. L. Pye (London, 1975), p. 80.

About the Contributors and Conference Participants

Byung-joon Ahn is a visiting fellow at the Institute of East Asian Studies, University of California, Berkeley, on leave from Yonsei University, Seoul, Korea; he received his Ph.D. in 1972 from Columbia University. His publications include *Chinese Politics and the Cultural Revolution: Dynamics of Policy Processes* (1976).

Marie Claire Bergère is director of the Centre de Recherches et de Documentation sur la Chine Contemporaine de l'École des Hautes Études en Sciences Sociales and is also professor at the Institut National des Langues et Civilisations Orientales (Université de Paris 3); she received her Ph.D. in 1966 from the Sorbonne and completed her State Thesis in 1975. Her publications include *La bourgeoisie chinois et la Révolution de 1911* (1968), *Capitalisme national et impérialisme: La crise des filatures chinoises en 1923* (1980), and *L'Économie de la Chine populaire* (1983).

Thomas P. Bernstein is professor of political science, East Asian Institute, Columbia University; he received his Ph.D. from Harvard University. His publications include *Up to the Mountains and Down to the Village: The Transfer of Youth from Urban to Rural China* and numerous articles and book chapters, the most recent being "The Soviet Union, China, and Korea" (with Andrew J. Nathan) in Gerald Cortis and Hansoon Joo, eds., *U.S.-South Korean Alliance.* He is currently involved in a comparative study of Soviet and Chinese rural politics.

Lucien Bianco is director of studies, École des Hautes Études en Sciences Sociales; he received his Ph.D. in 1968 from the Sorbonne ("La Crise de Sian, décembre 1936"); his publications include *The Origins of the Chinese Revolution* (Paris and Stanford, 1967 and 1971) and as coauthor, *Regards froids sur la Chine* (1976). He is presently studying the peasant movements in the Republican period.

Parris H. Chang is professor of political science and chairman of Asian area studies, Pennsylvania State University; he received his M.A. from the University of Washington and his Ph.D. from Columbia University in 1969. His publications include *Radicals and Radical Ideology in China's Cultural Revolution* (1973), *Power and Policy in China* (2nd ed., 1978), *Elite Conflict in Post-Mao China* (1983), and articles in *Asian Affairs, Asian Survey, China Quarterly* and many other journals; he often writes articles for *Newsweek.* In 1976/1977 he served as president of the Mid-Atlantic Region Association for Asian Studies.

Hungdah Chiu is professor of law at the University of Maryland School of Law; he received his S.J.D. from Harvard Law School. He has published thirteen books including *The Capacity of International Organizations to Conclude Treaties* (1966); *The People's Republic of China and the Law of Treaties* (1972); and *China and the Taiwan Issue* (1979); and he coauthored *People's Republic of China and International Law: A Documentary Study* (1974). He and Shao-chuan Leng also have a forthcoming book, *Criminal Justice in Post-Mao China.*

Lowell Dittmer is an associate professor of political science, University of California, Berkeley; he received his Ph.D. from the University of Chicago. His publications include *Ethics and Rhetoric of the Chinese Cultural Revolution* (1981).

Jean-Luc Domenach is a researcher, Fondation nationale des sciences politiques, and teaches courses at several Paris universities; he received his Ph.D. from the Sorbonne. He has published *The Origins of the Great Leap Forward* and numerous articles on Chinese political and diplomatic problems.

Jürgen Domes is professor of political science and director of the Research Unit on Chinese and East Asian Politics at the Saar University, Saarbrücken, Germany; he received his Ph.D. in 1960 from Heidelberg University and passed his professorial examination at the Free University of Berlin in 1967. He is a convener of the Standing Group on China and East Asia in the European Consortium for Political Research; his publications include *Vertage Revolution: Die Politik der Koumintang in China, 1923–1927* (1969).

June Teufel Dreyer is professor of politics and director of East Asian programs at the University of Miami, Coral Gables, Florida; she received her Ph.D. from Harvard University. Her publications, besides numerous articles, include *China's Forty Millions: Ethnic Minorities and National Integration in the People's Republic of China.* She is currently studying civil-military relations in the PRC.

Dennis Duncanson is professor of politics, Centre for South-East Asian Studies, Keynes College, University of Kent at Canterbury; he is a former colonial administrator and diplomat. His publications include *Government and Revolution in Vietnam* and *Changing Qualities of Chinese Life.*

Joachim Glaubitz is professor of international relations, University of Munich, and senior research fellow, Research Institute for International Relations and Security in Ebenhausen; he received his Ph.D. in Japanology from Hamburg University. His publications include *Opposition gegen Mao: Abendsprache am Yenshan und andere politische Dokumente* (1969), *China und die Sowjetunion: Aufbau und Zerfall einer Allianz* (1973), *Die Vereinten Nationen als Instrument der Chinesischen Aussenpolitik* (1974), and *Akzentverschiebungen in der Aussenpolitik in Europa-Archiv* (1983). He is currently studying Sino-Soviet relations with Japan.

Merle Goldman is professor of history, Boston University; she received her Ph.D. from Harvard University. Her publications include *Literary Dissent in Communist China* (1967) and *China's Intellectuals: Advise and Dissent* (1981), and she was editor of *Modern Chinese Literature in the May Fourth Era* (1974).

David S. G. Goodman is a lecturer, Department of Politics, University of Newcastle-upon-Tyne, England; he was educated at the Universities of Manchester, Peking, and London. His latest book is *Groups and Politics in the People's Republic of China,* and he is currently engaged in a research project on provincial leadership in the PRC.

Hsin-huang Michael Hsiao is professor of sociology at National Taiwan University; he received his Ph.D. from the State University of New York at Buffalo in 1979. He will soon be a Fulbright Fellow at the Center for Asian Development Studies, Boston University; his publications include *A Historical and Social Analysis of Agricultural Development on Taiwan.*

John Fu-sheng Hsieh is professor of political science, National Chengchi University, Taiwan; he received his Ph.D. in 1981 from the University of Rochester. He is presently working on a study of the Chinese-Vietnamese War.

James C. Hsiung is professor of politics, New York University; he received his Ph.D. in 1967 in political science from Columbia University. His books include *Ideology and Practice: The Evolution of Chinese Communism* (1970), *Law and Policy in China's Foreign Relations* (1970), and *U.S. Asian Relations: the National Security Paradox* (1983); he is also an executive editor for *Asian Affairs.*

Teh-hou Jen is professor of political science, National Taiwan University, Taiwan; he received his Ph.D. from the New School for Social Research, New York. His publications include *Comparative Constitutional Politics* (1981) and many journal articles in ROC publications, among them "Constitutional Change and Political Development of the Republic of China" (1981), "Psychoanalysis and Contemporary Political Theories" (1982), and "State and Society under Communism: A Theoretical Analysis" (1983).

Ellis Joffe is professor of political science, Hebrew University of Jerusalem; he received M.A.s from both the University of Hong Kong and Harvard University, and his Ph.D. from Harvard in 1967. He has written a large number of articles that have been published in books of collected essays and in journals such as *China Quarterly*. The Harvard East Asian Monograph series has published two of his works: *Party and Army: Professionalism and Political Change in the Chinese Officer Corps, 1949–1964* (1965, 1967, 1971) and *The Chinese Red Army, 1927–1963: An Annotated Bibliography* (1964).

Chalmers A. Johnson is professor of political science, University of California, Berkeley, from which he also received his Ph.D. His major works include *Peasant Nationalism and Communist Power, An Instance of Treason, Revolutionary Change, Conspiracy at Matsukawa, Autopsy on People's War, Japan's Public Policy Companies,* and *MITI and the Japanese Miracle*. He is currently working on the theory of the capitalist development state in East Asia.

Ying-mao Kau is professor of political science, director of Mao's Writing Project, and director of the East Asian Security Project, all at Brown University, Providence, Rhode Island; he received his Ph.D. from Cornell University. His publications include *The People's Liberation Army and China's Nation Building* (1973) and *The Lin Piao Affair* (1975); he also serves as editor of the journal *Chinese Law and Government.*

Gottfried-Karl Kindermann is full professor of political science, University of Munich, and founding director, Seminar für Internationale Politik, Munich; he received his Ph.D. from the University of Chicago, having studied as well at the University of Vienna and at Stanford. His publications include *Grundelemente der Weltpolitik* (1977, 1981); *Der Ferne Osten in der Weltpolitik des Industriellen Zeitalters* (1970); *Konfuzianismus, Sunyatsenismus und Chinesischer Kommunismus* (1963); and as editor and coauthor, *Sun Yat-sen; Founder and Symbol of China's Revolutionary Nation-Building* (1981). He is currently working on a history of post-war Japanese diplomacy, and he serves as editor of *Ost-West Synthesen.*

Ladislao La Dany, S.J., was the publisher of *China News Analysis,* Hong Kong (1953–1982); he received his Dr. Juris Utr. from Pazamy University of Budapest, Hungary, and studied philosophy and theology for seven years to be received into the Society of Jesus.

Ch'en Ming (Philip M. Chen) is professor of political science, Tamkang University, Taiwan; he received his Ph.D. from the University of Massachusetts. His major publications include the editorship of *Problems Among Nations, Law and Justice: Legal System in Communist China* and *American World Role of the Next Twenty-five Years;* he has also published several articles in English.

Ramon H. Myers is curator-scholar of the East Asian Collection and senior fellow at the Hoover Institution, Stanford, California, and he also teaches courses in the Food Research Institute of Stanford University; he received his Ph.D. from the University of Washington (Seattle). His publications include *The Chinese Peasant Economy* (Cambridge, Mass., 1970), ed., 44 vols., *The Modern Chinese Economy* (1980), *Two Chinese States* (1978), *The Chinese Economy Past and Present* (1980), and *A U.S. Foreign Policy for Asia in the 1980s and Beyond* (Stanford, 1982); he is also coeditor of *The Japanese Colonial Empire* (forthcoming).

Mineo Nakamima is professor of international relations and contemporary China studies, Tokyo University of Foreign Studies; he received his Ph.D. from the University of Tokyo in 1980. His publications include (titles given in English) *On Contemporary China: Politics and Ideology* (1971), *Introduction to Today's China* (1966), *Verification for China's Image* (1972), *Peking in Flux,* 2 vols. (1980), and *Shock of the Sino-Soviet Alliance* (1982); he has also published many articles in English.

Jan S. Prybyla is professor of economics, Pennsylvania State University. His publications include *The Political Economy of Communist China, The Chinese Economy: Problems and Policies, Issues in Socialist Economic Modernization,* and the forthcoming *Comparative State Socialist Economies.*

Lucien Pye is Ford Professor of Political Science, Massachusetts Institute of Technology, and consultant to the Rand Corporation; he received his B.A. from Carleton College and his Ph.D. in political science in 1951 from Yale University. His more recent publications include *The Spirit of Chinese Politics* (1968), *Warlord Politics* (1971), *China: An Introduction* (1972), *Mao Tse-tung: The Man in the Leader* (1976), *The Dynamics of Chinese Politics,* and *Chinese Commercial Negotiating Styles.*

Robert A. Scalapino is Robson Research Professor of Government and director of the Institute of East Asian Studies at the University of California, Berkeley. He is also editor of *Asian Survey,* a monthly journal. His most recent publications are *Elites in the People's Republic of China, Asia and the Road Ahead, The Foreign Policy of Modern Japan,* and the forthcoming *Modern China and Its Revolutionary Process.*

Yu-ming Shaw is director of the Institute of International Relations, Taipei, Taiwan, ROC, and professor of international relations at the National Chengchi University. He was formerly director of the Asia and World Institute, and before then, associate professor at the University of Notre Dame, Indiana; he received his Ph.D. in history from the University of Chicago. His publications include *Sino-American Relations in the Twentieth Century* (1980), *From the Open Door to the Diplomatic Rupture Between the U.S. and the ROC* (1983), and "John Leighton Stuart and U.S.-Chinese Communist Rapprochement in 1949: Was There Another 'Lost Chance in China'?" in *China Quarterly* (1982).

Noriyuki Tokuda is professor of political science, University of Tsukuba, Japan, currently serving as a cultural attaché at the Japanese Embassy in Peking; he received his Ph.D. in 1976 from Keio University and worked from 1960 to 1979 at the Institute of Developing Economies in Tokyo. His publications include (title in English) *Political Dynamics of Maoism* (1977). He is currently studying Post-Mao provincial politics.

Jiun-han Ts'ao is professor of political science, National Taiwan University, and research fellow, Institute of American Culture, Academia Sinica, ROC; he received his Ph.D. in 1974 from the University of Oklahoma. His publications include "U.S. Energy Policy in the Carter Administration: A Functional Analysis," in *Seminar on American Political Culture in the Seventies* (1977); "Acceptability and Adaptability of American Democratic Ideas to the Chinese Political Mind: A Cross-Cultural Analysis," *Journal of American Studies* (1978); and "Normalization As a Testing Factor for Better Security of the Western Pacific: Equilibrium or Confrontation?" in *Proceedings of the Seminar on Security in the Western Pacific* (1979).

Chi-wu Wang is secretary for international affairs, Academia Sinica, and vice-chairman of the National Science Council, Taiwan; he did his graduate work at Columbia University and was editor of many Chinese magazines in the United States before returning to Taiwan. He has published many articles in Chinese and English.

Liang-ts'ai Wei is research fellow at the Institute of American Culture, Academia Sinica, and associate professor at the National Chengchi University, Taipei; he received his Ph.D. in history from Oklahoma State University. His publications include *Peking Versus Taipei in Africa 1960–1978* (1982), *Trilateral Balance or Neo-Containment? Northeast Asian Realignment in the Eighties, Forum on the Pacific Basin* (1981), and several articles in *American Studies* (Taipei).

Wou Wei is professor of economics, National Taiwan University; he received his Ph.D. from St. Louis University, Missouri, in 1972. He has published ten books in Chinese and has written many articles, some in English. From 1980 to 1982 he served as chief adviser to the Ministry of Economic Affairs, ROC.

Yung Wei is adjunct professor of political science, National Taiwan University, and chairman of the Research, Development and Evaluation Commission, Executive Yuan, ROC; he received his Ph.D. from the University of Oregon. He has been a National Fellow at the Hoover Institution, visiting scholar at the Brookings Institution, and Eisenhower exchange fellow. His publications include *The Nature and Method of Social Sciences* (1971), *Science, Elites, and Modernization* (1980), and "A Methodological Critique of Current Studies on Chinese Political Culture" in *Journal of Politics* (1976).

Martin King Whyte is professor of sociology and associate of the Center for Chinese Studies, University of Michigan, Ann Arbor; he received his Ph.D. from Harvard University. His publications include *Small Groups and Political Rituals in China* (1974) and, in collaboration with William Parish, *Village and Family in Contemporary China* (1978) and *Urban Life in Contemporary China* (1984). He is currently interested in stratification and the selection of marriage partners and is conducting a survey on that topic in Detroit, Michigan.

Abbreviations

ASEAN	Association of Southeast Asian Nations
CC	Central Committee
CCP	Chinese Communist party
CCPCC	Chinese Communist Party Central Committee
CEC	Central Executive Committee
COMECON	Council for Mutual Economic Assistance
CPPCC	Chinese People's Political Consultative Conference
CPSU	Communist party of the Soviet Union
CRG	Cultural Revolution Group
DPRK	Democratic People's Republic of Korea
GNP	gross national product
MLM	Marxism-Leninism-Maoism
MP	member of parliament
NATO	North Atlantic Treaty Organization
NCNA	New China News Agency
NPC	National People's Congress
OPA	ordinary political actor
PLA	People's Liberation Army
PLO	Palestinian Liberation Organization
PRC	People's Republic of China
ROC	Republic of China
SSB	State Statistical Bureau
SSRC	Social Science Research Council

Index